THE AGE
OF SOCIAL RESPONSIBILITY

OF SOCIAL

Gospel in the

MERCER

THE AGE RESPONSIBILITY

The Social Progressive Era 1900-1920

Donald K. Gorrell

ISBN 0-86554-316-X

∞ The paper used in this publication meets
the minimum requirements of American National Standard
for Information Sciences—Permanence of Paper for Printed
Library Materials, ANSI Z39.48-1984.

Library of Congress Cataloging-in-Publication Data

Gorrell, Donald K.
The age of social responsibility:
The social gospel in the progressive era, 1900–1920

Includes index.
1. Social gospel—History.   2. Church and social
problems—History—20th century.   I. Title.
BT738.G64   1988   261.8'0973   88-13914
ISBN 0-86554-316-X

CONTENTS

PREFACE

This is the story of a turning point in American church history. This book traces the evolution of the Social Gospel movement from modest accomplishments by a few individuals and groups to the achievement of official recognition and then full status in American Protestantism. It is the account of the way Protestant denominations, challenged by the needs of a changing social order, accepted responsibility for the welfare and reform of a nation, and finally the world. The fundamental commitments made during the years 1900 through 1920 have continued to the present time.

In contrast to previous histories of the social gospel, this narrative deals primarily with the thought and action of social activists who worked in and through denominational and ecumenical Protestantism. Admittedly, this is institutional history, for that is the significant segment of Christianity where the turning point occurred in the first two decades of twentieth-century America. Many of the persons in the action are well known, but a number have hardly been noticed as important contributors to social Christianity, although these unheralded leaders were often most responsible for making the social gospel a permanent part of Protestantism. Despite their commitment to social ideals and programs, supporters of the movement shared in the larger dimensions of Protestantism in their day. Contrary to common interpretations that often polarize the social gospel and revivalism, many leaders of social Christianity thought, wrote, and spoke as evangelicals who valued campaigns for conversion. Their conceptions of social awakening, social salvation, and social evangelism were expressed in revival terms; what they did was to add a social dimension to the prevailing emphasis on individual salvation, not deny it. Nevertheless, they differed from more conservative evangelicals, and the years that witnessed the official recognition of the social gospel also were the years in which *The Fundamentals* were published and conflicts began to arise between the emerging factions. Moreover, the lively involvement of social activists in the budding ecumenical movement is as much a part of the story as their denominational leadership.

Additionally, this book relates the development of social ministry to events, movements, and trends in the United States during the Progressive Era because that was the context in which acceptance of the social gospel took place. While its sense of mission had deeper roots than mere response to current events, social Christianity was aware of its times and developed in close relationship to the changing national scene.

Although both the interpretation of developments and the mix of source materials are mine, I owe much to the advice and assistance of other persons. Robert T. Handy, Leonard I. Sweet, Newell J. Wert, and Kenneth W. Krueger read part or all of the book and helped me clarify and refine the story. Each made a unique contribution, but I especially acknowledge the help of Professor Handy, who provided correction and counsel from the beginning.

Before I wrote a word, I was indebted to the staffs at the libraries of the American Baptist Historical Society, Barnard College, Columbia University, Dayton and Montgomery County Public Library, DePauw University, New York Public Library, Ohio Historical Society, Ohio Wesleyan University, Union Theological Seminary (New York), and United Theological Seminary (Dayton, Ohio). Special appreciation is expressed to two librarians, my colleague Elmer J. O'Brien at United Theological Seminary and Robert Beach at Union Theological Seminary, the two places where the bulk of the research was done.

This volume is the product of years of study funded in part by financial assistance from two sources. A Faculty Fellowship awarded by the Association of Theological Schools made possible a year of study at Union Theological Seminary and Columbia University in New York City, which was the origin of the book. Several leaves for research and writing were granted by United Theological Seminary. I thank both institutions for this help.

In the preparation of the book I was aided by several faculty secretaries and by two typists who deserve special thanks, Dorla Morgan and Patricia Tutwiler. My greatest gratitude is to my wife Lois, whose encouragement, suggestions, and patience enabled me to complete the project. I happily dedicate the book to her.

Despite the help of so many over the years, I alone am responsible finally for what follows. I hope this work will provide new understanding and data concerning the movement and the church during this decisive period in social-gospel history.

INTRODUCTION

When some historian a hundred years hence undertakes to describe the present social transition, it will be an interesting task for him to make a comparative estimate of the influence which the various denominations have exerted on the awakening of the nation and the founding of a new social order.

(Walter Rauschenbusch,
Christianizing the Social Order, 1912)

"All whose recollection runs back of 1900 will remember that as a time of lonesomeness," wrote Walter Rauschenbusch of the pioneers of Christian social thought and action. "We were few, and we shouted in the wilderness." Yet by 1912 the same man, by then the acknowledged leader of the Social Gospel movement in American Protestantism, recognized a remarkable change in the nation. "The social interest in the Church has now run beyond the stage of the solitary pioneer. It has been admitted within the organizations of the Church." Whereas early in the twentieth century speakers on social issues had to compel their people to hear messages on social Christianity, ten years later audiences applauded what previously had seemed "shockingly radical." As a result of that amazing transformation, Rauschenbusch believed that his age had experienced the social awakening of the American churches. "Whenever men hereafter write the story of how Christendom became Christian," he said, "they will have to begin a new chapter at the years in which we are now living."[1]

With an eye to the significance of what had transpired in his time, the church historian and social prophet went on to state in 1912: "When some historian a hundred years hence undertakes to describe the present

---

[1]Walter Rauschenbusch, *Christianizing the Social Order* (New York: Macmillan Company, 1912) 9, 11-12, 28, 29.

social transition, it will be an interesting task for him to make a comparative estimate of the influence which the various denominations have exerted on the awakening of the nation and the founding of a new social order."[2] Although I have waited only seventy-five years, my study of social Christianity seeks to fulfill the task he suggested and offers somewhat more because additional needs have developed since he wrote.

My purpose in the book is to explain the basic developments in American Protestantism between 1900 and 1920 that enabled the social gospel to achieve an official status in the organizational life of denominational and ecumenical religious bodies. This important transition occurred during the Progressive Era, and it established the fundamental involvement of Protestant churches in social issues that continues to the present time. By recounting what happened several decades ago, my narrative describes the foundation of denominational social action today.

Although the impetus for this analysis came from Walter Rauschenbusch, I determined the precise periodization partly by the era itself and partly by the historiography of the Social Gospel movement. The first two decades of the twentieth century are commonly regarded as the Progressive Era in American history. Admittedly, historians differ over the precise years for that designation,[3] but one can make a reasonable case for regarding the beginning of the epoch as the inauguration of Theodore Roosevelt as president of the United States in September 1901. Whether one views the end of the period as the death of Roosevelt early in 1919, or the increasing preoccupation of America with the war in Europe in 1915, or the final rejection of Woodrow Wilson's League of Nations idea by the Senate in 1920 depends on what aspect of American history is being studied. Since the grass-roots stages of Progressivism preceded Roosevelt's succession to the presidency, and since there is a close affinity of social-gospel idealism with League of Nations idealism, it seems justified to regard the period from 1900 to 1920 as a legitimate era for study.

This dating also fits a need in the present state of social-gospel historiography. Of the several histories examining the movement, only

---

[2]Ibid., 22.

[3]A brief sample can be found in the following: Richard Hofstadter, ed., *The Progressive Movement, 1900–1915* (Englewood Cliffs NJ: Prentice-Hall, Inc., Spectrum Book, 1963) 1-15; Arthur Mann, ed., *The Progressive Era: Liberal Renaissance or Liberal Failure?* American Problem Studies, ed. Oscar Handlin (New York: Holt, Rinehart and Winston, 1963) 1-5; George E. Mowry, *The Progressive Era, 1900–1918: Recent Literature and New Ideas,* 2d ed. (Washington: Service Center for Teachers of History, 1964); David A. Shannon, *Twentieth Century America,* 3d ed., 3 vols., vol. 1: *The Progressive Era* (Chicago: Rand McNally, 1974).

INTRODUCTION

one modern history deals with the important change to which Rauschenbusch referred. More than forty years ago Charles Howard Hopkins published his pioneering study, *The Rise of the Social Gospel in American Protestantism, 1865–1915*,[4] which regarded the movement's official recognition by mainstream denominations and the Federal Council of Churches as the culmination of his account. However, his interpretation did not set that accomplishment in its historical context or explain it in light of the larger national scene because he saw it in a much-longer chronological survey. Later Aaron Abell's *The Urban Impact on American Protestantism, 1865–1900*[5] and Henry F. May's *Protestant Churches and Industrial America*[6] (which covered the years 1828 to 1895) amplified the Hopkins data up to 1900. Essentially, both men corroborated Hopkins's conclusion that the social gospel was "American Protestantism's response to the challenge of modern industrial society."[7]

Several years after, three other historians published diverse examinations of the social gospel during the years between the two world wars: Paul A. Carter, *The Decline and Revival of the Social Gospel*[8] between 1920 and 1940, Robert Moats Miller, *American Protestantism and Social Issues, 1919–1941*,[9] and Donald B. Meyer, *The Protestant Search for Political Realism, 1919–1941*.[10] Given the effective end of the Hopkins account in December 1912 and the diverse starting points of these later studies in 1919 or 1920, there is a period from 1913 to 1919 or 1920 that constitutes the missing years of social-gospel history that have not yet been studied carefully. More recently, Robert T. Handy's *The Social Gospel in America, 1870–1920:*

---

[4]Charles Howard Hopkins, *The Rise of the Social Gospel in American Protestantism, 1865–1915* (New Haven: Yale University Press, 1940) 316.

[5]Aaron Ignatius Abell, *The Urban Impact on American Protestantism, 1865–1900* (Cambridge: Harvard University Press, 1943; Hamden CT: Archon, 1962).

[6]Henry F. May, *Protestant Churches and Industrial America* (New York: Harper & Brothers, 1949).

[7]Hopkins, *Rise of the Social Gospel*, 318.

[8]Paul A. Carter, *The Decline and Revival of the Social Gospel: Social and Political Liberalism in American Protestant Churches, 1920–1940* (Ithaca NY: Cornell University Press, 1954).

[9]Robert Moats Miller, *American Protestantism and Social Issues, 1919–1939* (Chapel Hill: University of North Carolina Press, 1958).

[10]Donald B. Meyer, *The Protestant Search for Political Realism, 1919–1941* (Berkeley: University of California Press, 1960).

Gladden, Ely, Rauschenbusch[11] and Ronald C. White, Jr.'s and C. Howard Hopkins's *The Social Gospel: Religion and Reform in Changing America*[12] included those two decades in their coverage, but neither volume provides any major interpretation for that time. Consequently, I have added these missing years to the crucial years identified by Rauschenbusch to form a vital twenty-one-year period in social-gospel history that fills a gap in the overall evolution of the movement.

An additional word of a different nature needs to be said about my use of the basic literature of social Christianity. Concerning the years from 1900 to 1912, I found the first two chapters of Rauschenbusch's *Christianizing the Social Order*, published in 1912, a more-accurate depiction of what he calls "the social awakening of the churches" than the traditional topical analysis employed by C. Howard Hopkins. That earlier account pointed to a number of forces, organizations, and movements that have not been part of the standard story of the social gospel, so I studied those more carefully and integrated them into my history of the period. Consequently, there is more in this book about the relation of social Christianity to the muckrackers, Progressivism, revivalism, and the social crisis of the age than has been the case previously.

Before identifying other distinctive emphases in this study, I want to clarify my use of terminology and sources. The term *social gospel* was not as widely used as the term *social Christianity* in 1900, but it became increasingly common during the era. In light of that trend, and the popular use of *social gospel* in the years since, I have given preference to it in the book. In my wording in the text, I have used the terms interchangeably, but the quotations best demonstrate how the terms were used at the time. Actually, *social gospel* conveys multiple meanings: sometimes it designates a movement within Protestantism, but other times it is contrasted to individual salvation or it identifies a faith commitment to and responsibility for the social order. To compound the problem, Protestants did not always agree on the terminology. It is my hope that the context will clarify the proper meaning.

To convey the expressions of the era, I have quoted abundantly. It was an articulate time and advocates of social Christianity stated their ideas interestingly.

As a general principle, I developed my understanding of the social gospel in the Progressive Era on the basis of primary sources. By

---

[11]Robert T. Handy, ed., *The Social Gospel in America, 1870–1920: Gladden, Ely, Rauschenbusch* (New York: Oxford University Press, 1966).

[12]Ronald C. White, Jr. and C. Howard Hopkins, *The Social Gospel: Religion and Reform in Changing America* (Philadelphia: Temple University Press, 1976).

INTRODUCTION

immersing myself in the books, periodicals, sermons, and reports of the period, I sought to see the time through the eyes of the participants rather than to discuss or solve later scholarly quarrels. In order to clear up problems of motivation and cause and effect, I sampled several archival collections and worked manuscript materials into the research and analysis. In the collected papers of Walter Rauschenbusch, Washington Gladden, Frank Mason North, and Worth M. Tippy, along with the manuscript minutes of the Methodist Federation for Social Service, I uncovered little-known data concerning the degree of participation of individuals and groups, their opinions and strategies, their underlying values and goals, as well as their attitudes about what was happening in society, the nation, and the church. Autobiographical accounts also afforded perspective and value judgments not always evident in periodicals and denominational records. I think this mix of resources provides a fresh perspective on the movement in the first two decades of this century.

The development of the social gospel in those years occurred in uneven stages and with diverse causes and consequences. Social Christianity began the period in weakness and ended it in flux, but in the interim there was notable progress, success, and recognition. My part designations and chapter headings convey the varying pace and shifting emphases of the movement. The dating of the subperiods within the era is based on my reading of the primary sources and attempts to indicate the times when major changes occurred in the evolution of social Christianity. Part designations indicate the central tendency of each change but do not imply that former dominant motifs disappeared as new emphases emerged. While the changes identified in 1907–1908, 1912, and 1917 were determined in this way, the beginning and ending dates of the period were based, as noted above, on political history and social-gospel historiography. Thus, what happened from 1900 to 1902 was a continuity from the 1890s and what occurred in 1919–1920 persisted into the 1920s. The particular changes and developments in the era stand in sequence with social-gospel history before and after the years of this study. The distinctive schematic arrangement of the book evidences the pattern of my comprehensive interpretation.

Another characteristic of my study is its central attention to the institutional and organizational aspects of social-gospel development. Five denominations were more socially active than other Protestant churches; hence they became the focus for my investigation. The religious bodies themselves determined which would be studied, for I examined the records of those churches that not only espoused social ideas but also created official organizations for social and economic concerns and employed full-time persons to staff them. These were the Congregationalists, Episcopalians, and the northern branches of the Baptists, Methodists, and Presbyterians. For those interested in the continuity of social Christianity, these are the same primary denominations studied by Hopkins, May, and Carter. Occasional references are made to other groups, but Protestantism was too diverse to study every group and I thought it best to examine carefully the work of those most active in social ministry. Some earlier presentations of denominational accomplishment were organized topically by groups—as in Harry F. Ward's *A Year Book of the Church and Social Service in the United States*[13]—but that method obscured the interactions of the groups and ignored the different ways the bodies responded to common stimuli. Instead, I studied denominational activities within the subperiods identified above, which revealed that denominations became active in social service at different times and with varying degrees of commitment, and that leadership of the movement passed from pioneering groups to late-blooming ones that lent new vigor to the cause.

Organizations other than denominations also contributed significantly to the growth of the Social Gospel movement. Some of these were short-lived, but others were founded in the era and became permanent institutions. Foremost of these interdenominational institutions was the Federal Council of the Churches of Christ in America, which became a clearinghouse for social ministry, especially when it created a council of denominational social-service secretaries. Two other groups that were surprisingly committed to social concerns were the New York State Conference of Religion and the Religious Education Association. My study is the first to show that both relied heavily on social-gospel speakers in their programs and publications. In addition to providing platforms for the dissemination of social ideology, both groups made interpretative evaluations of the cause that were as perceptive as those by the denominations. The active involvement of social-gospel leaders in two ephemeral campaigns, the Men and Religion Forward Movement and the Interchurch World Movement, demonstrated the broadening influence of social Christianity during the period.

Following social-gospel advocates into the various organizations where they shared their ideas and gave their time and energies showed how broadly such persons were engaged in the agitation and reforms of the Progressive movement. Social activists were associated with the muckrackers and even with the politics of the Bull Moose campaign. There was important interaction of social-gospel leaders and groups with many social agencies associated with Progressivism, especially in the second

---

[13]Harry F. Ward, *A Year Book of the Church and Social Service in the United States* (New York: Fleming H. Revell, 1914) 31-67.

decade of the study. The one organized movement I have not included was the temperance crusade, which was so much larger in scope than the entire social-gospel cause that it was funded and staffed differently than other social ministries by Protestant denominations. Temperance was the primary social cause of the time and had the support of most proponents of social Christianity, but it was a massive single-cause campaign that dwarfed the entire Social Gospel movement and needed little help from it. Pointing to evidence of religious reformers' participation with other reform agencies is another contribution of this study.

Although many books dealing with the development of the social gospel describe its theological tenets, this book sheds new light on the major ideas and books that appeared in this period by examining them in their historical settings. Rather than discussing the kingdom of God concept abstractly, I show its expressions in such subthemes as the church and the kingdom, the city and the kingdom, and the nation and the kingdom. Moreover, I indicate how some advocates of social Christianity modified the kingdom-of-God idea to the democracy of God following the First World War. Similarly, one can see a fundamental concept like the Christianization of the social order transformed from the context of a Christian nation to the world. The movement's continuing reference to Christianizing the social order seemed to imply that Christianity should shape the new order of things, but contextual analysis demonstrates that it was the church that adapted its ideas as situations changed. During this period the pattern of social-gospel thought proved more diverse and complex than it was in the decades before 1900.

While dominant ideas of social Christianity such as the kingdom of God and Christianizing the social order stand out, I argue that an underlying concept, which runs throughout the entire era, really conveyed the essence of the movement: that concept was social responsibility. It was expressed by Progressive reformers as well as by proponents of the social gospel. Already in February 1900 the editor of the New York *Christian Advocate* maintained that "public affairs must become our daily, never-ceasing responsibility,"[14] even though it was still a dream at the time. By 1914, however, the dream became much more real after Progressive reforms had taken place and social Christianity had been officially endorsed by Protestant denominations and the Federal Council of Churches. That year, when the social gospel was at the zenith of its influence and activity, the Declaration of Principles of the Religious Education Association stated: "We believe that the age of sheer individualism is past and the age of so-

---

[14]*Christian Advocate* (New York), 22 February 1900, pp. 9-10.

cial responsibility has arrived." Applying this conclusion to its own organization, the association said: "Without any abandonment of the
educational ideals of our fathers we must now exalt the newer ideals of
social justice, social service, social responsibility."[15] It was the fact that
national religious organizations had committed themselves officially to
social responsibility that convinced Rauschenbusch that a significant shift
had occurred in Protestantism since the turn of the century.

By 1920 that commitment enlarged to envision the whole world, although it again was more of a dream. In light of this recurring theme
among social-gospel champions, a theme that united their cause to that
of persons with similar commitment in the various facets of Progressive
reform, I think it is appropriate to title this volume *The Age of Social Responsibility*. The chapters that follow trace the slow and uneven evolution
of that sense of social responsibility through the first decades of twentieth-century America.

---

[15]*Religious Education* 9 (April 1914): 98.

INTRODUCTION

PART 1

From the Social Question to the Social Crisis, 1900–1907

CHAPTER 1

The Social Question

What is it, then, to which we are brought as the special problem
which presents itself to the Christian Church in the age of the social
question? It is the problem of communicating to the social movement
that social energy which the teaching of Jesus originates and conserves. . . . Yet all these profound effects of the teaching of Jesus,
its reconstruction of theology and its regeneration of individual life, are
consummated and justified by being gathered up into a sense of power
which can create a better world. After all, the test of religion is in what
it will do. . . .

(Francis Greenwood Peabody,
Jesus Christ and the Social Question, *1900)*

IN 1900 SOCIAL CHRISTIANITY was identifiable as a body of ideas espoused
in books and on platforms by a few recognizable persons and was evident
in a small number of programs and buildings. But its existence as a
movement in America exerted little influence and attracted only small
numbers in some Protestant denominations. Sponsored and supported
by interested persons, the movement resembled many other voluntary
causes at the time, since it had not yet achieved official standing among
organizations authorized by the churches.

While social Christianity did not find wide recognition or support,
its efforts were appreciated and encouraged by some. The Department of
Social Economy for the United States Commission to the Paris Exposition
of 1900, for instance, asked Josiah Strong, a pioneer leader of the social
gospel and president of the League for Social Service, to prepare a report
for that event that was published under the title *Religious Movements for
Social Betterment*. Pointing out that a basic change was occurring in
American religious activities so that "they are now beginning to be

directed to the uplifting of the whole man instead of a fraction of him, and to the salvation of society as well as to that of the individual," Strong explained that this change required religious groups to find "new methods to meet new conditions."[1] He described the work of the Salvation Army, the Young Men's Christian Association, and the Young Women's Christian Association, but emphasized innovative efforts inaugurated by some denominations such as deaconess homes, manual training schools, social settlements, and institutional churches. The so-called institutional church had even produced a new form of church architecture, since the provision of resources directed to social as well as individual needs required the inclusion of parlors, classrooms, reading rooms, gymnasiums, and even baths and shops in addition to the traditional large auditoriums for worship and public meetings.[2] Citing 112 institutional churches and social centers as illustrations, Strong affirmed that such efforts attracted persons to Christianity when many were describing the period as a time of spiritual decline. "There will be no lack of growth on the part of the churches," he insisted, "as soon as they recognize their social mission and adapt their methods to changed conditions."[3]

Josiah Strong was an ardent and articulate spokesman for the cause of social Christianity, and his personal religious experience exemplified what occurred in the lives of others who reached a similar conclusion. Following a conscious religious commitment at age thirteen, he spent twenty-five years under the dominance of what he termed the "individualistic point of view" typical of late-nineteenth-century Protestantism. Gradually, however, he realized that great changes were taking place in society and the realm of ideas. Scientific method, economic and social disruption, and the discovery of the kingdom of God as a unifying principle led him to "the social interpretation of Christianity" about 1885. As he realized that the idea of the kingdom of God comprehended both the sacred and the secular, his life centered on the conviction that "everything must be made a means to the service of the kingdom," which he believed was an ideal to be attained in the world through service, love, and sacrifice.[4]

---

[1]Josiah Strong, *Religious Movements for Social Betterment* (New York: Baker & Taylor, 1900) 13-24.

[2]Ibid., 27-32.

[3]Ibid., 130-32.

[4]Josiah Strong, *My Religion in Everyday Life* (New York: Baker & Taylor, 1910) 18-21, 32-33, 37, 43, 50, 53, passim.

Concretely, that religious journey resulted in a flood of books, lectures, and conferences, as Strong devoted his restless energy to preserving the Anglo-Saxon culture he saw threatened in America, to reforming that culture, to spreading it throughout the world, and to enlisting others in these causes. The change in his life in 1885 was evident with the publication that year of his book *Our Country*, which dealt with such problems as wealth, labor unrest, conflict of capital and labor, and the city, and challenged Christians to work for the solution of these social problems. In *The New Era* (1893) and *The Twentieth Century City* (1898) he developed the same basic themes.

Accepting the leadership of the American branch of the Evangelical Alliance, he had that group sponsor conferences dealing with "National Perils and Opportunities" (1887), "National Needs and Remedies" (1889), and "Christianity Practically Applied" (1893). Following the third convention he reported, "A spirit of hope and even of confidence seemed to pervade the conference, due partly perhaps to the unwavering conviction that the principles of the gospel were fully equal to solving all existing problems before the church, provided only those principles are applied."[5] His optimism was not fulfilled as rapidly as he desired, however, and in 1898 Strong left the overly conservative Evangelical Alliance to establish his own organization, the League for Social Service, which focused its energies on gathering, interpreting, and disseminating facts bearing on social and industrial betterment. It was his conviction that through the education of public opinion persons would understand the problems and desire to correct them.

Such confidence in the power of education to enlist Christians in support of social ministry, as well as satisfaction from religion's modest accomplishments in social betterment, had to sustain Strong and other exponents of social Christianity, for there were few signs of encouragement in the early months of 1900. During the first quarter of the year, for example, editorials in the *Christian Advocate*, central voice of the Methodist Episcopal Church's chain of newspapers, complained that the nation's largest Protestant denomination was "a dying church" in need of "a true revival." Such weakness had seldom occurred in Methodist history, and it animated the bishops to issue "a weighty and solemn appeal to the Church to awake."[6]

---

[5]"Report of the General Secretary," *Annual Report of the Evangelical Alliance for the United States of America* (1893), 9-10.

[6]*Christian Advocate* (New York), 18 January, 15 February, 1 March 1900.

When the Northern Methodists met at Chicago in May for their quadrennial General Conference, the Episcopal Address contained sections on social problems that, on the surface, seemed encouraging. In words that might gladden Josiah Strong, the bishops asserted that "the question of the city has become the question of the race," and they urged the denomination to adopt legislation "determined by the necessities and perils of great cities."[7] Later in the Episcopal Address there was a section headed "The Church and Social Problems" in which disquieting facts were noted and the question was asked, "What is the relation of the Church to these questions of the hour?" The bishops concluded that "the Church has no authoritative message concerning trusts or labor unions, lockouts or strikes, capital or wages, tariffs and taxation, currency and colonies. It is neither appointed nor fitted to dictate social or economic laws." Although church pulpit and press need not abstain from such questions, they "must avoid partisanship toward classes," have a word for all groups, and avoid sanctioning particular measures.[8] Nevertheless, in a section on "The Church and Citizenship" the bishops urged the laity to apply their Christian convictions to their duties as citizens: "The Christian man cannot neglect or trifle with his political function; cannot separate it from his religion; must, as a member of the body politic, be as truthful, as honest, as pure in aim as he is in his membership of the Church."[9] Thus, while Methodist churches could take no official stands and were to avoid particular measures, its members were encouraged to apply Christian principles as responsible citizens. Officially, the General Conference took no action on social, economic, or political problems in 1900.

During the year no other major Protestant denominations took any more decisive authoritative action or stand than the Methodists. Consequently, Christian social ministry was left in the hands of Christian laity and clergy acting individually or through voluntary organizations. There was no paucity of such groups for the *New York Charities Directory* listed 3,449 organizations, "each in its own way striving in a common cause."[10] Most clergy and laity at the time viewed this situation as neither negligent nor irresponsible, for Protestantism in America had functioned in this voluntary fashion through most of the nineteenth century, with a record of considerable achievement. But as Christianity prepared to enter

---

[7]*Journal of the General Conference of the Methodist Episcopal Church* (1900), 63-64.

[8]Ibid., 69-70.

[9]Ibid., 76-77.

[10]*The Churchman* (New York), 10 February 1900, p. 70.

a new century, some believers wondered whether single-cause voluntary societies were any longer able to exert the influence or to effect the changes needed in the social order.

At the time, the most effective denominations in utilizing the voluntary-appeal approach were the Episcopalians and the Baptists. A number of Congregationalists, like Strong, were productive and influential as individuals, but there was little social expression yet among Methodists and Presbyterians.

That the Protestant Episcopal Church actively encouraged social ministry was evident in the fact that 42 of the 112 institutional churches Josiah Strong listed in New York City in 1900 were sponsored by that denomination.[11] Undergirding that activity was a long tradition of social concern in urban and industrial ministry that Episcopalians inherited from the work of Frederick Maurice and Charles Kingsley in England. Led by Bishops Henry C. Potter in New York City and Frederick Dan Huntington in central New York, prodded by clergymen such as R. Heber Newton, James Huntington, and W. D. P. Bliss, and informed by laity such as Richard T. Ely and Vida Scudder, the Protestant Episcopal Church was continuously challenged to social activity. A decade earlier, within a four-year period, three voluntary organizations were founded by Episcopalians to stimulate and support social concerns: the Church Association for the Advancement of the Interests of Labor founded by ministers in New York City in 1887, the Society for Christian Socialists organized in Boston in 1889 by two clergymen, W. D. P. Bliss and Philo W. Sprague, and the Christian Social Union created in New York in 1891 with Richard T. Ely as a leader. Chapters of these groups were established in other cities, providing a web of interest, education, and support that kept the denomination informed about social problems.[12]

By way of illustration, the Church Association for the Advancement of the Interest of Labor, popularly referred to as CAIL, believed both clergy and laity should be interested and informed about industrial problems of the time and created methods to achieve that end. While its methods were primarily educational, the association worked for beneficial legislation and attempted to arbitrate between employer and employee.[13] At the Annual Conference of the Church Association for the Advancement of the Interest

---

[11]Strong, *Religious Movements*, 81-82.

[12]William D. P. Bliss, ed., et al., *The Encyclopedia of Social Reform* (New York: Funk & Wagnalls 1897) 67-68, 258, 275-76, 1141-43.

[13]Strong, *Religious Movements*, 98-104.

of Labor, 30 April 1900, there were reports, addresses, papers, and extemporaneous speeches on varied interests "of immediate and practical bearing," such as the needs of motormen, Washington alley life, child labor, sweatshops, industrial organization of women, factory conditions, trade unions, conciliation and arbitration, and the church and the state.[14] Monthly meetings of the Church Association for the Advancement of the Interest of Labor concentrated on specific agendas such as tenement housing, factory legislation, or machinery replacing manual labor.[15]

Despite these encouraging and long-standing influences favoring social concern by Episcopalians, editorials in the weekly periodical *The Churchman* revealed that many in the denomination did not differ greatly from Northern Methodists. On one occasion the editor affirmed a statement by Bishop Potter that the Church must not be indifferent to grave social and industrial problems because "it is as much the function of the Church to save society as to save man." Yet the editor went on to say that this must be done by evolutionary reform: "not by a change of laws, but by a change of heart."[16] In another instance, an editorial insisted that "leadership in the readjustment of social and commercial relations belongs to the Church," but later it was stated that "when the Church appears too prominently in the work of redemption, the success of the whole matter is endangered."[17] With such a mixed outlook, it is not surprising that some questioned the use of institutional churches and that many Episcopalians criticized church involvement in the social-reform movement.[18] The diversity of denominational opinion on social issues was obvious in the papers read at the annual Church Congress of the Protestant Episcopal Church.[19]

Northern Baptists also expressed their views of social ministry at the Baptist Congress, a similar yearly gathering of clergy and laity to discuss current questions. Modeled after its Episcopal counterpart, the Baptist Congress provided an open platform for the debate of social and religious subjects, with no action taken. A number of young ministers concerned with

---

[14]*The Churchman* (New York), 12 May 1900, pp. 588-89.

[15]Ibid., 20 January 1900, p. 89; 10 March 1900, p. 311; 24 March 1900, p. 373.

[16]Ibid., 3 February 1900, pp. 125, 129.

[17]Ibid., 10 March 1900, p. 287; 21 July 1900, p. 76.

[18]Ibid.

[19]Protestant Episcopal Church in the U.S.A. Church Congress, *Papers, Addresses and Discussions* (1900–1909), passim.

social aspects of Christianity participated in the Baptist Congress, even assuming leadership responsibilities. One of Walter Rauschenbusch's early responsibilities was to serve as its corresponding secretary during 1893 and 1894, and he was a member of its General Committee throughout his ministry. During the 1880s and 1890s he also read papers and shared in discussions. Friends of Rauschenbusch, such as Leighton Williams and Samuel Zane Batten, also participated in the Baptist Congress.[20]

Finding Baptist platforms where they could develop and test the new understanding of social ministry that was slowly becoming clear to them was important to these young ministers. As Rauschenbusch looked back on these years he remembered that "the Church held down the social interest in me. It contradicted it; it opposed it; it held it down as far as it could; and when it was a question about giving me position or preferment, the fact that I was interested in the working man was actually against me—not for me."[21] Following his graduation from Rochester Theological Seminary, he became the pastor of a small congregation of German immigrant working-class families in the Hell's Kitchen area of New York City in 1886. Through his contacts with poverty and hardship in that situation, he developed the social concern that the church had not provided, and he benefited from his association with kindred spirits such as Leighton Williams, who ministered at Amity Baptist Church a few blocks away. From the traditional church he learned personal religion; from his pastorate he discovered the need for social information and social passion.

While struggling to reconcile those seemingly contradictory forces in his life, Rauschenbusch discovered the unifying conception that motivated his life thereafter.

> Then the idea of the kingdom of God offered itself as the real solution for that problem. Here was a religious conception that embraced it all. Here was something so big that absolutely nothing that interested me was excluded from it. Was it a matter of personal religion? Why the kingdom of God begins with that! . . . Was it a matter of world-wide missions? Why, that is the kingdom of God, isn't it—carrying it out to the boundaries of the earth. Was it a matter

---

[20]Walter Rauschenbusch, "The Relation of Church and State," *Proceedings of the Baptist Congress* 8 (1889): 138-40; idem, "The Pulpit in Relation to Political and Social Reform," *Proceedings of the Baptist Congress* 10 (1892): 127-29; Leighton Williams, "Baptists in Relation to Social Reform," in Bliss, *Encyclopedia of Social Reform*, 141.

[21]"The Kingdom of God," *Cleveland's Young Men* 27 (9 January 1913) unpaginated, reprinted in Robert T. Handy, *The Social Gospel in America, 1870–1920: Gladden, Ely, Rauschenbusch* (New York: Oxford University Press, 1966) 266.

of getting justice for the workingman? Is not justice part of the kingdom of God? Does not the kingdom of God simply consist of this—that God's will shall be done on earth, even as it is now in heaven. And so, wherever I touched, there was the kingdom of God. That was the brilliancy, the splendor of the conception—it touched everything with religion. It carries God into everything that you do, and there is nothing else that does it the same way.[22]

As he came to this understanding Rauschenbusch worked with Williams and others to publish a little journal titled *For the Right*, but it lasted only eighteen months because of inadequate financial support. In December 1892, however, they turned their social interests in another direction; the two shared in a small conference of Baptist ministers at Philadelphia, which decided to form the Brotherhood of the Kingdom. By design, the Brotherhood was a nondenominational society to study the social teachings of Jesus, to disseminate those ideas, and to energize persons to assist in the practical realization of the kingdom of God in the world. Beginning in 1893, the Brotherhood met annually for several days each summer, usually at the Williams farm near Marlboro on the Hudson River, to present and discuss papers on theological and social subjects. Based on warm fellowship and spiritual devotion as well as social interest, the Brotherhood sought to sustain, educate, and inspire its members to self-sacrificing work for "the social welfare of the common people." Samuel Zane Batten, who provided the germinal idea for the uniquely committed voluntary group, served for years as its secretary.[23]

During 1894–1895 Samuel Batten worked as associate pastor of Amity Church in New York City, where Williams was pastor. Amity Church was one of the Baptist institutional churches, and Batten carried some of its practices and concepts to Morristown, New Jersey, where he was pastor in 1900. The year Batten, Williams, and Rauschenbusch all ministered in New York City enabled them to solidify the Brotherhood and to cement their personal friendship for future work together. Their increasing potential was emerging, but Williams admitted in Bliss's *Encyclopedia of Social Reform* that "as yet the relation of Baptists to social reform is not so important for any distinct contribution that they have made to its literature

---

[22]Ibid., 267.

[23]"Baptists in Relation to Social Reform," "Brotherhood of the Kingdom," in Bliss, *Encyclopedia of Social Reform*, 141, 192; Leighton Williams, "The Brotherhood of the Kingdom and Its Work," *The Kingdom* 1 (August 1907–July 1908) 5-7; Walter Rauschenbusch, "Suggestions for the Organization of Local Chapters of the Brotherhood of the Kingdom," Walter Rauschenbusch Collection, American Baptist Historical Society, Rochester NY.

or to its institutions."[24] Reflecting on these years, Rauschenbusch on one occasion said, "I realized that God hates injustice and that I would be quenching the life of God within me if I kept silent with all this social iniquity of the world around me."[25] But some of his frustration with being unable to move others to recognize the injustice through either his own efforts or in collaboration with others was evident when he wrote, "All whose recollection runs back to 1900 will remember that as a time of lonesomeness. We were few, and we shouted in the wilderness."[26]

Honest appraisal of the Social Gospel movement in 1900 leads to the recognition that there was more latency than accomplishment. Episcopalians and Baptists were the only denomination with organized associations and platforms for promulgating Christian social responsibilities, and even those denominations had not made any official commitment to the cause of social Christianity. To restless, committed advocates of that cause, it seemed that new approaches were needed. During the year three new shaping influences became factors that were to affect the future of the emerging movement: an organization, a book, and a person.

The first was the founding of a new organization, an interreligious conference on social concerns in New York State initiated by Leighton Williams and Josiah Strong. On 23 May 1899, R. Heber Newton, rector of All Soul's Episcopal Church; James M. Whiton of the editorial staff of *The Outlook*; and A. C. McGiffert, professor at Union Theological Seminary, joined Strong and Williams to form a General Committee to plan such a meeting. During the months that followed they were joined by other interested leaders: Lyman Abbott, editor of *The Outlook*; Frank Mason North, corresponding secretary of the Methodist New York City Evangelization Union; W. S. Rainsford, rector of St. George's Episcopal institutional church; Theodore Roosevelt, governor of New York; and Augustus H. Strong, president of Rochester Theological Seminary. Williams served as general secretary. Agreeing to follow the form and procedures for papers and discussion developed by both the Episcopal Church Congress and the Baptist

---

[24]Bliss, *Encyclopedia of Social Reform*, 141-42.

[25]Rauschenbusch to Lemuel Call Barnes, 10 May 1918; reprinted in *Rochester Theological Seminary Bulletin* (November 1918): 38-39.

[26]Walter Rauschenbusch, *Christianizing the Social Order* (New York: Macmillan Company, 1912) 9.

Congress, the General Committee scheduled the first public meeting for 20-22 November 1900 in New York City.[27]

The distinctive nature of the New York State Conference of Religion was obvious in its purpose and membership. Its aim was to unite all the religious forces of New York State to promote observance of the Ten Commandments in order to achieve "social as well as individual betterment." As its motto the conference stated: "There are many religions, but religion is one. Accordingly, it is a Conference of Religion, not of religions." In contrast to other ecumenical gatherings that normally included only evangelical Protestants, the new conference included Jews and Unitarians among its speakers and members. Seeking a religious spirit that could appeal to persons of various faiths to cooperate religiously, the conference affirmed that the moral interests of religion should be supreme in dealing with the symptoms of moral decay in American society.[28] While this broad-based aim and constituency gave it potential appeal in the Progressive Era, it also stimulated enough criticism to require explanation. During 1901 the Conference of Religion justified its continued existence alongside the New York State Federation of Churches, also founded late in 1900, by stating that the latter promoted evangelization of individuals first and social reform second, while the former felt both needs were equally important and would not neglect social and civic needs.[29] Leighton Williams eventually felt it necessary to express an *apologia* by evangelicals who participated in the conference.[30]

Another unique feature of the New York State Conference of Religion was its ability to bring together a number of persons who emerged as leaders of social Christianity during the first decade of the twentieth century, and to provide them a platform for the fertilization of ideas across denominational lines. In this way Walter Rauschenbusch in 1900 heard the renowned Washington Gladden, pastor of First Congregational Church, Columbus, Ohio, speak on "Religion Vital to Democracy," and

---

[27]New York State Conference of Religion, correspondence, printed folders, and newspaper clippings in a pamphlet box, Union Theological Seminary, New York NY.

[28]Conference programs, 20-22 November 1900, 18-20 November 1902, 12-13 November 1903, ibid.

[29]"New York State Conference of Religion," printed folder dated January 1902, ibid.

[30]"The New York State Conference of Religion," *The Christian Register*, 27 November 1902, 1405, ibid.

learned that his views were similar to those of the more famous social prophet. Drawing on his new political involvement as a member of the Columbus City Council, as well as on his long-standing concern about government, Gladden in that address lamented the prevalent notion that politics and religion were regarded as separate realms, which produced "a great deal of practical atheism" in American political affairs. To counteract this, said Gladden, Americans needed to recognize that the power of religion is necessary to democracy.

> Something there must be in the appeal that democracy makes to its citizens which is deeper than self-interest, and diviner than the will of the majority. If we can believe that in the nation, not less truly than in the individual, it is God that worketh; that there is a Power not ourselves, that makes for righteousness in the ongoings of the state; that there is a moral ideal toward which He is leading us and which it is our business to discern and realize; that thus . . . we may be co-workers with God in the building of His Kingdom in the world, then there are motives to be drawn from the life of the state that are higher than mere expediency, that appeal to faith and imagination and self-devotion.[31]

Although Rauschenbusch at the time lacked the reputation of Gladden, Lyman Abbot, Josiah Strong, or even Leighton Williams, some who attended the conference in 1900 may later have remembered hearing him encourage the audience not to ignore the importance of the personal religious life in their preoccupation with social salvation.[32] The quality of the speakers at the conferences was noted by one reporter who commented on "the eminent and recognized ability of . . . those who took part."[33]

In addition to its speakers, the New York State Conference of Religion was also distinctive for its concentration on the moral dimensions of national and civic life. Not only were there themes dealing with moral mission, crisis in morals, and national righteousness, but also there were opening interpretations by Leighton Williams and closing messages by Josiah Strong that stressed this dimension.[34] By 1903 an Executive Committee of the conference had emerged, and James M. Whiton, as its chairman, annually

---

[31]"Religion Vital to Democracy," *Proceedings of the New York State Conference of Religion, November 1900* (New York: New York State Conference of Religion, n.d.) 116-24.

[32]"Religion The Life of God in the Soul of Man," ibid., 35-36.

[33]*The Christian Register,* 27 November 1902, 1405.

[34]Conference programs, 1900, 1901, 1902.

presented what amounted to a report on the moral state of the nation. Like a physician with his fingers on the national pulse, Whiton kept close watch on America's moral health. These reports provided a regular analysis in a time when moral decline became a dominant concern in the nation and served as a corrective to the moral sensitivities of denominational bodies that were neither as consistent nor as finely tuned on this issue as Whiton and the New York State Conference of Religion.[35]

Such concern for national morality and righteousness was present in 1900, but that conscience further evolved as the Conference of Religion became a continuing institution. At the turn of the century, proponents of social Christianity generally were more attracted by economic problems and their consequences. In the same month as the first New York State Conference of Religion, November 1900, Francis Greenwood Peabody's *Jesus Christ and the Social Question* reached bookstores. It was the second new influence to shape the movement that year. With a fresh interpretation of perennial problems confronting socially concerned Christians, Peabody, who was Professor of Christian Morals at Harvard University, produced his first major book beyond published college meditations, and it attracted such a wide reading that it had been reprinted twenty times by 1913. Its ideas permeated and influenced the expression of social-gospel ideas during the Progressive Era.[36]

Peabody's essential contribution in that volume was his combination of several problems into a single term. In effect, his analysis reduced a number of problems to what he called "the social question." Considering such modern social questions as the family, wealth, poverty, and the industrial order, he presented them as concentric circles that affected individual lives. "The area of each problem in succession is seen to be an essential part of a more comprehensive problem with a larger circumference and content." As a consequence, there is a mutual dependence that makes it impossible to identify neatly cause and effect. On this basis, Peabody argued that it was impossible to solve any one of the social questions, for "each has a part in the solution of all the rest, and all are in a measure dependent on the progress of each." Only by recognizing that the whole social body moves together or it does not move at all is one able to comprehend fully the problem and work

---

[35]*Addresses before the New York State Conference of Religion,* ser. 2 (March 1904): 5-6; ser. 3 (April 1905): 8-10; ser. 5 (February 1907): 4-7; ser. 7 (February 1909): 9-11; ser. 9 (February 1911): 8; ser. 10 (June 1912): 29-30; ser. 11 (February 1913): 6-12.

[36]Francis Greenwood Peabody, *Jesus Christ and the Social Question: An Examination of the Teaching of Jesus in Its Relation to Some of the Problems of Modern Social Life* (New York: Macmillan Company, 1900).

toward its solution. According to Peabody, "The correlation of the social questions gives to the scattered movements of social reform a unity and interdependence so vast and complex that one must dismiss the notion of a panacea for each separate social ill, and content himself with an imperfect and contributory service."[37]

On the surface the social questions appear to be industrial or political, Peabody said, but underneath they are really ethical questions because they are manifestations of the moral life of the times. Modern conscience thus becomes a source of social energy and "finds its main channel of expression in the social forces of modern reform." Maintaining that "social progress is but the expression of moral energy," he concluded that "in every social question the problem of guiding and directing social energy lies behind the problem of developing social organization." For Professor Peabody, the teachings of Jesus form an abundant source of social energy, and the main problem facing the Christian Church is to communicate "to the social movement that social energy which the teaching of Jesus originates and conserves." If only the church could be the "power-house" the social order needs, that would be its contribution in what Peabody designated "the age of the social question."[38]

By correlating several social questions into "the social question," Francis Peabody broadened the perception of the task confronting the Christian Church in the United States. Through institutional churches and social settlements, Christians could minister to the immediate needs of individuals, families, and communities, but the interrelated nature of social problems made it impossible to eliminate the causes simply by alleviating the symptoms. As a result, the problems facing champions of social Christianity were larger than formerly recognized; no longer was it enough for committed individuals or voluntary associations to minister to needs alone, they also needed to solve the causes of the problems. Since the basic concerns were so large, they required new strategies designed on a communitywide and nationwide basis. Peabody's interpretation affected the whole understanding of social salvation and challenged the social movement in Christianity not just to correct problems but to Christianize the social order.

During November 1900 the presidential election produced a third component that would influence the development of social Christianity for many years. The election of Theodore Roosevelt as William McKinley's vice-president on 6 November brought to the national scene a man who

---

[37]Ibid., ch. 7, 327-35.

[38]Ibid., 335-59.

was a Progressive in politics, a reformer in society, and a social activist in religious outlook. While the reelected McKinley continued as president, the influence of Mark Hanna and Republican machine politics made Roosevelt's presence little more than a popular name on a national ticket; but with the assassination and death of McKinley, the political destiny of the nation was significantly affected. When Theodore Roosevelt took the oath as the twenty-sixth president of the United States at age forty-two on 14 September 1901, he enabled the Progressive movement to attain recognition and ushered in a new political era.

Even before Roosevelt became nationally prominent, he was favorably regarded by Protestants in New York. Sponsors of the New York State Conference of Religion were delighted not only that Roosevelt as governor was interested in their effort but also that he was willing to be part of its General Committee.[39] Jacob Riis, social reformer and author, wrote an appreciative sketch of their mutual relationships in the cause of social service and better government that appeared in the *American Monthly Review of Reviews*.[40] *The Churchman* publicly endorsed Roosevelt "as the best possible candidate," noting that he had been "so useful to the public as Governor of New York" and "so obnoxious to the Republican machine."[41] Earlier in the year the weekly Episcopal periodical praised Roosevelt's address on "The Ideal and the Practical" delivered to the Sewanee College alumni, in which the governor stated characteristically that "men must work for ideals, but they must work in practical fashion . . . 'I do not pardon the politician who steals. I do not pardon the reformer who is a fool,' nor him who is more anxious to be independent than right."[42]

Similar advice was expressed by Governor Roosevelt in an article for *The Churchman* titled "The Best and the Good." Indicating that every leader of reform has to contend not only with those who oppose the reform but also with extreme advocates for the cause, he argued that both extremists were mistaken and dangerous. Roosevelt warned that zealots need "to realize that healthy growth cannot normally come through revolution," and he concluded, "We do only harm if, by intemperate championship

---

[39]"New York State Conference of Religion," printed folder dated June 1900, in pamphlet box, Union Theological Seminary.

[40]"Mr. Riis on Governor Roosevelt," *American Monthly Review of Reviews* (1 September 1900): 281.

[41]*The Churchman* (New York), 30 June 1900, p. 793.

[42]Ibid., 27 January 1900, pp. 118, 96.

of the impossible good, we cut ourselves off from the opportunity to work a real abatement of existing and menacing evil."[43] His moral pragmatism and moderation appealed to most Protestant supporters of social Christianity, who widely supported his views and actions in the years to come.[44] The editor of *The Churchman* voiced the high regard in which Roosevelt was held when endorsing his nomination for the vice-presidency: "Governor Roosevelt is to-day one of the most useful men in American public life. The force of his example is very great."[45]

That Roosevelt used his influence in positive ways was obvious late in December when as vice-president elect and governor he addressed the Young Men's Christian Association on "Christian Citizenship," urging his audience to base their social and political life on the Ten Commandments and the Golden Rule. "Christianity teaches," he concluded, "not only that each of us must so live as to save his own soul, but that each must also strive to do his whole duty by his neighbor," and he challenged his hearers to strive toward that end.[46]

Examination of the Christian social movement in America in the year 1900 has revealed that the cause had its advocates, who had achieved modest accomplishments. Social Christianity's most obvious evidences were found in institutional churches and social settlements, in a growing number of books, and in a few voluntary groups whose meetings provided platforms for vital concerns and fellowship for lonely advocates of a cause that did not have widespread support. Most of what occurred during the year had originated in the 1890s. By November, however, there were new signs that provided hope for the future. Organization of the interreligious New York State Conference of Religion furnished a broader platform for considering the moral basis of American social and civic life. Publication of Francis Greenwood Peabody's *Jesus Christ and the Social Question* proposed a new perception for understanding the larger dimensions of social responsibility. And election of Theodore Roosevelt as vice-president

---

[43]"The Best and the Good," ibid., 17 March 1900, p. 320.

[44]Washington Gladden, "The Church and the Social Crisis," *Minutes of the National Council of the Congregational Churches of the United States* (1907), 9-10; Walter Rauschenbusch, *Christianity and the Social Crisis* (New York: Macmillan Company, 1907) 386.

[45]*The Churchman* (New York), 30 June 1900, p. 793.

[46]Theodore Roosevelt, *The Works of Theodore Roosevelt*, National Edition, 20 vols., ed. Hermann Hagedorn (New York: Charles Scribner's Sons, 1926) 13:492-99.

of the United States, while taking advantage of a popular name, enabled a reform-minded official to reach national office. These three factors offered new perspective, new platform, and new political potential as socially concerned Protestants approached the beginnings of the twentieth century in 1901.

Despite the lack of widespread acceptance and influence in Protestant denominations or the nation, advocates of the social gospel were persistent optimists whose faith in the social teachings of Jesus, in the social mission he entrusted to them, and in their role in reviving a morally pure democracy in America made them confident they could not be overcome. That optimism was well evidenced in 1900 by Charles Ferguson in his book *The Religion of Democracy*. Believing that democracy would be inconceivable without religion, he affirmed that "democracy stands to-day at the grand junction and crossroads of history." "This is the very whirlwind of moral revolution," he insisted, and democracy is to achieve the new order and the new spirit. Not just democracy in general, for he was convinced that European democracy was passing away and "the moral hegemony of the world" was passing to the United States. "This land, America, shall be the land of the incarnation"; in it the new democracy would emerge. As a symbol of what he envisioned, Ferguson described the dome of the Capitol in Washington, D.C. Viewing it in the sunlight it reminded him "of things that have been, but are passing away." But looking at the dome from his window at night with the moon shining on it, he saw it as "a symbol of the new age and the America that is in the making." Admitting that "there is no social question anywhere that is not in the United States," he had no doubt that democracy in this land would prevail because of the "faith in the heart of America."[47] Such confidence in the power to solve the social question motivated champions of social Christianity, even if many other Christians were not equally convinced. Whether or not they agreed about the social question, Protestants generally agreed that a revival in America was needed as the nation entered the new century.

---

[47]Charles Ferguson, *The Religion of Democracy: A Memorandum of Modern Principles* (New York: Funk & Wagnalls, 1900) iii-iv, 36, 41-42, 55-61.

CHAPTER 2

The Next Great Awakening

If neglected Scriptural truth precisely adapted to the peculiar needs of our own times can be pointed out, is there not a strong presumption that the next great spiritual awakening will come when this truth is faithfully preached?

It is quite obvious that the great questions peculiar to our times are social. . . . That is, a social conscience is growing, though as yet it is uninstructed.

(Josiah Strong,
The Next Great Awakening, *1902)*

"THE NEW CENTURY was ushered in with many kinds of celebrations in all parts of the country," wrote the editor of *The Outlook* in January 1901. Among these was "a movement for a revival of religion" as an appropriate way for Protestants to inaugurate the twentieth century.[1] For most, the expected revivals were of the type that had become familiar under the leadership of Dwight L. Moody, who had died in 1899. But for others, a new type of awakening was envisioned, a social awakening.

Typical of the traditional pattern was the campaign sponsored by the Evangelical Alliance for the United States. Designated the "Twentieth Century Movement to Evangelize the Nation," this program was led by both clergy and laity who believed that God would bless the nation if only church people generated a genuine concern for "the salvation of souls through existing organizations and agencies." An appeal issued by the movement declared: "An extraordinary development of spiritual unrest is now taking place at many points in the United States. There is a widely

---

[1]"The New Century" and "The Social Apostolate," *The Outlook* (New York), 12 January 1901, pp. 92, 93-94.

extended expectation of the coming of a mighty awakening."[2] A Week of Prayer to usher in the new era was set for 6-13 January 1901.[3]

Preparation for such programs had been stimulated by publication in 1900 of John R. Mott's challenging book *The Evangelization of the World in This Generation.* As executive secretary of the Student Volunteer Movement for Foreign Missions, Mott wrote to explain the title, which was the watchword of his organization. Rather than proposing a new program for quick results, he emphasized the basic need to proclaim the Christian Gospel to people who had not heard it so that God might move as he willed in their lives. When the book and phrase caught hold in the popular mind, Mott was surprised because the motto had been adopted when the organization was formed in 1888. Mott hoped that missionary and other Christian organizations would accept the watchword, but he stressed that individual Christians had to implement it if it was to be realized. Although he elaborated the social dimensions and expectations implied in the evangelical slogan, the individualistic part of his message made the greater impact at the time. While the evangelization of the world might encompass the social order, most readers saw it in terms of individual salvation in America as well as in missions around the world. Mott's book contained both social and individual emphases, but the latter dominated, which reflected the prevalent Protestant view of evangelism and revivals at the turn of the century.[4]

A contrasting emphasis was sounded early in 1901, however, by Josiah Strong. Speaking on "The Next Great Revival" to the organizational meeting of the new National Federation of Churches and Christian Workers the first week in February, Strong said that the fundamental law of the kingdom of God contained two requirements: to love God and to love one's neighbor. In recent years only the first had been stressed, and it was time for the church to begin to put greater accent on the second. "When the social aspects of Christianity are thus insisted on," he asserted, "the next great revival will come."[5] Later in the year there was a "Demand for a Moral Revival" by the New York State Conference of Religion, which

---

[2]*Annual Report of the Evangelical Alliance for the United States of America,* (1900) 7-8.

[3]Ibid., 3-7.

[4]John R. Mott, *The Evangelization of the World in This Generation* (New York: Student Volunteer Movement for Foreign Missions, 1900) esp. chs. 1 and 9.

[5]"A National Organization," *The Outlook* (New York), 16 February 1901, p. 380.

declared that it was impossible to correct "the moral corruption and conscienceless commercialism in politics that infect the civic body" unless these were extirpated by "a religious revival of the dormant moral sense of the people."[6]

During October 1901 the first official actions demonstrating social concern on the part of Protestant denominations occurred, but they were not momentous and seemingly had little relationship to the religious revivals. By joint legislation of the House of Bishops and the House of Deputies, the Protestant Episcopal Church voted to establish a Joint Commission on Capital and Labor and assigned it several duties: to study the aims and purposes of labor organizations, to investigate the causes of industrial disturbances, to serve as arbitrators between employers and workers "should their services be desired," and to report back to the General Convention when it reconvened in three years.[7] Meeting the same month, the National Council of the Congregational Churches also voted to appoint a Committee on Labor and ordered it to prepare a report for the next triennial meeting.[8] Thus, the initial official actions of both the Episcopal and Congregational Churches were directed at industrial problems and indicated that the lengthy emphasis on economic issues had finally made an impact and elicited attention. Protestantism's first authoritative steps were cautious and required little of the denominations, but they constituted a modest beginning of official social concern.

Though simultaneous with the general emphasis on evangelism and moral awakening, these hesitant actions concerning economic problems mirrored the basic discrepancy in Protestantism between individual and social salvation. That difference attracted the attention of social gospel partisans at all levels in the early 1900s.

In a local situation, for example, Worth M. Tippy, a Methodist minister at Indianapolis, read a paper on the kingdom of God to a ministerial meeting in that city in December 1901. As he neared the close, Tippy argued that the gospel of the kingdom

> must be interpreted to the entire life of man, individual and social; to the home, to social customs, to the organization of industries, to education, to

---

[6]"New York State Conference of Religion," printed folder dated January 1902, p. 2, in the organization's correspondence, printed folders, and newspaper clippings pamphlet box, Union Theological Seminary, New York City.

[7]*Journal of the General Convention of the Protestant Episcopal Church in the U.S.A.*, (1901) 271, 296.

[8]National Council of the Congregational Churches, *The National Council Digest* (Boston: Under direction of the National Council, 1905) 47.

government, to diplomacy, to literature and the fine arts, to the correction of social evils, etc., as well as to the eternal welfare of human hearts. In short the Gospel that we teach should be one of world regeneration as well as of personal regeneration and they should go hand in hand, as one great unified message. To Jesus there was no distinction, such as we make between a social gospel and an individual gospel. It was all one mighty organic movement to him.[9]

Stressing that Jesus always emphasized "the necessity of transformed men for a regenerated society," the little-known Methodist pastor warned that dividing the message into individual and social components distorted the truth. "But if these two elements be preached together," he maintained, "they will issue some day . . . into a redeemed society upon the earth."[10]

Three months later, in March 1902, the more renowned Washington Gladden expressed similar ideas in his Lyman Beecher Lectures at the Divinity School of Yale University. Addressing himself to the social question as Peabody had expressed it, Gladden asked whether it could be better answered through the individual or through social organization. He was certain that putting the whole emphasis on personal experience was an inadequate way to answer society's cry, "What must I do to be saved?" The individual and social ideas "can no more be separated in Christian morality than the outside of a curve can be separated from the inside . . . . No individual can be right with his God who is not in right relations to his neighbors." On this basis Gladden urged,

> There can be no adequate social reform save that which springs from a genuine revival of religion; only it must be a religion which is less concerned about getting men to heaven than about fitting them for their proper work on earth; which does not set itself over against the secular life in contrast, but enters into the secular life and subdues it by its power and rules it by its law, and transfigures it by its light.[11]

In proposing his approach to what he called "social salvation," the experienced Gladden suggested to the future ministers he addressed that some awakening of conscience and development of ideas already had occurred in the last years of the nineteenth century and they might learn

---

[9]Worth M. Tippy, "The Need of a Synthesis of the Social and Individual Elements of the Christian Religion," Worth M. Tippy Papers, File DC614, Folder 13, Archives of DePauw University and Indiana Methodism, Greencastle IN 39-40.

[10]Ibid., 41-43.

[11]Washington Gladden, *Social Salvation* (Boston: Houghton Mifflin and Co., 1902) iv-v, 1-31.

from both. By his estimation, the primary goal was the Christianizing of society, and the most important function in that task was not to develop machinery but to provide motive power for achieving that end. Christian leaders ought to inspire others to "the spirit of social service" and "the feeling that [the] business of citizenship is a high and sacred function."[12] Although expressed in light of Peabody's *Jesus Christ and the Social Question*, Gladden in his second series of Beecher Lectures harkened back to his first series delivered in 1887, which was especially devoted to the idea of the Christianization of society.[13] In the earlier lectures he dealt almost totally with economic problems, but in this second series his perspective was more inclusive. When he emphasized "The Redemption of the City," he also drew on part of the argument in his previous book *Social Facts and Forces*.[14] Thus, Gladden helped pass on the ideas of the late nineteenth century as he spoke to his audience of ministerial students.

The social prophet from Columbus was not the only champion of social Christianity who provided continuity with America's previous religious experience. Josiah Strong enlarged his ideas on "The Next Great Revival" that he had shared with the National Federation of Churches and Christian Workers in 1901 into a book titled *The Next Great Awakening*, which appeared in 1902. In his book he again called for a new revival, but this time he set his appeal in the long history of Christian revivalism. "Is there to be during the twentieth century a mighty religious awakening, such as occurred in the sixteenth, seventeenth, and eighteenth centuries, and in both the first and second half of the nineteenth?" he asked. Studying those movements, he observed that Moody's message did not repeat that of Finney, who had not reiterated the message of Wesley, the Puritans, or Luther. Each revival had its own message because it made God real to its generation. According to Strong, "each of these great religious awakenings came in connection with the preaching of a neglected Scriptural truth which was precisely adapted to the peculiar needs of the times." If this was a correct reading of history, he concluded that finding the neglected biblical truth in the twentieth century would stimulate the desired spiritual quickening because the earnest efforts for new awakening in America and Great Britain in this new century had not met with notable success. Applying this historical interpretation to his day, Strong

---

[12]Ibid., 229-35.

[13]Washington Gladden, *Tools and the Man: Property and Industry under the Christian Law* (Boston: Houghton Mifflin and Co., 1893) esp. ch. 1.

[14]Cf. Washington Gladden, *Social Facts and Forces* (New York: G. P. Putnam's Sons, 1897) ch. 5 with *Social Salvation*, ch. 7.

believed that "the great questions peculiar to our times are social," and the central scriptural idea that was new and fit the needs of the industrial age was the kingdom of God as revealed in the social teachings of Jesus.[15] In several chapters on the kingdom and Jesus' teachings, Strong noted that modern Christians were slowly achieving self-consciousness about the industrial revolution, and from this "new social consciousness is coming the new social conscience." Only when it became obvious that Christians were different from other citizens would others see any reason to change. Thus, Christians themselves needed to apply the social teachings of Jesus to existing conditions if there was to be another time of spiritual quickening. For Strong, the next great awakening had to be a social awakening.[16]

Two years later, Walter Rauschenbusch also evidenced the central place of the evangelical motif in the thinking of social-gospel leaders. Now Professor of Church History at Rochester Theological Seminary, Rauschenbusch used historical perspective when writing his essay "The New Evangelism," which appeared in *The Independent* in May 1904.[17] Convinced that "the evangelizing power of the Church depends on its moral prestige and spiritual authority," he showed that the old evangelism was no longer effective because modern life was changing rapidly and the church had not kept pace. Noting that it was unfair to charge that churches had not tried to reach people because they had concentrated unparalleled energy into urban evangelism in the last generation, he maintained that such massive efforts had been futile because the message had not been stated in terms of new conditions. Commercial and professional classes dominated church life in many congregations, which in turn reflected their ethics and values, and consequently the laboring class felt uncomfortable and alienated in such groups. To reach them, Christians should be open to two influences: the spirit of Jesus in their lives and a clear vision of "the life of our own time." Those influences would produce a new evangelism by showing how a Christian should live under modern conditions, which would be less individualistic and more social.

At the opening of the twentieth century, advocates of social Christianity shared with other Protestants the desire for a new spiritual awakening. In attempting to achieve that common goal, the differences between

---

[15]Josiah Strong, *The Next Great Awakening* (New York: Baker & Taylor, 1902) 34-50.

[16]Ibid., 188-226.

[17]*The Independent* (New York), 12 May 1904, pp. 1056-61.

an individual gospel and a social gospel became more apparent, and that discrepancy continued to affect social ministry in the years to come. To the disappointment of partisans of both convictions, the expected awakening at the dawn of the new century did not materialize, whether it was formulated as a movement to evangelize the nation or the world on the one hand, or as a new evangelism, a social awakening, or social salvation on the other.

That some advocates of both persuasions struggled to hold on to the concern of the other was evident during 1902. When the Evangelical Alliance issued the invitation to its Week of Prayer in 1903, it noted signs of spiritual progress but confessed that there were sins, evils, and woes that were "more than enough to make the whole head sick and whole heart faint" and that "society [was] marred by wrongs and rent by strifes, which the full presence of the Kingdom would remove." In light of these conditions they urged, "Let us plead for the saving of souls, for the redemption of society, for the Christianizing of the nations, and for the doing of God's will on earth as it is done in heaven."[18] When the New York State Conference of Religion met in November 1902, a journalist commented on the session on "social salvation" by saying, in part, "Men are thinking now of saving society, and their souls are saved as they go along."[19] While differing in emphasis, the two organizations still sought to hold on to both individual and social salvation.

But the condition of social Christianity at the end of 1902 had not improved much, if the experience of the New York State Conference of Religion was a fair barometer. The reporter who attended its meeting in New York City observed that the session on "The Present Crisis in Morals" attracted the largest attendance, but he concluded that "the absence of great crowds" was evidence that the conference was "in advance of popular thought." "The interest it awakened was profound and intelligent," but for an elite group of leaders primarily.[20] A comment in a letter to Leighton Williams, general secretary of the conference, verified the reporter's perception: "Of course we must all have been disappointed at the very small attendance & little interest shown by even that part of the public whose interest might have been expected."[21]

---

[18]*Annual Report of the Evangelical Alliance* (1902), 8.

[19]*The Christian Register*, 27 November 1902, 1405.

[20]Ibid.

[21]A member of the executive committee to Leighton Williams, 28 November 1902, in New York State Conference of Religion, correspondence, printed folders, and newspaper clippings pamphlet box, Union Theological Seminary, New York City.

For proponents of the social gospel there was no more cause for rejoicing at the end of 1902 than there was for those who supported the cause of a religious awakening at the opening of the twentieth century. To that point no new spiritual vitality was evident in social Christianity. The major books by Gladden and Strong that year were evidence of expectations that were still unfulfilled. Social salvation and social awakening continued to be goals rather than accomplishments; but the dominance of traditional Protestant evangelical terminology and hopefulness was obvious in the continued use of such language by social advocates even when they sought to enlarge the conventional understanding to include the redemption of society.

CHAPTER 3

A Good Deal
of Moral Anarchy Prevailing

Those who have read the papers and the periodical literature of the last year are aware of a good deal of moral anarchy prevailing. Yet the churches, if we may judge by the sermonic literature that appears in print, if we may judge by what one hears in churches, or what one sees taking place in their great assemblies, do not seem to be very greatly disturbed by the situation, although it has been getting worse and worse for the past twenty years.

(James Whiton,
New York State Conference on Religion, December 1904)

ALTHOUGH SOCIAL-GOSPEL ADVOCATES had been studying social problems for years, they, and other Americans, were appalled by a steady flow of revelations that began to appear in popular periodicals late in 1902. For the next several years journalists shocked the nation with one exposé after another that disclosed corrupt practices in business and government that affected the lives of everyone. Revealing in specific detail what had been discussed previously in a general way as the social question, writers in ten-cent magazines informed the populace of the extent, depth, and complexity of the problems caused by those who sought to gain their own advantage by various immoral or illegal means. In the process, the sensational journalists aroused the populace to revulsion and demands for reform more effectively than proponents of social Christianity. Indeed, to some Protestant leaders it seemed clear that the social awakening had started not through the churches but outside them.

In the month that the New York State Conference of Religion bemoaned the lack of interest in social issues among church people, *McClure's Magazine*, one of the new low-priced periodicals, published the first installment of Ida Tarbell's series "The History of Standard Oil." The preceding month the same periodical had printed Lincoln Steffens's article "Tweed Days in St. Louis." Two months later editor S. S. McClure noted that his journal contained three articles on one subject: "We did not plan it so; it is a coincidence that the January *McClure's* is such an arraignment of American character as should make every one of us stop and think." That number included another installment of Tarbell's series on John D. Rockefeller's Standard Oil Company, an article by Steffens on "The Shame of Minneapolis," and one by Ray Stannard Baker on "The Right to Work." The cumulative effect led editor McClure to write, "Capitalists, workingmen, politicians, citizens—all breaking the law, or letting it be broken. Who is left to uphold it?"[1]

While the Steffens article on the Tweed Ring in October pioneered the literary style, the January 1903 issue of *McClure's* first evidenced the self-awareness that generally has been acclaimed as creating the muckraking movement. The form of literature was widespread before the name "muckraker" was applied to it derisively by Theodore Roosevelt in 1906. Likening exposé writers to "the Man with the Muck-rake" in Bunyan's *Pilgrim's Progress* because they concentrated "with solemn intentness only on that which is vile and debasing," the president of the United States sought to warn the nation of excesses and inaccuracies by such authors. But at the same time he recognized that "there should be relentless exposure of and attack upon every evil man, whether politician or business man, every evil practice, whether in politics, in business, or in social life."[2]

For the next decade muckraking articles probed into virtually every problem area: corruption in city, state, and national governments; manipulation by corporations; exploitation of labor, especially of women and children; contamination of food and drugs; injustice in the legal system; dishonesty in insurance; distortion by the press; and even hypocrisy in religion.[3] Utilizing the inexpensive magazine that had emerged in the 1890s with a price workers could afford, and in contrast to the older twenty-five- and thiry-five-cent magazines like *Harper's* and *Atlantic*, the

---

[1]*McClure's*, January 1903; quoted in Richard Hofstadter, ed., *The Progressive Movement, 1900–1915* (Englewood Cliffs NJ: Prentice-Hall Inc., Spectrum Books, 1963) 16-17.

[2]"The Man with the Muck-Rake," *The Outlook* (New York), 21 April 1906, pp. 883-87.

[3]Examples of the variety of this literature can be found in an anthology by Harvey Swados, ed., *Years of Conscience: The Muckrakers, An Anthology* (Cleveland: World Publishing Co., Meridian Books, 1962).

muckrakers nevertheless appealed primarily to middle-class morality rather than to the laboring masses. This further enlarged the circulation of these periodicals and constituted a new stage in the evolution of American journalism. Beginning late in 1902, the muckraking movement became militant in 1903, sensational in 1904 and 1905, and in vogue by 1906. It continued fitfully for several years, experienced a revival in 1911 and 1912, and then lost its force as a movement.[4]

Muckrakers worked with a sensitive social conscience that was essentially Protestant as well as middle class in its morality. Using such words as *sin, greed, guilt, salvation, righteousness,* and *soul* in their descriptions of the flaws they discerned in society, these writers expressed an evangelical understanding of human nature. It was their conviction that most Americans were ignorant of the true condition of democracy in the country, and they determined to reveal it. The muckrakers sought to stimulate public conscience by appealing to personal morality, with the expectation that citizens would act morally when informed of the evil conditions in their environment.[5] Leaders of the Social Gospel movement recognized their kinship with those ideas and drew heavily on the data uncovered by the muckrakers, as we shall see later. In turn, muckrakers evidenced the influence of social-gospel advocates in developing their own values, even though a number abandoned the organized church.[6]

Despite the influence of their efforts in shaping opinion, the muckrakers also reflected the views of their times. The muckraking movement was closely related to the progressive movement for reform, much of which had originated before the journalists began their revelations. Progressivism was so wide-ranging in its interests and issues that it defies precise definition, but three main tendencies of its political expression were identified by Benjamin Parke DeWitt: (1) "that special, minority, and

---

[4]Frank Luther Mott, "The Magazine Revolution and Popular Ideas in the Nineties," *Proceedings of the American Antiquarian Society,* n.s., 64 (1954): 195-96, 205-208; C. C. Regier, *The Era of the Muckrakers* (Chapel Hill: University of North Carolina Press, 1932) 49-50, 194-95.

[5]Stanley K. Schultz, "The Morality of Politics: The Muckrakers' Vision of Democracy," *The Journal of American History* 52 (1965): 527-47.

[6]Ray Stannard Baker to Washington Gladden, 7 October 1907, Gladden Papers, Ohio Historical Society, Columbus OH; John Graham Brooks to Walter Rauschenbusch, 29 November 1908, Upton Sinclair to Rauschenbusch, 4 February 1907, Rauschenbusch Papers, American Baptist Historical Society, Rochester NY; Ray Stannard Baker, *The Spiritual Unrest* (New York: Frederick A. Stokes Co., 1909) ch. 7.

corrupt influence" in all levels of government be removed, (2) that the machinery of government should be controlled by the many rather than the few, and (3) that the functions of government should "be increased and extended to relieve social and economic distress."[7] These concerns were larger than any political party, section of the country, or reform movement, and they were already expressed by the time the first muck-raking article appeared. For example, Washington Gladden was elected to the Columbus City Council in 1900, where he opposed efforts by the street-railway company and the gas company to extend their franchises at the expense of the citizens; Tom L. Johnson was elected reform mayor of Cleveland, Ohio, in 1901; and Oregon instituted the initiative and referendum by constitutional amendment in 1902.

Since the progressive movement transcended political parties it would be inaccurate to identify any single person as exemplifying its essence, but Theodore Roosevelt came close. In the first decade of the twentieth century he worked for the three goals defined by DeWitt and thought of himself as a progressive. More important, through the various offices he held at city, state, and national levels Roosevelt was able to articulate as well as implement progressive values. William Allen White, one of the muckrakers, later described Roosevelt as a preacher whose ideas had great influence because the offices he held were like a sounding board over his pulpit to magnify the sound.[8] Many of his political speeches were homilies that were simple to understand. He made no effort to be profound, but with clarity and vigor he preached the ideals of honesty, courage, common sense, and citizenship, based on living the Ten Commandments and the Golden Rule.[9] Like the muckrakers, Roosevelt voiced a popular version of Protestant morality, and champions of social Christianity viewed him as both hero and colleague in a common cause.

On 14 September 1901, Theodore Roosevelt took the oath as president of the United States after William McKinley died earlier that day from a wound inflicted by an assassin. That change in leadership produced a

---

[7]Benjamin Parke DeWitt, *The Progressive Movement: A Nonpartisan, Comprehensive Discussion of Current Tendencies in American Politics* (New York: Macmillan Company, 1915) 4-5.

[8]William Allen White, "Saith the Preacher," *The Works of Theodore Roosevelt*, National Edition, 20 vols., ed. Hermann Hagedorn (New York: Charles Scribner's Sons, 1926) 13:xi-xiii.

[9]"Latitude and Longitude among Reformers," *The Century* (June 1900) and "Christian Citizenship" (30 December 1900) both published in *The Strenuous Life* and reprinted ibid., 13:351-54, 492-99.

remarkable impact on the nation. Whereas McKinley had been a quiescent leader who cooperated with business leaders, Roosevelt was an activist who envisioned a stronger federal government that would regulate the great national corporations, especially the new trusts. That same year, 1901, the first trusts were legally incorporated, the United States Steel Corporation in March and the Northern Securities Company in November. When the new president sent his first annual message to Congress in December, he called attention to the trusts and stated his basic policy toward them. Viewing these large corporations as an inevitable product of industrial growth, he said they should not be broken up but should be regulated and their activities publicized.[10] The following summer Roosevelt again addressed what he termed "the trust question" and asserted that the "trusts are the creatures of the State, and the State has a right to control them" as necessary.[11]

During his presidency the trust issue arose from time to time, but Roosevelt did not seriously engage in "trust busting," for basically he was more concerned with extending the power of the national government in all areas than he was with dealing with a single economic problem. That assertion of greater power for the federal government was at the heart of his political policy, and the implementation of that policy led to legislation and presidential action that altered the political life of the nation. Thus, when White called Roosevelt a preacher he went on to say,

> We must not forget that Theodore Roosevelt was also accompanying his sermons with exercises in the practice of his preaching. He was sponsoring new laws, institutional changes of government, revolutionary attitudes toward politics and life. Along with all the uproar about righteousness came "the Roosevelt policies." The simplicity of the moralities was only the foundation upon which a political leader was building a rather complicated structure of social and industrial justice.[12]

By 23 October 1903 the critique by the muckrakers had already made an impression. That day President Roosevelt literally preached a sermon on " 'God Save the State' " at the Cathedral of St. Peter and St. Paul in Washington, D.C. Addressing the assembled Episcopal bishops, clergy, and laity he declared, "We need civic righteousness," and he argued that

---

[10]H. R. Richardson, *Messages and Papers of the Presidents*, 16:6645-49; quoted in Hofstadter, *The Progressive Movement*, 141-44.

[11]"The Control of Corporations," address at Providence RI, 23 August 1902, in Hagedorn, *Works of Theodore Roosevelt*, 16:61-68.

[12]White, "Saith the Preacher," ibid., 13:xii-xiii.

honest citizens could provide it. "Surely in every movement for the betterment of our life," he challenged, "we have a special right to ask not merely support but leadership from those of the Church."[13]

Three weeks later James Whiton quoted those remarks to the annual meeting of the New York State Conference of Religion. But as he examined the church he concluded that "few signs of that leadership appear. The great assemblies of the Church are mainly concerned with ecclesiastical and theological questions." The denominations seldom went beyond condemnation of drinking, divorce, and desecrating the Sabbath to address any other moral evils in society. Thus, in Whiton's estimation, it was necessary for the conference to promote the central ethical issues: "Religious men must combine to save the State from the commercialism in politics which corrupts citizenship, to save the Church from the refined materialism which threatens religion and democracy with a common overthrow."[14] In the spring of 1904 he again challenged the conference "to offset the moral degeneracy which now so seriously menaces our National life in America."[15] And when the conference convened the following December, Whiton called Christians to work for "a moral revival, a revival of righteousness, a re-awakening of the social conscience." Noting that the newspapers and periodicals during the past year revealed "a good deal of moral anarchy prevailing," he saw little evidence that churches seemed very disturbed by the social situation.[16] Evidence in the official records of five Protestant churches generally corroborated Whiton's charges, although there were some signs of new activity by the middle of the decade.

When the triennial General Convention of the Protestant Episcopal Church met in October 1904, there was little reference to the moral deterioration in society. However, the awareness of industrial problems that was recognized three years earlier continued. The Committee on the State of the Church asserted that the church was friend of both capital and labor and praised the Church Association for the Advancement of the Interests of Labor for its work. The pastoral letter delivered at the closing session by the bishops declared industrial conflict and racial strife to be

---

[13]"God Save the State," ibid., 13:549-53.

[14]"A Brief Statement of the Conference," 12 November 1903, *Addresses before the New York State Conference of Religion,* ser. 2 (March 1904): 5-6.

[15]"The Purpose of the Conference," 27 March 1904, ibid., 11.

[16]"Statement of the Conference," 1 December 1904, ibid., ser. 3 (April 1905): 8-9.

"the two supreme problems confronting the Republic." Nevertheless, the report of the Joint Commission on Capital and Labor contained little substantive advance. Although it condemned child labor and said some good things about labor generally, the report also deprecated excesses by workers. Otherwise the report did little more than refer to the committee's creation in 1901, reiterate its assigned duties, and show that it was beginning to function with an educational emphasis. By adopting the report, the General Convention approved the continuation of the Joint Commission.[17]

Similarly, the National Council of the Congregational Churches, which also had created a Committee on Labor in 1901, focused its social interest primarily on the report of that small group. Observing that concern for industrial problems had been indicated by the National Council's joint meeting the preceding Sunday afternoon with the local Trades and Labor Assembly of Portland, Maine, the committee felt this action evidenced an improved social and religious spirit that was "prophetic of a better day both for labor and the church." The committee's recommendation to change the name from the Commission on Labor to the Industrial Committee was approved. In contrast to the Episcopalians, Congregationalists heard addresses on subjects of broader social range, such as one on "The Preparation Required for a Spiritual Awakening" by Henry Churchill King, president of Oberlin College.[18]

More significant than any of these actions was the National Council's election of Washington Gladden as moderator of the Congregational Churches for the next three years. The office was an honor for the articulate minister and social prophet, who was then sixty-eight years of age. A moderator served without power or pay in addition to his regular ministry. Nevertheless, the position enabled him to be on various denominational boards and committees since the office symbolized congregational unity and fellowship, and it gave him the privilege to call the next meeting of the council, preside until his successor was selected, and deliver an address on the first evening.[19] Within six months after his election,

---

[17]*Journal of the General Convention of the Protestant Episcopal Church in the U.S.A.*, (1904), 311, 339, 395, 417, 530-32.

[18]National Council of the Congregational Churches, *The National Council Digest* (Boston: Under direction of the National Council, 1905) 12, 47-48. Interestingly, the editor of this compilation commented that assembling the actions of the committees revealed "how often the procession which seemed to be advancing was moving in its own footsteps" (ibid., v-vi).

[19]Washington Gladden, *Recollections* (Boston: Houghton Mifflin Co., 1909) 399-401.

Gladden was embroiled in a public controversy that was divisive for Congregationalism and indicative of his moral conscience.

In the spring of 1905, the American Board of Commissioners for Foreign Missions, overseas mission agency of the Congregational churches, announced a one hundred thousand dollar gift from John D. Rockefeller. Along with others, Gladden protested receiving money gained by what he regarded as "predatory wealth," especially a voluntary contribution from one who did not belong to the denomination. Later he learned that the gift had been solicited by the American Board, part of it already had been spent before the announcement, and the remainder never was returned. In the meantime, Gladden led the protest at the meeting of the board in September, and publicly as well. The tendency of his argument was evident in the titles of three public pronouncements in the controversy: "Shall Ill-Gotten Gains Be Sought for Christian Purposes?," "The Relation of Moral Teachers to Predatory Wealth," and "The Education of Conscience." His attack was as deliberate as that of muckrakers like Ida Tarbell, on whose data he based his critique. To him the protest was a matter of conscience because he felt that the way Rockefeller acquired his money corrupted character and undermined the social order.[20] In addition to voicing his conscience, which he believed was the faculty God used to speak to humanity, Gladden in this controversy strengthened the status of the moderator's office in Congregationalism.

Baptists in the years from 1903 through 1906 were remarkably uninvolved with social matters. The once socially conscious Baptist Congress paid scant attention to such matters in this period.[21] Despite a number of articulate writers and speakers, there was no unified denominational body for Northern Baptists. Instead, a number of organizations represented the churches, with each implementing only one aspect of the work, such as the Foreign Missionary Society, the Home Missionary Society, or the Publication Society. When Samuel Zane Batten tried in May 1905 to get the Home Missionary Society to create a committee " 'to study

---

[20]Ibid., 401-409; Gladden, "Shall Ill-Gotten Gains Be Sought for Christian Purposes," reprinted in Robert T. Handy, ed., *The Social Gospel in America, 1870–1920: Gladden, Ely, Rauschenbusch* (New York: Oxford University Press, 1966) 119-34; Gladden, "The Relation of Moral Teachers to Predatory Wealth," *Addresses before the New York State Conference of Religion,* ser. 4 (1906): 4-33; Gladden, "The Education of Conscience," manuscript sermon, 8 October 1905, Gladden Papers; cf. Ida Tarbell, *The History of Standard Oil;* quoted in Swados, *Years of Conscience,* 86-89.

[21]*Proceedings of the Baptist Congress,* 21 (1903), 22 (1904), 23 (1905), 24 (1906), showed only a half-dozen topics on social problems during these years.

the relation of the church to the social questions of our time,' " with power to call the attention of Baptists to preaching issues and recommend " 'social and reform measures,' " the matter was referred to the Executive Board. Meeting the following year that body decided, "After much consideration your Board is not prepared to recommend that the Society should assume responsibility for the appointment of such a committee, thereby practically creating a department of Christian Economics, with the numerous debatable questions involved." As an alternative it proposed to refer the concern to the General Convention of the Baptists of North America when it met in the future. Not until 1908, when the first regular meeting of the newly created Northern Baptist Convention gathered, would Baptists have the opportunity for official action.[22]

In contrast, Northern Methodists heard a sizable section of the Episcopal Address to their General Conference in May 1904 devoted to "Some of the Evils and Perils of Our Age." That ten-page portion constituted one-quarter of Bishop Cyrus D. Foss's two-hour address, and it urged the Methodist Episcopal Church to "meet and master" such concerns as political corruption, industrial relations, lynching, and the Negro problem, as well as more traditional problems like intemperance, divorce, and degrading amusements.[23] Despite such urging from its leaders, and petitions concerning social problems from two Annual Conferences, no serious consideration of these matters was given by this General Conference. Upon recommendation of the Committee on the State of the Church, the General Conference adopted the following:

> A memorial was referred to this Committee which asked for the appointment of a commission which should report to the General Conference of 1908 what principles and measures of industrial, political, and moral reform should receive the specific indorsement [sic] and support of the Church.
>
> Your Committee begs to report that they deem it advisable to take no action upon it at this time.[24]

An editorial on the General Conference in the New York *Christian Advocate* concluded that the sessions were "conservative, progressive, and aggressive." With regard to church law the conference was conservative,

---

[22]"The Department of Social Service and Brotherhood of the Northern Baptist Convention," in Harry F. Ward, ed., *A Year Book of the Church and Social Service in the United States* (New York: Fleming H. Revell Co., 1914) 32-34.

[23]*Journal of the General Conference of the Methodist Episcopal Church* (1904), 139-49.

[24]Ibid., 390, 475; *Christian Advocate* (New York), 19 May 1904, p. 9.

said the editor, but "it was quick to recognize new needs and new conditions."[25] Methodist proponents of social Christianity did not concur in the latter judgment, but they were still scattered, disorganized, and virtually voiceless.

The only new denominational action during the period from 1903 to 1906 was by the Presbyterian Church in the United States of America, which to that time had been inactive in social ministry. Consistent with its previous position, the General Assembly in these years made no official statement about social problems. However, one of its boards took an innovative step in 1903 that indicated that Presbyterians intended to do something about the industrial problem. That year the Board of Home Missions reported to the General Assembly in May that Charles Stelzle had been called "to a special mission to workingmen."[26]

Charles Stelzle was uniquely qualified for this new ministry to workers. Born and raised in the tenements of the Bowery in the lower east side of New York City, he left school at eleven to go to work. Five years later he became an apprentice in a machine shop and worked for eight years as a machinist. That experience of laboring ten hours a day, six days a week, as well as being fired during an economic depression, made him sensitive to the conditions of workers in practical ways most ministers did not know. When he felt a calling to be a minister he went to Moody Bible Institute in Chicago because he lacked the formal education to be admitted to more traditional Presbyterian seminaries. Stelzle became a successful lay preacher in Minneapolis but failed as a leader when he returned to his home chapel in New York. Moving to St. Louis he again experienced success and was ordained by the St. Louis Presbytery, ending a five-year lay ministry.[27] By 1901 his ordained ministry attracted national attention when *The Outlook* reported on a survey he conducted to discover the attitudes of labor leaders toward the church. The survey showed that workers felt the church was not for them because it seemed to be "a rich man's club" in which the poor were not welcome and because it seemed to be "organized hypocrisy."[28]

---

[25]"The General Conference," ibid., 9 June 1904, pp. 3-4.

[26]*Minutes of the General Assembly of the Presbyterian Church in the United States of America*, n.s. (1903), 240.

[27]Charles Stelzle, *A Son of the Bowery: The Life Story of an East Side American* (New York: George H. Doran Co., 1926) 13-66.

[28]*The Outlook* (New York), 9 February 1901, pp. 333-34.

Challenged by an executive of the Presbyterian Board of Home Missions to undertake a mission to change such attitudes by workers, as well as the atmosphere toward labor in the churches, Stelzle in 1903 agreed to head a new Workingmen's Department in that board. For two years he traveled and studied conditions; then he began to organize the work. Seeking to interpret the church to labor and labor to churchmen, Stelzle attended union meetings and made it possible for other ministers to do the same. Representing the church, he attended annual conventions of the American Federation of Labor, which slowly acknowledged his work by including an opening prayer and by adopting a formal resolution of appreciation to the Presbyterian Church.[29] In addition, he wrote a weekly column that was furnished free to labor papers, and it was printed in three hundred papers by 1907. A volume of these articles was published as a book in 1906 under the title *Messages to Workingmen*.[30] That same year the Presbyterian General Assembly upgraded his special mission to the Department of Church and Labor within the Board of Home Missions. Stelzle's success was evident the next year when "a monster labor meeting" attended by seven thousand persons was held in conjunction with the General Assembly's sessions in Columbus, Ohio, and all the expenses were paid by labor unions. Also it was reported to the assembly that several other denominations, in Europe as well as America, were inquiring about this ministry to workers, which was "unchallenged by any other Church throughout the world."[31]

Although the Presbyterian Church in the United States of America began its social ministry late, within five years it had developed a distinctive and influential labor ministry and had placed Stelzle in a leadership position where he would be able to continue to contribute to the social-gospel cause. The success of his pioneering efforts on a full-time basis were acknowledged when other Protestant churches sought more information about his work. But neither other denominations nor his own church was ready yet to take any official stands concerning the social

---

[29]Stelzle, *Son of the Bowery*, 67-96; *Minutes of the General Assembly* (1904), 79; (1905), 292; (1906), 79, 318; Charles Stelzle, "Presbyterian Department of Church and Labor," *The Annals of the American Academy of Political and Social Science* 30 (1907): 28-32.

[30]Charles Stelzle, *Messages to Workingmen* (New York: Fleming H. Revell Co., 1906).

[31]*Minutes of the General Assembly* (1906), 79; (1907), 336; Stelzle, "Presbyterian Department of Church and Labor," 28-32; Joseph Wilson Cochran, "The Church and the Working Man," *Annals of the American Academy* 30 (1907): 26.

problems confronting the nation. Nevertheless, Stelzle's ministry to workingmen, coupled with the hesitant support Episcopalians and Congregationalists gave to their committees on labor, indicated that the first official concern in social matters by Protestant churches was in the economic realm. These modest signs of denominational activity seemed to confirm James Whiton's contention that the churches were not very disturbed by the social situation, despite the revelations of moral corruption by the muckrakers or the challenges to civic righteousness by President Roosevelt. By the middle of the first decade of the twentieth century, supporters of social Christianity looked to whatever new signs of vitality they could find, for, despite the evils they deplored, they remained persistent optimists.

One of the new signs was the formation of the Religious Education Association in 1903. Germinated by an organization of biblical teachers who were bothered by the inadequacy of religious and moral instruction, the national organization was created with a structure like that of the National Education Association. The first meeting at Chicago, 10-12 February 1903, had an agenda that was basically oriented to education, but among its original members were several social-gospel partisans such as Walter Rauschenbusch, Josiah Strong, and Lyman Abbott. Others with similar interests included: Graham Taylor, Congregational clergyman, professor and head of Chicago Commons social settlement; Shailer Mathews, professor at the University of Chicago Divinity School; and George Albert Coe, professor of philosophy at Northwestern University. Coe was elected to be recording secretary, and William Rainy Harper, president of the University of Chicago, was elected as president of the nascent organization.[32]

The large number of persons from Chicago in the leadership of the Religious Education Association was distinctive, and it indicated the conscious emergence of that city as a center for social Christianity. The association maintained its headquarters in that metropolis, and it reflected the influence of the Midwest. Benefiting from the presence of Jane Addams at Hull House, and of Richard T. Ely and John R. Commons at the University of Wisconsin, and of a number of other professors not far away, Chicago became the focal center of social-gospel activity in the middle of the country, as New York was in the East.

Another evidence of the conscious emergence of Chicago as a center was the decision of President Harper to take over a dying monthly mag-

---

[32]*Proceedings of the First Annual Convention, Chicago, February 10-12, 1903* (Chicago: Executive Office of the Association, 1903) 230-40, 297-300, 317-39; Stephen A. Schmidt, *A History of the Religious Education Association* (Birmingham AL: Religious Education Press, 1983) 30-36.

azine and remake it into a journal to do for the Midwest what *The Outlook* and *The Independent* were doing for New York. The new magazine was called *The World Today,* and Shailer Mathews became its editor in the summer of 1903. Its purpose was not to be another religious periodical but "a new point of contact between religious idealism and political and social trends." Although the periodical had one hundred thousand subscribers in time, its influence never attained that of the Eastern magazines that were its models. However, in editing *The World Today* Mathews became very conscious of the social scene and developed a broadened, deepened social understanding. From the inception of the Religious Education Association, he was involved in its development and served as a member of its Executive Committee.[33]

With a portion of the leaders so conscious of social concerns, it was not long before a more prominent social theme emerged in the Religious Education Association. By the second annual meeting in 1904, the revelations in the popular press led the Resolutions Committee to declare, "An emergency has arisen in respect to the training of the young in the matters that pertain to character. To turn the heart of our people . . . will require a general revival of religious and moral education." In its first Annual Survey of Progress that year the importance of religious conviction in education for citizenship was discussed.[34] When the association held its third meeting in February 1905, the statement of purpose was broadened from the original "to promote religious and moral education" to the following:

> To inspire the educational forces of our country with the religious ideal;
> To inspire the religious forces of our country with the educational ideal; and
> To keep before the public mind the ideal of RELIGIOUS EDUCATION, and the sense of its need and value.

Translating that purpose into practice, the association sought to bring together leaders and workers "of all ecclesiastical, evangelical, educational, cultural, and social organizations" who wanted to achieve citizenship, morality, social goodness, and service.[35] In such a context it was not un-

---

[33]Shailer Mathews, *New Faith for Old* (New York: Macmillan Co., 1936) 90-93, 248-49.

[34]*Proceedings of the Second Annual Convention, Philadelphia, March 2-4, 1904* (Chicago: Executive Office of the Association, 1904) 89, 525-26.

[35]*The Aims of Religious Education: The Proceedings of the Third Annual Convention of the Religious Education Association, Boston, February 12-16, 1905* (Chicago: Executive Office of the Association, 1905) 474-75.

usual to hear addresses on "The Sacredness of Citizenship" or "The Ethical Education of Public Opinion."[36]

At the fourth annual meeting, 5-7 February 1907, the evolution of interest on social issues reached the point that the Resolutions Committee declared,

> The Association was born in a deep sense of our national need of a great new emphasis upon moral and religious education, and of the interpenetration of education and religious ideals.
> If it did not exist, patriotism alone would demand that another agency to do exactly its work should be formed without delay.[37]

What had started as a concern of biblical teachers resulted in an organization that was extremely sensitive to moral education and responsible citizenship. Thus, it was not strange for Walter Rauschenbusch to write later that the association "from the first dealt with its large problems from the social point of view, and the social emphasis seems to grow stronger every year."[38]

Another new sign of vitality that evidenced interest and potential for proponents of social Christianity occurred in the area of church cooperation. At the end of 1903 the *Federation Chronicle,* an occasional publication of the National Federation of Churches and Christian Workers that organized in 1901, printed an article on "The Social Mission of the Church." Arguing that if the church was "the agency by which the world is to be regenerated and saved," then the church needed to work to apply the moral teaching of Jesus to every sphere of life. Trusting that the gospel of Christ provided the primary solution to the problems evident in industry and social life, the federation asserted that "the churches should exert a more potent influence in the interests of social and civic righteousness."[39] During the next two years that social emphasis was a secondary but evident theme as the federation concentrated its energies to implement another stage of ecumenical development in the United States.

---

[36]Ibid., 47-51, 56-60.

[37]*The Materials of Religious Education: Being the Principal Papers Presented at, and Proceedings of the Fourth General Convention of the Religious Education Association, Rochester, New York, February 5-7, 1907* (Chicago: Executive Office of the Association, 1907) 295-96. There was no annual meeting in 1906.

[38]Walter Rauschenbusch, *Christianizing the Social Order* (New York: Macmillan Co., 1912) 17.

[39]*Federation Chronicle* (New York), November-December 1903, p. 8.

The new step for the National Federation of Churches and Christian Workers was the calling of an Inter-Church Conference on Federation to meet in Carnegie Hall, New York City, 15-21 November 1905. Acting in response to an overture from the National Council of the Congregational Churches, the National Federation in 1902 agreed to act as the agency to call the various Protestant denominations to a delegated conference. The invitation circulated by the appointed Committee of Correspondence recognized the need for a cooperative body that was "more organic and permanent than the Evangelical Alliance," and that had more authority and resources than the National Federation of Churches and Christian Workers, and its predecessor organizations, which was limited to state and local levels. Frank Mason North, who was involved in all the planning and served as vice-chairman of the Arrangements Committee, believed that the significance of the Inter-Church Conference on Federation of 1905 lay primarily in the fact that it was the first officially delegated council to represent the denominations in the history of American Protestantism. When the conference convened there were official delegates from thirty-two denominations.[40]

Prior to the gathering of the delegates, the editor of *The Independent* called attention to the social implications of the meeting. Feeling that the Christian Church was losing its influence, he wondered "if we are not mistaken in supposing that the Church can control the moral tone of the community." As evidence he cited "the sad exposures of the last year in public life in St. Louis, in Philadelphia, in New York, involving great financial institutions controlled by many church members, as well as in political life." Obviously influenced by the work of the muckrakers, the editorial pointed to the potential harmony and effectiveness of "federated fellowship" as a way to meet the moral needs of the time.[41]

In light of such expectations of social mission by cooperative Protestantism, it was not surprising that social awareness and responsibility were part of the program of the Inter-Church Conference on Federation. Three of the fifteen themes addressed, with a total of twelve presentations, dealt with "A United Church and the Social Order," "A United

---

[40]Frank Mason North, "The Inter-church Conference on Federation," *The Methodist Review* 87 (September-October 1905): 748-60; *Inter-church Conference on Federation to Be Held in Carnegie Hall, 56th Street, Seventh Avenue and 57th Street, New York, November 15-20, 1905* (New York: Office of the Executive Committee, n.d.) 3-9; "A Federal Congress of Churches," *The Independent* (New York), 16 November 1905, pp. 1135-41; 23 November 1905, pp. 1234-36.

[41]"The Inter-Church Conference," *The Independent*, 9 November 1905, pp. 1123-24.

Church and the National Life," and "A United Church and Evangeliza-tion."[42] With striking directness two federal judges told the delegates how federated Protestantism could serve the national life. Supreme Court Jus-tice David J. Brewer indicated that municipal corruption should have "the united force of the Christian Churches" hurled against it. Such awak-ened Christian conscience would "ere long redeem New York, make Philadelphia good and Chicago clean." "Let a Federation of all the Chris-tian Churches in this nation come into being," said Brewer, "and it will show to the world that this is in the highest sense a Christian nation."[43] And Circuit Court Judge Peter S. Grosscup declared that "the Church balances and steadies the national life" because it develops conviction, conscience, and love of justice.[44] Henry Wade Rogers, dean of the law de-partment of Yale University, noted that the conference assembled "at a time when thoughtful men are deeply concerned with great moral issues which existing conditions in the commercial and political life of the coun-try have made exceedingly prominent." In response, he challenged the churches to federate "that we may have a more effective agency for the prevention of that corruption," that it will thereby make impossible "a government by privileged classes," and that "a more determined effort may be made to establish the kingdom of God upon the earth."[45]

With the stimulus of such challenges, the Inter-Church Conference on Federation took two actions that related to the social order. First, it adopted resolutions on several subjects "which are most pressing at the present time." Among these was one "Concerning the Social Order" that addressed several problems ranging from discord between capital and la-bor to gambling to impurity in various forms. One of the most forceful paragraphs in this section resolved,

> That we see in the numerous revelations of "graft" in many high places of business and politics the system of a widespread commercialism which Jesus called "covetousness" and condemned more severely than any other vice, and which has in our time sanctioned many customs that are not only wicked, but criminal; and we urge that, while public indignation is aflame, all unrighteous political and commercial customs of rich and poor shall be

---

[42]Elias B. Sanford, ed., *Church Federation: Inter-Church Conference on Federation, New York, November 15-21, 1905* (New York: Fleming H. Revell Co., 1906) ix-xiii.

[43]David J. Brewer, "Law and Justice," ibid., 552-53.

[44]Peter S. Grosscup, "The Popular Conscience," ibid., 543-45.

[45]Henry Wade Rogers, "Government by the People," ibid., 563-64.

brought to the bar of conscience by faithful preachers, teachers and publicists.[46]

The second conference action was the inclusion of a social objective in the Plan of Federation that was recommended to the constituent denominations for approval. Fourth of the five objects of the proposed Federal Council of the Churches of Christ in America stated: "To secure a larger combined influence for the Churches of Christ in all matters affecting the moral and social condition of the people, so as to promote the application of the law of Christ in every relation of human life."[47] Thus, in their long-range vision, as well as in their response to immediate conditions, the first delegated assembly of Protestant churches projected that the denominations combine their influence for moral and social betterment.

In spite of the resolute intentions, at the time these proposals actually did little more than indicate the opinion of delegates and express their hopes for future action. While indicative of growing social concern at the cooperative level, the social objective and the resolution on the social order in no way committed the denominations represented. Frank Mason North understood the tentative nature of these statements better than most, and consequently it was not unusual that two months later he was preaching to convince Christians about the needs of the social order. Maintaining that the church casts a shadow in the world that influences "industries, the intellectual pursuits, the social ideals, the ethical standards and the spiritual aspirations of men" because its members exercise leadership in society, North argued that Christians need not regard atheists or immoral persons as responsible for recent disclosures of "the tremendous cross currents of greed and infamy" because the conditions were caused by "men who bow at the church's altars, enter her confessionals, accept her creed, support her propaganda and advocate her Faith." Visualizing the unfulfilled potential for dominant influence that Christians could exert, North asked,

> Why is the agitation for the redemption of children from industrial oppression necessary, and for the most part outside the organized church? Why is the agitation against starvation, hunger and destitution not a part of the church's enterprise? Why is the church's effort for the securing and enforcement of just laws confined principally to spasmodic pulpit declamation which entertains many but sets no one in motion?[48]

---

[46]Ibid., 108.

[47]Ibid., 77.

[48]"The Shadow of the Church," 17 January 1906, manuscript sermon, Frank Mason North Papers, Drew University, Madison NJ.

Washington Gladden also tried to arouse his congregation in February 1906 when he preached the sermon "Where Are We in Democracy?" Stressing the importance of democracy, he said that although political theories had not changed, conditions had. The old-fashioned democracy of the New England town meeting no longer worked because modern democracy was perverted by the presence of corrupt political bosses in cities, denial of voting rights to Negroes in the South, and economic tyranny and exploitation throughout the nation. Bad as conditions were, Gladden still remained hopeful because conditions really were not worse than earlier; citizens just knew more about them. Those revelations had driven bosses into hiding and led to control of the centralization of business. In Gladden's estimation, democracy was at a turning point. "I believe that the years ahead through which we are passing are critical and epochal. We are not yet through our times of trial . . . but we shall win." His confidence rested on the conviction that in democracy the citizen is ruler because God granted him the right to rule. "Thus the foundation of democracy is religion," and religious faith, as demonstrated by Washington, Lincoln, and President Roosevelt, was "the only principle upon which the voter can safely rely."[49] While North sought to challenge his hearers to action by pointing to current social needs, Gladden reminded his congregation that God undergirded democracy and would lead them through the time of testing they were experiencing. Both leaders, however, based their messages largely on their reading of conditions in the social order.

One of the difficulties of the time was the fact that various people read the conditions differently. While Christians committed to social concern still tried to activate the churches, political Progressives were beginning to feel that conditions were improving. Actually, the latter could point with some satisfaction to better circumstances. By the time of the North and Gladden sermons early in 1906, the United States Supreme Court had dissolved the Northern Securities Company railroad trust, Ray Stannard Baker had started a muckraking series entitled "The Railroads on Trial" in *McClure's*, and President Roosevelt had recommended regulation of the railroad industry in his message to Congress in December 1905. The meatpacking industry experienced similar treatment, with the Supreme Court's ruling against the Beef Trust and Charles Edward Russell's publishing a serialized exposé entitled "The Greatest Trust in the World" in *Everybody's* magazine. Public confidence in the insurance companies, which had been undermined by several authors in a number of periodicals, began to

---

[49]"Where Are We in Democracy?" 25 February 1906, manuscript sermon, Washington Gladden Papers; *Ohio State Journal* (Columbus), 26 February 1906.

revive when the Armstrong Insurance Investigating Committee began hearings in Albany, New York, in September 1905, with Charles Evans Hughes as the prosecuting attorney. Gladden rightly noted the critical state of the times in February 1906, for the resolution of several issues still in process then was achieved by summer. In April the New York State Legislature adopted reform legislation for life insurance companies, and on 29 and 30 June, the United States Congress enacted the Hepburn Act to regulate railroads, the Pure Food and Drug Act, and the Meat Inspection Act. An aroused citizenry saw evidence of reform through political processes used to correct the problems uncovered by muckraking journalists.

To Philip Loring Allen, a political Progressive, these changes amounted to "an awakening of the American people." Using terms like "this revival," "moral upheaval," and "civic renaissance" to describe the limitations imposed on political bosses and privileged corporations, he felt there was concrete evidence that "the moral sense of the country" was becoming effective. Even though he was aware that he wrote about "movements still in progress, policies only half worked out and men still active," Allen felt it was important to publish a book to celebrate "the record of success" that was under way. By his reading of events, the effects of "this moral wave over the country" were apparent "about the beginning of the year 1905" and continued to manifest themselves in what he termed "The New Politics" that Theodore Roosevelt evidenced when he congratulated Congress for the valuable legislation it had enacted through June 1906. He titled his book *America's Awakening: The Triumph of Righteousness in High Places*.[50]

In contrast to Allen's optimism and satisfaction, James Whiton in February 1907 still criticized the churches for "not leading in the struggle for social righteousness." That charge led some to accuse him of "abusing the churches," and in April he defended himself by arguing that not only did he see little activity in the social realm by organized Christianity, but "many competent observers testify to the existing fact of a *moral crisis*." Voicing the frustration of social-gospel advocates generally, Whiton declared, "When one looks at the Councils, Conferences, and Conventions, in which the churches of various denominations come together to consider the things which concern them at large, how small a part of their attention, if any, appears to be given to the interests of moral and social righteousness in the State, in comparison with what is spent on ecclesi-

---

[50]Philip Loring Allen, *America's Awakening: The Triumph of Righteousness in High Places* (New York: Fleming H. Revell Co., 1906) 5-9, 231-32, 279.

astical machinery and order!"[51] His charge sounded very much akin to his accusation in 1904 that there was "a good deal of moral anarchy prevailing" in the country. Obviously, Allen was correct in pointing to conditions that had changed for the better, but for social activists like Whiton that meant that such an awakening was occurring outside the churches, and organized religion had not yet acted. How could the churches be aroused to action?

---

[51]James Whiton, "Criticism of the Churches," *Addresses before the New York State Conference of Religion*, ser. 5 (April 1907): 4-5.

CHAPTER 4

The Church
and the Social Crisis

What has the Christian Church been doing while these powers of
piracy and plunder have been gathering their forces and spreading
their nets and heaping up their spoils? Where was the Christian
Church when the grafters were ravaging the cities and the rebate
robbers and frenzied financiers and the insurance sharks were getting
in their work? For the most part she has been standing by and looking
on, winking her eyes, and twiddling her thumbs, and wondering
whether she had any call to interfere.

(Washington Gladden,
"The Church and the Social Crisis," 1907)

IN LIGHT OF THE STEADY STREAM of sensational stories corroborated by
official hearings, reports, and corrective legislation, many Americans
began to feel that the condition of social morality in the nation had reached
crisis proportions. Between March 1907 and March 1908 books with a crisis
theme were published by four social gospel leaders who attempted to
interpret the meaning of the social crisis for the church. Each writer had
his own purpose and approach, but beneath that diversity were common
convictions that indicated a fundamental understanding of social
Christianity concerning the church's relationship to the social order.

Walter Rauschenbusch had long felt a debt to the working people of
New York City, among whom he had ministered for eleven years. Once
while in that work, and twice after he moved in 1897 to be a professor at
Rochester Theological Seminary, he tried to fulfill his obligation by starting
a book that would explain how to wed Christianity and the social

movement, since faithful working people were affected by both.[1] Each time he had to return to other work before completing his writing, although he managed to set down some of his germinal ideas in papers or published articles.[2]

In 1905 Rauschenbusch again felt inspired to write his book. Taking his family to Canandaigua Lake in New York, between late May and mid-July he prepared a book manuscript that he entitled "The Christian Movement and the Social Movement." Although he was once again unable to finish his work, he had achieved a basic formulation of his ideas that provided the major portions of his next manuscript. The following summer in Canada he was able to revise and expand that work in six weeks, and he sent the finished product, now titled "Christianity and the Social Crisis," to the Macmillan Company for possible publication. The nature of the revisions he made for the completed version indicated how the sense of social crisis altered his interpretation, and especially his perception, of the task of the church.[3]

---

[1]Rauschenbusch's autobiographical account of the origin of the book was noted by a reporter in the *Rochester Democrat and Chronicle,* 25 January 1913, and was reprinted after his death in the *Rochester Theological Seminary Bulletin* (November 1918): 51-53. Also, it was reproduced in full in Dores Robinson Sharpe, *Walter Rauschenbusch* (New York: Macmillan Co., 1942) 232-34. Sharpe indicated that the dates were 1891, 1902, and 1905 in a note on p. 233. Cf. Walter Rauschenbusch, *Christianity and the Social Crisis* (New York: Macmillan Co., 1907) xv. (Hereafter cited in this chapter as *CASC*.)

[2]Rauschenbusch's "The Pulpit in Relation to Political and Social Reform," *Proceedings of the Baptist Congress* 10 (1892): 127-29; "The Ideals of Social Reformers," *The American Journal of Sociology* 2 (July 1896-May 1897): 202-19; "What Help Does Modern Christianity Give Us?" *The Examiner* (New York) 82 (3 November 1904): 1292; "The New Evangelism," *The Independent* (New York) 56 (12 May 1904): 1056-61. Walter Rauschenbusch, *The Righteousness of the Kingdom,* ed. with an introduction by Max L. Stackhouse (Nashville: Abingdon Press, 1968) made available a previously unpublished manuscript of Rauschenbusch that may have been the earliest version of the book. See 16-19, passim.

[3]"The Christian Movement and the Social Movement," book manuscript in the Walter Rauschenbusch Papers, The American Baptist Historical Society, Rochester NY. (Hereafter cited as CMSM.) Comparison of this manuscript with his published book shows: the original title for ch. 1 was "The Prophet-Reformers of Israel"; the insertion of the word *Impetus* in place of *Character* in the title of ch. 3; the change from the assertion "Why Christianity Has Not Undertaken Social Reconstruction" to a question form for the title of ch. 4; the alteration of the title of ch. 5 from "The Call of the Present," and the addition of a final ch. 7 that used information from various parts of the 1905 recension as well as new material.

Essentially, Rauschenbusch transformed a scholarly treatise into a more lively account by amplifying the crisis concept, by updating the data to support that interpretation, and by suggesting ways for Christians to function in light of his analysis. His change of chapter title from "The Call of the Present" to "The Present Crisis" probably best illustrated his more enlivened and challenging approach, but a number of less obvious changes also transformed that section. Not only did Rauschenbusch change the order and data of his earlier material, but he also updated and rewrote other parts. At one point he deleted a sermonic analogy to expand references to the work of the muckrakers and Progressives.[4] At another place he inserted several pages of new text.[5] In another instance, he transformed a paragraph largely by rewriting. Thus, one sentence that dealt with the fraud businessmen perpetrated on consumers was changed from "Deviled chicken made of hog, coffee beans made of sweet potato pulp, fruit jam made without fruit, ground soap-stone advertised as an adulterant for flour" to "They sell us fruit-jam made without fruit; butter that never saw the milk-pail; potted chicken that grunted in the barnyard; all-wool goods that never said 'baah,' but leave it to the buyer to say it. If a son asks for bread, his father will not offer him a stone; but ground soapstone is freely advertised as an adulterant for flour."[6] And another sentence was modified from "Is it not rapacity when medicines, on the purity of which the life of a mother or a child may depend, are commonly adulterated?" to "But when fruit flavors are made with coal- tar and benzoic acid, and when the milk of our children is preserved with formaldehyde, the rapacity becomes murderous."[7] A footnote on the same page commented on the Pure Food Law, which was approved 30 June 1906, and showed that he kept abreast of current happenings as he completed his book that summer.

The crisis idea was most evident at the end of the chapter entitled "The Present Crisis" where Rauschenbusch wrote, "The cry of ' Crisis! crisis! ' has become a weariness." Interestingly, those words were in his 1905 manuscript and make it impossible to generalize that the whole notion of crisis was interpolated in 1906 and that it alone accounted for the transformation of his book. In 1905 he saw that the continuity of Christian civilization depended "almost wholly on the moral forces which

---

[4]Cf. the paragraph on pp. 254-56 of *CASC* to p. 59 of ch. 6 of CMSM.

[5]*CASC*, 260-64 were not in the 1905 manuscript.

[6]Cf. *CASC*, 269 with CMSM, 67 (ch. 6).

[7]Ibid.

the . . . nations can bring to the fighting line." "If those forces fail to be energized by the power of religion," he said, "the outlook is shrouded in the storm-clouds of the Deluge."[8] Clearly Rauschenbusch felt a sense of crisis already in 1905, but his modifications to enlarge that feeling in his finished book not only interjected more uses of the word but also affected his basic interpretation. At several places he worked the concept of social crisis into his vital chapter on "The Stake of the Church in the Social Movement," adding power and continuity of thought to his argument.[9] However, the central thesis of the book was stated in that chapter, and it was a totally new insertion in the final 1906 recension.[10]

> We have seen that the crisis of society is also the crisis of the church. The church, too, feels the incipient paralysis that is creeping upon our splendid Christian civilization through the unjust absorption of wealth on one side and the poverty of the people on the other. It cannot thrive when society decays.
> . . .
> But on the other hand the present crisis presents one of the greatest opportunities for its own growth and development that have ever been offered to Christianity. The present historical situation is a summons of the Eternal to enter on a larger duty, and thereby to inherit a larger life.[11]

Rauschenbusch's double concept of crisis, in the church as well as in society, was insightful and distinctive. It focused his earlier understanding of the Christian movement and the social movement by viewing the crisis as a God-given opportunity. At an earlier point in the book he traced the two movements, indicating that as Christianity reached "moral maturity" it was threatened by the social movement that was strangling civilization. "The converging of the two lines of development is providential," he said. "We are at the turning of the ways. . . . It rests upon us to decide if a new era is to dawn in the transformation of the world into the kingdom of God, or if western civilization is to descend into the graveyard of dead civilizations."[12] After stating his crisis thesis, Rauschenbusch posed the issue again in these terms: "This is the stake of the church in the social

------

[8]CMSM, 84; cf. to *CASC*, 286, where the challenge continued but with improved wording.

[9]See *CASC*, 287, 316-17, 340-41.

[10]The paragraphs on pp. 331-32 of *CASC* were inserted between two paragraphs on p. 49 of ch. 7 of CMSM.

[11]*CASC*, 332.

[12]*CASC*, 210.

crisis. If society continues to disintegrate and decay, the church will be carried down with it. If the church can rally such moral forces that injustice will be overcome and fresh new blood will course in a sounder moral organism, it will itself rise to higher liberty and life."[13]

Having posed the present crisis and pointed to the stake of the church in the social movement, Rauschenbusch went on to suggest what the church could do if it accepted the challenge to "rally the moral forces." He warned that the church as "the organized conscience of Christendom" must guard against subtly working for its own benefit rather than for the good of the people if it set out "to Christianize social life." To avoid this he urged the church to "be content with inspiring the social movement with religious faith and daring." Christians should combine religious faith, moral enthusiasm, and economic information and apply them through existing and natural relationships to public morality. To do so required a faith that believed "that God saves not only the soul, but the whole of human life," which Rauschenbusch called "social evangelization." Creating moral sensitivity in everyday life was more vital than seeking to control the social order through legal and political power. Rather, religion should concentrate on creating moral convictions. As Rauschenbusch said, "Religion creates morality, and morality then deposits a small part of its content in written laws." In his view, both religious and political forces should mingle and cooperate, for it was the purpose of both "to transform humanity into the kingdom of God." However, the two forces should not directly interfere with the machinery of the other or the important principle of separation of church and state would be compromised. Admitting that the task of establishing a Christian social order often seemed like a futile dream, Rauschenbusch nevertheless called upon Christians to work toward that end by accepting the challenge of what he termed "the new apostolate." "At best there is always an approximation to a perfect social order," but since God called the faithful to this duty they must remember that the kingdom of God is always in process. Typically, Rauschenbusch closed his book with an apt analogy. Like the blossoms on the fruit trees last May, which were the unfolding of a long process of sap running for weeks and months within the tree, social renewal may be a miraculous result of the religious faith and moral strength of the church.[14]

Despite the optimism implicit in his analysis, as well as explicit in his critique of "The Present Crisis" where he said he was "not a despiser of my age" and was appealing hopefully "to the educated reason and the moral insight" of modern Christians, Rauschenbusch admitted later that

---

[13]*CASC*, 341.

[14]*CASC*, 287, 343- 422.

he anticipated a poor reception for *Christianity and the Social Crisis.* "I wrote the book with a lot of fear and trembling. I expected there would be a good deal of anger and resentment." To avoid that anticipated reaction he left for a sabbatical year of study in Germany just after the book appeared in print.[15] To his surprise, the response was favorable and widespread. During the summer in a letter from Marburg, Germany, to the Brotherhood of the Kingdom he acknowledged the changed conditions and urged his colleagues to rejoice.[16] Leighton Williams, at the meeting of the Brotherhood in August, recognized the success of the book when he stated, "Our brother, Dr. Rauschenbusch, has now set forth our contentions in a systematic way and his book is received with wide and cordial approval."[17] In retrospect, Rauschenbusch explained what had happened: "The social movement had got hold of me, just as the social awakening was getting hold of the country. The book came out at the psychological moment, and was taken as an expression of what thousands were feeling."[18] Its sales were so numerous that the Macmillan Company reprinted his book in October and again in November 1907. With this first book, Rauschenbusch gained a national reputation for the first time.

A publisher takes on an unknown author with hesitancy, and the Macmillan Company must have accepted Rauschenbusch's manuscript with some uncertainty. Probably the editors felt more secure in publishing the book of another social gospel author, Shailer Mathews. The University of Chicago professor had already published several volumes and edited a series of New Testament handbooks for Macmillan. Mathews thus seemed to offer Macmillan a more certain investment. A month after Rauschenbusch's book reached the bookstores, Macmillan printed Mathews's *The Church and the Changing Order* in April 1907.

As editor of *The World Today* magazine since 1903, Mathews kept alert to social change, and in his new book he "attempted to bring the results of a developing science of religion to bear upon social conditions" with

---

[15]*CASC,* 220; *Rochester Democrat and Chronicle,* 25 January 1913; quoted in *Rochester Theological Seminary Bulletin* (November 1918): 52 and also in Sharpe, *Walter Rauschenbusch,* 137-38.

[16]Rauschenbusch, "To the Brotherhood of the Kingdom, Marlboro, New York," 20 July 1907, *The Kingdom* 1 (September 1907) unpaginated; quoted in full in Sharpe, 137-38.

[17]Leighton Williams, "The Reign of the New Humanity," *The Kingdom* 1 (December 1907): 2.

[18]Rauschenbusch, *Rochester Theological Seminary Bulletin* (November 1918): 52.

which he came in contact.[19] Although as a Baptist and a seminary professor trained in both Bible and religious history he was similar to Rauschenbusch, his book had a different style and approach. Nevertheless, its stated purpose was closely akin: "To-day . . . the church must face the vital decision as to what part it shall have in producing the new world."[20]

Shailer Mathews faced the matter of crisis more immediately than any of the four social gospel authors. His first chapter was titled "The Crisis of the Church" and helpfully defined the meaning of crisis. Using the term *crisis* to describe a situation "that assures radical change in the immediate future," he indicated that such conditions are not always precipitated by great events but are simply the culmination of slowly gathering forces that compel a choice between sharply drawn alternatives. Historically, he said, "an age is usually aware of its crisis," as during the American and French revolutions. According to Mathews, "Men of our own day are growing increasingly alive to the fact that we are facing remarkable social changes in the immediate future. In fact . . . it is apparent that those changes are already taking place."[21]

Applying this understanding to the church as institutionalized Christianity, Mathews insisted that the church had to decide how it would relate to the formative forces at work then. To him, it was more than an academic question how the church related to various religious, intellectual, and social phases of the crisis; it was "a matter of life and death for both the church and the new social order." The church could not control the forces creating the new order, but he believed it was out of touch with some of them and could work more closely with them. Should the church be brought into closer union with those forces? Answering that question posed the real crisis of the church for Mathews.[22]

For the Chicago professor and editor the forces that threatened Christianity included scholarly and theological methods and ideas, but more than half his book dealt with issues concerning the church's relationship to the changing social order. Although he believed that social reform needed to be strengthened and social and political discontent needed to be resolved, Mathews urged that the church recognize its

---

[19]Shailer Mathews, *New Faith for Old* (New York: Macmillan Co., 1936) 95- 96.

[20]Shailer Mathews, *The Church and the Changing Order* (New York: Macmillan Co., 1907) 3. (Hereafter cited in this chapter as *CACO*.)

[21]*CACO*, 1-2.

[22]*CACO*, 3-9.

proper function in the changing world. Since church members could hold differing opinions about socialism, trusts, prohibition, unions, and other issues, the church as a social institution needed to realize that it did not have to resolve those concerns. Instead it should educate its members in the principles of Christian conduct and trust them to make their own decisions on such matters. "It is not the business of the church, as an institution, to go into the field of economics or politics. The church is not a sociological lectureship. Its function is spiritual in the largest sense." By that he meant that the church should develop the morality that lay beneath all social and political issues.

> It is so much easier to assail economic and political wrongs than to train up a generation of men who shall be morally and religiously sensitive, and who shall go out into the world to do actual reconstruction in accordance with their own regenerate lives. The pulpit should attack the abuses, but its chief function is not that of denunciation, but that of the development of a moral sensitiveness on the part of its followers.[23]

Only as the church assumed leadership in training the conscience would it be able to educate and direct social impulses in the proper way.

As Mathews encouraged the organized church to take the slow and difficult method of education and conversion of individuals rather than that of attempting to achieve social betterment through legislation, he became involved in the controversy over individual or social salvation. His way of resolving that problem was to affirm the need for both: "If there can be no regenerate society without regenerate men, neither can there be regenerate men without a regenerate society." It was not enough to preach individual salvation without teaching social right and wrong.[24]

Looking at the contemporary scene, Mathews was unable to determine the extent to which the church was the source of the new public conscience. But he was certain that the reforming zeal of men and women between thirty and fifty years of age was indirectly the product of the Sunday school and young people's movements of the church in which they were reared. Moreover, he believed that such conscience and reform in the social order was evidence of a religious revival already under way, and the church should recognize it and cooperate with it rather than bemoan the fact that more traditional revivals had not occurred. Christianity should look to such persons, for the social leadership of the church would be exercised by what Mathews termed "the vicarious tenth

---

[23]*CACO*, 105-106, 113, 116-48.

[24]*CACO*, 150-82.

of society." Those were the people who faced the future with creative thinking, Christian values, and a willingness to carry the burdens of the whole community.[25] Rauschenbusch in his book referred to a similar group as the "new apostolate,"[26] and Josiah Strong looked to those he called "Christian patriots."[27]

The influence of Mathews's book is difficult to ascertain because it was overshadowed by the unexpected success of Rauschenbusch's volume. Determining the real influence of Josiah Strong's *The Challenge of the City* is also hard, but there is no questioning that it achieved wide circulation. As a volume in the Forward Mission Study Courses sponsored by the Young People's Missionary Movement, it enjoyed a print run of 40,000 within six months of the time Strong signed the preface on 10 August 1907.[28] Such extensive distribution for a book on social Christianity was still unusual and may have been the reason that the author chose to repeat a number of the ideas he had previously expressed.

At the outset Strong admitted that two-fifths of the book constituted a revision and an updating of his *The Twentieth Century City*, originally published in 1898.[29] In addition, however, the volume included information about socialized churches and religious social settlements that had appeared previously in *Religious Movements for Social Betterment*,[30] and also contained writings about the social teachings of Jesus on the kingdom of God and the social laws of service, sacrifice, and love that were included in *The Next Great Awakening*.[31] There was a consistency and continuity to Strong's convictions about the needs of the city, the effective ways to minister to those needs, and the biblical and theological basis for such work.

---

[25]*CACO*, 223-25, 245-55.

[26]*CASC*, 414-21.

[27]Josiah Strong, *The Challenge of the City* (New York: Young People's Missionary Movement of the United States and Canada, 1907) 84, 271-73. (Hereafter cited in this chapter as *COC*.)

[28]Religious Education Association, *Education and National Character* (Chicago: Religious Education Association, 1908) 118.

[29]Preface of *COC*, xiv; cf. Josiah Strong, *The Twentieth Century City* (New York: Baker & Taylor, 1898) passim.

[30]Cf. *COC*, 209-24 with *Religious Movements for Social Betterment* (New York: Baker and Taylor, 1900) 42-90.

[31]Cf. *COC*, 169-93 with *The Next Great Awakening* (New York: Baker & Taylor, 1902) 51- 151.

What made Josiah Strong's new book distinctive was its use of the crisis concept. When he declared that "the problem of the city forces upon us a national crisis," he went on to remind readers that "the city is the microcosm of the new industrial world" and "to solve its problems for America is to solve them for mankind."[32] Later he argued that existing tendencies would "precipitate a crisis" in due time if they were permitted to continue. The only way to avoid that result was to rely on "a new evangelism" based on the use of socialized churches and social settlements. Warning that a social or political crisis would result in twenty or thirty years if action were postponed, he referred to conditions in his time as "a national emergency to-day." Only the "Christian patriotism of the churches" could transform both the people and their environment and solve "the city problem."[33] Strong's view of crisis was unique in that he regarded it to be a potential problem that only had reached the dimensions of an emergency, and the solution for the crisis was to work hard to head it off.

To arouse the necessary commitment and implement the needed changes was the work of the church, according to Strong. Affirming the instrumental view of the church that was characteristic of the social gospel—"that the church is not an end in itself, but a means to the kingdom [of God] as an end"—he insisted that it was the sacred duty of the church to educate the social conscience.[34] The essence of his argument was embodied in these sentences:

> Twentieth century Christianity will instruct the social conscience, will teach that the kingdom of God fully come in the earth is the true social ideal; that the brotherhood of the kingdom creates the true social spirit, and that the three fundamental laws of the kingdom—those of service, sacrifice, and love—are the only laws by obedience to which society can be perfected.
> In a word, twentieth century Christianity will be the Christianity of Christ,

---

[32]*COC*, 84-85.

[33]*COC*, 241-46, 268-71.

[34]*COC*, 182, 190-91. Cf. his statement with Gladden's analogy of the distinction: "The kingdom of heaven is the entire social organism in its ideal perfection; the church is one of the organs—the most important of them all—having much the same relation to Christian society that the brain has to the body. The body is not all brain; but the brain is the seat of thought and feeling and motion." *The Church and the Kingdom* (New York: Fleming H. Revell Co., 1894); quoted in Robert T. Handy, *The Social Gospel in America, 1870–1920: Gladden, Ely, Rauschenbusch* (New York: Oxford University Press, 1966) 105.

and will teach that he is the only Savior of society as well as the only Savior of the individual.[35]

When the church could forget her own life to serve gladly in these ways, it would save the city, the nation, and civilization. "Will not this be the next great awakening?" asked Strong.[36] Just as he regarded the crisis as something in the future, so he regarded the next awakening as being ahead. Just as his national crisis was still only a national emergency, so his view of the kingdom required a social perfection that remained an ideal. Although the main pattern of his argument went in the opposite direction, there was more truth than he would admit in his comment following the question about the next awakening: "We make pleas for social Christianity, but it seems vague and impracticable to most people."[37]

Compared to his friend and fellow Congregationalist Josiah Strong, Washington Gladden was equally committed to repeating long-held views, but with more realistic application and impact in the midst of changing circumstances. Indeed, his book *The Church and Modern Life*— which was not completed until mid-December 1907 and did not reach bookstores until the following March—can only be fully appreciated when it is set in the context of the realities Gladden experienced during its writing in the autumn of 1907. At the time he was seventy-one years old, was completing twenty-five years as pastor of the First Congregational Church in Columbus, and concluding his three-year term as moderator of the National Council of the Congregational Churches. After reading Rauschenbusch's *Christianity and the Social Crisis* and agreeing with its thesis that "the crisis of society is also the crisis of the Church," Gladden felt a new impulse to arouse the church to work more actively to achieve the kingdom of God in America. Much of his energy in the last half of 1907 was devoted to stimulating a sense of urgency concerning this need at all levels of his involvement. During those months his reading and preparation was focused in three areas: preaching to his congregation, confronting the triennial meeting of the Congregational churches, and preparing a book manuscript for a broader audience.

Although Gladden had written thirty books, held political office, and worked for numerous reforms, he regarded himself as primarily a pastor. For him the central function of pastoral ministry was preaching, and con-

---

[35]*COC*, 178-179.

[36]*COC*, 272.

[37]*COC*, 272-73.

sequently he gave large amounts of time to his pulpit preparation. Each Sunday he developed two sermons, one for the morning that usually concentrated on personal religion, and the other for the evening that dealt with a wide range of religious, theological, biographical, and social topics. All but six of his books were printed volumes of sermons and lectures that were prepared initially for the pulpit.[38] His work during the latter part of 1907 followed this long-established pattern, and it was not surprising that Gladden's three foci interacted.

Most indicative of his preaching emphasis at the time was his sermon "The New Reformation" in September. Using the text "Repent: for the kingdom of heaven is at hand" (Matt. 4:17), Gladden maintained that the church was responsible for the evil conditions in the nation because "the social structure has been reared under the supervision of the Christian church." While the church as an organization was not to engage in business or politics, its function was "to furnish the constructive ideas and sentiments by which every part of our social life should be controlled." In Gladden's estimation, it was unfaithfulness to this trust that was responsible for the injustice, oppression, exploitation, inequalities, and enmities that had been revealed in society. Reflecting his reading of Rauschenbusch, the Columbus pastor told his people, "Between the ruling principle of the existing social order and the ruling principle of the Christian church there is deadly enmity, and one or the other must prevail. Either the church must Christianize society or society will de-christianize the church." With the conviction that things could not go on indefinitely as they had been, Gladden argued that the church needed to settle the question quickly. At the conclusion the issue was clearly stated.

> What American civilization needs is a new heart. New ideals, new motives, new principles of action must take the place of those now ruling. The kind of work must be done for it that the Christian Church is here in the world to do.
>
> But in order that the church may be fitted for its work a reformation of the church itself is called for, no less radical than that of the sixteenth century. And the question confronting her today, the most momentous question, in my judgment, that she has faced in all her history, is whether she will rouse herself from her slumber, and repent from her defiling complicities with Mammon and take up with resolute purpose the one task which from the beginning has been awaiting her—the Christianization of the social order.[39]

---

[38]Washington Gladden, *Recollections* (Boston: Houghton Mifflin Company, 1909) 410-12.

[39]*The Ohio State Journal* (Columbus), 7 September 1907, p. 3.

In this sermon Gladden put the responsible choice more squarely upon the church than he had in earlier sermons like "Where Are We in Democracy?" in February 1906 or "The Education of Conscience" during the tainted money controversy in October 1905.[40]

His own commitment to direct confrontation of the church was obvious as the social prophet prepared for the triennial meeting of the National Council of the Congregational Churches at Cleveland, Ohio, in October. Exercising control of the agenda, he saw to it that social concerns were considered several times during the ten days from 8 to 17 October. His own Moderator's Address on "The Church and the Social Crisis" came the first day[41]; the last day had addresses on social themes by four ministers during the morning, afternoon, and evening[42]; and on 11 October the Industrial Committee Report was considered.[43]

Gladden's "The Church and the Social Crisis" address not only focused the problem but also directed it to the organized Church in bold, unequivocal terms. Whereas each of the other three social-gospel writers addressed the church generally, Gladden challenged his denomination specifically. And he did so as its official leader reporting on what had happened during the past three years. While he included the world in his scope, he concentrated on "upheavals that have taken place in the industrial and social order" in America, which he likened to the impact of the recent San Francisco earthquake. His list of social problems was a catalogue of major muckraker disclosures: the shame of the cities, the insurance and packing house investigations, the railroad, shipping, and public service combinations, the widening breach between workers and employers.[44] Lest his hearers miss his point, Gladden stated forthrightly,

It is idle, it is fatuous, to hide from ourselves the fact that we are facing, here in the United States of America, a social crisis. The forces which are at work here—the forces whose operation I have been pointing out—mean de-

---

[40]Manuscript sermons in the Gladden Papers, Ohio Historical Society, Columbus OH.

[41]*Minutes of the National Council of the Congregational Churches of the United States* (1907), 1-21.

[42]"The Church as Witness of Civic Righteousness," "The Church as Champion of Social Justice," "The Church and the Industrial Problem," and "A New Day for Congregationalism in Social Service," ibid., 77-107, 133-39, 426-30.

[43]Ibid., 310-20, 427.

[44]Ibid., 3-8.

struction. The tendencies which have been gathering strength since the Civil War—the tendencies to the accumulation of power in the hands of a few; the tendencies to use this power predaceously; the tendencies to boundless luxury and extravagance; the tendencies to the separation and the antagonism of social classes must be arrested and that speedily, or we shall soon be in chaos. A social order which makes possible the rise of a Harriman or a Rockefeller is a social order which cannot long endure.[45]

Despite his appreciation for the efforts of President Roosevelt and others to "restrain and extirpate these unsocial forces," the Congregational social prophet was more concerned about what the church should do about such conditions. Pointedly he asked the delegates,

> What has the Christian Church been doing while these powers of piracy and plunder have been gathering their forces and spreading their nets and heaping up their spoils? Where was the Christian Church when the grafters were ravaging the cities and the rebate robbers and the frenzied financiers and the insurance sharks were getting in their work? For the most part she has been standing by and looking on, winking her eyes, and twiddling her thumbs, and wondering whether she had any call to interfere.[46]

Although Gladden concluded that all this was "a sad and shameful business," his optimism led him to wonder if "in this hour of the nation's testing, the church is beginning to awake to some sense of her past infidelity and her present opportunity. I wonder if she knows that *now*, NOW, is for her the accepted time and the day of salvation." If the church only recognized that the threatening social conditions of the past three years were due to the absence in society of elements that the church could have provided, then it could assume its rightful responsibilities "to organize industrial and civil society on Christian principles." Realizing that instant change was impossible, he advised that it would be enough if the church grasped the need and believed it was possible to act. But the church had to admit that it had lost its grip on society and had to begin to grapple with its assigned task. "The responsibility now resting on the Church in America is something tremendous. If this nation is destroyed the guilt will lie at the door of the Church," he warned. He hoped that such destruction would not come to pass, for he believed that "the Church will hear the call of her Master in this great crisis, and put away her weaknesses and scandals, and rise to the mighty task that awaits her."[47]

---

[45]Ibid., 9.

[46]Ibid., 10-11, 15.

[47]Ibid., 16-20.

Washington Gladden had been a champion of social Christianity during all of his twenty-five years as pastor in Columbus, but never had he addressed the church so resolutely as in his Moderator's Address. A few years earlier he was glad to speak to the social question when he wrote about the need for social salvation, but the striking and continuing disclosures by muckrakers and reformers convinced him that there was a social crisis and that aroused him to new levels of bravery.[48] Stimulated by Rauschenbusch's provocative handling of social crisis, and aware of the unique opportunity he possessed as moderator of the Congregational churches, Gladden determined to confront the organized church in a direct manner in his address "The Church and the Social Crisis."

Newspapers gave the address front-page coverage. " 'Says We Face Social Crisis' " proclaimed the headline in the *Cleveland Plain Dealer:* "Rev. Washington Gladden Makes Dire Prophecy" in a "stirring valedictory address."[49] In Columbus the *Ohio State Journal* headline read, "Nation Faces Social Crisis . . . It Is Idle to Attempt to Disregard the Fact."[50] However, Gladden's correspondence during the following weeks gave evidence that the speech had received a cool reception, which bothered him. His friend James Whiton wrote back, after Gladden had described the Cleveland meeting, to say, "Of course there must have been dissent: if conditions tending to such dissent had not existed, the address could never have been born. It is most encouraging to know that the dissenters were far outnumbered."[51] Another correspondent said, "When formidable words are said a silence ensues, and the man who has had the temerity to speak is liable to feel lonely."[52] Josiah Strong requested a copy of the address after Whiton, who had an advance copy to read, had called him the day before the speech to express his enthusiasm. The call motivated Strong to phone his son living in Cleveland to urge him to hear it.[53] Cyrus Osborne, secretary of the Congress of Religion, commended the address as "magnificent and inspiring," assured that it was "exactly the

---

[48]Cf. Washington Gladden, *Social Salvation* (Boston: Houghton Mifflin Co., 1902).

[49]*Cleveland Plain Dealer*, 9 October 1907, p. 1.

[50]*The Ohio State Journal* 9 October 1907, p. 1.

[51]James M. Whiton to Gladden, 22 October 1907, Gladden Papers.

[52]John McCarthy to Gladden, 12 October 1907, Gladden Papers.

[53]Josiah Strong to Gladden, 21 October 1907; James M. Whiton to Gladden, 12 October 1907, Gladden Papers.

fitting word which needs to be spoken today," and concurred that "the church holds the key to the situation and that it can and must move along the lines pointed out in your address."[54]

Despite these assurances, the cool reception accorded the address by the Congregational National Council apparently had a significant effect on Washington Gladden. The most obvious evidence of this was in the manuscript of his new book *The Church and Modern Life*, in which he avoided any mention of a social crisis. The closest approximation to that term was his statement in the preface that "the church is passing through a critical period"; otherwise he limited himself to phrases such as "recent exposures of social decay" or "present deplorable conditions."[55] Failure to use social-crisis terminology had to be intentional because he again referred to the crisis and the need for urgency in facing it when he preached his twenty-fifth anniversary discourse on 29 December, twelve days after he signed the preface to the book, and two days after the editor of Houghton, Mifflin & Company wrote to acknowledge receiving it.[56]

"A serious crisis is that that confronts us, my countrymen!" declared Gladden in the discourse he delivered at morning worship that anniversary Sunday. Titled "Memories and Visitations," the address reflected on changes during the past twenty-five years. Observing that the notable material progress of the nation during that time had not been accompanied by a comparable moral development, he told the large congregation that gathered to honor him that it was unfortunate that the church had not done more to achieve the kingdom of God on earth, for that was "the main business of the church." The serious responsibility to which the church was called was the work of "invigorating the morality of the land," and the aged social-gospel advocate confessed that he had "been trying to do a little of this kind of work in the quarter century behind us." However, in assessing his own role he admitted, "As for myself I must own that I have never discerned, as I think I am coming to discern, in these later years, the essential value of the service to which the Christian Church is called. If I could have seen it twenty- five years ago as clearly as I see it

---

[54]Cyrus A. Osborne to Gladden, 5 November 1907, Gladden Papers.

[55]Washington Gladden, *The Church and Modern Life* (Boston: Houghton Mifflin Co., 1908) v, 167, 170, 213. (Hereafter cited in this chapter as *CAML*.)

[56]*CAML*, vi; F. G. of Houghton Mifflin & Co. to Gladden, 27 December 1907; "Memories and Visitations," *The Twenty-fifth Anniversary of the Commencement of the Pastorate of Rev. Washington Gladden, D. D. over the First Congregational Church of Columbus, Ohio, 1882–1907: Sermons and Addresses* (N.p., n.d.) in the Edward J. Converse Papers, Ohio Historical Society, Columbus OH, pp. 11, 15.

now, I believe that we might have had larger reasons for rejoicing to-day."[57] That clearer vision of the church's mission seemed to be the compelling force behind his more aggressive preaching, writing, and advocacy in the last four months of 1907.

The most lasting product of those months was his book *The Church and Modern Life*. Although it contained no reference to the term *social crisis*, his other statements and actions from the time the manuscript was finalized indicated clearly that the crisis dimension was basic to his understanding. Nevertheless, the book was much less barbed in tone than either his "The Church and the Social Crisis" address or his "The New Reformation" sermon. In the book was a chapter titled "The Coming Reformation," but it was not nearly as probing as his sermon of similar title. It concentrated much more on an analysis of the Protestant Reformation itself and was much less specific about modern life. Its general message was stated in one sentence: "The coming reformation will consist in the awakening of the church to its social responsibilities."[58]

While the tone of the entire volume was less confrontational than his other statements at the time, Gladden in the final third of the book did state his basic ideas about social redemption, which were similar to those expressed by the other three social-gospel writers in 1907. In contrast to countries such as England and Germany where church and state were not separate, the church in America could not coerce, dictate, or prescribe the forms of industrial or political society. "Its concern is not with the machinery of society, but with the moral motive power," he insisted. Believing that the existing social order could be Christianized, he argued that the first step needed to redeem it was "the education of the Christian conscience," which was the business of the church. Like Rauschenbusch, Gladden felt that there must be moral insight and social passion underlying the laws of society, and providing that foundation was the business of the church too. To him, "the recent exposures of social decay" made it obvious that "social morality must have a religious foundation." But was the church ready for the effort and cost that were necessary to redeem society?[59]

To achieve the desired goal would require a new evangelism and a new leadership, according to Gladden. Rejecting the old type of personal evangelism as outmoded, he maintained that the redemption of society was the

---

[57]Gladden, "Memories and Visitations," 13-15, 17.

[58]*CAML*, 147.

[59]*CAML*, 148-72.

objective of the new evangelism. In the new style, emphasis should be on transforming self-love into love that identifies the self with the neighbor. In developing this concept he paid Rauschenbusch an unusual compliment by quoting four full paragraphs from the section on "the new apostolate" in *Christianity and the Social Crisis* and by saying that Rauschenbusch's book was "one that no intelligent student of present-day Christianity can afford to neglect."[60] Gladden felt that the new evangelism would be fulfilled by young men and women, to whom he looked for the new leadership in the church.[61] In sum, he recalled the ominous nature of the social conditions depicted to the nation and indicated that the only way to cure such evils was the power of public opinion, which the church must educate. "The church is therefore called to the redemption of society. But the work of redemption to which it is called is not a reconstruction of economic or political machinery; it is the quickening of the social conscience, and the reenthronement of justice and love in the place of selfishness and strife as the ruling principles of human society."[62]

Although Washington Gladden wrote these words, Rauschenbusch, Strong, or Mathews could have stated the same convictions. Despite the unique purpose and emphasis of each of the four social-gospel writers in 1907, there was a common understanding of the social scene and a remarkable similarity in the response that was expected from the church. The following emphases were common to the four writers.

Social Crisis. Three of the four used the term *social crisis* itself, and Gladden, while avoiding those words, conveyed their meaning in his book. His open use of the term in other circumstances during the months while he composed the book indicated that he viewed society in crisis dimensions and felt the urgency of such an understanding. Frequently, references to the crisis were general, but Rauschenbusch's chapter on "The Present Crisis" and Gladden's "The Church and the Social Crisis" address indicated specific problems that constituted the social crisis. Only Strong regarded the crisis as a future danger if the "national emergency" of the time continued to worsen; the others viewed it as a present reality to which the church ought to respond immediately.[63]

---

[60]*CASC*, 414-16; quoted in *CAML*, 177-79.

[61]*CAML*, 220.

[62]*CAML*, 200-201.

[63]*CASC*, 332, 340-42, 285-86; *CACO*, 3-9, 247; *COC*, 84, 270-71, 241; *CAML*, v, 167, 170-71, 213-14.

Church. Each of the social-gospel authors looked to the church "as the organized conscience of Christendom" that should rise up to meet the needs of a troubled social order.[64] The argument of each writer was to be read by individual Christians, but the recommended actions consciously or unconsciously presumed activity by organized institutional denominations. All four men accepted the instrumental understanding of church held by Christocentric Liberalism. Gladden stated that view in 1894 when he wrote of the kingdom of God as comprehending "the entire social organism" and of the church as the central organ of the social organism. According to him, "There is a pretty strong tendency, in many churches, to forget the instrumental character of the church; to forget that it is a part and not the whole, a means and not an end."[65] Similarly, Rauschenbusch warned that the church did not exist for its own sake, but rather to be "a working organization to create the Christian life in individuals and the kingdom of God in human society."[66] Facing the call to achieve the kingdom of God in the world forced the church to make one of three choices: to withdraw from the evil world, "to tolerate the world and conform to it," or "to condemn the world and seek to change it."[67] For the social-gospel writers only the third option was reasonable.

Christianize the Social Order. Since the church was intended to be the instrument to facilitate the achieving of the kingdom of God on earth, according to social-gospel advocates, its task was to work for the redemption of society. Although the four writers were vitally concerned about social problems and wanted to see them corrected, all four argued that the basic job of the church was not to work for social reforms.[68] As Mathews put it, "Reforms are for church members, not for churches."[69] Instead, the church was to work primarily for the Christianization of the social order.

---

[64]These were Rauschenbusch's words but similar ones were expressed by each (*CASC*, 287). Cf. *CASC*, 287, 185; *CACO*, 2-9, 179-81; *COC*, 190-91, 272; *CAML*, 92, 97.

[65]Washington Gladden, *The Church and the Kingdom;* quoted in Handy, *The Social Gospel in America*, 105, 111.

[66]*CASC*, 185.

[67]*CASC*, 342.

[68]*CASC*, 314, 347; *CACO*, 135, 142-44; *COC*, 173, 259; *CAML*, 86, 154, 149, 164.

[69]*CACO*, 177.

Uniformly these writers said the basic function of the church was to educate the Christian conscience. Selfish, misguided conscience had created the social crisis; only right Christian conscience could correct it. If Christians were taught the social teachings of Jesus and the Hebrew prophets, as well as the moral principles developed by Christianity, they would be able to awaken public conscience to social injustice and the conviction of sin that would lead to social righteousness. Each of the authors believed that sin lay behind the abuses in the social order[70] and called for its removal by a transformation of social values that they called social evangelism.[71] There was no salvation for society that did not involve a change of motives in citizens, and there was no agency except the church that could accomplish that purpose. Thus, social redemption was impossible unless the church awakened to its responsibility to Christianize the social order.

Two of these three common emphases—the instrumental understanding of the church and the Christianizing of the social order—were fundamental tenets of social Christianity since its early days late in the nineteenth century. Indeed, Washington Gladden constructed his first Lyman Beecher Lectures, *Tools and the Man*, on the two concepts in 1887.[72] It was the emphasis on social crisis that was the new common feature evident in the four social-gospel authors in 1907. Earlier, it was customary to refer to the social question, but, significantly, that term seldom appeared in these books.[73] In one instance Rauschenbusch observed that "to most thoughtful men to-day the social question is the absorbing intellectual problem of our time." But he went on to point out that for the working class the social question involved not just people's minds but their entire social existence.[74] Like the workers, Rauschenbusch moved beyond intellectual formulation and discussion to a level of emotional involvement. By adding passion to analysis, he abandoned his long-held scholarly interest in relating the Christian movement to the social movement and wrote instead about Christianity's relation to the

---

[70]*CASC*, 349; *CACO*, 5, 222, 224; *COC*, 173; *CAML*, 157.

[71]*CASC*, 357-58; *CACO*, 177, 180-81; *COC*, 241; *CAML*, 185, 173-98.

[72]Washington Gladden, *Tools and the Man: Property and Industry under the Christian Law* (Boston: Houghton Mifflin Co., 1893) 6, 12-16.

[73]Comparison of Gladden's 1907 book to his previous volume, *Social Salvation*, showed that the first chapter in the earlier one was titled "Religion and the Social Question," while the later one said only that it was "one question which Christianity . . . never ceases to ask" (*CAML*, 84).

[74]*CASC*, 318-19.

social crisis people faced daily. The social gospel movement took a distinctive step in its development when it moved from the social question to the social crisis.[75]

Why was the move from the social question to the social crisis so significant? On the one hand, it shifted the social gospel from the abstract to the concrete level. The problems described by the muckrakers were specific and detailed, and people could feel indignation as well as exercise their minds. When advocates of social Christianity followed the same pattern, they discovered that the laity better comprehended and felt their message. On the other hand, the change of emphasis enabled social-gospel leaders to unite their energies and cause with the efforts of the muckraking journalists and Progressive reformers. By doing this, their cause moved into the mainstream of American life where it became more visible. Although much of their message repeated earlier themes that were part of what had been designated the social question, the shift to the emphasis and detail of the social crisis enabled champions of social Christianity to communicate their ideas in terms that were more readily comprehended by Christians generally. Movement from the social question to the social crisis did not mean rejection of the earlier understanding; it meant better communication and implementation of these ideas. As a result, it was feasible that Christians might be more easily motivated to assume greater responsibility for the social order. If proponents of social redemption were successful, perhaps the organized church would be ready to act, to move beyond recognition of social crisis to some form of response. That would mark still another stage of development for social Christianity.

_____

[75]Francis Greenwood Peabody would have disputed this interpretation. In an address entitled "The Universities and the Social Conscience" in February 1908 he said that "it is the age of the Social Question" (Religious Education Association, *Education and National Character*, 15-27). However, he acknowledged the distinction between emotional and intellectual to which I have referred when he wrote: "The social question of the present time has just reached the point where emotional power needs a new degree of intellectual direction." Peabody viewed the emotional power negatively; I regard it as positive and empowering for the social gospel at the time.

PART 2

From the Social Crisis to the Social Creed, 1907–1908

CHAPTER 5

The Social Application of Religion

At all hazards, the Church must throw herself into the current social agitation, not as a reluctant laggard, but as the informing genius and the controlling mind of the movement which she has really inspired by her teaching.

(George P. Eckman,
The Social Application of Religion, *1908)*

WALTER RAUSCHENBUSCH'S ANALOGY of fruit trees blossoming in May as being the culmination of a long process of sap rising and distending unseen within the trees was a fitting prediction of the way the social gospel was accepted by American Protestantism.[1] Its blossoming was not evident until 1908, but that budding had already commenced the preceding year.

When Washington Gladden tried unsuccessfully to stimulate the Congregational Church to respond to the social crisis at its triennial meeting in October 1907, there was only a modest achievement by forces of social Christianity during those sessions. The report of the Industrial Committee to the Congregational National Council received serious hearing, and its recommendations were officially adopted. Indicative of the conservative mood of the assembly, however, that approval was limited in ways the committee and its social-activist members did not appreciate. One of the recommendations urged that the Industrial Committee be made a standing committee, which was endorsed. But when its new membership was assigned, only one of the seven members

---

[1]Walter Rauschenbusch, *Christianity and the Social Crisis* (New York: Macmillan Co., 1907) 422. See p. 59 above.

of the previous committee, Graham Taylor, was reappointed, which limited continuity of thought and action by partisans of social concern. Another recommendation praised the work of Charles Stelzle and the Department of Church and Labor of the Presbyterian Church and urged the National Council to "provide a secretary for a similar purpose." While the recommendation was approved, the appointment of such an official was left to the Executive Committee of the Congregational Home Mission Society in communication with leaders of the National Council, which at the time effectively rendered the authorization inoperative. Thus, the Industrial Committee report was authorized on the one hand, but its action recommendations were limited on the other.[2]

Similar conditions prevailed at the triennial General Convention of the Protestant Episcopal Church, which met at the same time as the Congregationalists. Its Joint Commission on Relations of Capital and Labor also commended the Presbyterian Department of Church and Labor and endorsed the principles on which it was based. The Episcopalians thereby agreed that " 'the labor question is fundamentally a moral and religious question' " and that "the chief mission of the Church at large in dealing with the economic questions of the present is to determine, proclaim, and to insist upon this moral and religious basis." In addition, the Joint Commission recommended that it be made a permanent commission and that its powers be extended to enable it to coordinate the various existing organizations involved with social questions. Both parts of the resolution were enacted. With no Gladden presiding, the Episcopal Church was spared a direct confrontation with the social crisis, and that term nowhere appeared in the denomination's official proceedings.[3] When the General Convention ended, Episcopalians joined Congregationalists in making the Labor Commission permanent and in avoding any official recognition of the social crisis. Since neither group would convene for another three years, these actions put both beyond the area of potential action on social matters for that length of time.

While official national bodies of Protestants ignored all but economic aspects of the prevailing social problems as the year 1907 came to a close, President Theodore Roosevelt in December sent a message to Congress that recommended several new measures for dealing with the problems confronting the nation. By the end of January 1908 Congress had not

---

[2]*Minutes of the National Council of the Congregational Churches of the United States* (1907), 310-21, 407, 427.

[3]*Journal of the General Convention of the Protestant Episcopal Church in the U.S.A.* (1907), 383, 388, 427-28, 527-29.

responded, and Roosevelt sent a more radical message to the legislators. Those two messages contained "practically every reform that was to be made during the Taft and Wilson administrations," according to historian George E. Mowry. Noting that the president was a politician whose ears were attuned to the public mood, Mowry concluded that "the country was moving, and Roosevelt, being a good democratic politician, was ready to move with it and guide it in the ways of moderation, expediency, and righteousness."[4] Praising the 31 January message to Congress as the greatest state paper Roosevelt had written to that time, the editor of *The Independent* went on to say, "This message is essentially the most serious and earnest appeal that has ever been made by a public man in America to the moral sense of the nation."[5]

Twelve days later that moral sense of the nation was evident when the Religious Education Association assembled at Washington, D.C., for its annual meeting. The theme, "Education and National Character," marked a new stage of development for the organization and reflected the social consciousness of Henry F. Cope, who became its general secretary in February 1907. In its first four conventions the association had considered various phases of religious pedagogy: improvement of methods in religious training, the biblical basis for such training, the aims of this education, and the materials to be used in such instruction. Building on this foundation, the association in 1908 proceeded to consider the relation of the religious life to the duties of citizenship and the contribution of religion to the national life. By intention, the sessions were held in the nation's capital city. The organization's concern for civic morality and its leaders' general social outlook was noted earlier, and this concern accounted for the association's almost- total concentration on national morality at the 1908 meeting. Actually there had been a gradual development of such interest over the years; for example, there were addresses on "The Quickening of Public Conscience" and "What Is a Christian Nation?" at the 1907 meeting, although its theme was "The Materials of Religious Education." Rauschenbusch set the stage for the Washington convention with his "What Is a Christian Nation?" paper. In it he said that a Christian nation was not one that simply referred to God in the Constitution, had daily prayer in Congress, administered the oath

---

[4]George E. Mowry, *The Era of Theodore Roosevelt and the Birth of Modern America, 1900–1912*, The New American Nation Series, ed. Henry Steele Commager and Richard B. Morris (New York: Harper & Row, 1958; Harper Torchbooks, 1962) 220-23.

[5]*The Independent* (New York), 6 February 1908, pp. 322-23.

of office using the Bible, or maintained a state church. More important to him in determining the nation's character was "the spirit pervading the nation's life."[6]

In the addresses at the 1908 convention the delegates were reminded that "the Religious Education Association was born out of a profound conviction . . . of the national need of a deeper and steadily deepening moral and religious life," and that it was still committed to that ideal of national greatness because "our national need is a religious need." The organization was "an expression of the moral and religious aspirations of democracy."[7] That emphasis was evident in all the papers, which were published as a book bearing the theme as its title: *Education and National Character*. The volume constituted a contemporary commentary on the religious foundation of social conscience in a troubled time. It contained major addresses by Washington Gladden, Francis Peabody, and Lyman Abbott, and others by Shailer Mathews, Henry Cope, and George Albert Coe. A social-gospel orientation and basic understanding was evident throughout the conference.

Discovery and development of a social conscience was the unifying theme of the addresses. It was social conscience that would produce a sense of social responsibility, social justice, and social morality that in turn would find expression in moral-reform and political-reform societies, in social settlements, in philanthropic groups, and in churches. "Never in human history were so many people . . . concerning themselves with social amelioration, dedicating themselves to philanthropy, organizing for industrial change, or applying the motives of religion to the problems of modern life," said Francis Peabody. Although he believed these activities confirmed that "it is the age of the social question," he feared that too much sentimentality and emotion were involved and urged that the real answer to the social question lay in leadership by more disciplined minds.[8] Washington Gladden pointed out that the civil state was created by God to serve religious ends and that the state shared with the church and the

---

[6]*The Materials of Religious Education: Being the Principal Papers Presented at, and Proceedings of the Fourth General Convention of the Religious Education Association, Rochester, New York, February 5-7, 1907* (Chicago: Executive Office of the Association, 1907) 25-30, 37-42.

[7]Religious Education Association, *Education and National Character*, by Henry Churchill King, Francis Greenwood Peabody, Lyman Abbott, Washington Gladden, and others (Chicago: Religious Education Association, 1908) 7-15, 90-92.

[8]Ibid., 15-27.

home the obligation and opportunity to work for social righteousness. Also, he argued that all moral and religious forces ought to unite their energies because they had a common educational function in the nation.[9]

Such an educational role was the proper domain of the Religious Education Association, and resolutions adopted by the convention thanked God that educational organizations like it could work with other religious and moral agencies to achieve industrial and social reconstruction.[10] President Roosevelt held a reception for the association in the East Room of the White House, and there he expressed gratitude for the association's efforts and urged it to continue to work for the dominance of spiritual ideals in the nation. "Any failure to train the average citizen to a belief in the things of the spirit no less than the things of the body must in the long run entail misfortune, shortcoming, possible disaster upon the nation itself," declared Roosevelt.[11] When reporting on the convention, *The Outlook* concluded that the existence of the Religious Education Association was "an encouraging sign of the ethical awakening of our time—an awakening which it is hoped will make our education more spiritual and our religion more rational and practical."[12]

Identification of a voluntary religious organization like the Religious Education Association with "the ethical awakening of our time" was one of the first recognitions that Protestants were part of the social revival occurring in the nation. Since the program for the Washington convention was planned months earlier and at least some of its speakers began their preparation the preceding year, the process that bloomed in February actually had started in 1907. While it is difficult to date precisely when the renewal began, the earliest overt evidence began to appear early in 1908. In succeeding months several religious sources confirmed that changes were beginning to happen. For instance, the March issue of *The Kingdom*, published by the Brotherhood of the Kingdom, had a front-page article on "The Passion for Righteousness" that began: "For some time a wave of moral earnestness has taken possession of the thinking element of the country's citizenry." Citing economic and political evidence, the article concluded that such action was "a part of the moral revival that has been taking place."[13]

---

[9]Ibid., 33-42.

[10]*Religious Education* (Chicago) 3 (April 1908): 35.

[11]Ibid., 34-35, 45; *The Outlook* (New York), 29 February 1908, p. 478.

[12]*The Outlook* (New York), 29 February 1908, p. 478.

[13]*The Kingdom* 1 (March 1908): 1.

Another sign of growing change was the increasing frequency of lectures on social ministry that were delivered at colleges and seminaries in the same period. During the winter of 1907–1908 John R. Mott, leader of both the World's Student Christian Federation and the Student Volunteer Movement, presented a series of lectures at three schools. Later published by the Student Department of the Young Men's Christian Association, the lectures revealed how much social questions had become part of Mott's message to young men and women. When he published his *The Evangelization of the World in This Generation* in 1900 the importance of individual salvation dominated his thinking, but in these lectures— published in 1908 as *The Future Leadership of the Church*—a responsible social Christianity was emphasized. Still pointing to the importance of individual salvation as "the chief business of the Church," he went on to say, "Nevertheless, the social aspects of the programme of Christianity constitute one of the distinctive calls of our generation." Quoting Rauschenbusch's statement that the church should awaken to rally moral forces in communities, Mott warned that the church should not hold back "in the present social crisis." "Not only are social questions an important concern of the Church," he said, "but it is essential to the Church that it should give itself whole-heartedly to their solution." Thus, the organized church should accept its social responsibility to create the ideas and sentiments in society that would make it "impossible for social wrongs to endure." Only as the nation was "steadied, guided, and inspired by Christian principles" could it be saved and fulfill its destiny.[14] Although Mott took time arriving at his understanding of a social gospel, he had learned its basic tenets rather well.

At Ohio Wesleyan University the renowned Merrick Lectures in April 1908 departed radically from the eleven previous lectures by virtue of having a social theme. President Herbert Welch, who advocated "The Social Application of Religion" theme, explained that the unusually large attendance was due in part to the fame of the speakers and in part to the topics that were addressed. The five speakers and their subjects indicated the range of interest: Charles Stelzle on "The Spirit of Social Unrest," Jane Addams on "Woman's Conscience and Social Amelioration," Charles Patrick Neill on "Some Ethical Aspects of the Labor Movement," Graham Taylor on "Industry and Religion: Their Common Ground and Interdependence," and George P. Eckman on "Christianity and the Social Situation." Interpreting the theme in an introduction to the published lectures, Welch explained, "There is a genuine social awakening—which

---

[14]John R. Mott, *The Future Leadership of the Church* (New York: Student Department, Young Men's Christian Association, 1908) 42-53.

has shown itself in philanthropy, in political reform, in vigorous discussion of family problems and commercial morality, in ardent and not unsuccessful efforts for industrial and social betterment." He felt not only that the church should be closely identified with the social crusade of the day but that the church was largely responsible for the awakening.[15]

Each of the lectures underscored, to greater or lesser extent, Welch's interpretation, but three of them spoke directly to the need for the church's involvement. Stelzle said that the church was responsible for the spirit of social unrest at the time. However, having created dissatisfaction among the people, the church should not "step aside and permit the unprincipalled [sic] agitator of materialism" to take over and finish the job. The church must continue to be involved, but primarily to build up the people rather than organized religion.[16] Taylor also indicated that "the present crisis . . . tests the capacity of the Christianity of the Church to adapt itself to the modern conditions of life."[17] Eckman emphasized not only the need for the church's efforts but also the nature of the participation: "At all hazards, the Church must throw herself into the current social agitation, not as a reluctant laggard, but as the informing genius and the controlling mind of the movement which she has really inspired by her teaching."[18] The cumulative message of *The Social Application of Religion* well reflected the state of the social gospel at the time, for the church did begin in 1908 to get more involved in the social unrest.

During May the national legislative assemblies of three denominations devoted some of their attention to ministry to the social order. The General Assembly of the Presbyterian Church in the United States of America heard with pride that other denominations had praised the ministry among workers conducted by Charles Stelzle's Department of Church and Labor. It was reported that Stelzle had added an Immigration Department as well, since so many workers were immigrants. Another testimony to Presbyterian efforts among workers was a great meeting on the relation of the church and labor that attracted

---

[15]*The Social Application of Religion*, by Charles Stelzle, Jane Addams, Charles P. Neill, Graham Taylor, and George P. Eckman. *The Merrick Lectures for 1907–1908 Delivered at Ohio Wesleyan University, Delaware, Ohio, April 5-9, 1908* (Cincinnati: Jennings and Graham; New York: Eaton and Mains, 1908) 5-7.

[16]Ibid., 11-38.

[17]Ibid., 96.

[18]Ibid., 136-37.

12,000 people during the assembly sessions at Kansas City.[19] In the "Narrative of the State of Religion" report was a statement that "it is the duty of the Church not only to save the lost, but also to inform, to mould, to strengthen public opinion in the sphere of morals and religion." Noting "the tide of unrest that is rising in our land," the report stated that it was the duty of the church, "before and above all other societies and organizations," to minister to needy persons and to be the "champion of righteousness in Church and State." Significantly, these assertions of social responsibility were only indirect commitments of the Presbyterian Church, for they were part of an endorsement of the Inter-Church Federation movement and its potential for "regaining the Church's grip upon the masses, and of defending the cause of civic righteousness." While showing that they were aware of the needs and possibilities in social ministry, Presbyterians made no official commitment to such outreach by their own denomination, other than Stelzle's distinctive work with labor.[20]

Charles Evans Hughes, Progressive governor of New York, was elected the first president of the Northern Baptist Convention when it was officially organized in May 1907.[21] However, the real business of the new denominational body, which combined the previously disparate activities of Baptists, did not occur until its meeting 21-27 May 1908. A Commission on Social Service was created at that time to study Baptist social activity and report the results to the convention in 1909. Samuel Zane Batten was appointed its chairman, and Walter Rauschenbusch and Shailer Mathews were among the other ten members.[22] Thus, the new commission of the nascent Baptist Convention began its existence with a constituency of interested and experienced social-gospel partisans. That a generally favorable attitude toward social involvement prevailed in the convention was evident in the thirteen resolutions that it adopted, five of which showed social concern. Most significant of these was the third resolution, which urged "our ministry and churches to emphasize the social significance of the Gospel, and to lend their aid to the united efforts of Christian men to arouse the civic conscience and to compel social righteousness in politics, commerce and finance." Other resolutions

---

[19]*Minutes of the General Assembly of the Presbyterian Church in the United States of America*, n.s. (1908), 326-27; Walter Rauschenbusch, *Christianizing the Social Order* (New York: Macmillan Co., 1912) 13.

[20]*Minutes of the General Assembly* (1908), 88, 259.

[21]*Annual of the Northern Baptist Convention* (1907), 3.

[22]Ibid. (1908), 19, 79, 93.

praised prohibition agitation, called for the abolition of child labor, and supported the formation of the Federal Council of Churches as enhancing "the Kingdom of righteousness on earth." Another commended the Religious Education Association to Baptist churches and urged support of "this organization which seeks to avert national evils and to promote true morality and religion."[23]

Northern Methodists were the third church that met in national assembly during May 1908. Since their actions and activity that year were significant in the history of the social gospel, and especially since they occurred with little previous social involvement, Methodist developments will be examined in more detail in the next chapter.

Episcopalians also reflected the growing social interest, although their General Convention did not meet that year. The Church Congress, which for several years had not scheduled social subjects on its agenda, in May 1908 had several addresses on two social themes: "The Civic Mission of the Church" and "The Place of Organized Christianity in Modern Life." The first speaker on the second theme explained its importance when he said, "The appearance of this subject upon the programme is significant. It is the recognition of a great social movement which has forced its way into the councils of the Church." Describing the social agitation and unrest in the nation as a crisis, he called upon the church to transform the turbulent forces into "effective powers for social righteousness."[24] Speakers on the first theme noted that "we are on the verge of a great revival of religion, . . . a revival of patriotic religion," and the church should "perform her civic mission." If the church developed "the social conscience of the community," it would fulfill its great purpose "to transform human society into the Kingdom of God."[25] While the Church Congress had no official standing, its papers in 1908 showed that Episcopal clergy and laity were akin to other Protestants that year in their thinking about the Church's role in the social crisis.

These signs of increasing awareness and interest in the denominations at the national level indicated that the appeals of social-gospel proponents were being heard more favorably. As this evidence was corroborated by other religious sources, it seemed likely that Protestantism might finally be ready to take some more formal official action. Such verification appeared at intervals during the latter half of 1908. In July an editorial in *The Independent* denied charges in the *International Journal of*

---

[23]Ibid., 101-102.

[24]Protestant Episcopal Church in the U.S.A., Church Congress, *Papers, Addresses and Discussions* (1908), 159-67.

[25]Ibid., 73-100.

Ethics that the nation was "morally decadent" and insisted that "there has never been any time in our national life when the evidences of moral virility were more numerous and encouraging than they are today."[26] By November when the New York State Conference of Religion met, even James Whiton had abandoned his usual jeremiad to affirm that "something like a moral revival has set in." He admitted that "the winter is past, and the spring is at hand."[27] And the November 1908–January 1909 issue of *The Kingdom* contained two articles confirming desired changes in society. One assured that there were "constantly arising evidences of a new spirit taking hold of the problems of life." The other asserted that a combination of individual consciences had effected desirable social changes so that a social conscience was discernible. "It is seen at work in the movement to restrict child labor; to provide adequate protection for womanhood and the home; safeguards against danger from machinery in factories, railroading and the like."[28]

It was precisely those concerns that the Methodist Episcopal Church officially committed itself to work for in 1908, and considerably more. Consequently, it is important to turn our attention to the social application of religion taken by that denomination, and to the larger impact that its actions had upon the development of social Christianity. Looking back to those events at a later time, Rauschenbusch declared that "the honor of making the first ringing declaration in a national convention belongs to the Methodist Church North," but that achievement, like his fruit trees blossoming in May, had its origins in processes that started months earlier.[29]

[26]*The Independent* (New York), 8 July 1908, pp. 107-108.

[27]*Addresses before the New York State Conference of Religion*, ser. 7 (February 1909): 9-11.

[28]*The Kingdom* 2 (November 1908-January 1909): 13, 15.

[29]Rauschenbusch, *Christianizing the Social Order*, 13.

CHAPTER 6

Methodism to Serve the Present Age

And now we summon our great Church to continue and increase its works of social service. . . . Upon every member rests a solemn duty to devote himself with his possessions, his citizenship, and his influence to the glory of God in the service of the present age. And thus by their works, as by their prayers, let all "the people called Methodists" seek that kingdom in which God's will shall be done on earth as it is in heaven.

("The Church and Social Problems" report,
Journal of the General Conference of the Methodist Episcopal Church,
1908)

MANY OF THE SAME SIGNS were present in the Methodist Episcopal Church that marked nascent social Christianity in other religious groups after 1900, but they had not coalesced into a movement to nurture its advocates or enable them to influence the denomination's institutional life. Consequently, the vitality of the social-gospel cause in northern Methodism was scarcely evident before the social crisis in America made the need for church action very apparent. With concerted efforts by a small group, however, the Methodist Episcopal Church, when it acted, did so in such a convincing manner that it quickly moved to the leadership ranks in social ministry.

Methodism was not so moribund that sparks of social concern were totally missing. In 1892, 1896, and 1904, some Annual Conferences petitioned the quadrennial General Conference to take some action concerning social problems or social reform, but invariably the requests were ignored. Such inaction was not the result of a lack of knowledge because the bishops pointed to social needs in their Episcopal Addresses. But preoccupation with a constitutional crisis and withdrawal of holiness sympathizers in the 1890s, and fear of declining membership after 1900, distracted attention from social questions. Furthermore, no charismatic leader or group attained national recognition as the champion of the social cause.

Absence of renowned leaders did not mean that Methodists were inactive in social matters, but it did mean that those who espoused social Christianity were limited largely to local influence. Nonetheless, Edward T. Devine was head of the New York Charity Organization Society, Homer Folks guided the New York State Charities Aid Association, J. W. Magruder led the Federated Charities of Baltimore, and E. J. Helms was minister at the Morgan Memorial institutional church in Boston, where he established Goodwill Industries. Moreover, a number of pastors demonstrated genuine social interests; among these were George P. Eckman, Harry F. Ward, Worth M. Tippy, and William M. Balch. Methodist scholars also produced books dealing with social issues; for example, Samuel Plantz, president of Lawrence University, wrote *The Church and the Social Problem* in 1905,[1] and Edwin L. Earp, chairman of the sociology department of Syracuse University, published *Social Aspects of Religious Institutions* in 1908.[2] Both volumes had Methodist publishers and dealt with the same themes of social crisis, civic consciousness, awakening, and social redemption as had the books of other authors noted earlier, but they attracted no wide interest and exerted little influence.

Frank Mason North was the only Methodist who was consistently involved in the various social-gospel meetings noted previously. Since he usually preferred to work unobtrusively behind the scenes, it was easy to miss his presence. Nevertheless, he had led the efforts in the New York East Conference that sent social petitions to the 1892 and 1896 General Conferences; he was among those who initiated the New York State Conference of Religion; he was involved in the Open and Institutional Church League; and he was actively engaged in several groups concerned with cooperative Protestantism: the Evangelical Alliance, the Federation of Churches and Christian Workers in New York City, the National Federation of Churches, and the Inter-Church Conference on Federation.[3] As vice- chairman of the Arrangements Committee of the latter group, he

---

[1]Samuel Plantz, *The Church and the Social Problem: A Study in Applied Christianity* (Cincinnati: Jennings and Graham; New York: Eaton and Mains, 1906).

[2]Edwin L. Earp, *Social Aspects of Religious Institutions* (New York: Eaton & Mains; Cincinnati: Jennings & Graham, 1908).

[3]Creighton Lacy, *Frank Mason North: His Social and Ecumenical Mission* (Nashville: Abingdon Press, 1967) 80-82, 113-22.

made one of his infrequent addresses on "The Evangelization of American Cities," which was his primary concern. In that address he said that the early years of the twentieth century were giving birth to a new civilization. Despite the crises and hardships involved in that upheaval, he regarded it as a great epoch filled with great opportunities. For him the city was the center of the new society because in it both the problems and the opportunities were the greatest. "If the new civilization is to be mastered by Christ, the city must be taken for him," said North, and he challenged the churches to unite to achieve that end through vigorous evangelization.[4]

Since 1892 North had been employed as the corresponding secretary of the New York City Church Extension and Missionary Society, through which Methodism carried on its urban mission. A small magazine titled *The Christian City* was edited by North to promote his program and interests. From that base he also served without pay as head of the National City Evangelization Union, which coordinated Methodist urban ministry across the country. Through those contacts North was aware of nationwide social and industrial problems, as well as those he faced directly in his own New York City work. From his pivotal position he was a vital cog in the evolution of Methodist social concern, although his low profile approach did not focus attention on his endeavors.[5]

Several of those concerned about broadening the impact of the social gospel in Methodism recognized the value of a coordinated program or agency, but they had been unable to achieve that goal by the winter of 1906. At that time, Worth M. Tippy and Elbert Robb Zaring, in a natural correspondence between former college classmates, considered the need for an organization to promote thought and action on social problems, and then they involved Herbert Welch in the communications. All three had moved to Ohio during 1905 to undertake diverse ministries: Tippy as pastor of the prestigious Epworth Memorial Church in Cleveland, Zaring as assistant editor of the *Western Christian Advocate* weekly newspaper in Cincinnati, and Welch as the president of Ohio Wesleyan University in Delaware. The three perceived that English Methodism was in advance of America in social ministry, and they considered that they might use the recently established Wesleyan Methodist Union for Social Service in

---

[4]Frank Mason North, "The Evangelization of American Cities," *Church Federation; Inter-Church Conference on Federation, New York, November 15-21, 1905*, ed. Elias B Sanford (New York: Fleming H. Revell Co., 1906) 501-509.

[5]Frank Mason North, "The National City Evangelization Union," *The Methodist Year Book* (1910), 139-41; Lacy, *Frank Mason North*, 87-109, 122-26.

England as a possible model. Welch had spent a sabbatical year at Oxford University in 1902 and had some familiarity with the work of Hugh Price Hughes and English social programs, but the idea became more enticing when a wealthy friend offered to pay Tippy's expenses for a three-month trip to Europe and England. When his congregation granted him a leave from May to July 1907, Tippy decided to make the voyage and agreed to learn all he could about the work of the Wesleyan Methodist Union for Social Service and of the Methodist Central Missions in London, Manchester, and Leeds. On his return in July, Tippy stopped in New York to visit Frank Mason North, a long-time friend of Welch, and learned that North and Harry F. Ward, a socially concerned pastor of working-class churches in Chicago, were considering plans for an organization with the same purpose as that of the three men in Ohio. By these events a bridge was established between interested persons who were then able to formulate plans for social service in Methodism.[6]

Through correspondence and occasional meetings, the five ministers initiated efforts to create a new organization. They agreed to accept North's suggestion to schedule the initial meeting just prior to the annual meeting of the National City Evangelization Union because persons who would attend it probably had similar social interests.[7] Consequently, a social service meeting was scheduled in Washington, D.C., for a day and a half before the Evangelization Union met in nearby Baltimore. A printed letter of invitation that expressed the combined thinking of North, Tippy, Ward, Welch, and Zaring went out over their names. According to the letter, their purpose was to form "a society to stimulate a wide study of social questions by the church, side by side with practical social service, and to bring the church into touch with neglected social groups." While stimulated by the success of the Wesleyan Methodist Union for Social Service in England, and by movements by Episcopalians and Presbyterians in America, the organization was motivated mainly by the need for such a group in the Methodist Episcopal Church. It would be

---

[6]"Minutes of the Methodist Federation for Social Service, 1907-1930," unpublished manuscript, Rose Memorial Library, Drew University, Madison NJ, p. i; Worth M. Tippy, "Autobiography," unpublished MS, Worth M. Tippy Papers, Archives of DePaul University and Indiana Methodism, Greencastle IN, Box DC627, "Europe 1908," pp. 1-2; Herbert Welch, *As I Recall My Past Century* (Nashville: Abingdon Press, 1962) 51-52. For a more extensive presentation of the argument and data for the rest of this chapter, see my "The Methodist Federation for Social Service and the Social Creed," *Methodist History* 13 (January 1975): 3-15.

[7]Frank Mason North to Worth M. Tippy, 1 November 1907, Tippy Papers.

"an effort to apply the sane and fervent spirit of Methodism to the social needs of our time."[8]

Twenty-five of the fifty-one persons who responded favorably to the invitation attended the first meeting at the Ebbitt House Hotel in Washington, D.C., 3-4 December 1907. Frank Mason North called the meeting to order, and the group elected Herbert Welch as temporary president and Worth Tippy as temporary secretary. Tippy reported that the "conference was dominated by a singular unity of purpose and by a spirit of earnest comradeship, and was carried on in an atmosphere of prayer." Several addresses were presented on current social needs, and the efforts for the promotion of social service by the Protestant Episcopal and Presbyterian churches were held up as examples. But special attention was given to the work begun two years earlier by the Wesleyan Methodist Union for Social Service in England. Those in attendance agreed that the American Methodists needed a social- service organization and proceeded to create it: they selected the name, adopted a constitution, elected officers, and pledged four hundred dollars to enable the new movement to get started. The organization was called the Methodist Federation for Social Service, and the following purpose was stated in the constitution: "The objects of this Federation shall be to deepen within the Church the sense of social obligation and opportunity to study social problems from the Christian point of view, and to promote social service in the spirit of Jesus Christ." Since much of the work of the organization would be carried out through an Executive Committee, its membership was important. Welch and Tippy were regularly elected as president and secretary; John Williams, commissioner of labor, Albany, New York, and Harry F. Ward were vice-presidents; and the three members-at-large were North, J. W. Magruder, and E. J. Helms. A General Council with twenty-one members, including Edward T. Devine, Homer Folks, John R. Mott, and George Albert Coe, also was created. Following adjournment, the group was received at the White House by President Roosevelt, who encouraged their efforts because without such work by the church, the nation was not strong enough to endure the grave problems and social evils that menaced her at the time.[9]

---

[8]Undated printed letter to those invited; also a second printed letter dated 27 November 1907, Tippy Papers, Box DC615, Folder 14.

[9]"Minutes of the Methodist Federation for Social Service," 3-4 December 1907, pp. viii, 1-16; *Western Christian Advocate* (Cincinnati), 18 December 1907, pp. 4, 20-21; 25 December 1907, p. 2; Worth M. Tippy, "The Methodist Federation for Social Service," unpublished address, Tippy Papers, Box DC615, Folder 14, pp. 3-5, 8.

In an address delivered several times in the succeeding months, Worth Tippy interpreted the thinking of those at the founding meeting. After noting the range of problems in America that motivated the group to organize, he listed four ways by which the new federation hoped to relieve them. First, they hoped "so to stimulate the spirit of social reform in Methodism as to give to the church that commanding and influential place in social reform and social betterment which it is possible for her to assume." Second, they wanted to encourage clergy and laity to undertake "widespread and careful study of social questions." Third, they anticipated inspiring Methodist churches to minister to actual need and suffering. And fourth, they were convinced that "the church must not stop with remedial effort; it must also have a part in the more difficult work of rectifying conditions that make for social waste." When Tippy went on to assert that "the church must take a large place in the efforts for social reform," his list revealed both the pressing concerns that the Methodist Federation saw in the current social order and the direct way their thinking was affected by the values of the muckrakers and Progressives.

> It must work unselfishly with the forces that are making for efficient government and for government in the interests of the people; for the regulation of the monopolies which control the necessities of life, particularly food stuffs, transportation, light, heat and water; in the movement against the granting of special privileges of whatever form by which those who possess them prosper at the expense of the public; in the control of child labor and the protection of the labor of women; in the effort to provide safety appliances in dangerous forms of industry; in movements for tenement house reform, popular education, parks, and play grounds in crowded sections of cities, in the reform of taxation and in other constructive movements of a similar character.[10]

The needs indicated by Tippy revealed the wide range of interests envisioned by the federation at the outset. They also showed that the organization was more directly influenced by immediate problems than by the general shaping of conscience and that America's social problems outweighed the prior activity and pattern of English Methodist social ministry. That the initial stance of the new Methodist Federation was more pragmatic than ideological was evident too when Tippy declared that the group "will have no sociological or economic creed. It is not a radical and not a conservative movement." Rather he stated that it proposed "to create a broad platform upon which men of the most divergent opinions may stand as brothers, working for the redemption of the world."[11]

---

[10]Tippy, "The Methodist Federation for Social Service," 6-13.

[11]Ibid., 16; Welch, *As I Recall My Past Century*, 53-54.

In addition to this general outlook and commitment of the Methodist Federation for Social Service, there were several actions approved by the Washington conference that established the strategy and program for the organization. Crucially important was its decision "that the Federation shall be kept wholly unofficial in its relation to the General Conference, and to the other official societies of Methodism." This fundamental commitment to its own autonomy was intended to provide prophetic freedom on social issues, but its strategy to influence official Methodist action sometimes clouded its role. Despite its concern to preserve its own autonomy, the federation proceeded to plan ways to influence the denominational General Conference that was to meet in May 1908. "On motion of F. M. North, the Executive Committee was asked to prepare a statement for the use of Bishop Goodsell, in drawing up the Bishop's address for the ensuing General Conference, this statement to cover that which, in the judgment of the Executive Committee, is the church's obligation and opportunity in relation to social service." Moreover, the Executive Committee was "requested to bring the matter of Social Service before the General Conference." A publication emphasis also was given priority, and an effort to establish local organizations in cities and colleges was encouraged.[12]

During the next six months members of the Executive Committee of the federation endeavored to implement these goals. On 19-20 December 1907 the committee met in the office of the federation established at the Epworth Memorial Church in Cleveland. Welch, Ward, and Tippy were the only members present, but they planned the publications empahsis. According to plan, the constitution was printed in February, and by April two pocket-size pamphlets titled "What Is It?" and "How to Organize" were published. To gain wider exposure, "A Statement to the Church" appeared in the church press of Methodism in March 1908. The statement, the constitution, simple plans for local branches and individuals, and an introductory bibliography comprised the contents of the pamphlet titled "What Is It?," which was distributed to interested delegates at the Methodist General Conference in May.[13]

---

[12]"Minutes of the Methodist Federation for Social Service," 12-14; *Western Christian Advocate* (Cincinnati), 25 December 1907, p. 2.

[13]"Minutes of the Methodist Federation for Social Service," 19-20 December 1907, pp. 18-19; "What Is It?," Federation Publications No. 2 (N.p., [Spring 1908]); "How to Organize," Federation Publications No. 3 (N.p., [Spring 1908]); "What Has It Done?," Federation Leaflets No. 2 (N.p., [late 1908 or early 1909]) 5-7, Tippy Papers, 1908.

"A Statement to the Church" told of the formation of the Methodist Federation for Social Service in December 1907 and of the social needs that occasioned its birth. Noting its unofficial but Methodist origin and purpose, the statement referred to the growing social conviction evident in various petitions and resolutions adopted by denominational groups, the increasing number of church committees for social betterment, and the sending of delegates from ministerial fellowships to labor-union meetings. Brief reference was made to the need for righteousness and justice in the political, industrial, commercial, and social conditions of the day. The historical roots of social redemption in the Hebrew prophets, the teachings of Jesus, and the ministry of the Wesleys in England were summarized, and the Wesleyan Methodist Church in England and the Presbyterian, Protestant Episcopal, and Congregational churches in America in 1908 were cited as examples for the new federation. Following a general description of the federation's purpose and methods, the statement appealed to Methodists to join in "the social awakening of the Church."[14]

When "A Statement to the Church" appeared in the *Central Christian Advocate*, published in Kansas City, it was one of several items addressed to General Conference delegates under the heading "Methodism to Serve the Present Age." The section was nearly two full pages in length and was dominated by a social interest. In addition to the statement, there also were references to Charles Stelzle and the Presbyterian Department of Church and Labor, to several petitions on social problems coming to General Conference from several Annual Conferences, and to expected references to social issues in the forthcoming Episcopal Address. While commenting that he expected no instant or revolutionary panacea for social problems, editor C. B. Spencer called upon the delegates to face the needs that would come before the General Conference. Paraphrasing a famous statement from Rauschenbusch's book, he asked, "Are we to have a revival of social religion, or are we to have the deluge?"[15]

The statement also was printed in the *Western Christian Advocate* at Cincinnati, but its editorial comment seemed more cynical.

> It has long been evident that other Churches—notably the Protestant Episcopal, the Presbyterian and the Congregational—have far outdone us on these lines. We know from experience that it is next to impossible to awaken

---

[14]"What Is It?," 3-8.

[15]C. B. Spencer, "Methodism to Serve the Present Age," *Central Christian Advocate* (Kansas City), 18 March 1908, pp. 6-7; cf. Walter Rauschenbusch, *Christianity and the Social Crisis* (New York: Macmillan Co., 1907) 287.

our congregations or our Church officials to any effectual interest in these present-day experiments and efforts. They simply could not be aroused to undertake anything out of the ordinary.

Nevertheless, the editorial expressed a hope that the General Conference "will have the wisdom and courage to recommend something worthwhile along the lines we have indicated."[16] Thus, in the Methodist weekly papers at both Cincinnati and Kansas City, the "Statement to the Church" occasioned challenges to the General Conference to take positive action on social problems—to create a "Methodism to serve the present age," as one stated.

Such favorable opinion in the church press was not accidental. The editors of the two regional editions of the *Christian Advocate* just noted, Levi Gilbert at Cincinnati and Claudius B. Spencer at Kansas City, along with James R. Joy of the main edition at New York, were among the forty-three friends of the Methodist Federation for Social Service who publicly added their names to the "Statement to the Church." Also adding their names were professors Edwin Earp and Samuel Plantz. Thus, on the eve of the General Conference of the Methodist Episcopal Church, the federation had elicited the support of many of the socially concerned ministers and laity in the denomination. Several of these persons were in vital positions for interpreting the organization's purpose and work to the church's membership through the weekly newspapers and other periodicals. Some of them also were in crucial leadership positions of the General Conference if recommendations on social matters were processed. For instance, Daniel J. Dorchester, Jr., a Pittsburgh pastor, was among the forty-three friends, and he chaired the Committee on the State of the Church, while Levi Gilbert headed the subcommittee that dealt with the report "The Church and Social Problems," which eventually was presented to the General Conference.[17]

While leaders of the federation trusted the power of persuasion and propaganda, they were also political realists and made specific plans to influence the 1908 General Conference. When together in March, Welch and Tippy scheduled a meeting of the federation's Executive Committee in conjunction with the General Conference and arranged for a large public session at which social concerns would be presented to interested

---

[16]"New Occasions Teach New Duties," *Western Christian Advocate* (Cincinnati), 11 March 1908, p. 8.

[17]"What Is It?," 8-11; *Western Christian Advocate*, 27 May 1908, p. 6.

delegates.[18] They also agreed to urge members of the Executive Committee who were not delegates to attend the conference at their own expense so that the federation's purposes might be achieved. Since North was the only elected delegate from its ranks, and he would be busy as chairman of the Committee on Home Mission and Church Extension, that action brought Welch, Tippy, Ward, Helms, and Magruder to Baltimore to work for the social-service cause. Of these persons, Herbert Welch and Harry Ward played the most important roles at the General Conference, since the two men contributed directly to the writing of the report "The Church and Social Problems," which was presented to the Committee on the State of the Church.[19]

A flood of petitions to the General Conference led to the subcommittee report. A petition on the relationship of the church to social problems submitted by the Nebraska Conference early in the General Conference initiated the process. William M. Balch, a pastor from Lincoln, Nebraska, with a strong sympathy for workers, had written the petition, presented it to the conference, and was appointed secretary of the subcommittee to which it and similar petitions were referred by the parent Committee on the State of the Church.[20] Federation leaders decided to endorse the Nebraska petition and had it printed so that Annual Conference caucuses would have it for consideration. As a result, at least four other conferences supported the same petition.[21] Additional support for the Nebraska petition was expressed by the editors of both the *Central Christian Advocate* and the *Western Christian Advocate*.[22] Several similar petitions were submitted by other Annual Conferences and ministerial groups. Careful use of the petition process enabled the federation and other interested persons to ensure that the General Conference could not ignore social concerns. By their voluntary presence at the month-long

---

[18]"Minutes of the Methodist Federation for Social Service," 24 March 1908, 20.

[19]Welch, *As I Recall My Past Century*, 54.

[20]*Journal of the General Conference of the Methodist Episcopal Church* (1908), 195, 204-205.

[21]Methodist Episcopal Church, General Conference, 1908. Committee on the State of the Church, General Conference Manuscripts. Rose Memorial Library, Drew University, Madison NJ. The New England, New Hampshire, Northern New York, and Troy Annual Conference memorials.

[22]*Central Christian Advocate* (Kansas City), 18 March 1908, p. 7; *Western Christian Advocate* (Cincinnati), 1 April 1908, p. 8.

General Conference, Welch and Ward were actually able to write "The Church and Social Problems" report, but not without careful planning. The minutes of the federation indicated that Levi Gilbert and William Balch, chairman and secretary of the subcommittee charged with that report, met with the federation's Executive Committee during the conference. At that session it was agreed that the Nebraska-petition request for the creation of a Commission on Labor to study a series of issues should be directed instead to the Federation on Social Service.[23] Such an assignment would not only guarantee their direct input but also would provide unofficial recognition of the new organization by the General Conference. Welch, Ward, Tippy, and Magruder labored on the subcommittee report, but Ward performed the major work. "To him more than to any other man, was due the substance and phrasing of our group contribution to the General Conference committee," Welch later acknowledged.[24] Although the contributions of the federation members were informal and unofficial, they were not secret. When editor Gilbert reported to his readers in the *Western Christian Advocate*, he stated that Welch and Ward had "collaborated long and patiently" in preparing the document.[25]

While these behind-the-scene preparations were going on in committee, federation leaders also sought to influence the mood of the delegates in other ways. One of the strategies agreed to the previous December, when the organization was founded, was to make suggestions to Bishop Daniel Goodsell for inclusion in the quadrennial Episcopal Address. Although there is no direct evidence of such influence, a quarter of the speech was devoted to social issues, and nearly half of that section referred to child labor, working men, and unions. Reforms and civic righteousness also were discussed, along with comments on temperance, divorce, polygamy, and peace. According to the *Western Christian Advocate*, "The Bishop's Address gave unusual space to social, civic, and moral conditions and issues—possibly the larger part. It is eulogized on every hand."[26] After the General Conference, the federation reprinted the social portions of the address and made wide use of it.[27]

---

[23]"Minutes of the Methodist Federation for Social Service," 13 May 1908, 21.

[24]Welch, *As I Recall My Past Century*, 54-55.

[25]*Western Christian Advocate* (Cincinnati), 27 May 1908, p. 6.

[26]Ibid., 13 May 1908, p. 10; *Daily Christian Advocate*, 8 May 1908, p. 1.

[27]"The Church and Social Problems; Including the Statement of the General Conference of 1908 and The Social Problem in the Episcopal Address," Federation Publications No. 5 (N.p., [late summer 1908]).

Most obvious of the strategies to influence delegates was the public meeting on 21 May to promote the interests of the Methodist Federation for Social Service. Herbert Welch presided and introduced Edward T. Devine, professor of social economics at Columbia University and general secretary of the New York Charity Organization Society, who presented an address on charity and reform work. Governor Edward W. Hoch of Kansas gave a challenging closing speech. The "What Is It?" pamphlet was distributed to the more than one thousand persons in attendance. One reporter commented that the several petitions pending before the General Conference concerning social and industrial questions added interest to the session. Worth Tippy noted in the federation minutes that "it was generally agreed that the meeting was a real success."[28]

On Saturday, 30 May, the report "The Church and Social Problems" was considered for action by the General Conference. Based on the simple theological affirmation that the ultimate solution of all the problems of the social order will be found in the teachings of the New Testament, the body of the report attempted to show a practical application of these ethics for the church collectively and its members individually. There were references to specific industrial problems such as the exploitation of child labor, dangers to workers, and chronic warfare between employers and employees. While admitting the good that industrialists do, the report declared a "primary interest" in the conditions of workers and urged both parties to seek "industrial peace and human brotherhood." A section of the report that soon was designated "The Social Creed of Methodism" read as follows:

> The Methodist Episcopal Church stands:
> For equal rights and complete justice for all men in all stations of life.
> For the principles of conciliation and arbitration in industrial dissensions.
> For the protection of the worker from dangerous machinery, occupational diseases, injuries, and mortality.
> For the abolition of child labor.
> For such regulation of the conditions of labor for women as shall safeguard the physical and moral health of the community.
> For the suppression of the "sweating system."
> For the gradual and reasonable reduction of the hours of labor to the lowest practical point, with work for all; and for that degree of leisure for all which is the condition of the highest human life.
> For a release for [from] employment one day in seven.
> For a living wage in every industry.
> For the highest wage that each industry can afford, and for the most equitable

---

[28]"Minutes of the Methodist Federation for Social Service," 26; *Daily Christian Advocate*, 19 May 1908, p. 1; 23 May 1908, p. 2.

division of the products of industry that can ultimately be devised. For the recognition of the Golden Rule and the mind of Christ as the supreme law of society and the sure remedy for all social ills.[29]

A final portion of the report praised the growing sense of responsibility evidenced by the Christian Church. "Our own Church in particular, historically and traditionally in close sympathy with the common people and ever diligent for their welfare, does not fail to recognize the greatness of its own opportunity in the present crisis and the consequent urgency of its duty." The Episcopal Address and numerous petitions to the General Conference were viewed as "signs of encouragement." Attention was called to the formation of the Methodist Federation for Social Service, and its purpose and plans were praised. In addition, the federation was asked to study and submit answers to the General Conference of 1912 concerning principles and measures of social reform, how the Methodist Episcopal Church could be used or altered to promote such principles and measures, how the denomination might best cooperate with other Christian bodies in such activities, and how better to prepare "our preachers for efficiency in social reform." Finally, a paragraph summoned the Methodist Episcopal Church "to continue and increase its works of social service" at all levels of its ministry and organization, including every individual member.[30]

Although the report was adopted unanimously, the official *Daily Christian Advocate* made no mention of it when summarizing the outstanding events of the General Conference. However, conference summaries in the *Central Christian Advocate* and *The Western Christian Advocate* evaluated it more highly. Editor Spencer of the former delared that "the Church moved to a front place on questions of labor and capital. The cry of the toiler is in her ears."[31] And Levi Gilbert's résumé in the latter declared that "the Conference adopted a ringing preamble and resolutions which made a Methodist platform on social problems." Moreover, adoption of the report also meant that "the Methodist Federation for Social Service was recognized as an unofficial Methodist organization." Calling this "a new departure for the Church," Gilbert remarked that the federation would now enable Methodism "to keep in touch with all the delicate problems relating to social problems and industrialism."[32]

---

[29]*Journal of the General Conference* (1908), 545-47.

[30]Ibid., 547-49.

[31]*Central Christian Advocate* (Kansas City), 10 June 1908, p. 10.

[32]*Western Christian Advocate* (Cincinnati), 10 June 1908, p. 6.

In short, General Conference approval of "The Church and Social Problems" report meant two things: recognition of the Methodist Federation for Social Service as an "unofficial Methodist organization" and provision of "a Methodist platform on social problems." The concerted efforts of leaders of the federation resulted in an improved position for their organization as well as a platform on which to base their organization's future work. Consciously evaluating the influence of the report at the end of the summer, the federation leadership found that it had "aroused a new interest throughout the church in social questions," and it had favorably impressed the labor press and leading religious and sociological periodicals, which led to this conclusion: "The great Methodist Church, with its heritage from the Wesleys, is awakening to the urgent needs of this day, and with the Wesleyans in England, is pressing into the battle lines of the Social Crisis."[33]

Invigorated by the positive action of the General Conference and the cordial support in much of the denominational press, the federation's Executive Committee decided that rather than have a convention of those interested in the federation it would sponsor a National Conference of Methodist Social Workers at St. Louis, 17-19 November 1908. It was the philosophy of the Executive Committee that "the social work of Methodism ought not and cannot be done by the Federation for Social Service, nor any other special organization," but should be implemented by the pastors, social workers, colleges, seminaries, periodicals, Book Concern, and other agencies of the church. "The work of the Federation is primarily one of education and agitation and only secondarily one of organization," the Conference of Social Workers was told.[34] In keeping with that philosophy, the federation in September published a leaflet on behalf of unemployed workers, and at the conference in November the addresses dealt with topics of interest to social workers. Despite their noble motives, federation members were disappointed by the poor attendance at the St. Louis meeting. "This first meeting can hardly be called great, for it lacked the numbers for a meeting of that description," wrote the *Central Christian Advocate*. "It could not be called a practical meeting entirely, for too little has been accomplished to make practical

---

[33]"The Church and Social Problems," pamphlet, 4, 17. This evaluation also was printed in the appendix to Worth M. Tippy, ed., *The Socialized Church: Addresses before the First National Conference of the Social Workers of Methodism, St. Louis, November 17-19, 1908* (New York: Eaton & Mains, 1909) 288.

[34]Tippy, *The Socialized Church*, 7-8.

workers numerous."[35] While the St. Louis Conference of 1908 may have expressed the social concern of Methodism and pointed to its future possibilities, the immediate reality was somewhat disillusioning.

There was further reason for disappointment when the Executive Committee met during the Conference of Social Workers. The employment of a full-time salaried secretary to lead the Methodist Federation, which had been strongly suggested in the report to the General Conference, proved impossible to put into effect because of lack of funds. This financial inadequacy forced the federation to reorganize on a functional basis so its work could be carried on by the voluntary efforts of individuals. As reconstituted, the Executive Committee included thirteen persons: six officers, three members-at-large, and the chairpersons of four committees. It was agreed that those in the Midwest would meet occasionally to facilitate communication and planning. Although unhappy because of poor attendance and inadequate finances, the spirit of the federation leaders remained positive and expansive. Even with the necessary restructuring, the Executive Committee broadened its work into more areas by creating the new committees and by encouraging increased publication efforts.[36]

Despite the chastening impact of events in the autumn of 1908, the Methodist Federation for Social Service took pride in the work accomplished during its first year of existence. Worth Tippy rightfully expressed their conclusion that "the Federation has . . . made a decided impression upon the Methodist Episcopal Church in arousing a stronger conviction of its social duty and opportunity."[37] Within a few months' time, those who founded that organization had achieved a great deal. Not only had they created a functional voluntary society dedicated to the cause of social Christianity, but by conscious planning, effective collaboration, and earnest effort they had led Methodism to assume its social responsibilities in the United States. More significantly, a handful of committed social advocates accomplished what no other social-gospel Protestants had yet done: they secured the official commitment of their denomination to the social needs of the time. The Social Creed of Methodism, which its members authored and the Methodist General Conference approved, embodied that commitment in concrete terms

---

[35]*Central Christian Advocate* (Kansas City), 25 November 1908, pp. 5-6; *Western Christian Advocate* (Cincinnati), 25 November 1908, pp. 22-23; "What Has It Done?," 8, 14.

[36]"Minutes of the Methodist Federation for Social Service," 10 July 1908, 28; 17-19 November 1908, 31-43; "What Has It Done?," 14-15.

[37]"What Has It Done?," 13.

that symbolized the Methodist pledge to do something about the nation's social crisis.

Editor Levi Gilbert correctly understood that the General Conference had done two important things in 1908: it had recognized the Methodist Federation for Social Service "as an unofficial Methodist organization" and it had adopted "resolutions which made a Methodist platform on social problems." Additionally, federation leaders had confirmed by their actions that they were able to initiate and implement responsible social-service programming beyond their influential efforts at the General Conference. As a consequence, Methodism reached the vital turning point in social-gospel history before other Protestant churches; it was the first denomination to respond officially to the social needs of the day, even though it was late in getting started. In the process, the Methodist General Conference fulfilled Editor Spencer's challenge to create a "Methodism to serve the present age," and the conference entrusted most of the responsibility to the new Methodist Federation for Social Service.

CHAPTER 7

The Social Conscience
of the Churches

No action of any church body in recent years surpasses in importance the adoption by the Federal Council of Churches of resolutions concerning the relation of the Church to modern industry, in fact, to the whole social order of the day. They may be said to constitute a charter, a bill of rights, which the Protestant Churches of America recognize on behalf not only of those who toil but also of society.

("The Social Conscience of the Churches,"
The Outlook, 19 December 1908)

METHODISM'S ACCOMPLISHMENTS DURING 1908 not only served to enrich the social ministry of that denomination but also contributed to the broadening of the social gospel in other Protestant churches. The spirit that enlivened the Methodist Episcopal Church was communicated to the newly forming Federal Council of the Churches of Christ in America through Frank Mason North. From this cross-fertilization emerged an ecumenical social service that transformed and enlarged the cause of social Christianity for succeeding years.

Cooperative Protestantism's interest in social righteousness and moral reform had been evident already in 1902, and it was clearly apparent at the Inter-Church Conference on Federation in 1905. The addresses on social themes and the resolutions concerning the social order that were part of the latter meeting were discussed earlier, when it was noted that the words spoken and the principles espoused were not binding on the delegates or representative of the churches because the constituent denominations had not yet voted to form a federated organization.[1] However, in the following years that condition altered. When the 1905 conference adjourned, it sent back to the denominations a Plan of Federation for ratification, with the stipulation that when two-thirds of the bodies voted approval, the proposal would become operative. That affirmative action was achieved by November 1907, and the first meeting of the Federal Council of the Churches of Christ in America was announced for 2-8 December 1908 at Philadelphia.[2]

William H. Roberts, stated clerk of the northern Presbyterian General Assembly, served as chairman of the Executive Committee chosen by the conference in 1905, and he signed the call to the churches to unite formally. In that leadership capacity he also was the presiding officer at the organizing session of the Federal Council of Churches, at which he gave a welcoming address that outlined the character, purpose, and spirit of the council. As he concluded the address, he remarked that "a new order of things is beginning" because "the churches realize the need for co-operation, as churches, for the moral and spiritual welfare of the nation and of the world."[3] That notion of cooperative social responsibility also was manifest in the fourth purpose of the federation, which read, "To secure a larger combined influence for the churches of Christ in all matters affecting the moral and social condition of the people, so as to promote the application of the law of Christ in every relation of human life."[4] Both the constitutional affirmation and the presiding officer's remarks indicated that there was an appropriate context for the report "The Church and Modern Industry," which was presented by Frank Mason North.

When North prepared for the organizational meeting of the Federal Council, he was able to combine his social concern with his ecumenical commitment in a document that embodied the Christian principles for social betterment that he had long envisioned. As chairman of the Committee on the Church and Modern Industry, he was one of sixteen persons who presented papers at the assembly. North had the opportunity to do the paper because of his years of active involvement in ecumenical organizations and because he had even more years of involvement with

---

[1]See pp. 48-51 above.

[2]*Western Christian Advocate* (Cincinnati), 27 November 1907, p. 29.

[3]Elias B. Sanford, ed., *Federal Council of the Churches of Christ in America: Report of the First Meeting of the Federal Council, Philadelphia, 1908* (New York: Revell Press, 1909) 325.

[4]Ibid., 513.

social and industrial problems in his own urban ministry in New York City and in the Methodist Federation for Social Service. Also, he was able to draw on the report "The Church and Social Problems" that had been adopted by the recent Methodist General Conference.

Even though he had little part in preparing the Methodist report because of his busy duties as chairman of the General Conference Committee on Home Missions and Church Extension, North recognized that the contents of the document were pertinent to his own presentation. However, when he employed its social and industrial analysis he rearranged the data to fit his own order and context. And when he used the Social Creed of Methodism section he felt free to add and delete items. Beneath those obvious modifications lay two basic differences of interpretation: he appealed to ecumenical Protestantism as the best basis for confronting problems in the social order, and he provided a more elaborate theological framework for such action. Thus, as Methodism's new social commitment was passed on to other denominations of the Federal Council, it clearly was modified by the mind and values of North.[5]

Theologically, the Methodist report's simple assertion that "the ultimate solution of all the problems of our social order" will be found in the teachings of the New Testament and the spirit of Jesus was transformed by "The Church and Modern Industry" report into an extensive Christ- centered basis for church social service. Placing primary emphasis on the redemptive work and authority of Jesus, as well as on New Testament teachings, North declared, "Christ's mission is not merely to reform society but to save it. He is more than the world's Re-adjustor. He is its Redeemer." This conviction served as the basis for several premises. First, in contrast to all other organizations for human well-being, the church was motivated by a "two-world theory of life" that saw the kingdom of God instituted on earth but finding its fulfillment in heaven. Second, the gospel of Christ was not a class gospel; it should be preached to all persons as persons, not as laborers or capitalists, rich or poor. Third, the church did not exist as an end in itself: "Through it is revealed the meaning of righteousness, of justice, of salvation, not for its own sake, but that sinners may be redeemed and that these ideals may be worked into the lives of men and become the principles of the new social order." And, fourth, as the representative of Christ, the church was appointed to establish the kingdom of God on earth, and therefore it should be less

---

[5]For a more detailed argument and data on North's role, see my "The Methodist Federation for Social Service and the Social Creed," *Methodist History* 13 (January 1975): 16-22.

concerned with the services of the church and more concerned with the church's services to humanity.[6]

Using his ecumenical vision to apply these theological premises, North told the assembled delegates that it was their primary task as representatives of the churches of Christ in America to establish Christ's kingdom in the United States. "It is the Church of America which must deal with the social and industrial problems of America." Unfortunately, in North's opinion, the American church had been hampered too much by denominationalism. "At no time have the disadvantages of the sectarian divisions of the Church been more apparent than when the call has come for a common policy or a united utterance concerning such problems as modern industry now presents," he warned. The basic problem for North was this: "Nowhere has there been formulation of principles, or statement of aims which represents in an authoritative sense the attitude of American Protestantism toward the tremendous problems of our industrial and social order."[7]

Following a review of social and industrial conditions in the nation, North attempted to face the fundamental problem by appealing to the Federal Council to do two things. First, it should "give utterance, by appropriate resolution, to its convictions touching the industrial conditions which concern the multitude." And, second, it should "extend to all the toilers of our country and to those who seek to organize the workers . . . the greetings of sympathy . . . and co-operation" in the name of Christ. It was in response to these needs that North proposed fourteen responses to practical industrial problems that formed a social platform for which the churches must stand. As a basis for that declaration, he used the Social Creed of Methodism but freely adapted it to express his own convictions. Comparison of the two declarations shows that he deleted the final assertion about the Golden Rule because he already provided a larger theological groundwork in the report, and that he added four additional items:

> For the rights of all men to the opportunity for self-maintenance, a right ever to be wisely and strongly safeguarded against encroachments of every kind.
> For the right of workers to some protection against the hardships often resulting from the swift crises of industrial change.

---

[6]Frank Mason North, "The Church and Modern Industry," in Sanford, *Federal Council*, 226-29.

[7]Ibid., 229, 231.

For suitable provision for the old age of the workers and for those incapacitated by injury.

For the abatement of poverty.[8]

In addition, several general suggestions for improving the relationship of the churches to workers were recommended by North. These included: an appeal to churches to recognize "the great work of social reconstruction which is now in progress" and to publicize it in the pulpit, press, and public meetings; the creation of study classes on social questions and the social teachings of Jesus; and the formation of official denominational bureaus or agencies on the church and labor.[9]

More significant than these proposals in the long run was a final recommendation that the Federal Council should create its own Commission on the Church and Social Service that would be representative of the constituent denominations and of various industrial interests. According to North, the commission would cooperate with similar church organizations to study social conditions, act to express the purpose of the Federal Council, promote the spirit and practice of social service in the member bodies, and especially secure better understanding and relations between workers and the church.[10]

North's report took an hour to deliver, but despite its length the delegates "listened most intently and applauded roundly."[11] Six speakers responded warmly to the presentation, but none with more effect than Charles Stelzle of the Presbyterian Department of Church and Labor, who asserted that "the statement presented by Dr. North is the greatest paper on this subject that I have ever heard or read." As the Protestant leader most involved with workers, Stelzle went on to say, "If I can say to workingmen of America that the Federal Council really means it it will be the biggest thing I can say or that I have ever yet said." With such praise it was not surprising that the report was unanimously adopted by the council on Friday, 4 December 1908.[12] The following Sunday, at a mass meeting of conference delegates and labor-union members, Dennis Hays,

---

[8]Ibid., 235, 238-39. These additions were inserted into the Methodist resolutions, becoming items 2, 3, 13, and 14 in the final Federal Council recension. Cf. the original Methodist text above, pp. 100-101.

[9]Ibid., 239-42.

[10]Ibid., 242.

[11]*Western Christian Advocate* (Cincinnati), 16 December 1908, p. 6.

[12]Sanford, *Federal Council,* 68-76.

a union leader, congratulated the Federal Council for "the fair and outspoken declarations it has made in regard to organized labor." Then he read the Social Creed section and said that it not only showed "keen insight into social and industrial conditions" but was so sympathetic to trade unions that it read "like measures passed in a convention of the American Federation of Labor."[13]

Similar favorable reactions to North's address appeared in the religious press. The editor of the *Central Christian Advocate* called the report "a masterly pronouncement" and wrote with obvious pride that "this first formal deliverance of federated Christian sentiment in America as to the place of the Church in the seething industrial world as it lies about us today, a deliverance representing the position of eighteen million people, was prepared by a Methodist."[14] In the *Western Christian Advocate* the report was considered to be one of the two most important events during the meeting in Philadelphia.[15]

Particularly impressive was the editorial evaluation in Lyman Abbott's *The Outlook*, the most widely circulated Protestant periodical in 1908. One editorial, titled "The Social Conscience of the Churches," pointed to the significance of North's statement.

> No action of any church body in recent years surpasses in importance the adoption by the Federal Council of Churches of resolutions concerning the relation of the Church to modern industry, in fact, to the whole social order of the day. They may be said to constitute a charter, a bill of rights, which the Protestant Churches of America recognize on behalf not only of those who toil but also of society.[16]

Another editorial, bearing the heading "The Social Programme of the Churches," stated,

> *The Outlook* wishes that the resolutions of this Council might be put into the hands and stored in the mind of every minister in the land. It is certain that

---

[13]Ibid., 442-48.

[14]*Central Christian Advocate* (Kansas City), 16 December 1908, p. 6.

[15]*Western Christian Advocate* (Cincinnati), 16 December 1908, pp. 4-6. Other favorable comments appeared in various journals and were kept in a file by North: *Christian Advocate,* 17 December 1908, p. 2101, 24 December 1908, p. 2139; *Southwestern Christian Advocate,* 17 December 1908, p. 3; *Zion's Herald,* 9 December 1908, p. 1518; *The Interior,* 24 December 1908, p. 1770; *The Congregationalist and Christian Worker,* 12 December 1908, p. 833. Frank Mason North Papers, Rose Memorial Library, Drew University, Madison NJ, "The Social Creed" folder.

[16]*The Outlook* (New York), 19 December 1908, pp. 849-50.

the churches have drawn a line behind which they can never afford to retreat and up to which every church may feel itself summoned. If any man hereafter doubts whether the churches of America really understand their duties and responsibilities toward the grim problems of to-day, he will have no excuse for his doubts if he reads these resolutions.[17]

Although Frank Mason North used ideas that were initially endorsed by the General Conference of the Methodist Episcopal Church through the efforts of the Methodist Federation for Social Service, he apparently acted unilaterally, for there were no references to his endeavor in federation records. "The Church and Modern Industry" report was compatible with the federation's purposes and plans, but it significantly broadened the scope of responsible church social concern from a denominational to an ecumenical base. What North did was distinctive. By securing the endorsement of all the Protestant denominations that comprised the Federal Council, he extended the responsible involvement of the church in the social order.

For North, both single denominations and voluntary organizations were "non-representative and without authority," which greatly limited their effectiveness. To remedy this problem, his report purposely included principles that could officially represent the attitude of Protestant churches concerning industrial and social problems. The appeal of the Federal Council of Churches for North was that it was an officially and ecclesiastically organized body, in contrast to the earlier cooperative movements that were only voluntary interdenominational fellowships.[18] Thus, when his report concluded with an appeal that "the Church must witness to the truths which should shape industrial relations," he meant the thirty-three denominations represented in the council, not just one of them. By sharing what already had been popularly designated the Social Creed of Methodism with other churches, North transformed it into the Social Creed of the Churches.

Adoption of "The Church and Modern Industry" report not only achieved the long-hoped-for official response of Protestant Christianity to the crisis in the social order, it also provided a visible symbol of that commitment. When the delegates unanimously approved the report, they also directed the council's Executive Committee to publish it " 'so that it will be spread abroad throughout the country in the widest possible

---

[17]Ibid., 850- 51.

[18]See North's statements on this in his report in Sanford, *Federal Council*, 229, 231, 235, and compare them with those in Charles S. Macfarland, *The Progress of Church Federation* (New York: Fleming H. Revell Co., 1917) 31.

manner.' "[19] Such distribution served a dual purpose: it communicated the Federal Council of Churches' social commitment, and it also testified to the existence of the council itself. In time, the entire report became too large for popular reading and easy distribution, and the visible sign was reduced to the resolutions that constituted what *The Outlook* had called "a charter, a bill of rights" that represented "the social conscience of the churches." Soon that statement was designated the Social Creed of the Churches. In effect, the Social Creed became the symbol of both the social and the ecumenical dimensions of the new Federal Council of Churches. It was a powerful symbol in that it was visible and it communicated the same meaning to those outside the churches as to those who were church members. Since the council was a product of the convergence of the cooperative ecumenical movement and the social Christianity movement, the Social Creed was an appropriate symbol because it represented both dimensions.

The importance of visibility in a newly emerging movement also was evident in the recognition of authorship of that symbol. In relating the account of the writing and adoption of the Social Creed, the names of both Harry F. Ward and Frank Mason North have been evident, and over the years it has been argued whether one or the other was its author.[20] Actually each man had a rightful claim to authorship if a distinction is made between the two versions of the Social Creed, for Ward wrote the Methodist recension and North composed the Federal Council recension. Since Ward was out of the country when the latter was written and adopted, there has been little conflict over that version. But as noted in the last chapter, it was apparent that Ward authored the first form of the creed and that North had little to do with it because of other responsibilities during the General Conference. Unfortunately for Ward, his work on the initial text was informal and behind the scenes; with such scant public recognition, few persons knew he was the primary author. In contrast, everyone present at the Federal Council meeting on 4 December heard North present his report, which also carried his name in print. Consequently, in the public eye North was the recognized writer of the Social Creed, and he was accorded that honor for the rest of his life.

---

[19]Sanford, *Federal Council*, 76.

[20]The most obvious example was in the four-volume Methodism and Society series where Richard Cameron (*Methodism and Society in Historical Perspective* [Nashville: Abingdon Press, 1961] 323) credited Harry F. Ward as the author, while Walter G. Muelder (*Methodism and Society in the Twentieth Century* [Nashville: Abingdon Press, 1961] 50) acclaimed Frank Mason North.

Later Ward published two editions of a book titled *The Social Creed of the Churches*,[21] but in neither was there any indication of authorship. Nevertheless, his authorship was acknowledged in 1912 by the editor of the *Central Christian Advocate*[22] and much later in Herbert Welch's autobiography.[23] The most conclusive proof, however, appeared only a few years ago when a letter from Ward to his wife, dated 17 February 1909, was printed. In part, Ward wrote,

> Have been amused at something more to see in church papers how other men have been reaping glory from the little labor platform that I drew up at General Conference. It was my idea to begin with, that we should have a definite platform that should mean something to labor men and I drafted it with a few minor changes from Magruder. Now at the big Church Federal Council North gets great glory for preparing the Labor report and he did a fine piece of work, but he incorporates my platform with a few generalizations and the Council adopts it and the Labor men get on to it, see that it means something and enthusiastically, this wipes out all the present indifferences of the Church. Hence North is a great man [illegible] but I am waiting to see whether he acknowledges my credit to anyone else.[24]

North never publicly acknowledged that credit or disavowed the honors attributed to him as author of the Social Creed, although he never claimed to be the author of any more than "The Church and Modern Industry" report. Since the effect of the adoption of the report was that the Social Creed of the Churches absorbed and expanded the Social Creed of Methodism, the question of his authorship really was not raised. Whether the two men ever resolved this matter between themselves remains a mystery, but they continued to work side by side for the cause of social Christianity for many years, in both Methodism and the Federal Council.

That matters of authorship and symbolism of the Social Creed deserve attention in itself testifies to the significance of what happened to social Christianity in 1908. With the adoption of "The Church and Social Problems" report by the Methodist General Conference in May, and "The

---

[21]Harry F. Ward, *The Social Creed of the Churches* (New York: Eaton & Mains; Cincinnati: Jennings & Graham, 1912; Nashville: Abingdon Press, 1914).

[22]"Report of the Federal Council," *Central Christian Advocate* (Kansas City), 18 December 1912, p. 230.

[23]Herbert Welch, *As I Recall My Past Century* (Nashville: Abingdon Press, 1962) 54-55.

[24]Quoted in Eugene P. Link, "Latter Day Christian Rebel: Harry F. Ward," *Mid-America* 56 (October 1974): 226-27.

Church and Modern Industry" report by the Federal Council of Churches in December, the social gospel achieved another major stage in its development in America. Indeed, the fact that these two endorsements constituted official actions of organized churches in response to crises in the social order constituted a turning point in the history of social Christianity. For years, those who had hoped to arouse Christians to get involved in the work of social redemption in America had looked to official church councils or conferences for action, but they were disappointed. Finally, in 1908 the Methodist Episcopal Church became the first denomination to act officially when it adopted the Social Creed of Methodism and directed the Methodist Federation for Social Service to guide its work of social ministry. With a similar endorsement on behalf of its constituent denominations, the Federal Council of Churches in December enabled mainline Protestantism officially to respond to social and industrial problems by approving a social platform. At last Protestant churches had moved beyond the nineteenth-century practices of single-cause declarations or condemnations and encouragement to their lay members to achieve social change solely through voluntary societies. As an officially approved statement, the Social Creed evidenced that the social awakening that had been recognized in society for months had finally reached the councils of the organized church.

In the eyes of the church press, the new commitment to social responsibility marked an important turning point. One editorial called it "a new chapter in Protestant Christianity,"[25] and another said, "This meeting marks an epoch in the history of the American Church, if we have the faith and grace to make it so."[26] Although Walter Rauschenbusch had only returned from his sabbatical leave in mid-1908, and was not a delegate at the Federal Council meeting, he no doubt shared in the rejoicing over the development of social Christianity during the year. After all, it appeared that his fruit trees that bloomed in May had borne fruit.

[25]*Central Christian Advocate* (Kansas City), 16 December 1908, p. 5.

[26]*The Independent* (New York), 17 December 1908, p. 1500.

PART 3

From the Social Creed to the Social Awakening, 1908–1912

CHAPTER 8

The Spiritual Unrest

So the church wanes and sickens in New York. A few earnest churches and missions drag men here and there from the gutter, but the gutter itself, the gutter of unbrotherliness, of the oppression of the weak and luxury of the strong, still engulfs its thousands and carries them down to ruin. Much of the reconstructive power and vision is outside the churches, not inside; it is found in settlements, charity and civic organizations and among socialists.

(Ray Stannard Baker,
The Spiritual Unrest, *1910)*

GENERAL RECOGNITION OF THE CHANGED SITUATION in the nation and the church was expressed by social-gospel advocates who were leaders of the Religious Education Association when it convened at Chicago, 7-13 February 1909. In the Annual Survey of Progress in Religious and Moral Education, George Albert Coe remarked that a moral awakening had been evident during the six years since the organization was founded, "and most of all in the last year."[1] And Francis Greenwood Peabody in his presidential address said that "the awakening of the social conscience has been so abrupt and startling" that it caused a "sense of apprehension" in devout people.[2] The remarkable achievements by advocates of social Christianity during 1908 produced restlessness as well as rejoicing. During

---

[1]George Albert Coe, "Annual Survey of Progress in Religious and Moral Education," *Religious Education* 4 (April 1909): 7.

[2]Francis Greenwood Peabody, "The Social Conscience and the Religious Life," ibid., 1-2.

the next few years circumstances in the nation again altered and affected the way Protestant churches developed their ministry to the social order.

By design the 1909 Religious Education Association theme of "Religious Education and Social Duty" built on the previous emphasis on religion's contribution to the development of national life. That life rested on questions of citizenship, said Peabody, but beneath such questions lay a "vast complexity of social conditions and obligations." For the association the vital question was: "Does religious education fortify social duty?" Two of the most celebrated speakers addressed that issue. Jane Addams suggested that it was natural to appeal to traditional religious sanctions for human conduct if the nation was to find relief from domination by commercial ideals. But she discovered that it was impossible to rely on such motives and values because they had not been worked into the character of the present generation. As a result, she urged religious educators to do more to assert the reality of spiritual forces "against that rank materialism that threatens to engulf us all."[3] And James Bryce, ambassador from Great Britain to the United States, argued that events and influences of the day required greater need for religious instruction in public schools. He believed that "a more material and less spiritual view of the ends and scope of human life had gained ground" in recent years. To him, the causes lay in the progress of scientific discovery, historical criticism, loss of biblical and church authority, and a tendency to make amusement "the chief end of man." While avoiding an outright charge of moral decline, Bryce observed "that the notions of duty and self control seem less present in the minds of most people than they once were."[4]

Through his own struggle with the question of social duty, Peabody accepted that religion, like other institutions, "must submit itself to the test of social utility." For him, therefore, the main defense of religious education was evidence that it produced leadership, wisdom, efficiency, and peace in society. But, he asked, "Is the Christian Church to be reckoned with as a factor in the social problem; or is it—as so many agitators frankly assert— the shell of a discarded faith, a club of the prosperous, a bulwark of the capitalist, a social menace rather than a social force?" The Harvard professor also asked whether the current interest in social duty did not divert the church from its primary function of redeeming the individual soul. Further, he inquired, "Is not the Church

---

[3]Jane Addams, "The Reaction of Modern Life upon Religious Education," ibid., 23-29.

[4]James Bryce, "Religion and Moral Education," ibid., 30-33.

in our day less frequented than the parish house, and the preacher drawn to a gospel of social reform rather than to a gospel of salvation?" His concern was not to lose "the practice of the presence of God" in favor of "the practice of the service of man." In the end, however, Peabody concluded that the way of social duty was "one way toward the religious life." President Roosevelt had addressed the conscience of the nation and found it to be an instrument for industrial peace; therefore, the Religious Education Association should educate the social conscience to understand that what seems to be an economic, legislative, or philanthropic movement really was a "contemporary expression of the spirit of God touching the hearts of men." After all, the brotherhood of man and the Fatherhood of God were not two Commandments but "opposite sides of One Law."[5]

Although Peabody and the Religious Education Association were able to reconcile the social-service and individual-salvation emphases of Christianity for themselves in February 1909, the fact that such a dichotomy was discussed evidenced a new state of restlessness in the church and the nation. The fuller impact of the suggested inadequacies of religion to provide dynamic Christian motives and values in a needy society, or to arouse a sense of social duty among Christians, did not become clearer until later in the year. By then, even the association was more sensitive to the growing unrest, and its themes for the next three years shifted from social concerns to training persons for work in the church and the home.[6] With a nationwide membership of more than 2,000, the Religious Education Association was unusually sensitive to the national mood, and both its themes and the insights of its socially concerned leaders served as a more broadly based nondenominational barometer of the social gospel than the New York State Conference of Religion during the remaining years of this study.

A primary cause of the new discomfort in Protestantism was the frontal attack on the church by the muckrakers and the resulting negative reaction among the populace to the apparent hypocrisy and ineffectiveness of religion. As depicted in the popular press, the church, rather than providing the resources for social redemption, seemed to be another institution corrupting and weakening the social order.

The immediate focus of attention was Trinity Protestant Episcopal Church in New York City, which was widely attacked in January 1909 for

---

[5]Francis Greenwood Peabody, "The Social Conscience and the Religious Life," ibid., 1-6.

[6]The themes were: "The Church and Education" (1910), "Religious Education and the American Home" (1911), and "The Training of Religious Leaders" (1912).

its tenement holdings in lower Manhattan. Several New York periodicals described and ridiculed the poor condition of the buildings, the vast extent of the properties, and the Trinity Church Corporation's conduct as landlord of facilities that violated public-health provisions and supported the worst brothels and saloons in the city. Similar disclosures had been made in 1895 and 1905, but they had ceased when promises of correction and improvement were made. In 1909 muckraker Charles Edward Russell felt reforms had not been made, and he renewed the attack with articles such as "Trinity Church: A Riddle of Riches" in *Hampton's* in May and "The Tenements of Trinity Church" in *Everybody's Magazine* in July. Attempting to respond to those critiques, the rector on 1 January 1909 issued the first financial report on the church's holdings to correct misunderstandings in the public mind. The report showed that Trinity Church owned real estate with an assessed valuation of $13,646,300 and total gross assets of $14,079,330! A number of New York newspapers published the report, and the parish stood branded in public as the richest church in America, as well as a corrupt landlord. An independent investigation and report was authorized to allay public opinion, and following a thorough study by a distinguished group headed by Lawrence Veiller of the National Housing Association, systematic improvements were instituted.[7] While the situation at Trinity Church improved in the long run, the immediate effect was a negative reaction against churches generally.

Trinity Church was not the only religious institution condemned by the muckrakers. Mary Baker Eddy and the Mormons also were assailed, but they were not part of mainstream Protestantism. As noted earlier, muckraking journalists shared basic Protestant values and were not inclined to condemn the churches. But their dislike for hypocrisy and corruption, triggered by the revelations about Trinity Church, led them to examine organized religion more extensively. Beginning in May 1909 Harold Bolce ran a series on current religious thought in colleges and universities that appeared in *Cosmopolitan* and attracted extensive interest and comment. Most significant of the critical examinations, however, was a series in the *American Magazine* during 1909 entitled "The Spiritual

---

[7]Charles Thorley Bridgeman, *A History of the Parish of Trinity Church in the City of New York: Part VI, The Rectorship of Dr. William Thomas Manning, 1908-1921* (New York: the Rector, Churchwardens and Vestrymen of Trinity Church in the City of New York, 1962) 116-32.

Unrest" by Ray Stannard Baker. Because of the large correspondence and interest that resulted, Baker published the series as a book in 1910.[8]

Claiming that his material represented neither an attack nor a defense, Baker maintained that "The Spiritual Unrest" was written by a lay observer for everyday men and women, both within the church and outside it, because he was convinced "the people can be trusted with the facts."[9] The seven-article series told the story of Trinity Church, evaluated the condition of the Protestant Church, examined the disintegration of immigrant Jewish communities in New York City, and then evaluated four sources of vitality: the institutional churches and slum missions, the Emmanuel Movement of faith healing, the religious dynamic outside the churches, and the "Vision of the New Christianity" represented by Walter Rauschenbusch. Essentially, Baker did not dispute the charge that people were avoiding the church or that organized religion was not holding its own. "But religion is not decaying; it is only the church," he insisted. "More religion is to be found in our life to-day than ever before. . . . As ever, it demands, not observances, nor doctrines, nor a habitation in magnificent temples—but self-sacrifice and a contrite heart."[10]

Baker's analysis of the condition of Protestant churches was incisive in its protrayal of spiritual unrest. Studying churches in New York City, he discovered a "general tone of discontent and discouragement among church workers themselves." To his astonishment, he found that much of the voluntary giving that formerly flowed to the churches was diverted now to other philanthropic purposes. When he began, Baker had the impression the city was underchurched, but he concluded in the end that it was overchurched for what was accomplished. The churches were populated by the rich, but nearly all the poor were outside. Revivals intended to reach poor had accomplished little. "The churches, as churches, have not waked up. They are still dallying with symptoms: offering classes and gymnasiums to people who are underfed and underpaid who live in miserable and unsanitary homes!" They tried to help the poor but did nothing about the conditions that made people poor. "They have no vision of social justice: they have no message for the

---

[8]Louis Filler, *Crusaders for American Liberalism* (New York: Harcourt, Brace and Company, Inc., 1939; New York: Collier Books, 1961) 273-82; Harvey Swados, *Years of Conscience: The Muckrakers; An Anthology* (Cleveland: World Publishing Co., Meridian Books, 1962) 295-320.

[9]Ray Stannard Baker, *The Spiritual Unrest* (New York: Frederick A. Stokes Co., 1910) preface.

[10]Ibid., 46-47.

common people." Rather than giving their money, they needed to reach the people, and that required personal self- sacrifice that Baker found little of in church members. They needed cooperation, but scarcely two ministers, let alone two denominations, agreed on either doctrine or what to do. A Federation of Churches existed in the city, but it consisted only of one energetic man and had "almost no significance as a directing or centralizing power."[11]

Looking for signs of vitality, Baker studied the institutional churches and slum missions that churches sponsored. However, he concluded that while they evidenced genuine concern and achieved some good, both institutional churches and city missions tended to be paternalistic efforts by the rich for the poor, which really alienated the impoverished. In contrast, Baker discovered signs of religious vitality outside church influence in more secular activities like the social-settlement movement, hospitals, municipal and political reform, and several charities. The tendency in each of these was to have direct contact with the needy by going to them and cooperating with them, which was the direct reverse of the church movement, which tended to flee from tenement neighborhoods to build new buildings elsewhere while hiring workers to maintain missions to serve the poor who were left behind.[12]

Church leaders, Baker found, agreed about the waning influence of organized Christianity, but they were unable to produce a common plan or purpose to remedy the situation. When he asked progressive religious leaders for a positive sign, they referred most frequently to Walter Rauschenbusch's *Christianity and the Social Crisis* as the book offering the best hope of renewal. Baker read the book, went to Rochester where he interviewed Rauschenbusch and sat in his classes, and concluded that the social prophet's ideas provided a legitimate and exciting vision for Christianity. While much of his article summarized ideas in Rauschenbusch's book, other parts described the social prophet's work, life-style, and involvement in neighborhood and city affairs. His interview elicited further explanation of Rauschenbusch's idea of the new evangelism as the source for the rebirth of society. The Rochester professor's conviction that the new American church would have to make important changes in religious expression and worship impressed Baker, who printed two prayers from Rauschenbusch's book *Prayers of the Social Awakening*[13] because they illustrated the creativity possible in worship and

---

[11]Ibid.,49-100.

[12]Ibid.,142-82, 232-59.

[13]Walter Rauschenbusch, *Prayers of the Social Awakening* (Boston: Pilgrim Press, 1910).

devotional life. In light of his negative evaluation of much of Protestant church activity, it was obvious that Baker presented Rauschenbusch favorably as an encouragement to his readers.[14]

With a typical muckraking approach, Baker's series of seven articles in the *American Magazine* began in June 1909 with his initial indictment of the churches in "The Condition of the Protestant Church" and ended in December with his hopeful portrayal of Rauschenbusch in "A Vision of the New Christianity." Despite its ultimate optimism, the primary impact of *The Spiritual Unrest* was critical. Seemingly applying the test of social utility that Francis Peabody felt was justified for religious institutions in society, Baker found that much that the organized church was doing was inadequate and ineffectual. When such a general critique was applied in addition to the disclosures concerning the tenements of Trinity Church, the credibility of the church in the nation was questioned. It was one thing for the church to be prodded from within by advocates of social Christianity; it was another matter for the church to be evaluated by external and apparently impartial negative appraisals. Why should the public accept the social conscience of Protestant churches concerning matters of civic righteousness and social redemption when evidence indicated that Protestant churches were themselves corrupt, hypocritical, and ineffectual? That was the question posed by the spiritual unrest in 1909.

Another change of circumstances affected the nation, the church, and the social gospel in 1909. On 4 March William Howard Taft was inaugurated as president of the United States, and Theodore Roosevelt lost the sounding board of the presidency that had amplified his message of righteousness for years. Later that month Roosevelt and some friends left on a year's hunting expedition in Africa, followed by a brief world tour, and he did not return to America until 10 June 1910. While Roosevelt had handpicked his political successor, Taft differed in many ways from his bumptious, articulate, and publicly righteous predecessor. During the 1908 election Roosevelt had defended Taft's Unitarian affiliation as of no concern to voters because a religious test for office was forbidden by the Constitution.[15] Nevertheless, evangelical Protestants found Taft's religion bothersome, and champions of social Christianity missed a clarion voice for moral righteousness in the White House. Theodore Roosevelt had been a hero to social-gospel advocates and was missed. After his return in 1910,

---

[14]Baker, *Spiritual Unrest*, 260-85.

[15]"Religion and Politics," 6 November 1908, *The Works of Theodore Roosevelt*, National Edition, 20 vols., ed. Hermann Hagedorn (New York: Charles Scribner's Sons, 1926) 16:45-48.

he became a contributing editor for *The Outlook,* and his ideas once again reached the public with their previous vigor. When he delivered his address "The New Nationalism" at Osawatomie, Kansas, on 31 August 1910, Roosevelt began a new political movement that transformed *The Outlook* into a political journal and brought political Progressivism to a feverish climax in the election of 1912. In that address he stated the need for "a genuine and permanent moral awakening" in the country, and his political cause contained that message, which paralleled the advocacy of a social awakening of the churches in the same years.[16] Both by his absence and his presence Theodore Roosevelt influenced the evolution of the Social Gospel movement.

Beneath the ebb and flow of these tides of political and spiritual unrest ran an undercurrent that provided stability and continuity for social Christianity during this period. The long evolution of social- gospel thought provided ballast during the unsettling storms, and its presence became evident in new statements of basic concepts by leaders of the movement. On 21 July 1909, for instance, Frank Mason North delivered an address on "The City and the Kingdom" at Chautauqua, New York, that gave new expression to his fundamental interest in urban ministry. This time he focused not on the evangelization of the city but on the centrality of the kingdom of God in the teaching of Jesus and how that message related to the church's mission in the city. Maintaining that the central importance of the kingdom was evident in the Lord's Prayer petition that God's kingdom come on earth as in heaven, North said that the city had more to do with the kingdom than to threaten it and oppose its coming. "The way to the Kingdom is not over the ruins of the city, but through its streets," he declared, as he pointed to the potential for metropolis to become the City of God. "The Kingdom is coming! We dream of it, we await it, we work for it. The city is here, the very heart of the divine strategy, the key of the mighty campaign." By winning the cities for Jesus, Christians could hasten the coming of the kingdom "by making real, here and now, the City of God," because, he concluded, "in the City of God is the Kingdom of Heaven."[17]

In similar fashion, Washington Gladden sought to clarify the relation of the nation to the kingdom of God that same year. Preaching the annual

---

[16]Theodore Roosevelt, *The New Nationalism* (New York: The Outlook Co., 1910) with intro. and notes by William E. Leuchtenburg (Englewood Cliffs NJ: Prentice-Hall, Inc., Spectrum Books, 1961) 38.

[17]Frank Mason North, "The City and the Kingdom," in *Social Ministry: An Introduction to the Study and Practice of Social Service,* ed. Harry F. Ward (New York: Eaton & Mains; Cincinnati: Jennings & Graham, 1910) 293-318.

sermon to the American Board of Commissioners for Foreign Missions in October, he affirmed that "the nation is to be an important agency in the kingdom." In 1908 he had reminded the Religious Education Association in Washington that the civil state was created to serve religious ends,[18] but already in 1900 he had declared, "The nation is a divine institution. . . . Love of the nation, in its true conception, is a religious devotion."[19]

Building on the message of the prophet Isaiah, Gladden stated that the kingdom of God was to be set up in the world by the nation. Nations that God had purified and made holy would be the means by which other nations would be transformed. Thus, Christians should look to God's use of nations in evangelizing the world. "If we want the nations of the earth to understand Christianity," he said, "we have got to have a Christianized nation to show them." Working with the seeming contradiction that Isaiah's prophecy of a godly nation was coming true in America, and yet that American society was imperfectly Christianized, Gladden argued that conditions at the time were considerably improved over the past and, despite its imperfections, the American social order embodied principles, forces, and resources by which other nations might be Christianized. Believing that the nation was part of God's providence, and that God needed the efforts of every Christian, he climaxed his address with this challenge: "We must make this nation fit to be a witness for him, so that when the banner of our country and the banner of the cross are seen floating together, it shall be evident to all men that the day has come when mercy and truth are met together, and righteousness and peace have kissed each other."[20]

Gladden's ideas in 1909 about the God-given role of the nation in achieving righteousness, and ultimately the Christianization of the social order, were an expression of long-held convictions. Moreover, his understanding of the role of the nation in achieving the kingdom of God was similar to North's view of the city and the kingdom, and this view harkened back to Gladden's earlier clarification of the church and the

---

[18]Washington Gladden, "Bringing All the Moral and Religious Forces into Effective Educational Unity," *Education and National Character* (Chicago: Religious Education Association, 1908) 35.

[19]"Our Country, Right or Wrong?," 30 September 1900, manuscript sermon, Washington Gladden Papers, Ohio Historical Society, Columbus OH, pp. 25-26.

[20]Washington Gladden, *The Nation and the Kingdom: Annual Sermon before the American Board of Commissioners for Foreign Missions* (Boston, 1909), in Robert T. Handy, *The Social Gospel in America, 1870–1920: Gladden, Ely, Rauschenbusch* (New York: Oxford University Press, 1966) 135-53.

kingdom. In social-gospel thought, the nation, city, and church were all instruments to be utilized to achieve the larger kingdom of God. "The Nation and the Kingdom" address simply refined and expanded Gladden's own classic definition written fifteen years earlier.

> Every department of human life—the families, the schools, amusements, art, business, politics, industry, national policies, international relations—will be governed by the Christian law and controlled by Christian influences. When we are bidden to seek first the kingdom of God, we are bidden to set our hearts on this great consummation. . . . The complete Christianization of all life is what we pray for when we work and pray for the coming of the kingdom of heaven.[21]

But Gladden's interest also reflected both the general Protestant interest in a Christian America and an immediate concern about the whole matter of the relationship of church and state in the process of Christianizing society.[22] This immediate interest had been evident at the Religious Education Association's convention on "Education and National Character" in 1908, but it was examined more thoroughly in 1909 by another leader of social Christianity, Samuel Zane Batten.

Batten's massive 450-page book *The Christian State* was the most comprehensive analysis of the relation of Christianity to political government to emerge in this period of the social gospel. The underlying theme of his careful analysis was the fact that both the church and the state were aspects of the kingdom of God, which was the larger unifying factor. In arriving at that synthesis, Batten traced the origins of both church and state, pointed to the role each played, and indicated the need to find a workable relationship for the two. To avoid the subordination of one to the other, or the failure to recognize that they exist side by side, it was necessary to find a conception that would bring them into harmony, and he found that in the ideal of the kingdom of God. For him, the way to implement that ultimate ideal was by seeking to create the "Christian State." According to Batten, "The kingdoms of this world become the kingdoms of our God by the realization of the life of the kingdom in the life of the State and the transformation of the institutions of the State into

---

[21]Washington Gladden, *The Church and the Kingdom* (New York: Fleming H. Revell Co., 1894), in Handy, *Social Gospel in America*, 104.

[22]See Robert T. Handy, *A Christian America: Protestant Hopes and Historical Realities* (New York: Oxford University Press, 1971) 144-47, passim.

the kingdom of God. The Christian spirit must create the Christian State. The Christian State is only a matter of time and patience."[23]

That conclusion did not mean that Batten intended for Christians to sit back and patiently await the result; on the contrary, he advocated action by Christians and by the state. Periodically the lines of his argument converged at one point: "The State has one great end to seek in the world, and that is to organize and incarnate in the social and political life of man the righteousness, the peace, and the joy of the kingdom of God." It was the task of the Christian citizen to hasten this divinely approved work.[24] To achieve that end a number of problems had to be faced, but the preeminent one was "the social problem." In discussing that issue Batten showed wide familiarity with the literature of the first decade of the century, and he frequently cited the ideas of his friend Walter Rauschenbusch. When he pointed to new functions that the state had to assume to meet the problems of a new social order struggling to be born, Batten consistently called for a strong central government.[25] This was significant because his book was published six months before Herbert Croly's *The Promise of American Life,* which became the popular book advocating the same argument strictly in political terms and was viewed as a basic contribution to Theodore Roosevelt's emerging notion of the new nationalism.

Along with these new expressions of basic ideas of social Christianity concerning the nation, the city, and the church in relation to the kingdom of God, the first book bearing the term *social gospel* in its title was published early in 1910. Shailer Mathews's little volume titled *The Social Gospel* related New Testament teachings to current social problems, rather than providing an explanation or justification of the term.[26] Well aware that there had been much discussion "whether the individual or society is the great end of all social development," the professor and editor reiterated ideas already expressed in other publications, but in simplified form. Rather than defend a social interpretation of the gospel, Mathews presumed that the gospel had both individual and social implications. Without denying the importance of individual salvation, he stressed the

---

[23]Samuel Zane Batten, *The Christian State: The State, Democracy and Christianity* (Philadelphia: Griffith & Rowland Press, 1909) 287-89, 292-93, 444-45.

[24]Ibid., 398-99, 416-21.

[25]Ibid., 10-14, 76-77, 352-56.

[26]Shailer Mathews, *The Social Gospel* (Philadelphia: Griffith & Rowland Press, 1910) passim.

social ideal expressed in the New Testament. But in addressing such social problems as the family, the state, the economic life, and social regeneration, he emphasized their spiritual significance rather than their social solution. It was his conviction that the gospel taught by Jesus was capable of transforming persons, and they in turn were capable of transforming society. As for the church, Mathews believed its basic task was to proclaim the gospel so that persons were converted and then filled with a passion for righteousness and service. Christian individuals should work to solve problems in society, but they should be educated by the church about both the problems and the gospel so they could apply the principles of Jesus in all dimensions of social life. In 1910 Josiah Strong's little autobiographical book *My Religion in Everyday Life* also provided a personalized argument for the fact that "society must be saved as well as the individual."[27]

By a strange happenstance, the month of February 1910 not only witnessed the publication of Mathews's book *The Social Gospel* but also the printing of the first volume of a new series called *The Fundamentals*, which its sponsor intended as a response to "those infidel professors in Chicago University."[28] During the next five years the series grew by design to twelve volumes, which were distributed without cost "to every pastor, evangelist, missionary, theological professor, theological student, Sunday school superintendent, Y.M.C.A. and Y.W.C.A. secretary in the English speaking world." Funding for this massive project was provided by two brothers, Lyman and Milton Stewart, who believed "that the time has come when a new statement of the fundamentals of Christianity should be made."[29] Reflecting the spiritual unrest of the era, these men and their sympathizers sought to reaffirm the biblical basis of Christian beliefs, which they felt was being threatened by the recent biblical criticism emanating from German scholarship and American colleges and seminaries. Shailer Mathews represented that new scholarship on the one hand, while A. C. Dixon, whom Lyman Stewart secured to design and

---

[27]Josiah Strong, *My Religion in Everyday Life* (New York: Baker & Taylor Co., 1910) 50.

[28]Quoted by Ernest R. Sandeen, *The Roots of Fundamentalism: British and American Millenarianism, 1800–1930* (Grand Rapids MI: Baker Book House, 1978) 188-89.

[29]*The Fundamentals: A Testimony to the Truth*, 12 vols., published in 2 bound vols. (Chicago: Testimony Publishing Co., n.d. [1910–1915]) 1, foreword on back of title page.

direct the new venture, represented the conservative and millenarian forces that opposed it on the other hand.

Advocates of social Christianity generally were involved in the emerging struggle between the two contending viewpoints of evangelical Protestantism that were beginning to become quite distinct. Beneath the teachings of social-gospel leaders was an understanding of biblical truth that rested heavily on the teachings of the prophets and Jesus and that pointed to the establishment of the kingdom of God on earth. Since this goal seemed to play down the second coming of Christ and the establishment of a millennial kingdom, many conservative evangelicals felt that the social gospel was denying the basic tenets of Christianity. While the differences had begun to become openly apparent by 1910, they had long been latent in American Protestantism. Already in the 1890s Walter Rauschenbusch was distinguishing his social understanding from that of millenarian Baptists, feeling that their views were an unhistorical way to interpret the Bible, were pessimistic and antiworldly, and were so centered on catastrophies that faith and action became disjointed.[30] During 1903 he had engaged in an open skirmish with Isaac M. Haldeman, pastor of First Baptist Church in New York City, over millennial interpretation, which he questioned as legitimate Christian truth.[31] Years later Haldeman wrote an extended critique of Rauschenbusch's *Christianity and the Social Crisis* to indicate that it was based on church history rather than on the more authoritative New Testament.[32] The basic difference of understanding had been stated by conservatives in Article XIV of the Niagara Bible Conference Creed as early as 1878: "We believe that the world will not be converted during the present dispensation, but is fast ripening for judgment, while there will be a fearful apostasy in the professing Christian body, and hence that the Lord Jesus will come in person to introduce the millennial age."[33] The Christianization of the social

[30]Walter Rauschenbusch, "Our Attitudes toward Millenarianism," *The Examiner* (New York), 24 September 1896, pp. 878-79; 1 October 1896, pp. 897-98.

[31]Walter Rauschenbusch, "Mr. Haldeman's Millenarianism," *The Examiner* (New York), 18 June 1903, p. 779; cf. Isaac M. Haldeman, "The Coming of Christ: Is the Millennium to Come before Christ, Or Is Christ to Come before the Millennium?," ibid., 7 May 1903, pp. 585-86.

[32]I. M. Haldeman, *Professor Rauschenbusch's Christianity and the Social Crisis* (New York: Charles C. Cook, n.d. [1912]).

[33]Great Commission Prayer League, *The Fundamentals of the Faith: As Expressed in the Articles of Belief of the Niagara Bible Conference* (Chicago: Great Commission Prayer League, n.d. [1914]); also printed in full in Sandeen, *Roots of Fundamentalism,* Appendix A, 273-77.

order taught by social-gospel proponents stood in direct conflict with such millennial teachings of the fundamentalists. While the battleground of *The Fundamentals* lay primarily in biblical interpretation and theological doctrines rather than in social involvement, the divergent views concerning the former affected the latter, especially in the middle years of the next decade, as we shall see later.[34]

In 1910 the conflict between the two persuasions was not yet noticed by many people. While the volumes of *The Fundamentals* began to be published and distributed, their impact was still tentative, except as another sign of the spiritual unrest at the time. Meanwhile, with leaders like Josiah Strong, Shailer Mathews, Samuel Zane Batten, Washington Gladden, and Frank Mason North reaffirming or elaborating basic social-gospel ideas during 1909 and 1910, their movement found the stability to withstand the uncertainties of spiritual and political unrest. Anchored by a continuity of leaders and fundamental concepts, the cause of social Christianity was able to venture into advanced positions within the organized churches, despite the sharp criticisms and open attacks that were occurring at the time.

---

[34]See ch. 14 below and George M. Marsden, *Fundamentalism and American Culture: The Shaping of Twentieth-Century Evangelicalism, 1870–1925* (New York: Oxford University Press, 1980) 91-92.

CHAPTER 9

Social Christianity in Agencies
of the American Churches

The rise of social Christianity is felt in all the institutional agencies of the American churches. Those movements which are distinctively modern and devised to meet present-day needs are completely dominated by it.

(Walter Rauschenbusch,
Christianizing the Social Order, *1912)*

FOLLOWING THE EXPRESSION of "the social conscience of the Churches" at the first meeting of the Federal Council of Churches in December 1908, it remained to be seen what the constituent bodies would do about the commitment they had mutually affirmed. When they returned to their own official conventions and assemblies, how would the individual denominations seek to implement the platform that was adopted?

Of the churches that had shown interest in social Christianity, the northern Presbyterians were the first to meet. Their General Assembly convened in May 1909 and received a report that the Federal Council meeting had been "a great success," although it was impossible yet to estimate the value of such an organization. That report made no reference to the council's social resolutions, but a special committee report within the "Narrative of the State of Religion" supported the Federal Council's activities in "building up public opinion in support of civic righteousness, and in general securing other advances in social and religious betterment."[1] Little specific implementation of social matters was

---

[1] *Minutes of the General Assembly of the Presbyterian Church in the United States of America,* n.s. (1909), 77-78, 265.

attempted at this General Assembly, but the possibility for future advance was assured when the assembly voted to create the Committee on Social Problems, which was to submit a report to the next assembly on "the thought and purpose of our Church regarding the great moral questions arising out of the industrial and commercial life of the people."[2]

Despite the absence of concrete official action on the Federal Council recommendations, Presbyterians at the 1909 General Assembly received the Board of Home Missions report that told of the continuing work of Charles Stelzle's Department of Church and Labor. By this time an extensive and vigorous program with workers was being carried on across the country, with his weekly column for workers now syndicated in more than 350 labor papers. New efforts through his Immigration Department were being carried on in partnership with the Presbytery of New York; together they compiled data for extending the ministry among immigrant workers. The success of Stelzle's work was confirmed by the appointment of an assistant, Warren H. Wilson.[3] In 1910 William P. Shriver also was added to the staff, assuming responsibilities among immigrants while Wilson established a new Department of Church and Country Life. The next year another person joined Stelzle's staff to help with research and survey work. Also the publication of Stelzle's book *The Church and Labor* in 1910 attracted national attention to his program.[4] Thus, Stelzle's pioneering efforts achieved notable success and expansion in the church and "revolutionized, within a few years, the attitude of the trade unions towards the Church," according to one newspaper.[5]

As a result of the studies conducted in New York City, Stelzle decided to attempt a new approach in ministering to workers. Since laborers generally felt alienated in most local congregations, he considered creating a church specifically for workers. During 1910 a church building became available on a prominent corner in a congested tenement area of the lower east side of New York, and it was purchased to experiment with the practicability of getting workers to attend a congregation of their own laboring class. Called the Labor Temple, the new venture aroused public interest and reached the point that it sponsored thirty-three meetings each week, with such crowds that people were frequently turned away on

---

[2]Ibid., 47.

[3]Ibid., 330-31.

[4]Stelzle, *The Church and Labor* (Boston: Houghton Mifflin Co., 1910).

[5]*Minutes of the General Assembly* (1910), 359-60; (1911), 349-50; *The Outlook* (New York), 21 December 1912, pp. 849-50.

Sunday evenings. In this congregation, reported Stelzle, 90 percent who attended were men, and 50 percent were Jews. Since Stelzle permitted radical views to be expressed there, some members of the Presbyterian Board of Home Missions objected and attempted to close it down. Its continuity was assured only because Stelzle secured the support of prominent Presbyterian clergy and Theodore Roosevelt, who both preached there and wrote favorably about Labor Temple in *The Outlook*.[6] The Labor Temple project evidenced Stelzle's creativity and diligence, but the response it engendered also indicated the potential for objections to his freestyle and energetic methods. Its success was the culmination of several years of ministry to workers and symbolized an expanding multiple staff mission to social needs that was unique among Protestant denominations.

Equally important in 1910 was the official action taken by the Presbyterian General Assembly concerning the report of the Special Committee on Social Problems. The committee of five ministers and five laymen presented its report through its chairman, Rev. John McDowell. Reminding the delegates of the purpose of the report authorized by the preceding assembly, the committee affirmed its conviction that "an authoritative declaration of the attitude of the Church upon these matters is imperative." Several reasons for such a statement were cited: urgent questions of wealth and poverty and relations between capital and labor that resulted from the industrialism in society required answers; Christian principles to offset the exclusively secular basis of proposed programs of social betterment should be provided by Christianity; and moral and religious ideas addressed to the current state of industrial and commercial progress ought to be provided in order to relieve the perplexity of Christians whose conscience had been aroused. The committee endorsed the work of existing agencies of the church that addressed particular social problems and urged continued support of their efforts. Nevertheless, not all problems were being solved, and Christianity was largely responsible, on the one hand, for failing to discern the moral basis of economic relations and, on the other, for creating "the present demands for social and economic justice."[7]

On the basis of that rationale, the committee presented what it termed "The Christian Solution of the Social Problem." At the outset four beliefs

---

[6]*Minutes of the General Assembly* (1911), 349; Charles Stelzle, *A Son of the Bowery: The Life Story of an East Side American* (New York: George H. Doran Co., 1926) 117-33.

[7]*Minutes of the General Assembly* (1910) 229-30.

were affirmed: that Jesus was the final authority over the social as well as the individual aspects of human life; that righteousness in the complexity of modern human affairs was realizable only through the principles of the kingdom of God taught by Jesus; that the church was obligated "to show how these Christian principles apply to human affairs"; and that this teaching by the church should be related "to present practical conditions." "Therefore," continued the committee, "we hold that the time has come when the Presbyterian Church in the United States of America must speak its mind concerning particular problems now threatening society."[8]

The fourteen declarations that the report urged the Presbyterian Church to make were clearly rooted in the Social Creed of the Churches, but they did not simply reaffirm that pronouncement. Although the statements in both documents totaled fourteen, the Presbyterian declarations retained only nine duplicate items, and just two of those used identical wording. The rest were paraphrased, some with the original meaning but others with different emphasis. New statements concerning the obligations of wealth, the equitable distribution of wealth, the regulation of unsanitary dwellings, the care of "dependent and incapable persons," and the reformation of legal offenders were added. At five places, commentary paragraphs also were inserted to amplify meanings. A careful analysis revealed that the report thoroughly reworked the Federal Council platform and produced derivative Presbyterian declarations.[9]

A series of four recommendations applied Frank Mason North's suggested church actions to Presbyterian polity and practice. These recommendations urged ministers especially, but also laity generally and students particularly, to study both social problems and opportunities for service in light of the social teachings of Jesus. One important recommendation proposed that the General Assembly appoint a Bureau of Social Service, consisting of ministers and laymen, to work with similar organizations of other denominations, to study social conditions, to suggest to the church "practical ways of realizing the social ideals of the Gospel," and to report annually regarding its efforts. Significantly, the proposed Bureau of Social Service was to assume "the duties now performed by other agencies of the Church which deal with social and moral questions," including the Department of Church and Labor of the Board of Home Missions.[10]

---

[8]Ibid., 230.

[9]Ibid., 230-32.

[10]Ibid., 232-33.

This summary of the report of the Special Committee on Social Problems presents the contents of the document as it was finally adopted after amendments. Essentially, the Presbyterian General Assembly, by approving the report, adhered to the process followed by the Methodist Episcopal Church and the Federal Council of Churches: endorsing a platform of social declarations addressed to immediate needs in the social order, urging social service upon all levels of its membership, and authorizing an agency to deal with "the whole matter of social righteousness." Although the specific statements in the Presbyterian platform differed at a number of points from the preceding Social Creeds, the practice of addressing current social problems was uniform, and in effect the northern Presbyterians formed a parallel structure that facilitated cooperation with other denominations. The declarations of "The Christian Solution of the Social Problem" became the basic statement of the Presbyterian Church in the United States of America and constituted its ratification of the Federal Council's Social Creed of the Churches.

At the 1911 General Assembly a Bureau of Social Service was officially created, but with modification. Despite the approval of the idea in 1910, implementation was delayed for a year so that a second proposal to reorganize the Board of Home Missions could be correlated to it. By this maneuver the Executive Committee of the General Assembly avoided establishing the bureau as an independent agency, justifying the adjustment because of the reorganization of the Mission Board. While the reorganized board was directed to administer the bureau without losing any of "the present efficiency of the Departments of Church and Labor, and of Immigration," the authorization kept the new bureau directly responsible to the board and limited its autonomy.[11] The consequence of these changes was evident in 1912 when the Board of Home Missions report explained that the Department of Church and Labor formed nine years ago was "enlarged into a Bureau of Social Service, which is to include not only the relations of working men to the Church, but a consideration of all moral and social problems."[12] At the time when Presbyterian social ministry was being broadened beyond work with laborers, there was a suspicious statement in the "Narrative of the Church" that suggested future trouble: "For the safeguarding of Social Service in the life of the Church we should clearly mark its proper sphere."[13] Until that statement,

---

[11](1911), 154, 157.

[12]Ibid. (1912), 371.

[13]Ibid., 296.

a purposeful movement of the cause of social Christianity from 1909 to 1912 was evident among northern Presbyterians.

Although the Northern Baptist Convention had no full-time person like Charles Stelzle to organize its social ministry, it had created a Social Service Commission in 1908 and directed it to submit a report the next year. Thus, the Baptists were organized to implement the Federal Council's actions at Philadelphia in December 1908. Consequently, when the convention gathered late in June 1909, it received a report on social service that elicited official authorization of social Christianity.

Chairman Samuel Zane Batten presented the report of the Social Service Commission. On the basis of a survey of local churches, he said, it was obvious that Baptist churches were an indirect force for social righteousness but did "little in a direct way in social service, in philanthropy, in civic betterment, in child-saving, in community improvement, in prison reform, and public righteousness." Pointing to needs in these areas, Batten moved on to discuss "The Church and Labor and Industry," where he noted a "new social consciousness." That awareness was based on a growing realization that economic and political questions were "essentially moral and human questions" that churches could help to solve. As churches acknowledged that "society needs saving as much as the individual," they could begin to generate the power to transform the social order. To guide Christians in that task, the committee presented the Social Creed propositions taken without change from the "Church and Modern Industry" report of the Federal Council of Churches. "We approve and adopt these propositions and recommend that they be made a part of our social program," continued the report, which was enacted by the Baptist Convention.[14]

Following the now-familiar pattern used by the Federal Council and the Methodists, five recommendations to implement the propositions were urged upon the convention. Typically, they ranged from instructing "the people in the social duties of the churches" to cooperating with others "in behalf of better conditions in society." Two of the five involved institutional machinery. One called for the creation of a Commission on Religious and Moral Education that would serve primarily to coordinate existing activities. According to the honest appraisal of the committee: "We do not need much new machinery; but we do need to coordinate the machinery we now have. And above all we must see that this work of moral training is done by somebody in an adequate way." The second called for the establishment of a Social Service Department of the

---

[14]*Annual of the Northern Baptist Convention* (1909), 129-34.

Convention and the early appointment of a full- time "social service secretary." Delegates approved the first four recommendations and referred the last one to the Executive Committee with power to act.[15]

Finally, the report ended with an eloquent challenge, which in part declared,

> The men who have the vision of the Christ and seek his kingdom should never be willing that the agitation of social wrongs, the correction of great abuses, the destruction of social injustice, and the leadership of social reform should be left to outsiders, to agnostics often, to men who have no real vision of the kingdom and no impelling motive of loyalty to Christ. In fine, the men who know Christ and expect the coming of his kingdom are the very men who should assume the leadership of the social faith.[16]

While the recommendations were akin to those in other denominations, this wording appropriately expressed the long emerging ideas of the Brotherhood of the Kingdom and the Baptist authors previously described. Probably that was not accidental since Walter Rauschenbusch and Shailer Mathews, as well as Batten, were members of the committee that prepared the report. The convention's general approval of the report and its actions was a fitting endorsement of the longtime efforts of these advocates of social Christianity.

When the Northern Baptist Convention met again in May 1910, Walter Rauschenbusch's national fame was apparent in the invitation he received to deliver the honored convention sermon. Undoubtedly, he would have preferred that the Executive Committee had approved the employment of a social- service secretary, but that group recommended that the matter "be laid over until the next Convention." Several reasons were given for that action: finances did not justify it; even if money were available, it was questionable whether the convention should itself engage in active work; and employing such a person might set a precedent for persons in other fields. The Executive Committee's unwillingness to create such new machinery may have reflected foot dragging on social matters, but it seemed that the convention, which had only begun to function officially two years earlier, was struggling mostly with the polity and finances of a denomination little given to centralized programming and personnel.[17]

---

[15]Ibid., 134-36.

[16]Ibid., 136.

[17]Ibid. (1910), 69-70, 90.

Though the Baptists lacked full-time leadership, their Commission on Social Service reported in 1910 that it was working as diligently as possible in light of great needs. Two major program emphases were the production of literature on social concerns and cooperation with various state conventions to create social-service commissions at that level of the denomination in order to broaden social involvement. Batten's report also well evidenced the impact of the unrest in the nation.

> Many people have lost interest in the churches and no longer attend its meetings and assist in its work. Many people have taken up an attitude of indifference where it is not opposition to all forms of organized religion. There is much unrest to-day in the political world, in social life, and in religious thought. The present, every discerning man confesses, is a time of pressure and crisis. . . . A new social order is struggling to the birth; the old vine of the kingdom is producing some new wine that is bursting the wine skins.[18]

The following year Batten's report again stressed the work on publications and helping state conventions, and the report marked the "steady progress of the Social Service ideal in all denominations." Consequently, the commission again urged the employment of a full-time leader in the area of social service. And once again the convention referred the matter to the Executive Committee.[19]

At the Baptist Convention in May 1912 there was still no appointment of the desired full-time executive. Instead, the commission reported that it was fully organized by subdividing its work into manageable units that could be handled efficiently on a voluntary basis. Increasing cooperation with other denominations and with the Federal Council of Churches was now reported. Its philosophy was stated concisely: "The Commission is not seeking to create a new organization, but to serve the organizations already in existence."[20] Having enunciated that strategy and voluntary method, it was surprising when the American Baptist Publication Society created a Department of Social Service and Brotherhood and Samuel Zane Batten was elected to be its full-time leader, starting 1 October 1912.[21] As will be evident in the next chapter, the Baptist Brotherhood movement actively supported the Men and Religion Forward Movement during 1911–1912, whose unexpected success stimulated both the Brotherhood and the

---

[18]Ibid., 141-44.

[19]Ibid. (1911), 127-35, 140.

[20]Ibid. (1912), 161-70.

[21]Ibid. (1913), 128, 518-19.

now-popular social-concern emphasis. Among Northern Baptists this success resulted in the employment of a full-time executive to serve both interests, thus fulfilling one of the primary goals of the Social Service Commission since 1909: to include social Christianity in the official organizational life of the denomination.

Because of the triennial cycle of its meetings, the National Council of the Congregational Churches did not convene until October 1910. During the delivery of the moderator's address by Thomas C. MacMillan of Illinois, it sounded as if this assembly would have much less social interest than when Washington Gladden had spoken in 1907. MacMillan refered to "the remarkable revival in civic righteousness which we are now experiencing," but he attributed the main cause for it to preachers who stressed "a gospel of individual responsibility to God" every week in their sermons.[22] However, before the National Council adjourned it took several actions that moved it into the ranks of denominations supporting social Christianity.

The direct challenge to take such action was presented by another man from Illinois, Professor Graham Taylor of the University of Chicago and director of the Chicago Commons settlement. "The time has now come for action," he declared, "if the Congregational churches are to be recognized as having assumed any attitude whatever toward these vital issues of our time, upon which all the great fellowships of American churches have taken their position and have gone to work." Taylor's summons to action was part of the report of the Committee on Industry, which contained many of the same ingredients as the reports adopted by the Methodist General Conference and the Federal Council of Churches in 1908. There was a description of the present condition of industry in the nation, an indication of how other denominations had responded to the situation, a summary of the failure of Congregational agencies to support and enlarge activity in this field, and a series of recommendations by which the denomination could respond to the immediate needs. His words of challenge were embodied in a series of recommendations.[23]

When delineating what Congregationalism had not done, Taylor reviewed for the delegates what had happened to the Committee's previous recommendation to employ an Industrial Secretary, which had been approved by the National Council in 1907. Implementation of that action had been referred to the Executive Committee of the Congregational Home

---

[22]*Minutes of the National Council of the Congregational Churches of the United States* (1910), 32-33.

[23]Ibid., 222-33.

Missions Society in communication with the Provisional Committee of the National Council. The society took up the matter in January 1908, but delayed action until its next meeting in May. At that time the full Missions Society approved the establishment of a Department of Industrial Relations, but it left the details of implementation to the directors of the society.

In January 1909 the directors discussed the matter again and decided that it was "an utter impossibility under present conditions to contemplate the engagement of an executive secretary." A grant of one thousand dollars was voted to sustain the work temporarily, beginning 1 February, but on 2 March the Executive Committee took final action when it said there were no funds for such work. The report of the General Secretary of the Home Missions Society verified that action but indicated that the reason was that it seemed to fall outside the main interests of their board. With half of the assigned time of the Industrial Committee now consumed, they turned to the Provisional Committee to request the budget to employ the executive, but their appeal was declined due to lack of funds. Rather than question these past happenings, Taylor suggested that henceforth actions taken by the National Council should be cleared by the Finance Committee to be sure they were feasible. Lack of funds and delaying tactics had consumed most of the energies of the Industrial Committee for three years, and there was still no satisfactory result.[24]

In light of these frustrating experiences, and the committee's conviction regarding the importance of social service, five recommendations for action were proposed to the National Council. First, they recommended the adoption of the declaration of the Committee on the Church and Modern Industry of the Federal Council of Churches "as our own." Second, they proposed that the Congregational Council, through its Committee on Industry, cooperate with the Federal Council and its Committee on the Church and Modern Industry, and that other denominational agencies cooperate at national, state, and local levels. Third, it was urged that state conferences of Congregationalism create Committees on Industry "and get them working." Fourth, the committee suggested that the Congregational Brotherhood of America be requested to assume the function of executive agency for all matters pertaining to labor and social service, and at all levels "promote the study and knowledge of local industrial conditions and relations" and work for their solution. And, fifth, they called for the creation of a Committee on Industry during the next triennium. All five recommendations were approved and the committee was appointed. Taylor continued as a

---

[24]Ibid., 228-30, 169.

member, and Washington Gladden, Edward Steiner, and Charles Macfarland were among the other eight assigned.[25] By adopting the Federal Council's Social Creed, the Congregationalists joined the northern Baptists in affirming precisely the form mutually enacted at Philadelphia. Approval of the second recommendation kept the Congregational Churches associated with other denominations and the Federal Council in social-service activities.

This obvious interaction of Congregational and Federal Council interests was highlighted at two other points during the 1910 session of the National Council. In an evening address entitled "Industrial Obligations" following the adoption of the recommendations, H. M. Beardsley of Kansas City stated that there was "no need now for a new declaration of principles" concerning work problems and working people because the Federal Council of Churches already had "laid down a platform of principles." Much of the rest of his address elaborated on the items in that social affirmation.[26] When the Committee on Inter-Church Relations reported shortly after, it also described the organizing of the Federal Council and recommended the adoption of the resolutions in North's report "Church and Modern Industry." With the approval of that report, the Social Creed of the Churches was ratified a second time by the Congregationalists in 1910.[27] The denomination's willingness to cooperate was also obvious when it appointed a Committee on Cooperation with the National Conference of Charities and Correction, which included Gladden as a member.[28]

More important than it appeared at first glance was the National Council's endorsement of the recommendation to request the Congregational Brotherhood to assume executive responsibilities in the area of labor and social service. In the autumn the Brotherhood pursued this task and in December employed Rev. Henry A. Atkinson of Atlanta, Georgia, as Secretary of Labor and Social Service.[29] Atkinson wrote immediately to invite Gladden to the Service of Inauguration to launch the new department at Chicago on 20 January 1911. "I would consider it a great honor personally," he said, "to have you preach the sermon at

---

[25]Ibid., 230-33, 382.

[26]Ibid., 71-72.

[27]Ibid., 264-68, 373, 389.

[28]Ibid., 392.

[29]Ibid. (1913), 276.

that time and I am sure that your name on our program will give us just the sort of introduction that will be helpful in all we plan to do."[30] Although Gladden's schedule did not permit him to attend, both his presence and reputation were desired to give immediate credibility to the new venture and to tie the work into the long preparation stages in which he had pioneered. As was true with the Baptists, the men's Brotherhood became the channel through which social Christianity was integrated into the organizational life of Congregationalism.

Also meeting on a three-year cycle, the General Convention of the Protestant Episcopal Church was in session at the same time as the Congregationalists in October 1910. Its Committee on the State of the Church remarked on "the recent awakening of the civic and commercial conscience," but it admitted that allegations that the church as an institution was waning while its influence "as a pervasive force in the affairs of men" was increasing were partly true. The committee noted that there was a growth of interest in the cause of social service among church members and rejoiced that efforts to correct evils in the political order were no longer left only to individual Christians but now were being influenced by the organization and power of the church as an institution.[31]

In light of these growing and broadening interests, one of the recommendations brought to both the House of Deputies and the House of Bishops was to discharge the Joint Commission on the Relations of Capital and Labor and to establish a new Joint Commission on Social Service. The new Joint Commission should have a membership of five bishops, five ministers, and five laity, and its duties were listed as follows: ". . . to study and report upon social and industrial conditions, to coordinate the activities of the various organizations existing in the Church in the interests of social service, to cooperate with similar bodies in other Communions, to encourage sympathetic relations between capital and labor, and to deal according to their discretion with these and kindred matters."[32] Both houses approved the formation of the new Joint Commission with its broader responsibilities.[33]

---

[30]Henry A. Atkinson to Washington Gladden, 19 and 27 December 1910; Frank Dyer to Gladden, 19 December 1910, Washington Gladden Papers, Ohio Historical Society, Columbus OH.

[31]*Journal of the General Convention of the Protestant Episcopal Church in the U.S.A.* (1910), 438-39.

[32]Ibid., 538.

[33]Ibid., 110, 177, 304, 344-45, 404.

Prior to being discharged, the Joint Commission on the Relations of Capital and Labor reported on efforts of diocesan social-service committees and the preparation and distribution of literature on social issues. The death of Bishop Henry C. Potter, who was active in labor matters for many years, was noted and was one reason for ending this commission and forming another commission more broadly based on social service. Special reference was made to the reports and recommendations of the recently founded Federal Council of Churches. The report on social questions was considered "sane and forcible," and members of the Episcopal Church were encouraged to read it. Three of the Federal Council's appeals in behalf of labor were quoted from the Social Creed as deserving support—reduction of the hours of labor, one day's rest in seven, and a living wage—because they were "the direction in which improvement of labor conditions may move." No mention was made of the remaining resolutions of the ecumenical social platform, nor of the fact that these three measures were selected for immediate action by the Federal Council's Commission on the Church and Social Service. The work of Charles Stelzle and the Presbyterian Department of Church and Labor was praised as "the most notable work in any one Communion." A significant feature of the report was the declaration that the church needed to maintain a neutral position in the social order.

> The Church herself has concern not with any specific outward form of society, either political or industrial. Her concern is with the spirit which shall ultimately mould fit forms for its own expression. She cannot, therefore, stand officially for or against individualism or socialism, democracy or autocracy. But she must be hospitable towards every view which claims to utter her spirit and realize her own ideals. She must give its proponents a free hearing and trust in God's working through humanity to establish permanently only that which is of value.[34]

Such a statement in 1910 made the Protestant Episcopal Church different from the other denominations active in social Christianity, which believed the church had a more distinctive contribution to make in the Christianization of society. Beyond creating a new Joint Commission on Social Service to work in a larger social arena than the relations of capital and labor during the next three years, the General Convention committed itself to no social position, let alone a social platform of specific resolutions. And there was, up to this time, no overt effort made to create any full-time social ministry, either by a person or an agency, within the permanent organizational structure of this denomination.

---

[34]Ibid., 534-38.

Nevertheless, with an initiating independence that was feasible in the formidable-looking Episcopal polity, the Joint Commission on Social Service found a way to strengthen its work by securing a paid staff person. In the months following the 1910 General Convention the larger responsibilities of social service confirmed the need for more direction than voluntary effort could supply. In contrast to other denominations that had difficulty finding funds, the Joint Commission somehow found the money to employ a Field Secretary for Social Service, first on a half-time basis from October 1911 to October 1912, and then as a full-time position thereafter. The new field secretary was Reverend Frank M. Crouch, who previously served as assistant minister at a church in Brooklyn, New York. An office was opened in the Church Missions House in Manhattan on 1 October 1912.[35] It was not until the General Convention met again in 1913 that the Joint Commission on Social Service requested permanent standing in the church.

Despite Methodism's late start in the cause of social Christianity, its pattern of adopting a social platform and entrusting official social ministry to a recognized group was copied by other denominations in the years after 1908. Uniquely, however, by maintaining an unofficial relationship to the Methodist Episcopal Church, the Methodist Federation for Social Service enjoyed an autonomy that the other denominationally recognized agencies did not have. In its first four years, this independence was not emphasized because the advantage of official recognition by the General Conference was obvious to the leaders of the nascent federation. Thus, in spite of its legal autonomy, the Methodist Federation for Social Service functioned much like the other denominational commissions or committees. An examination of its official minutes showed more of its evolution than its cumulative quadrennial report did and revealed how a denominational program became involved in an emerging cooperative social-service effort through the Federal Council of Churches. The experience of the Methodist Federation will serve as a model for what developed similarly in the other denominations.

Following the reorganization of the Executive Committee in November 1908, when the Methodist Federation for Social Service realized it could not afford a full-time leader and had to divide the responsibilities functionally in order to carry on its program on a voluntary basis, its work was implemented by a small group of people who were hampered by limited finances. A called meeting of the General Council of the Federation at Chautauqua, New York, in July 1909, when North delivered his "The City

<hr>

[35]Harry F. Ward, *A Year Book of the Church and Social Service in the United States* (New York: Fleming H. Revell Co., 1914) 56, 186.

and the Kingdom" address, did not have a quorum, but the six members present met with the governing board of the Methodist Brotherhood to discuss ways to involve laymen in the cause. The main result was agreement that a monthly periodical, tentatively titled *The Gospel of the Kingdom*, would be a useful resource.[36]

When the Executive Committee met in New York City the next December, strategy for the future was developed. It was agreed that its mission should be "education and inspiration rather than to undertake executive functions." Also it was felt that the federation should not do the the social work of the church, but should seek to promote "the spirit of Social Service" throughout the denomination, and especially through its various agencies. To carry out these duties, it was recognized that they needed to expand the membership to get a larger number of persons working on the vast task. Their goal was to employ a full-time secretary to lead the federation when there was enough money. Faced with a large area of ministry and few members, and lacking the impetus to influence an imminent General Conference, the federation in its own records indicated the enormity of the tasks they took up.[37] However, when they submitted a description of the organization to the *Methodist Year Book* for 1910, they took a positive approach and listed activities that were being carried on at all levels of the church: organizing local branches, addressing groups, supporting legislation, collecting data, cooperating with Methodist Brotherhoods, preparing a course of social studies for ministers, relating to charity organizations, and publishing pamphlets and books.[38]

Actually, the federation's main accomplishment was in the area of publications, where a number of small pamphlets and leaflets were printed and two books were published. Worth Tippy edited a volume of the addresses at the National Conference of Methodist Social Workers that was published as *The Socialized Church* in 1909.[39] In 1910 Harry Ward began his work as editorial secretary by editing a volume of twelve papers titled *Social Ministry:*

---

[36]"Minutes of the Methodist Federation for Social Service, 1907–1930," unpublished MS, Rose Memorial Library, Drew University, Madison NJ, 20-23 July 1909, 55-59; 1 December 1910, 118.

[37]Ibid., 21 December 1909, 105.

[38]*The Methodist Year Book* (1910), 148-49.

[39]Worth M. Tippy, ed., *The Socialized Church: Addresses before the First National Conference of the Social Workers of Methodism, St. Louis, November 17-19, 1908* (New York: Eaton & Mains, 1909).

An Introduction to the Study and Practice of Social Service. Eight of the twelve papers were by persons active in the federation's leadership, and Ward's preface indicated frustration that all the promised contributors had not completed their work.[40] The continuing emphasis on publications was evident at the December 1910 meeting of the Executive Committee, when the editorial secretary "was requested to prepare at an early date a hand-book of Social Service, a Commentary on the Social Creed of Methodism, a plan of Social Service for village and rural churches, and several other publications."[41] One month later, the federation published the first number of *The Social Service Bulletin*, which was edited by Ward.[42]

Caught between recognized needs and noble motivations on the one hand, and disadvantages of geographic separation and voluntary leadership by persons who already had busy jobs on the other, the federation experienced frustration in these years. Securing full-time leadership seemed to be the most obvious solution to the dilemma, but insufficient funding only added to the disturbing condition. In light of the organization's emphasis on publications, which made the editorial secretary a central figure, and of Ward's ability, interest, and willingness to assume larger responsibilities, his gravitation to the leadership of the organization was a natural development that was stymied only by lack of money. In a letter to Worth Tippy, Frank Mason North accurately summarized the situation when he agreed that Ward's work "will be less than satisfactory unless he can give his entire time to the Federation. It would seem to me to be simply a matter of the raising of the budget." North concurred that "the plan suggested is the right one if it can be carried through," but he pleaded "great financial strain" in his own program.[43] Finally, in October 1911, President Herbert Welch announced that Harry F. Ward had been engaged as part-time executive secretary, and with that move the Methodist Federation for Social Service entered a new stage in its history.[44]

The announcement in October that the federation had an executive secretary, coupled with the beginning of the *Social Service Bulletin* in January,

---

[40]Harry Ward, ed., *Social Ministry: An Introduction to the Study and Practice of Social Service* (New York: Eaton & Mains; Cincinnati: Jennings & Graham, 1910).

[41]"Minutes of the Methodist Federation for Social Service," 1 December 1910, 105.

[42]*The Social Service Bulletin* (January 1911).

[43]Frank Mason North to Worth M. Tippy, 14 March 1911, Worth M. Tippy Papers, Archives of DePaul University and Indiana Methodism, Greencastle IN.

[44]*The Social Service Bulletin* (October 1911): 1.

marked 1911 as an important year in the organization's development. Since Ward was the central figure in both, that year also marked his emergence as the leader of the Methodist Federation for Social Service. In addition, during 1911 Ward became more involved in the social ministry of the Federal Council of Churches, where he served on the Committee on Literature and was added to the Committee of Direction.[45] In the latter he was part of the leadership that met monthly to guide the council, and on the former he coordinated publications with a group consisting of Samuel Batten, Graham Taylor, Jacob Riis, Walter Rauschenbusch, and Charles S. Macfarland. It was Macfarland, who was employed 1 May 1911 as full-time secretary of the Federal Council's Commission on the Church and Social Service, who added Ward to the Committee of Direction.[46] Those appointments brought Ward and the Methodist Federation more fully into Federal Council activities, although North already was a leader in the council, and Ward previously had gravitated to the ecumenical agency through his duties as editorial secretary of the federation.

Harry Ward's work as editor of a book on the Social Creed actually documented the subtle but steady meshing of the social-service activities of the Methodist Federation and the Federal Council of Churches. In December 1909 the federation's Executive Committee approved his preparation of a book "on the Social Creed of Methodism."[47] A year later they asked him as editorial secretary to prepare several books, among them "a Commentary on the Social Creed of Methodism."[48] Ward reported in November 1910 that "the handbook expounding the Social Creed of Methodism is in preparation."[49] However, in the first issue of the *Social Service Bulletin* in January 1911, Ward expressed hope that the first cooperative publication of the Federal Council Commission on the Church and Social Service would be "the little handbook which we have prepared, explaining and applying the 'Social Creed' that has been adopted by all the large Protestant denominations."[50] The October 1911 issue of the same peri-

---

[45]Ibid.

[46]*Annual Report of the Executive Committee of the Federal Council of the Churches of Christ in America* (1911), 33, 35.

[47]"Minutes of the Methodist Federation for Social Service," 21 December 1909, 87.

[48]Ibid., 1 December 1910, 105.

[49]Ibid., 29 November 1910, typed report of the editorial secretary, 122.

[50]*The Social Service Bulletin* (January 1911): 2.

odical announced that Ward's book "explaining and expounding the Social Creed of the Churches, will become the first common publication."[51] Ward's *The Social Creed of the Churches* appeared in print in 1912 with the following statement opposite the title page: "Authorized by the Commission on The Church and Social Service of the Federal Council of the Churches of Christ in America."[52]

Since the Methodist Episcopal Church already had approved the Methodist Federation for Social Service and adopted a Social Creed before the Federal Council met in 1908, it did not have to follow precisely the same steps as the other socially involved denominations. Nevertheless, the course of development taken by the Methodist Federation was remarkably similar in goals and emphases to the other agencies. Though the details varied from denomination to denomination, the programs developed, the problems faced, the need for funds, the difficulty securing full-time leadership, and the growing relationship of each church's social-service program to the Federal Council of Churches were much alike in each of the five Protestant bodies. While sufficient motive and causation existed in each tradition to justify some of the developments, it was apparent that the Federal Council of Churches was an outside influence that affected each of the denominations. Certainly the stimulus of the "Church and Modern Industry" report, with its platform of social principles, was clear. Not as obvious, but nonetheless real, were the accelerated efforts to secure full-time Social Service Secretaries in each of the churches during 1911 and 1912. Examination of the Federal Council's development after December 1908 indicates that its evolution had a catalytic effect upon the denominations.

Although it tended to get lost in the public acclamation over the Social Creed pronouncements, approval by the Federal Council of the recommendation to create its own Commission on the Church and Social Service was functionally important, not only for the cause of social Christianity but also for the continuity of the Council itself. Frank Mason North continued as its chairman following his rousing address, and representatives of various constituent bodies were appointed to its ranks. Among its members were several who were long active in social interests: Josiah Strong, Graham Taylor, Charles Stelzle, Samuel Batten, Shailer Math-

---

[51]Ibid. (October 1911): 2.

[52]Harry F. Ward, *The Social Creed of the Churches* (New York: Eaton & Mains; Cincinnati: Jennings & Graham, 1912).

ews, Walter Rauschenbusch, Herbert Welch, and Levi Gilbert.[53] Impressive as the list was, limited finances made it impossible to assemble the members, and only a small group of volunteers in the New York region and correspondence enabled the commission to function. Charles Stelzle volunteered his time and energy for administrative and executive services, carrying on extensive correspondence to stimulate interest, and establishing a relationship with labor for the Federal Council. Josiah Strong headed the Research Committee. Inexpensive pamphlets were distributed to publicize the commission's existence. A volunteer committee investigated problems in the steel industry in Pennsylvania. If not for Stelzle, there would have been no activity, but much of it was of a tentative and temporary quality during the first two years.[54] Provisional as the work of the Church and Social Service Commission was, it was the only active department of the Federal Council in the first years. While some envisaged the commission transforming the church and society overnight, the reality was that the constituent denominations provided blessing and encouragement but no resources. As the delegates went home from the Philadelphia meeting, they seemed to forget the organization they had created. Charles Macfarland remembered that in 1911 the Federal Council administratively "consisted of little more than a constitution, a small office and a typewriter."[55] The concepts of both church federation and social service were really held together by a very few people. If it had not been for small pamphlets published sporadically, its existence might have gone unnoticed. In "A Plan of Social Work," published in 1911, the rhetoric was impressive—"Social service is thus in part the basis of the Federal Council, and the Federal Council offers the basis for Social Service"— but that circular indicated little substance beyond words.[56] At that junc-

---

[53]Elias B. Sanford, ed., *Federal Council of the Churches of Christ in America: Report of the First Meeting of the Federal Council, Philadelphia, 1908* (New York: Revell Press, 1909) 242, 529.

[54]"Points of Progress in 1910" (N.p., n.d. [21 March 1910]); "Enlargement of Work in 1910. November Bulletin" (N.p., n.d. [1910]); Charles S. Macfarland, "The Kingdoms of This World; The Kingdom of Our Lord," *Christian Unity at Work: The Federal Council of the Churches of Christ in America in Quadrennial Session at Chicago, Illinois, 1912,* ed. Charles S. Macfarland (New York: Federal Council of Churches, 1913) 155-56.

[55]Charles S. Macfarland, *Across the Years* (New York: Macmillan Co., 1936) 88-90.

[56]"A Plan of Social Work. Prepared by the Federal Council Commission on the Church and Social Service, Charles S. Macfarland, Secretary" (New York: National Offices, n.d. [1911]; "Bulletin of Results: Inter-Church Federation at Work" (N.p., November 1911).

ture, only a radical move of faith to employ an executive for the faltering commission redeemed the situation.

Since the council's executive secretary, Elias B. Sanford, suffered poor health and could not get the new organization off the ground, it was decided to seek another secretary for the only functioning part of the organization, the Church and Social Service Commission. For months the volunteer leaders looked in vain because no one was willing to lead the struggling group. Charles Macfarland first encountered the organization when he attended its Executive Committee at Washington in December 1910 to urge that the commission should be adequately administered. When it was suggested later that he undertake the work, he declined because he knew that Frank Mason North also was being considered and felt North was more qualified. However, when North decided to continue his Methodist responsibilities, Macfarland accepted the invitation.[57]

Charles Macfarland was forty-five years old when he took up the work on 1 May 1911. He brought with him a genuine interest in the social ministry of the church, but only from the perspective of a pastor of Congregational churches. His outlook was admittedly opportunistic. An address to students at Yale Divinity School during the winter of 1908–1909 indicated that he was almost crassly pragmatic. Arguing that a minister should wield political power by openly and directly influencing the men in his congregation, Macfarland went on to explain, "He must do it by every means—by appeal, by rebuke, by exhortation, by condemnation, by persuasion, by every weapon or seduction at his hands. It is a splendid thing for a man to feel that he thus dominates the political, the social, and the civic life of a city—that he is a general commanding the very forces of the universe." Asked how ministers might gain such power, he answered, simply, "Above all things, such a minister needs to be (of course in the higher sense of the term) an opportunist."[58]

On the basis of such opportunism, Macfarland took the line of least resistance when he assumed his work with the Social Service Commission, because he believed it was also the line of greatest opportunity. To his thinking, social service should be the area of first advance by the Federal Council because it was the new area of service in which the denominations had not yet developed much programming. In that area they

---

[57]Macfarland, *Across the Years*, 87-88.

[58]"The Part and Place of the Church and the Ministry in the Realization of Democracy," in *The Christian Ministry and the Social Order: Lectures Delivered in the Course in Pastoral Functions at Yale Divinity School, 1908–1909*, ed. Charles S. Macfarland (New Haven: Yale University Press, 1909) 32-33, 34, 36.

wanted leadership; in other areas Federal Council activity was considered competitive. "It was, at one and the same time, the line of least resistance and of the greatest compulsion," he remarked later.[59] Macfarland's assessment of the opportunity was essentially accurate, and his outlook enabled him to take advantage of circumstances to move rapidly and strategically.

In December 1911 the Executive Committee of the Federal Council of Churches met at Pittsburgh and heard Macfarland present his first report as full-time secretary of the Commission on the Church and Social Service. Observing that social problems were urgent and serious, Macfarland stated his understanding of the church's role in the social order.

> The Christian Church has the three-fold vocation of conscience, interpreter and guide of all social movements. She should determine what their motive and conscience should be, and impose that conscience upon them. She should interpret their inner and ultimate meaning. Then, with a powerful hand and mind and heart, guide them towards their spiritual ends. The task of the Church is to transform a chaotic democracy into an ordered Kingdom of Heaven.[60]

That this concept was basic to his thinking was obvious in the next few months when it was repeated with only slight modifications in an address to the Religious Education Association in March[61] and in his book *Spiritual Culture and Social Service*, which consisted of utterances previously made to his congregations.[62]

Macfarland's functional style also was evident in three ways in the report. First, he added several more persons to the commission's Committee of Direction. Since this new group included Ward, Atkinson, and Gladden, it was clear that he wanted both functional denominational social leaders and persons with social-gospel reputations in its membership. Second, he made "elaborate plans for publications" through the Committee on Literature, which consisted of Batten, Taylor, Ward, Riis,

---

[59]Charles S. Macfarland, "Twenty Years in Retrospect," *Twenty Years of Church Federation: Report of the Federal Council of the Churches of Christ in America, 1924–1928*, ed. Samuel McCrea Cavert (New York: Federal Council of Churches, 1929) 29; idem, *Christian Unity in Practice and Prophecy* (New York: Macmillan Co., 1933) 60.

[60]*Annual Report of the Executive Committee* (1911) 39.

[61]Charles S. Macfarland, "The World of Toil as a Field of Religious Leadership," *Religious Education* 7 (June 1912): 146.

[62]Charles S. Macfarland, *Spiritual Culture and Social Service* (New York: Fleming H. Revell Co., 1912) 9, 17.

Rauschenbusch, and Macfarland. This membership combined some of the best minds in the field, and the committee was influential and effective in planning coordinated publications that made good use of limited funds. And, third, Macfarland by letter and at conferences attempted to instruct social workers in ways to work more closely with churches. By these methods, within seven months Macfarland strengthened his own organization, improved his coordination with denominational social-service programs, and reached out to related movements for social betterment. These were rapid and ambitious new steps for the commission, which quickly felt Macfarland's presence.[63] Such initiative and creativity continued to be evident during 1912.[64]

Significant as these steps were, Macfarland's wisest venture probably was to encourage the denominational Commissions on Social Service to employ staff persons and then to coordinate the efforts of these field secretaries. While there was recognized need for such personnel in each denomination, there was a remarkable correlation in timing between Macfarland's assuming his post with the Federal Council and the hiring of Ward, Crouch, and Batten by their denominations. When Macfarland organized a Secretarial Council within his commission to coordinate officially the social-service activities of denominations employing half-time or full-time personnel in that area, he created the means to unify the previously disparate activities of the individual church bodies. With that impulse, five denominations employed six full-time Social Service secretaries by the time the Federal Council of Churches met again in December 1912: Henry A. Atkinson, secretary of the Congregational Brotherhood; Samuel Z. Batten, secretary of the Baptist Department of Social Service and Brotherhood; Frank M. Crouch, field secretary of the Protestant Episcopal Joint Commission on Social Service; Charles Stelzle, superintendent of the Presbyterian Bureau of Social Service; Harry F. Ward, secretary of the Methodist Federation for Social Service; and Warren Wilson, superintendent of the Presbyterian Department of the Church and Country Life. Prior to that meeting, the Committee of Direction elected each as associate secretary of the Federal Council Commission. Macfarland's evaluation of this process was evident when he told the Federal Council in 1912: "The most important procedure in the mutual association of the denominational movements was the organization of a Secretarial Council."[65]

---

[63] *Annual Report of the Executive Committee* (1911) 33-35.

[64] Charles S. Macfarland, "Christian Unity in Fact and Practice. From January 1 to June 1, 1912" (N.p., 1 June 1912) 1-4.

[65] Charles S. Macfarland, "The Kingdoms of This World," *Christian Unity at Work*, 159.

During the four years from 1909 to 1912, there was a remarkable development of social-service interest and organization within the five denominations most active in social Christianity. Most of these bodies committed themselves to official social platforms, and all solidified their social-service agencies to the point of employing full-time personnel. Furthermore, the new Federal Council of Churches not only joined in this growing social ministry but also became the catalytic agency that helped the several movements reach fruition. In addition, the Federal Council then coordinated the developing programs so that it became the hub that centralized the programming and resources of the separate agencies. These developments led Walter Rauschenbusch to conclude in 1912, "The rise of social Christianity is felt in all the institutional agencies of the American Churches."[66] Although his assessment may have been an overgeneralization if all thirty-four denominations of the Federal Council were considered, it was a fair evaluation of what had emerged in the five most socially active denominations and in the Federal Council itself.

This growth of social activity in official Protestant agencies between 1909 and 1912 showed that the inner dynamic of the social movement in the churches had become strong enough for denominations not only to fulfill the commitment of conscience adopted in December 1908, but also to move beyond the expectations of that time. Moreover, the energy of that dynamic was sufficient to overcome the potentially negative impact of the spiritual and political unrest of the time. If anything, that unrest stimulated a simultaneous evangelistic campaign in the nation that coordinated with the advances of the social gospel.

---

[66]Walter Rauschenbusch, *Christianizing the Social Order* (New York: Macmillan Co., 1912) 17.

CHAPTER 10

The Men and Religion Forward Movement

The Men and Religion Forward Movement of 1911–1912 is another evidence of the ascendency of social Christianity. It was the most comprehensive evangelistic movement ever undertaken in this country and was planned with consummate care and ability. . . . All the varied departments of the movement found their spiritual center and unity in the idea of the Kingdom of God on earth, which is the doctrine of social Christianity. When the movement began to be tried out, it grew increasingly plain that it was the trumpet call of the social gospel which rallied the audiences and brought men under moral and religious conviction.

(Walter Rauschenbusch,
Christianizing the Social Order, *1912)*

DURING THE SAME YEARS THAT INSTITUTIONAL AGENCIES of the churches were organizing for social service, there was parallel planning for what Walter Rauschenbusch described as "the most comprehensive evangelistic movement ever undertaken in this country." The Men and Religion Forward Movement originated in 1910 and turned its work back to denominational and other church agencies in 1912. In its two-year existence, the revival movement attracted widespread attention and was "another evidence of the ascendency of social Christianity," according to Rauschenbusch.[1] Since the movement combined evangelism and social

---

[1]Walter Rauschenbusch, *Christianizing the Social Order* (New York: Macmillan Co., 1912) 19.

Christianity, it offered the promise of the long-expected great awakening of the church.

At a meeting in New York City, 18 May 1910, fifty-four representatives of denominational brotherhood organizations, the men's and boys' departments of the Sunday schools, and the Young Men's Christian Association agreed unanimously to undertake a campaign to vitalize Protestantism. The object of the movement was to secure the personal commitment of men and boys to Jesus Christ and to enlist them in a program to carry their faith into all their daily affairs in the world. To this end, six emphases were designated for special work: Bible study, boys' work, evangelism, community extension, missions, and social service. The formal declaration of the social emphasis revealed the following goals: "to increase the permanent contribution of the Church to the best life of the Continent, socially, commercially and physically, and to emphasize the modern message of the Church in social service and usefulness." The movement was sponsored by three groups: the men's brotherhoods of ten denominations, the International Committee of the Young Men's Christian Association, and the International Sunday School Association.[2]

This men's movement not only was "planned with consummate care and ability" but also was unique in the history of religion because it approached religion on what "amounts to a business basis." The business basis was evident in several ways. Preparations were started sixteen months prior to the start of the eight-month public campaign. Prominent business and professional men such as J. P. Morgan, Cyrus McCormick, John D. Rockefeller, Jr., John Wanamaker, and William Jennings Bryan played leading parts. The Committee of Ninety- Seven coordinated the planning on a voluntary basis and employed a staff of several persons, headed by campaign leader Fred B. Smith and executive secretary Roy B. Guild. Campaigns were planned in seventy cities, with each carefully organized by a chairman and executive secretary. In addition, teams of experts were created to serve as resources throughout the country for each of the six emphases. Moreover, the movement paid its own way and promised not to create any new permanent machinery in Protestantism.[3]

---

[2]"Report of the Committee of Ninety- Seven," *Messages of the Men and Religion Movement. Complete in Seven Volumes; Including the Revised Reports of the Commissions Presented at the Congress of the Men and Religion Forward Movement, April, 1912, Together with the Principal Addresses Delivered at the Congress* (New York: Association Press, 1912) 1:13-16, 19-20.

[3]Ibid., 1:16-27; *New York Times*, 15 May 1911, p. 10; 4 June 1911, pt. 5, p. 14; Rauschenbusch, *Christianizing the Social Order*, 19.

Its businesslike character also was evident in its functional style. The Forward Movement began with a banquet of 400 men at the Hotel Astor in New York City on a Friday evening, and the following Sunday special speakers filled the pulpits of many of the city's churches. When the public campaign approached its climax in New York in 1912, advertisements were published on the sports pages of the daily papers and also on a large electric sign at 23rd Street. The advertising approach was criticized by some as being too commercialized, but it exemplified the functional business orientation applied to the evangelistic endeavor.[4]

By design, the Forward Movement was announced on 15 May 1911, and its purpose and approach were publicized. However, the concentrated public portion of the campaign did not begin until 24 September when a Rally Day was held across the nation. In succeeding months local conventions were scheduled for seventy cities, with the culmination in Chicago and New York in mid- April. The central focus was the Christian Conservation Congress at New York City, 19-24 April 1912. At those sessions in Carnegie Hall, the Men and Religion Forward Movement claimed an attendance of 1,338 from 37 states, and on Sunday, 21 April, speakers in churches throughout the city were reported to have reached 100,000 people.[5]

In this evangelistic campaign, social Christianity was a primary ingredient. As noted previously, from the earliest stages a social-service interest was one of the six emphases. When the Men and Religion Forward Movement was launched on 15 May 1911, the announcement was made by social activist Charles Stelzle, and the headquarters was in his office. As interpreted by him, the program was "a new movement, with social reform as its aim." It represented leading churches that hoped to involve churchmen in consideration of such topics as housing, health, education, recreation, welfare, and industrial conditions.[6] His interpretation leaned more heavily to social themes than campaign leader Fred Smith's explanation: "The ultimate object of the movement in a nutshell is, of course, to make real the Christian ideal from the individual clear out into the last recesses of society."[7]

---

[4]New York Times, 4 June 1911, pt. 5, p. 14; 10 June 1911, p. 22; 6 March 1912, p. 1; 11 March 1912, p. 1; 12 March 1912, p. 12; 13 March 1912, p. 11; Western Christian Advocate (Cincinnati), 10 April 1912, p. 6.

[5]William T. Ellis, "The Christian Conservation Congress," Messages of the Men and Religion Movement, 1:1-4; New York Times, 15 May 1911, p. 10; 4 June 1911, pt. 5, p. 14; 22 April 1912, p. 13.

[6]New York Times, 15 May 1911, p. 10.

[7]Ibid., 4 June 1911, pt. 5, p. 14.

At the outset, the leaders did not intend to give the social message the prominence it gradually acquired, but the social-service component attracted the largest attendance in all but two or three of the city conventions. Such response may have reflected the energy and effort of Stelzle and the other social-service experts—J. W. Magruder, Graham Taylor, I. J. Lansing, and Raymond Robins—but it also evidenced the extent of social interest among men across the nation at the time.[8]

Unquestionably, Stelzle deserved much of the credit for the social interest. For eight months he served as dean of the Social Service Department of the Men and Religion Forward Movement, in addition to his duties as superintendent of the Bureau of Social Service of the Presbyterian Church in the United States of America. In that role he prepared survey forms, designed charts, and organized statistical data accumulated in the seventy principal cities involved in the Forward Movement. His office also prepared the exhibits displayed at the Christian Conservation Congress. Personally, Stelzle served as a leader in various cities across the country.[9] After the movement ended, he compiled the charts and statistics regarding conditions in the seventy cities, interpreted their meaning, and proposed recommendations based on them in a book titled *American Social and Religious Conditions*, which was published in 1912.[10]

Less obvious, but genuine, contributions were requested and provided by other social-gospel advocates during the evangelistic effort. On 1 May 1911 executive secretary Roy Guild wrote to Rauschenbusch asking that he write articles on the Forward Movement for *Harper's Weekly* for the last week in September and for the *North American Review* in October. Clearly desiring to make use of the professor's national reputation in conjunction with the Rally Day on 24 September, Guild appealed to him to "render the Movement a signal service," even after the teacher indicated he could not do so because of weariness from delivering sixty addresses, in addition to his professional duties and his need to complete a book by the beginning of September. "Even a willing horse can get winded," he apologized.[11] Nevertheless, he spoke at the

---

[8]"Report of the Committee of Ninety-Seven," *Messages of the Men and Religion Movement*, 1:22, 29.

[9]*Minutes of the General Assembly of the Presbyterian Church in the United States of America*, n.s. (1912), 374.

[10]Charles Stelzle, *American Social and Religious Conditions* (New York: Fleming H. Revell Co., 1912) esp. Appendixes A and B.

[11]Roy B. Guild to Walter Rauschenbusch, 1 May 1911; Rauschenbusch to Guild, 4 May 1911; Guild to Rauschenbusch, 8 May 1911, Walter Rauschenbusch Papers, American Baptist Historical Society, Rochester NY.

close of the Men and Religion Forward Movement in Chicago, presented an address at the Conservation Congress, and contributed to the report of the Social Service Commission to that mass meeting.[12]

In a similar way, Fred B. Smith asked Washington Gladden to help in the final stages of the movement. On 29 February 1912 he asked Gladden to be on an emergency roll of "Count on Me's," whose names would be "kept sacredly confidential" and not be part of the formal organization. After agreeing to be one of the "pledged 'minute men,' who may be counted on to do practical service," the Columbus elder statesman was asked to write a piece for use in the religious press, which Smith praised as the most helpful single statement of the past year. Also Smith requested that Gladden preach in a New York church on Sunday, 21 April, during the Conservation Congress.[13] Like Rauschenbusch, Gladden was a member of the Social Service Commission, helped to write its report, and presented a paper to that congress.[14]

The climax of the Men and Religion Forward Movement was the Christian Conservation Congress in New York City, 19-24 April 1912. In businesslike fashion, the statistics of 1911-1912 were reported by the Committee of Ninety- Seven: there had been 9,832 addresses at 7,062 meetings, plus 2,403 committee sessions; there were 7,580 conversions in an evangelistic attendance of 326,000, and 26,000 pledges to active personal service in the world in a total attendance of 1,491,245 at all the meetings; and all debts were paid.[15] The committee then handed over to the denominations and organizations of the Christian Church all the work and records of the Forward Movement, with the assurance that "this national meeting will be remembered as marking the entrance of American churches into a new era of comprehensive Christian service."[16]

---

[12]Walter Rauschenbusch, "The Conservation of the Social Service Message," *Messages of the Men and Religion Movement*, 2:121-25; *Record-Herald* (Chicago), 15 April 1912, in "Scrapbooks," Rauschenbusch Papers.

[13]Fred B. Smith to Washington Gladden, 29 February 1912; 21 March 1912; 23 March 1912. Washington Gladden Papers, Ohio Historical Society, Columbus OH.

[14]Washington Gladden, "The Church and Social Service," *Messages of the Men and Religion Movement*, 2:126-29; H.D.W. English to Gladden, 16 March 1912, Gladden Papers.

[15]"Report of the Committee of Ninety-Seven," *Messages of the Men and Religion Movement*, 1:23, 28; *New York Times*, 25 April 1912, p. 12.

[16]*Messages of the Men and Religion Movement*, 1:4, 10.

"What is Christian social service?" asked Henry Sloane Coffin, who, as chairman, introduced the Report of the Social Service Commission to the Conservation Congress. "It is everything that men plan and do to accomplish the purpose of God in Jesus Christ . . . for the whole world," he answered. With that all-inclusive sweep it included evangelism, missions, church unity, and every topic reported to the congress. "This entire movement is a conspicuous national social service," he declared. Accordingly,

> the report contains references to saved baseball, redeemed penitentiaries, regenerated government, sanctified tenements, to business born again. It recognizes the importance of the house in which a man lives, the food he eats, the conditions under which he works, the forms of recreation he takes, the system of political authority by which he is ruled—above all, the ideals of the home, of industry, of amusement, of government which control his conscience, shape his soul and affect his eternal destiny.[17]

The commission believed that Christianized social institutions created Christian men, although it recognized that Christians could differ over the directions the church should take when reconstructing society. Essentially, according to the report, the church's mission was to inspire rather than dominate, to furnish ideals rather than give directions, to supply motives rather than run agencies.[18]

The lengthy Report of the Social Service Commission reflected the definitions stated by Coffin, but certain portions provided additional clarification and insight. At one point the polarity between social service and evangelism was noted, since some disparaged the former because it dealt only with temporary relations while the latter dealt with eternal destiny. In contrast, the commission affirmed that "social service affects conditions which shape immortal souls, and social relations . . . have permanent significance" because those who are not good neighbors in an earthly city are hardly desirable tenents of the New Jerusalem. To them, the social outlook should be vitally connected to evangelism. Indeed, the commission's concept was so lofty that they declared, "Social reponsibility is the chief sacrament of religion in our age."[19] It was the conclusion of the Social Service Commission that the Men and Religion Forward Movement in the past six months had convinced American Christians that Christian churches had to be organically and vitally related to the

---

[17]"What Is Social Service?," ibid., 2:111-12.

[18]Ibid., 2:115-16.

[19]Ibid., 2:1-108. Specific references here are located on pp. 13-15.

communities with which they coexisted. Thus, the business of the churches was not "to edify and comfort and sanctify the people whom they are able to gather out of the community," but rather "to pour a constant stream of saving influence into the civic life and the industrial life and the professional life and the educational life and the philanthropic life and the social life, of the community."[20]

Gladden's address to the Conservation Congress expressed the theory of the report so closely that it added nothing new. But Rauschenbusch's address "The Conservation of the Social Service Message" provided supplementary understanding. On the one hand, he affirmed that the Men and Religion Forward Movement "marked a definite advance of the social gospel in the Christian Church in America" and would be memorable for that, if not for anything more. As a consequence, "the social gospel has now come to be one of the dogmas of the Christian faith." But since that progress had been achieved, it became important, on the other hand, to consider how to conserve the results. "I should like to prophesy that within a short time a reactionary movement is likely to take place," he warned. The old men who cared for the old points would not allow the new points to force their way in without contradicting them. Insisting that he did not blame or scorn such persons, he urged that it was necessary "to stand up against that reaction when it comes" if the motion of the Forward Movement was to be conserved. Another way to conserve the results of the social approach, he suggested, must be to "socialize our theology" and "make it part of the institutional church."[21] Once again keenly aware of the state of the American churches, Rauschenbusch foresaw the needs of the next several years in light of the progress of social Christianity in 1911–1912.

Late in April 1912, when Rauschenbusch spoke those words, the danger and direction to which he pointed did not seem nearly as apparent as the sense of destiny and achievement felt by the thousands touched by the Men and Religion Forward Movement. During the Conservation Congress a journalist reported, "In numerical attendance and emotional enthusiasm the meetings surpassed expectations."[22] An editorial in the *New York Times* commented that the object of the Forward Movement had been served: ". . . the practical application of religion to the enormous problems, social, political, and commercial, with which the country is

---

[20]Ibid., 2:90-91.

[21]Ibid., 2:121-23.

[22]*New York Times*, 22 April 1912, p. 13.

confronted. In the words of one of the members, the country must be cleaned up in the name of religion." The editorial concluded that no thinking person could question the movement's practicality: "From the purely practical point of view no recent effort at so-called 'social uplift' is nearly so encouraging."[23] In the estimation of the New York newspaper, the Men and Religion Forward Movement was evaluated solely in terms of its social application and outreach.

When Harry E. Fosdick reported as president of the Baptist Brotherhood to the Northern Baptist Convention a month later, he praised the enthusiasm for reform measures and for missions that resulted from the Forward Movement, but he also said that it remained for men in the local churches to implement the full dimensions of the Conservation Congress.[24] That same month a report on the Men and Religion Forward Movement to the General Assembly of the northern Presbyterians recognized the nationwide attention it had received and the great impression it had made on individual churches and communities, but the report stated that it was "too soon to judge the effects of this movement." On the basis of the press, the report continued, "the one great feature was the Social Betterment of Mankind"; however, it questioned whether that was a revival of religion and urged the church to pray for the manifestation of the presence of God's Spirit in the church that would mark a true revival of religion.[25]

During the year following the close of the Men and Religion Forward Movement, Fred B. Smith wrote a book titled *A Man's Religion*, in which he revealed insights gained in the campaign.[26] Among these was a chapter on "A Religion of Social Service," in which he admitted that no growth in Christianity during the past twenty years had been as marvelous as that which manifested itself in improvements in the social realm. "The social service message and its expositors have had much to do with bringing about this result," he acknowledged. Admitting that he had spent most of his life in the field of evangelism with an emphasis on the conversion of the individual, Smith went on to indicate the change the movement made in his thinking. At that juncture, he decided, "In this twentieth century, red-blooded, high-minded men, of large vision and keen

---

[23]Ibid., 26 April 1912, p. 10.

[24]*Annual of the Northern Baptist Convention* (1912) 159-60.

[25]*Minutes of the General Assembly* (1912) 295.

[26]Fred B. Smith, *A Man's Religion* (New York: Association Press, 1913) 147-50, 174-75.

intelligence, will no longer be found in any church or other organization which neglects the unlimited opportunities offered by social service in the name of the Lord and Master. This is the most powerful magnet in religion at the present time."

Because of long interest in a new evangelism with a strong social emphasis, it was not surprising to find that Rauschenbusch, Gladden, North, and Taylor appreciated the Men and Religion Forward Movement and willingly shared in its program. All four were among the eleven-member Social Service Commission chaired by Henry Sloane Coffin, and they contributed to the report it submitted. The significance of the evangelistic campaign in the development of social Christianity was obvious in the high appraisal of Rauschenbusch shortly after it ended.

> The movement has probably done more than any other single agency to lodge the social gospel in the common mind of the Church. It has made social Christianity orthodox. But in turn it has shown what spiritual power lies in store in the Kingdom ideal, and has proved that the present generation, in the nation and in the Church, will not be satisfied with any kind of Christianity that does not undertake to Christianize the social order.[27]

---

[27]Rauschenbusch, *Christianizing the Social Order*, 20.

CHAPTER 11

The Social Awakening
of the Churches

When a great spiritual movement like the social awakening shakes
our nation to the depths, we may be sure that the churches will
respond to it and have an active part in it. And so we find it.

(Walter Rauschenbusch,
Christianizing the Social Order, *1912)*

WHAT ADVOCATES OF SOCIAL CHRISTIANITY THOUGHT about the changes that
were going on around them in both church and nation affected the
meaning they found in these events. It was one thing to call for a response
by the churches in light of an obvious social crisis, but was the adoption
of social platforms and the creation of social-service agencies staffed by
full-time executives an appropriate answer? Earlier it had been enough to
recognize the need for a religious awakening as well as a social salvation,
but now that there had been an evangelistic awakening with a popular
social component, did it meet the intended need? During 1911 and 1912
such questions were pondered by some social-gospel proponents, and the
answers influenced the way those persons understood and interpreted
their times.

James Whiton, for instance, had long proclaimed that a moral crisis
existed in the nation, but by 1908 he saw signs that "something like a moral
revival" was occurring. During 1910 and 1911 he continued to tell the New
York State Conference of Religion that a moral awakening was under way,
but he felt it was neither complete nor sufficiently righteous to let up their
efforts.[1] Similarly, the Religious Education Association Declaration of

---

[1] *Addresses before the New York State Conference of Religion*, ser. 9 (April 1911): 45-
47; ser. 10 (June 1912): 29-30.

Principles in the same years noted "the great ethical passion of our time" and the "moral awakening" in recent years.[2] In 1911 Jane Addams's address to the educators said that no one could ignore "the great social awakening at present going forward in the churches," and she hoped that differences between progressive churchmen and social reformers could be amicably negotiated so that they might all live "in the sense of a religious revival."[3] By 1912 the Religious Education Association Declaration recognized "the social question as the burning issue of the day."[4] In November of that year, Whiton told the Conference of Religion, which he headed, that the current moral awakening seemed to be an auspicious sign that the churches qualified for the moral leadership of the nation.[5]

This emerging consensus in understanding seemed to be in accordance with the course of events at the time. But, interestingly, two long-time friends and colleagues, Samuel Batten and Walter Rauschenbusch, read the meaning of the events differently in 1911. That year Batten published a book titled *The Social Task of Christianity*, which read much like the volumes published in 1907. "It may be said that Christianity is passing through the most momentous crisis of its long history," he wrote. "And if the churches fail to read the signs of the times, or if they misread them, they will forfeit their election and lose the allegiance of mankind." Seeing both crisis and opportunity, Batten argued for the transformation and Christianization of the social, industrial, and political life of the nation. His subtitle conveyed the essence of his approach: "A Summons to the New Crusade."[6] In contrast, Rauschenbusch during 1911 declared in both a published article[7] and a series

---

[2]*Religious Education* 5 (April 1910): 52; 6 (April 1911): 128.

[3]Jane Addams, "Religious Education and Contemporary Social Conditions," ibid., 6 (June 1911): 151-52.

[4]Ibid., 7 (April 1912): 118.

[5]*Addresses before the New York State Conference of Religion,* ser. 11 (February 1913): 11.

[6]Samuel Z. Batten, *The Social Task of Christianity: A Summons to the New Crusade* (New York: Fleming H. Revell Co., 1911) 7-8.

[7]Walter Rauschenbusch, "The Church and Social Questions," in *Conservation of National Ideals, by Mrs. D. B. Wells, Prof. Edward A. Steiner, Ray Stannard Baker, Prof. Walter C. Rauschenbusch, Miss E. B. Vermilye, Rev. Charles L. Thompson. Issued under the Direction of the Council of Women for Home Missions* (New York: Fleming H. Revell Co., 1911) 103.

of lectures delivered at two universities[8] that the social awakening of the churches was already under way. That lecture series was the early formulation of the ideas he expressed in *Christianizing the Social Order*, which was published late in 1912. Part 1 of that book was titled "The Social Awakening of the Churches."[9] Like Batten, Rauschenbusch envisaged the Christianizing of the social order, but he claimed that the process had already commenced. His challenge was to continue the work already started in order to bring it to completion, whereas Batten contended that the social task of Christianity to impel Christians "to arise and build a Christian order of human society" still needed to be undertaken seriously.[10]

The difference in understanding between the men's viewpoints lay in their expectation of perfection and achievement. For Batten, the goal of Christianity was "a perfect man in a perfect society." Since the person and the society could not be separated, the perfection of one implied the perfection of the other. "If it is a Christian's duty to cherish the ideal of a Christian social order it is no less his Christian duty to build a Christian social order."[11] With more moderation, Rauschenbusch reasoned that fair-minded persons would not demand "that a great composite body like the Christian Church should be wide- awake and intelligent at the dawn of a new era, while political parties, the Law, the Press, the colleges, and the working class itself are just beginning to rub the sleep from their eyes." In his opinion, it would take at least a generation, under favorable conditions, to achieve the new social ideals; in the meantime efforts might be groping, timid, and inefficient. "But the Church is moving," Rauschenbusch rejoiced, and "the social awakening is an epoch in the history of the American churches."[12]

Although Batten's analysis and bibliography showed that he kept abreast of developments in society and Christian social thought, his argument approximated that in Rauschenbusch's book in 1907. He wanted Christianity to undertake the task of Christianizing society, whereas by

---

[8]*Wisconsin State Journal* (Madison), 21 January 1911; *Ohio Wesleyan Transcript* (Delaware), 13 April 1911, pp. 375, 384; 20 April 1911, pp. 395, 403, 404, 405; *Western Christian Advocate* (Cincinnati), 5 April 1911, in "Scrapbooks," Walter Rauschenbusch Papers, American Baptist Historical Society, Rochester NY.

[9]Walter Rauschenbusch, *Christianizing the Social Order* (New York: Macmillan Co., 1912) 1-29.

[10]Batten, *Social Task of Christianity*, 9.

[11]Ibid., 78-79, 227.

[12]Rauschenbusch, *Christianizing the Social Order*, 24-25, 28-29.

1911 Rauschenbusch believed the task was already in process. That was quite clear in the letter Rauschenbusch wrote to his editor at the Macmillan Company in May 1911 to describe briefly the approach of his new book.

"Christianizing the Social Order" is to take up the question where "Christianity and the Social Crisis" stopped. The former book called for a social awakening of the moral and religious forces: the new book will show that this awakening is now taking place, and to that extent is full of hopefulness. It will examine the present social order to determine what portions have not yet submitted to the revolutionizing influences of the Christian law and spirit. The process by which these unredeemed sections of modern life can be Christianized will be discussed. It will exhibit a Christian Social Order in the process of making. The closing chapter will show that in performing this great social task, religion itself will be rejuvenated and increasingly Christianized.[13]

Demands of teaching and speaking delayed the completion of Rauschenbusch's book until October 1912, but his essential argument did not change. When the volume reached bookstores on 20 November, just after the Progressive Movement reached its peak in Theodore Roosevelt's unsuccessful "Bull Moose" presidential campaign against Woodrow Wilson and William Howard Taft, most readers were attracted to his assessment of which portions of society were Christianized. Rauschenbusch concluded that "four great sections of our social order—the family, the organized religious life, the institutions of education and the political organization of our nation—have passed through constitutional changes which have made them to some degree part of the organism through which the spirit of Christ can do its work in humanity." He argued that the family was becoming assimilated to Christianity as the despotism and exploitation of the patriarchal family became more loving, decent, and democratic. Similarly, the church was increasingly Christianized as it moved from a corrupt and tyrannical organization thriving on superstitions to a more democratized structure that encouraged religious and intellectual freedom and "aroused the moral aspirations of the people." Education went through a Christianizing process as it changed from a privilege limited to the aristocracy to a more democratic public school system. And political life was redeemed when the special privilege of a dominant minority was replaced by "the principle of personal liberty and equal rights." Confessing personal misgivings about including politics among the Christianized portions of society, Rauschenbusch changed his mind as he realized how few years had been required for reformers in

---

[13]Walter Rauschenbusch to H. S. Latham, 20 May 1911, "Correspondence, 1904–1912," Rauschenbusch Papers.

America "to curb the extralegal power of the bosses by direct primaries, uniform accounting, direct legislation, and the recall."[14]

Despite the accomplishments noted, Rauschenbusch recognized the constant danger that any of the four sections could backslide. Nonetheless, he also believed that the fundamental changes currently in process proved that "Social Christianity is not, then, an untried venture." In his estimation, "The larger part of the work of christianizing our social order is already accomplished. . . . Christianity works."[15] By comparison, Batten dealt only with the family, the church, and the state, and argued that all three still needed to be Christianized in order to help in the larger work of social redemption.[16]

According to Rauschenbusch, other portions of the social order could be redeemed if they submitted to similar changes. The most difficult area for him was the economic one, and he devoted a large portion of his book to that problem. "Business life is the unregenerate section of our social order," he declared, and it "is the seat and source of our present troubles." He believed that capitalism was at fault because it placed ownership and control of industry and commerce in the hands "of a relatively small group of men." That group of investors differed from the workers in spirit and goal, thus creating a two-class system that was essentially antagonistic. As the capitalistic owners acquired political and social power as well as economic dominance, humane considerations were "trampled down" and a "fierce struggle" resulted. Christianity was involved because its spirit and teachings stressed the value of life, not profit, and pointed out "the sinfulness of our economic system" and of those responsible for it.[17]

Rauschenbusch's indictment of the economic order as "unchristian" concentrated so heavily on economic relations that many have regarded this volume as his most secular work. But he insisted that it was "a religious book from end to end. Its sole concern is for the Kingdom of God and the salvation of men." To him, "the Kingdom of God includes the economic life," and "a full salvation also includes the economic life." However, his solution proposed that economic readjustments would not suffice because the nation really needed "a new mind and heart, a new conception of the way we ought to live together," which only religion could provide. "We must begin at both ends simultaneously," he

---

[14]Rauschenbusch, *Christianizing the Social Order*, 123-54.

[15]Ibid., 154-55.

[16]Batten, *Social Task of Christianity*, 107-18.

[17]Rauschenbusch, *Christianizing the Social Order*, 156-68, 311-23.

proposed. "We must change our economic system in order to preserve our conscience and our religious faith; we must renew and strengthen our religion in order to be able to change our economic system."[18]

At the time, and since, most readers of *Christianizing the Social Order* have been so absorbed with Rauschenbusch's moral analysis of society that they have tended to overlook his historical analysis. Yet the latter analysis was central to his methodology and basic to his understanding. For instance, after explaining what he meant by "christianizing the social order" and listing Christian principles of social life by which to test the social order, he affirmed, "History will give us a better comprehension of the problem than the closest definition of terms. If we know how a thing has been done, we can see how it can and ought to be done." Thus, he traced "the moral evolution of those social institutions which have to some degree been christianized" as the way to conceptualize "the Christianizing process."[19]

That was also the way he concluded that a social awakening was in process in his day. His review of events in the nation since 1900 convinced him that a moral awakening had occurred. Although he cited specific data for his argument, an illustration effectively explained the change he saw. He likened the situation to his walking along the seashore. At one time he saw broad stretches of sand cluttered with seaweed and dead things, but a few hours later he traversed the same area and found brisk waves covered the sand and the debris. The transformation caused by the tide coming in was like magic, and the world smelled and felt differently. "The same sense of a great change comes over any one who watches the life of this nation with an eye for the stirring of God in the soul of men," he said in 1912.[20]

It was a similar perception of change in social Christianity, and in the church's acceptance of it, that convinced Rauschenbusch that there had been a social awakening of the churches. Remembering the lonesomeness felt by pioneers of social Christianity in 1900, he was amazed by their general acceptance at the time he wrote. In earlier years the church's social interest had been expressed by solitary individuals, but in the present "it has been admitted within the organizations of the Church." He compared Charles Stelzle's initial efforts with workers to his success in 1910. On the one hand, he noted that "since 1908 the denominations have begun to

---

[18]Ibid., 458-60.

[19]Ibid., 127.

[20]Ibid., 5.

adopt formal declarations defining their attitude to the social problems." On the other hand, "The leaders of the social awakening are now creating permanent organizations . . . to give practical effect to the new convictions." Furthermore, he regarded the Men and Religion Forward Movement as "the trumpet call of the social gospel." The meaning conveyed by Rauschenbusch's historical survey of the movement was clear: in his estimation something significant was happening to social Christianity and the nation at the very time he wrote.[21]

Sometimes what was happening attracted little attention but was significant as a small victory nevertheless. When the General Conference of the Methodist Episcopal Church held its quadrennial meeting 1-29 May 1912, the National City Evangelization Union reported that it was disbanding because its work had been achieved. Headed by Frank Mason North from its inception in 1892, the union had functioned primarily as an inspirational and educational agency. Its chief ends were "the agitation of the city question until the church should be profoundly aroused to its import" and the standardization of city societies so they had a permanent place in Methodism. Since both goals were accomplished, the work was transferred to the Board of Home Missions, and North was elected one of the corresponding secretaries of the Board of Foreign Missions. North must have felt satisfaction when he wrote in the report, "The church is at last awake to the problem of the city."[22]

As North's agency lost its distinct identity, the Methodist Federation for Social Service, with its broader social interests, submitted its first report to a Methodist General Conference. In contrast to four years earlier when the federation members had to work informally and behind the scenes, they now presented an eight-page report that was signed by members of the Executive Committee. That document in format fulfilled the responsibility that had justified the authorization of the federation; it answered the four questions assigned to it by the 1908 General Conference. By careful planning of those responses it was able to describe the federation's total program, to recommend its own continuity as "the recognized executive agency to rally the forces of the church in support of measures specifically approved by the General Conference in the

---

[21]Ibid., 9, 11, 12-13, 16, 19. Although his moral analysis proved to be inaccurate and the book became dated, his historical account in the first two chapters remains the most accurate record of the development of social Christianity from 1900 to 1912.

[22]*Journal of the General Conference of the Methodist Episcopal Church* (1912): 1418-21, 133.

adoption of this report," and to present a new revision of the Social Creed for approval.[23]

After the report was reviewed by the Committee on the State of the Church, it was submitted as Report 11, titled "The Church and Social Relations," of that Committee to the General Conference, which approved it. During the review within the committee, the main features of the federation report were endorsed, but with modifications. Most important to the organization was the authorization of its continued recognition as the executive agency of Methodism in the area of social service, and of the relationship of the Methodist Federation to the Commission on the Church and Social Service of the Federal Council of Churches. Since the federation now was recognized in its own right and not on the basis of a specific task, and since three bishops were now appointed to its membership, it had more status than it had previously had in the Methodist Episcopal Church.[24]

In the recommendation, review, and approval process several important things happened to the Social Creed that marked a new stage in its development. Whereas in 1908 the General Conference of the Methodist Church first approved the Social Creed resolutions written by Harry Ward, and then the Federal Council of Churches endorsed an enlarged version revised by Frank Mason North, the 1912 revision originated with the new Secretarial Council of the Federal Council. As the major Protestant denominations adopted the 1908 Social Creed of the Churches as their own platform, several made adaptations in its text. Those changes by Baptist, Congregational, Presbyterian, and Unitarian legislative bodies resulted in a plethora of different Social Creeds.[25] Believing that the value of the Social Creed would be enhanced if there was a common text ratified by the member bodies of the Federal Council, the Council of Secretaries prepared a revised and enlarged Social Creed of the Churches based on all the versions. Moreover, the Committee of Direction of the council's Commission on the Church and Social Service

---

[23]Ibid., 1324-32.

[24]Ibid., 636-38. In printing Report 11 in the *Journal*, the response to Question 1 was omitted, but its content dealt with the important revision of the Social Creed and can be found in the *Daily Christian Advocate*, 22 May 1912, pp. 546-48.

[25]A concise presentation of the various denominational additions and the revised Social Creed of 1912, as well as the earlier Methodist and Federal Council versions of 1908, appeared in Harry F. Ward, *A Year Book of the Church and Social Service in the United States* (New York: Missionary Education Movement of the United States and Canada, 1916) 197-201.

recommended that the scope of the declaration be broadened to include more than economic matters and that those be made more comprehensive. In the end, a seventeen-point revised Social Creed of the Churches was prepared for submission to the second quadrennial meeting of the Federal Council at Chicago, 4-9 December 1912.[26]

Prior to the presentation of the creed to the Federal Council, however, it was recognized that the Methodist Episcopal Church had a unique relationship to the declaration, since this denomination had approved the declaration first, and the revised statement was submitted to the denomination's General Conference through the report of the Methodist Federation for Social Service. In its report the federation described the revision as "the best form of what has come to be called the Social Creed of the Churches." During the review of the report, the Committee on the State of the Church deleted one of the seventeen items and reworded two others. As a consequence, the General Conference adopted a different version than that originally proposed by the Federal Council. Negotiations by the Methodist Federation with the Secretarial Council resulted in acceptance of the Methodist modifications in order to retain the possibility of a uniform Social Creed when the Federal Council met in December.[27] Such interaction and coordination was evidence of the new stage of cooperation among leaders of Protestant social-service agencies in 1912.

At the same time, the move to revise the Social Creed also revealed the fitful nature of cooperative social strategy. After years of preparation and evolution, Harry Ward's *The Social Creed of the Churches* finally was printed in 1912 as the first publication authorized by the Federal Council's Commission on the Church and Social Service, but ironically, the proposed revision of the Social Creed at the end of that year rendered its commentary on the 1908 creed obsolete. The book consisted of thirteen articles elaborating the meaning of the points in the 1908 creed and was intended to be a resource to broaden the discussion and understanding of the Social Creed in local congregations. Most of the articles were written by different authors, making the book an ecumenical venture. Ward wrote the preface in which he stated that adoption of the creed was "a significant

---

[26]Charles S. Macfarland, "The Kingdoms of This World; The Kingdom of Our Lord," *Christian Unity at Work: The Federal Council of the Churches of Christ in America in Quadrennial Session at Chicago, Illinois, 1912*, ed. Charles S. Macfarland (New York: Federal Council of Churches, 1913) 175-77.

[27]Ibid.; *Journal of the General Conference* (1912): 1324. Methodism's unique relation to the Social Creed was evident in the fact that the document was not submitted to the Baptist Convention or Presbyterian General Assembly that also met the same month.

fact in the history of religion. It marks the deliberate and conscious entrance of the Church upon the field of social action."[28]

Charles Macfarland's report on the work of the Commission on the Church and Social Service recommended that the Federal Council reaffirm the social declaration of four years earlier and then approve the additions and changes unanimously authorized by the General Conference of the Methodist Episcopal Church in May. The enlarged version included new statements about family life, children's development, liquor traffic, conservation of health, and prevention of poverty. "That we should thus make an advance," he explained, "is called for by the fact that the problems which face us, while probably no greater, are more plainly seen by us than they were four years ago."[29]

Suprisingly, the delegates also had expanded their vision and voted to enlarge the statement further: two additional items on the rights of both employees and employers to organize and on the acquisition and use of property were proposed from the floor and adopted.[30] One consequence of these latter actions was that the diversity of creeds continued, but at least the variety was limited to the Methodist Episcopal Church, which was unable to endorse the additions until it met again in 1916.[31] When the various additions and changes were completed, the following version of the Social Creed of the Churches was adopted 9 December 1912 and remained unchanged for twenty years.

> The Churches must stand:
>
> For equal rights and complete justice for all men in all stations of life.
> *For the protection of the family, by the single standard of purity, uniform divorce laws, proper regulation of marriage, and proper housing.*
> *For the fullest possible development for every child, especially by the provision of proper education and recreation.*
> For the abolition of child labor.
> For such regulation of the conditions of toil for women as shall safeguard the physical and moral health of the community.
> For the abatement *and prevention* of poverty.
> *For the protection of the individual and society from the social, economic, and moral waste of the liquor traffic.*
> *For the conservation of health.*

---

[28]Harry F. Ward, ed., *The Social Creed of the Churches* (New York: Eaton & Mains; Cincinnati: Jennings & Graham, 1912) 7.

[29]Macfarland, "The Kingdoms of This World," 175-77.

[30]*The Outlook* (New York), 21 December 1912, p. 851.

[31]*Journal of the General Conference* (1916): 602.

For the protection of the worker from dangerous machinery, occupational diseases, and mortality.

For the right of all men to the opportunity for self-maintenance, *for safeguarding this right* against encroachments of every kind, *and for the protection of workers from the hardships of enforced unemployment.* [This consolidates two points of the 1908 Creed and adds more.]

For suitable provision for the old age of the workers, and for those incapacitated by injury.

For the right of employees and employers alike to organize and for adequate means of conciliation and arbitration in industrial disputes.

For a release from employment one day in seven.

For the gradual and reasonable reduction of the hours of labor to the lowest practicable point, and for that degree of leisure for all which is a condition of the highest human life.

For a living wage as a minimum in every industry, and for the highest wage that each industry can afford.

For a new emphasis on the application of Christian principles to the acquisition and use of property, and for the most equitable division of the product of industry that can ultimately be devised.[32]

The broadening interests and enthusiasm concerning the church's part in the social unrest that were so evident in this enlarged Social Creed were actually part of changed conditions affecting the whole nation and not just the Federal Council of Churches. What was happening, and its implications for the delegates, was vividly proclaimed by Walter Rauschenbusch in a stirring address that he titled "The Social Revival."

The positions taken in 1908 marked a brave stand. It is not so brave anymore. The whole country has been catching up. The trusts are adopting our welfare measures. Some sections of the Progressive Party Platform read very much like the Social Creed of the Federal Council, and if you knew the inside facts, you would realize that the similarity is not accidental. They simply adopted the Federal Council platform. And when political parties are sitting down on its coat-skirts, it is time for the Church of Christ to move on.

In 1908 we lodged our protest against the outstanding inhumanities of our social life, against child labor, excessive female labor, the sweating system, a seven-day working week, wholesale mutilation by industrial accidents, old age left helpless, and a wage on which men can not live like men. That was the voice of Christian mercy, and it was a just and holy protest. God in heaven seems to have heard it. But it was not the last word of the Christian Church on our industrial questions. To demand a living wage is not incisive enough

----

[32]Additional clauses and phrases are italicized and other changes indicated. The clause "For the suppression of the 'Sweating System' " was the only complete deletion. Macfarland, "The Kingdoms of This World," 174-77. See my "The Methodist Federation for Social Service and the Social Creed," *Methodist History* 13 (January 1975): 25-28.

for those who speak in the name of Jesus Christ. A living wage is not yet a just wage. It will serve as a minimum, but only as a starter.

. . . We want not only mercy, but justice; not only social service, but social repentance, social shame, social conversion, social regeneration. Thousands of people are now passing through these religious experiences, feeling the pangs of social contrition and coming out into the gladness of a new surrender and peace. We are having a revival of religion. . . . On the scroll of the everlasting Gospel, God is today writing a flaming message of social righteousness, and you and I must learn to read it.[33]

In the religious and secular press, the outstanding features of the Federal Council meeting were the revised Social Creed and Rauschenbusch's address. *The Outlook* considered the "greatest meeting" to be the session when Rauschenbusch spoke,[34] while the *Central Christian Advocate* indicated "the outstanding event" was the adoption of the Social Creed.[35] Both events were sufficiently newsworthy that the *New York Times* carried two stories on the "new social creed," one on the front page, [36] and the *Chicago Tribune* headline read, "Church Planks Like Bull Moose. Dr. Rauschenbusch Cites Similarity in Federal Council and Progressive Platforms."[37] The whole meeting was important enough that it received extensive summaries in *The Outlook*[38] and the *Western Christian Advocate*.[39]

These lengthy interpretations were particularly useful because they were expressions of the meaning of the events by men who had been members of the Federal Council's Commission on the Church and Social Service during the quadrennium, Ernest H. Abbott of *The Outlook* and Levi Gilbert of the *Western Christian Advocate*. Of the two, Abbott's article had the larger reading and the larger perspective. Ernest Abbott, one of Lyman's sons who now ran the daily functions of the weekly periodical, was concerned about the question "What have they done?" Essentially, the Federal Council of Churches had created a system for the churches on a national scale. It was a good system that offset the wasteful lack of

---

[33]Macfarland, *Christian Unity at Work*, 205-206.

[34]*The Outlook* (New York), 21 December 1912, pp. 851-52.

[35]*Central Christian Advocate* (Kansas City), 18 December 1912, p. 230.

[36]*New York Times*, 2 December 1912, p. 7; 4 December 1912, p. 1.

[37]*Chicago Tribune*, 9 December 1912, p. 1.

[38]*The Outlook* (New York), 12 December 1912, pp. 846-52.

[39]*Western Christian Advocate* (Cincinnati), 11 December 1912, pp. 6-7; 18 December 1912, pp. 20-21.

system due to denominational rivalries, to which Rauschenbusch made reference at the beginning of his notable speech and repeated in his 1912 book,[40] because it represented "the conscience and unselfishness of the community." Also the council had broadened its social declaration with greater commitment and enthusiasm than even the Church and Social Service Commission had anticipated, and thus additions from the floor had amplified the more cautious enlargement initially proposed. That growing sentiment was demonstrated by what Abbott called "the greatest meeting of the sessions," which was devoted to social service. At that gathering Frank Mason North presided and read the newly enlarged Social Creed, and Rauschenbusch and Edward Steiner presented addresses. Despite the contrasting styles of the two professors, they made a combined impact on the audience, which was typified by one prominent minister from a denomination that stressed an extremely individualistic religion. He acknowledged that "he had been converted to the social view of religion." Abbott believed the churches had converted themselves as they discovered that the message entrusted to them did not concern merely individual men and women but also the city and the nation and the values they expressed. That represented "the most important thing 'they have done,' " concluded Abbott.[41]

The mood of the Federal Council's quadrennial meeting in Chicago offset the doubts that some persons had about the new cooperative organization. Shailer Mathews was asked by the Northern Baptist Convention to have his name submitted for the presidency of the council, but he was reluctant to do so on the basis of what he had seen it do during its first four years. His fears that the ecumenical body was moribund were corrected when he attended its sessions in Chicago. "There was an enthusiasm and initiative in the body that were inspiring," he said later.[42] And Francis J. McConnell, elected bishop at the Methodist General Conference in May where the Episcopal Address was very critical of the council, praised the power of the Federal Council to shape public opinion in the solution of social questions.[43]

---

[40]Walter Rauschenbusch, "The Social Revival," *Christian Unity at Work*, 203; idem, *Christianizing the Social Order*, 98, 463-64.

[41]*The Outlook* (New York), 21 December 1912, pp. 846-52.

[42]Shailer Mathews, *New Faith for Old: An Autobiography* (New York: Macmillan Co., 1936) 161.

[43]*Journal of the General Conference* (1912): 210; *Christian Unity at Work*, 28.

That was the first national appearance of Bishop McConnell as a new Methodist voice. Also it was a modest opportunity for the new president of the Methodist Federation for Social Service to become a part of the Federal Council and its social ministry. With Harry Ward's employment as a full-time secretary of the federation on 1 October 1912, a new team of leaders emerged on the scene that year, and Ward and McConnell served together in that capacity until 1944.[44] Although Ward joined the faculty of the Boston University School of Theology in 1913, a joint appointment enabled him to develop his social ideology while still directing the program of the federation.

Ward's increasing involvement in various phases of social ministry in the Methodist Episcopal Church, as well as his larger participation in the Federal Council's Commission and Secretarial Council, was typical of the advance of social Christianity in the leading socially active Protestant denominations at the end of 1912. By that time the cause of social Christianity seemed to have achieved its greatest recognition and opportunity. Unfortunately, during the preceding months the health of Elias B. Sanford, who headed the Federal Council, declined seriously, and Charles Macfarland was requested to assume the duties of acting executive secretary. Although his report did not indicate any limitation, he was not able to devote full attention to the Commission on Church and Social Service. In 1913 he assumed full responsibilities as executive secretary of the Federal Council of Churches, but continued to head the commission. According to Shailer Mathews, it was Macfarland's great energy and self-sacrificing commitment that provided efficient and able leadership despite the fact that he had to work out of offices that were still modest, struggle with a limited budget, and carry on too large a program for one man.[45] However, because of the inspiration and success of the Federal Council meeting in Chicago in December 1912, Macfarland was able to find increasing support for the program and finances for the Federal Council of Churches.

In a significant way, the churches had awakened to the needs of the social order and at last seemed committed and organized to function both denominationally and cooperatively to achieve the long-felt goals of social Christianity. In the view of the *Jefferson City Tribune* in Missouri, the Chicago meeting exemplified "The Church and Social Justice." The session

---

[44]*Journal of the General Conference* (1912): 636-37; *The Methodist Year Book (1913)*, 148.

[45]Macfarland, "The Kingdoms of This World," 157; Mathews, *New Faith for Old*, 163.

during which North read the newly adopted Social Creed of the Churches and Rauschenbusch delivered his stirring address particularly seemed to embody evangelical Christianity for the writer. "That platform is an epitome of Professor Rauschenbusch's theory of Christianizing the social order," wrote the reporter, who then concluded, "The church is in the transport of an admitted awakening to the demands and opportunities thrust upon it by society and this is encouraging."[46]

---

[46]*Jefferson City* (Mo.) *Tribune,* 17 December 1912, in "Scrapbooks," Rauschenbusch Papers.

CHAPTER 12

It Is Unwise
to Take Sides in Politics

Ordinarily it is unwise for a minister to take sides in politics. There is a deeper work for him to do. I do think it is necessary for him to see the great problems of the community, but he should approach public questions from the divine and not from the personal side.

It is his part to foster high ideals, and if he identifies himself with one party he shuts himself off from part of the people.

(Lyman Abbott, to students at University of Chicago,
quoted in New York Times, *28 April 1912)*

THE YEAR 1912 WAS CLEARLY A TIME of accomplishment and recognition for social Christianity in America. Most of the forces and influences expressed in that movement since the turn of the century reached a point of culmination during those twelve months. Like every other aspect of national life, the social gospel also was affected by the momentous political agitation of the time. Since the role of social morality and the nature of government were primary considerations in the election of 1912, certain tendencies and interests of Protestant churches were revealed in a new light.

When James Whiton reviewed the moral lessons of the past year for the New York State Conference of Religion on 11 November 1912, he commented on one unique feature: "It has never before happened that distinctly moral questions in an election have been put before the people by all political parties as they were last week—with varying fullness, indeed, and varying emphasis, not all in the same tone, not all in the same volume—in such a way, at any rate, that all the people have been summoned to consider great moral questions as never before."[1] His perception that the various political parties were concerned with moral questions was not the product of a blind devotion to morality by the conference but was also recognized by political observers. Benjamin Parke DeWitt remarked that Theodore Roosevelt and Woodrow Wilson were both progressive, and the significance of the election was not that Wilson defeated Roosevelt but that "the country for the first time had gone progressive." In that campaign, the people, who were upset by the corruption and immorality in the land, voted consciously and deliberately to restore the control of the government to the people, according to DeWitt.[2] An examination of the role played by advocates of social Christianity in that unique election provides helpful perspective on the goals and methods of the now-recognized Social Gospel movement.

Because of Walter Rauschenbusch's widely quoted comment in 1912 that the Progressive party platform "simply adopted the Federal Council platform,"[3] the impact of the Social Creed of the Churches on the new third party in American politics seemed to be the most obvious influence of social Christianity in that election. While it was true that evidences of the Social Creed could be found in the Progressive party platform of 1912, the influence of the Federal Council document was not as great as Rauschenbusch's comments suggested. The most apparent similarities occurred in the section on Social and Industrial Justice of the platform. Items four, five, nine, ten, eleven, twelve, thirteen, and fourteen of the sixteen-point Social Creed were clearly identifiable in content, but the wording often was changed.[4] An annotated edition of the platform published by the Progressive party indicated that the planks on Social and Industrial Justice, rather than being "a hodge-podge of catch- penny proposals," were based upon recommendations of the National

---

[1]*Addresses before the New York State Conference of Religion*, ser. 11 (February 1913): 10.

[2]Benjamin Parke DeWitt, *The Progressive Movement: A Nonpartisan Comprehensive Discussion of Current Tendencies in American Politics* (New York: Macmillan Co., 1915) 43-44.

[3]Walter Rauschenbusch, "The Social Revival," *Christian Unity at Work: The Federal Council of the Churches of Christ in America in Quadrennial Session at Chicago, Illinois, 1912*, ed. Charles S. Macfarland (New York: Federal Council of Churches, 1913) 205-206.

[4]"Progressive Party Platform," in Kirk H. Porter and Donald Bruce Johnson, *National Party Platforms, 1840–1956* (Urbana: University of Illinois Press, 1956) 175-82, esp. 177.

Conference of Charities and Corrections.[5] Jane Addams, who served as president of the Progressive Platform Committee, had worked on those recommendations, and she indicated that persons closely identified with the Men and Religion Forward Movement, as well as social workers, labored with her "to give political expression to the religious motive."[6] The major contribution of the Commission on the Church and Social Service of the Federal Council of Churches and of the Forward Movement apparently was in the formulation of the statement adopted by the National Conference of Charities and Corrections, which was approved in June 1912, and then within weeks that program "was swept into the insurgent political movement" of the Progressive party.[7]

According to Addams, political Progressivism offered an unusual opportunity for the implementation of ideas she valued. "In spite of our belief in our leader," she said later, "I was there, and I think the same was true of many others, because the platform expressed the social hopes so long ignored by the politicians." By that involvement, "measures of industrial amelioration and demands for social justice . . . were at last thrust into the arena of political action." Seeing politics as an opportunity to change the conditions of national life, she campaigned extensively across the country to speak on behalf of the measures stated in the Progressive platform. Miss Addams shared with political progressives and religious liberals the conviction that educating the people concerning social justice would lead them to enact needed changes. Even when Roosevelt and the Progressive party platform were defeated, Addams felt the effort was worthwhile because many of the planks she valued ultimately became parts of the platforms of other political parties. Moreover, Addams and other social workers discovered that only when their concerns became political issues did they attract national attention.[8]

It appears that the Progressive party platform included a number of the ideas contained in the Social Creed of the Churches, but primarily through their incorporation in the social platform endorsed by the National Conference of Charities and Corrections in June 1912. The

---

[5]*Annotated Edition of the Platform of the National Progressive Party of the State of New York. Adopted by the State Convention, Syracuse, N.Y., Sept. 5, 1912* (N.p., n.d.) 32.

[6]Jane Addams, *The Second Twenty Years at Hull-House; With a Record of a Growing World Consciousness* (New York: Macmillan Co., 1930) 29-30.

[7]Ibid., 12, 27.

[8]Ibid., 27, 30-31, 38-40, 45-46.

experience of Jane Addams seems to have typified the interaction of persons and cross-fertilization of ideas between various movements for social betterment. For example, at the June Charities and Correction meeting, Rauschenbusch preached the annual sermon,[9] and Addams spoke frequently to religious leaders at such organizations as the Religious Education Association[10] In light of similar interests and values regarding social improvement, a number of persons shared common concern for the measures stated in the Progressive party platform. Assuming that Rauschenbusch was correct in his statement that the Social Creed influenced that platform, it appears that the political declaration may have been an expression of a more general social concern and commitment evidenced by the Men and Religion Forward Movement and the increasing willingness to organize for social service evidenced by several denominations during 1912. Moreover, it should be recognized that the Republican party platform in 1912 also contained a brief plank on social betterment that reflected a general commitment similar to portions of the Social Creed. The Republican party, the platform declared,

> is prepared to go forward with the solution of those new questions, which social, economic and political development have brought into the forefront of the nation's interest. It will strive . . . to enact the necessary legislation to safeguard the public health; to limit effectively the labor of women and children, and to protect wage earners in dangerous occupations; to enact comprehensive and generous workman's compensation laws . . . and in all possible ways to satisfy the just demand of the people for the study and solution of the complex and constantly changing problems of social welfare.[11]

In contrast, the Democratic platform pledged little social commitment, while the Socialist party platform affirmed not reform but a revolution to replace capitalism with socialism.[12]

If it was the opportunity to work for a social platform that led Jane Addams to support the Progressive party, it was Theodore Roosevelt who

---

[9]Walter Rauschenbusch, "Ye Did It unto Me," *Proceedings of the National Conference of Charities and Correction* (1912), 12-19.

[10]Jane Addams, "The Reaction of Modern Life upon Religious Education," *Religious Education* 4 (April 1909): 23-29; "Religious Education and Contemporary Social Conditions," ibid., 6 (June 1911): 145-52.

[11]"Republican Party Platform of 1912," in Porter and Johnson, *National Party Platforms*, 183.

[12]"Democratic Party Platform of 1912," ibid., 168-75; "Socialist Party Platform of 1912," ibid., 188-91.

attracted others. Presbyterian social-gospel leader Charles Stelzle said, "When Mr. Roosevelt organized the Progressive Party, I accepted the candidacy for the Assembly in Essex County, New Jersey, where I lived at that time, mainly for the purpose of giving me a good excuse to make campaign speeches for Mr. Roosevelt throughout the State." With his usual enthusiasm, Stelzle won the nomination amid controversy and campaigned vigorously for Roosevelt, whose "interest in the welfare of the common man" had long appealed to him. With little regard for his own victory at the polls, Stelzle used his candidacy as an opportunity to stump for the man who had helped him solidify the work at Labor Temple.[13]

Most influential of those who supported Roosevelt's Progressive party campaign was Lyman Abbott and his weekly periodical, *The Outlook.* Lyman Abbott had known and admired Roosevelt for years and editorially supported most of his policies and actions when Roosevelt was president of the United States. Their fundamental agreement on the need for stronger central government was evident in 1910 when Roosevelt advocated his "new nationalism," which was published by *The Outlook,*[14] and Abbott explained the development of democratic government in his book titled *The Spirit of Democracy.*[15] As Abbott wrote in his *Reminiscences,* "I have steadfastly advocated the doctrine that not only railways, but the mines, the forests, the waterways . . . must be brought under Government regulation, State or National, and that this regulation must be extended to all forms of business—including the regulation of food, beverages, and drugs—as fast and as far as is necessary to conserve the public welfare."[16] It was because of that basic accord that Abbott stated that *The Outlook* "could not do otherwise than support what are popularly known as the Roosevelt policies without repudiating the political principles which it has been advocating for more than a score of years."[17]

Whereas previously it had been appropriate for *The Outlook* to support Roosevelt and his policies when he was the president, that became a questionable practice when Roosevelt ran for office again in 1912. In the

---

[13]Charles Stelzle, *A Son of the Bowery: The Life Story of an East Side American* (New York: George H. Doran Co., 1926) 243-46.

[14]Theodore Roosevelt, *The New Nationalism* (New York: The Outlook Co., 1910).

[15]Lyman Abbott, *The Spirit of Democracy* (Boston: Houghton Mifflin Co., 1910).

[16]Lyman Abbott, *Reminiscences* (Boston: Houghton Mifflin Co., 1915) 441-42.

[17]Ibid., 443.

meantime, Roosevelt had joined the staff of *The Outlook* as a contributing editor in 1909, and he occupied that position when he announced his candidacy for the presidency in 1912. Until early that year the journal had generally been favorable to President Taft, but it quickly changed its stance after Roosevelt sought the Republican nomination and then accepted the candidacy of the National Progressive party that summer. Abbott tried to maintain an impartial policy by publishing articles presenting the cause of the Republicans, the Democrats, and the Socialists, but editorially *The Outlook* backed the Progressives after 27 April, when it declared itself in favor of Roosevelt. When Roosevelt became a contributing editor, subscriptions to *The Outlook* increased significantly and it appeared on newsstands for the first time; when Roosevelt lost the election in 1912 subscriptions declined noticeably. *The Outlook* learned that a periodical could not claim to be independent politically when a party leader was on its editorial staff, even though he exercised no editorial judgment in this period and all his contributions were signed. In the eyes of many, *The Outlook* was the political mouthpiece of Roosevelt and the Progressive party.[18]

Unlike Abbott and Stelzle, Washington Gladden did not publicly campaign for Roosevelt's bid for reelection in 1912, but he was involved behind the scenes. Occasionally over the years, the staff of *The Outlook* had written to Gladden for political information and evaluation, as for example in 1910 when they sought his views on Warren G. Harding's attempt to unseat Governor Judson Harmon in Ohio.[19] Moreover, Gladden had known Roosevelt for many years, and when the latter planned to go to Columbus on 21 February 1912 to address the Ohio Constitutional Convention, he wrote on the letterhead stationery of *The Outlook* to inquire if he might have lunch with his pastor friend. "In the first place I want to see you, and in the second place I do not want to see any politicians. Are there any suggestions you have to make as to what I should say at the Convention?" wrote Roosevelt.[20]

---

[18]Ira V. Brown, *Lyman Abbott, Christian Evolutionist: A Study in Religious Liberalism* (Cambridge: Harvard University Press, 1953) 208-11; "Theodore Roosevelt, Preacher of Righteousness," in Lyman Abbott, *Silhouettes of My Contemporaries* (Garden City NY: Doubleday, Page & Co., 1921) 312.

[19]Elbert Baldwin to Washington Gladden, on *The Outlook* letterhead, 24 October, 1 November 1910, Washington Gladden Papers, Ohio Historical Society, Columbus OH.

[20]Theodore Roosevelt to Gladden, 7 February 1912; R. D. Townsend to Gladden, on *The Outlook* letterhead, 19 February, 24 February 1912, Gladden Papers; Jacob Dorn, *Washington Gladden: Prophet of the Social Gospel* (Columbus: Ohio State University Press, 1967) 341-44.

Gladden actively supported the effort to reform the Ohio Constitution and sat with Roosevelt at the convention. Just three days after that visit, on 24 February, Roosevelt publicly announced his candidacy for the presidency as a Republican insurgent.[21] In September Gladden was invited by Walter E. Weyl to assist Roosevelt and the National Committee of the Progressive party.[22]

What role a minister should play in party politics was a concern to advocates of social Christianity. The issue was focused clearly by Lyman Abbott on 27 April 1912. On that date an editorial in *The Outlook* favored Roosevelt over Taft for the Republican nomination. That same day Abbott told students at the University of Chicago that ministers should not take an active part in politics. " 'Ordinarily it is unwise for a minister to take sides in politics,' " he said. ' "It is his part to foster high ideals, and if he identifies himself with one party he shuts himself off from part of the people.' " Although he allowed that there may be times when ministers should become active politically, he regarded those as exceptions. Primarily, it was the minister's job to approach political issues from a divine perspective, not from personal involvement.[23]

By both taking sides and telling others that it was unwise to take sides in politics, Abbott exposed one of the complexities of social-gospel thought and action. For him, it was appropriate to take a definite political stand editorially in *The Outlook* and to advise readers how to vote on particular issues. According to his autobiography, Abbott reached this approach in 1896 when he found the editorial staff of *The Outlook* divided in opinion over the free coinage of silver issue. Shutting himself in his study for two or three days to struggle with the issue, he concluded that it was important to oppose William Jennings Bryan and the Democrats on this issue because of moral rather than political reasons. "This episode confirmed me in my belief that political questions are to be determined, not by considerations of political or commercial expediency only, but fundamentally by moral principles," he wrote later.[24] Through his utterances, Abbott attempted to interpret to others opinions they already held but had been unable to

---

[21]Arthur S. Link, *Woodrow Wilson and the Progressive Era, 1910–1917*, The New American Nation Series, ed. Henry Steele Commager and Richard B. Morris (New York: Harper & Row, 1954; Harper Torchbook, 1963) 14.

[22]Walter E. Weyl to Gladden, on Progressive party letterhead, 25 September 1912, Gladden Papers.

[23]*New York Times*, 28 April 1912, p. 6.

[24]Abbott, *Reminiscences*, 432-33.

crystallize and formulate. "These principles have prevented me from *belonging* to any party, and have made it difficult sometimes for perfectly honest-minded critics to classify me. I have believed in anti-saloon legislation but have not been a Prohibitionist, in social reform but have not been a Socialist, in individual liberty but have not been a Democrat, in a strong centralized government but have not been a Republican, in political progress and social justice but have not been a Progressive," he said. For clarification he explained that in order to vote in a direct primary in New York State, "I enrolled myself as a Progressive, but I none the less count myself an independent in politics."[25] In 1912 it was the affinity of the political principles of Abbott and *The Outlook* with Roosevelt's policies that led to the endorsement of Roosevelt rather than Woodrow Wilson or William Howard Taft.[26] The principles rather than the personality determined the endorsement, and in Abbott's opinion that was a legitimate area of concern for a social-gospel minister.

Washington Gladden, who was the same age as Abbott, shared a common concern for moral principles and a nonpartisan attitude in politics. However, his interpretation of those values was more activist than other proponents of social Christianity. In his *Recollections,* which was published in 1909 prior to Roosevelt's "Bull Moose" campaign, he said, "There have been times when I should have been glad to belong to a party, but, on the whole, I am inclined to think that, for me, it has been the right attitude. There are decided advantages in not being a member of any political party."[27] His decision was reached not on doctrinaire grounds but on the basis of practical expediency; he had been a Republican with pride when he ministered in Massachusetts, but he found Ohio Republicanism unfit to claim his allegiance and so became a political independent.[28] Nevertheless, Gladden's nonalignment did not preclude his sense of obligation to run for a seat on the Columbus City Council, where he served from 1900 to 1902. In that period, he was more motivated to oppose the monopolistic franchises of the street-railway and natural gas companies and to work for the principle of municipal ownership and control of public-service industries than he was to being representative of any political party. Moreover, he gave up his public office not because

---

[25]Ibid., 421- 22.

[26]Ibid., 443; Abbott, *Silhouettes of My Contemporaries,* 310-13.

[27]Washington Gladden, *Recollections* (Boston: Houghton Mifflin Co., 1909) 378-79.

[28]Ibid., 377-78.

he resented political responsibility in theory or practice, but because it demanded so much time that it interferred with his primary duties as a Christian pastor.[29] On other occasions he worked with both Republicans and Democrats to recommend capable candidates in each party and urged other Christians to form a Municipal Voters' League.[30]

In his autobiography, Gladden expressed genuine admiration and appreciation for the political contributions of Theodore Roosevelt. "Certainly no man since Lincoln has poured into the life of this nation such a stream of vitalizing influence," he affirmed.[31] Although he recognized Roosevelt's limitations and differed with him on issues such as peace and armaments, Gladden had known Roosevelt since Roosevelt's days as police commissioner in New York City and confidently asserted, "I have known him well enough to feel sure of his ruling motives." Appreciative of the Roosevelt policies of honesty, justice, and fair play, and of his actions in the critical period in which he served as president, Gladden described the political leader's achievements with words that conveyed almost a religious aura.

> Here was a man with eyes to see the extent and the enormity of this veiled injustice, with words to describe it, and with an arm to smite it. The service which he has rendered to his nation in bringing into the light these furtive plunderings, in awakening the conscience of the land against them, and in setting the machinery of the law in motion for their prevention and punishment, is one of the greatest services that it has ever fallen to any man to render.[32]

Little wonder, in light of such sentiments, that Roosevelt felt free to invite himself to lunch at Gladden's house in February 1912, when he came to play politics in Columbus and to make his final decision about running for the presidency again. Roosevelt enjoyed Gladden's hospitality, but whatever contributions the pastor made in that choice were behind the scenes, not public.

On the basis of his own experience in the pastorate, Charles Macfarland believed that a minister should participate in civic affairs but should keep fundamental purposes in mind. Sunday worship and sermons should provide spiritual uplift more than economic discussion,

---

[29]Ibid., 337-52.

[30]Ibid., 379-82.

[31]Ibid., 389.

[32]Ibid., 391, 388-97.

but community needs ought to be faced in one's total ministry. The minister should be primarily a pastor, not just a reformer. And "rarely should a minister seek political office." In civic interests, the wise pastor should seek the advice of leading laypersons, explain what is proposed and the reasons why, and then "he should tell them frankly that, unless they can show him that he is wrong, they should give him their unqualified support." Even though he was an admitted opportunist, Macfarland sought to preserve a working balance between pastoral ministry to his own flock and "social interest in humanity."[33]

As in so many areas, Walter Rauschenbusch expressed the basic social-gospel attitude of the minister's role in politics. While he refused to say that clergy never should identify with a political party, because he believed it was feasible for a national party to achieve the triumph of justice, he was convinced that party allegiance made ministers liable to the charge of partisanship. His advice was: "A minister has no business to be the megaphone of a political party and its catchwords. He should rather be the master of politics by creating the issues which parties will have to espouse." Christian preachers should discern the right before others and should use that prophetic insight to champion new causes. Believing that "the early work is the formative work," Rauschenbusch urged ministers to concentrate on shaping opinion "before a question is torn to tatters" in political conflict. "If the pulpit creates the public sentiment which will insist on the enactment and enforcement of such laws and ordinances, it will not be meddling with party politics."[34] In keeping with this interpretation, Rauschenbusch spoke in behalf of numerous social causes and against current problems, wrote letters to the editor in various newspapers, attended meetings of the school board and the city council to seek improvements, and served on advisory committees to effect social improvements.[35] But he did not run for political office or become active in partisan politics.

---

[33]Charles S. Macfarland, *Across the Years* (New York: Macmillan Co., 1936) 79-80.

[34]Walter Rauschenbusch, *Christianity and the Social Crisis* (New York: Macmillan Co., 1907) 362-63.

[35]For examples see Walter Rauschenbusch, "Scrapbooks," 5 August 1901; 1 January, 17 March 1902; 16 January 1911; "What Is the Matter with Rochester," manuscript address, 3, 22 April 1904; letter on streetcar abuses to the Mayor and Common Council of the City of Rochester, Spring 1905; "Rochester Public School Report" and related documents, 1907–1908, Walter Rauschenbusch Papers, American Baptist Historical Society, Rochester NY.

Nevertheless, Rauschenbusch had a different attitude toward the political function of the church. "Should the church ever exert its influence in politics?" he asked in 1911. His answer was negative insofar as the church sought to defend or acquire privileges for itself, as happened frequently in history. But his answer was affirmative if the church asked nothing for itself and worked for the moral protection of the people. "Then they are not one more selfish interest going into politics, but are the champions of the people and prophets of God." If only the church would get as politically involved to correct the evils caused by industrial life as it did against the liquor traffic, he argued, it would be able to reenforce "the interests that are bringing on a better day." In this way, the organized church would be able to exercise its special task "of Christianizing our national life."[36]

A similar understanding was evident in an address entitled "Political Integrity" that was presented to the National Council of the Congregational Churches in 1910. "Why should a church convention be concerned with political affairs?" asked Rev. George S. Rollins of Springfield, Massachusetts. Some political bosses and commercial interests would accuse the church of meddling outside its proper province, but religion deals with the whole of life, including politics, and has the responsibility to shape social conscience. Thus, the speaker concluded, "Christ commands us to make the age Christian—to make our nation Christian. Therefore to make politics Christian." Rollins also repudiated church efforts to create "a church party," or to acquire special favors, or to dominate the government. Rather, Christians should strive for Christian ideals in politics and civic affairs, for the support of good citizens and good measures, for righteousness in the nation, and for "Christian men in politics." In encouraging the latter, however, the speaker meant laypersons rather than clergy. While it might be unwise for ministers to take sides in politics, it was a necessity for laity if the Christian Church was to directly influence political life.[37]

Since the Christianizing of the social order was a central component of social Christianity, it was essential for the movement to find some way to relate to the political life of the nation. If ever the church was to get

---

[36]Walter Rauschenbusch, "The Church and Social Questions," in *Conservation of National Ideals, by Mrs. D. B. Wells, Prof. Edward A. Steiner, Ray Stannard Baker, Prof. Walter C. Rauschenbusch, Miss E. B. Vermilye, Rev. Charles L. Thompson. Issued under the Direction of the Council of Women for Home Missions* (New York: Fleming H. Revell Co., 1911) 104, 121-22.

[37]George S. Rollins, "Political Integrity," *Minutes of the National Council of the Congregational Churches of the United States* (1910), 52-61.

beyond criticism to the achievement of better conditions, it was vital to get beyond principles to legislation. While most social-gospel advocates agreed with Rauschenbusch that "laws do not create moral convictions; they merely recognize and enforce them,"[38] it was clear that laws and regulations had to be implemented through the political process in some fashion. As Alfred W. Wishart told the Baptist Congress in November 1912, "The crucial issue of the country is this: Is religion sufficiently vital and effective to become a socially controlling force?" He raised that question in a discussion of the effect of democracy on religion, which in itself evidenced the breadth and complexity of this basic social- gospel concern.[39] Christianizing the social order, according to Wishart, involved questions of democracy and a Christian nation, as well as of Christianizing, of educating conscience, and of relating to party politics. In his discussion of the same theme as Wishart, Samuel Batten pointed to the larger and interrelated scope of the issues facing the church: "The social question is up for a hearing because the Christian faith and the democratic principle are here today. It is sometimes supposed that the social question is a purely social and economic one . . . but this does not touch either the root or the meaning of the question." Batten was certain not only that "modern democracy is a Christian product and is the direct result of Christian principles," but also that democratic principles had the potency to change and reconstruct the entire social order.[40]

It was Lyman Abbott's conviction that the great need of America in 1912 was that the high ideals required to transform the social and political order should be maintained courageously in all political parties as well as in all churches. Ministers could foster those ideals in relation to community problems, but they should primarily focus on the divine rather than the human dimension. They should approach political questions, but they should not take an active part in politics. While Abbott did not say so, other social-gospel leaders concluded that such political activity was more properly the sphere of Christian laypersons.

That was the proper sphere for Woodrow Wilson, as well as for Theodore Roosevelt. He too was a Progressive politician with strong Christian convictions. When a correspondent asked in *The Outlook* why readers could not vote for Wilson, who was a progressive Democrat, the

---

[38]Rauschenbusch, *Christianity and the Social Crisis*, 363.

[39]Alfred W. Wishart, "The Effect of Democracy on Religious Thought and Practice," *Proceedings of the Baptist Congress (1912)*, 88.

[40]Samuel Z. Batten, "The Effect of Democracy on Religious Thought and Practice," ibid., 74, 83.

editor responded that he did not object to either the character or ideals of Wilson but to the corrupt city and state machines of the Democratic party organization and the inadequacy of its platform.[41] When Wilson won the election by plurality, the Federal Council of Churches extended the good will and prayer of its constituency to the victor. That letter also stated,

> Your warm and sympathetic sense of our democracy; your conviction expressed in so many ways, both by utterance and execution that our social order must be fashioned after the Kingdom of God as taught by Jesus Christ; together with your public faithfulness and your personal faith, lead the churches of the nation to look with confidence to the performance of the serious and solemn duties of the coming years.
>
> While you are planning for these four years, the Federal Council is also projecting for the same term of years. . . . It is to be hoped that, without unwise embarrassment, with both sympathy and discrimination, with social vision and social emotion; the political forces of the nation, and its moral forces as embodied in the churches of Christ, may feel and serve together for the social and spiritual well-being of the people.[42]

In that letter to President-elect Wilson, the Federal Council of Churches indicated its continuing confidence in the potential for the cooperation of the moral and political forces in the nation. The epistle also evidenced the ongoing nature of the Christianizing of the social order. Later, Shailer Mathews told about the bitterness generated by the election of 1912. Although Theodore Roosevelt was in the hotel in which the Federal Council held its meeting in December, it was not considered expedient to ask the defeated candidate to attend or to speak during its sessions. However, Ernest Abbott of *The Outlook* insisted that Mathews meet Roosevelt, but took him up to the former president's room secretly.[43] The vacillating nature of politics was clearly apparent in this little vignette, especially if one recalls the warmth of the letter from the Federal Council to Wilson. Together these incidents seemed to confirm the wisdom of Lyman Abbott's advice that "ordinarily it is unwise for a minister to take sides in politics."

Although the dominant political party changed with the election of Wilson, the progressive mood continued in the nation. The social awakening was obvious in the nation as well as the church. As

---

[41]*The Outlook* (New York), 20 July 1912, p. 610.

[42]Letter dated 20 February 1913, quoted in *Annual Reports of the Federal Council of the Churches of Christ in America* (1913), 4.

[43]Shailer Mathews, *New Faith for Old: An Autobiography* (New York: Macmillan Co., 1936) 162-63.

Rauschenbusch told the delegates to the Federal Council in December 1912,

> We are having a revival of religion. There is a big camp-meeting going on from Maine to Oregon, and if anyone has not yet come out on the Lord's side I invite him to come and get salvation. It would be a spiritual disaster to be left unsaved while others are moving up to a new level of religion, moral insight, and manhood. That is true of denominations as well as individuals. . . . God is today writing a flaming message of social righteousness, and you and I must learn to read it.[44]

That proclamation of the social revival fittingly climaxed the progress of the Social Gospel movement from the Social Creed to the Social Awakening during the four years from December 1908 to December 1912. The potential dangers of spiritual unrest were overwhelmed by the organizing zeal of the socially active denominations and the Federal Council of Churches, as well as the evangelical and social fervor of the Men and Religion Forward Movement. Those efforts eventually resulted in an awareness of God at work throughout the land in a widespread awakening that seemed to mark the birth of a new era. Despite a changing of the guard politically, the forces of progressivism continued unabated in the social order, and champions of social Christianity had greater expectations for their cause than ever before. When Woodrow Wilson was inaugurated on 4 March 1913 it appeared that the churches had only to program and publicize the social service that had finally won recognition in the churches and the nation.

---

[44]Rauschenbusch, "The Social Revival," *Christian Unity at Work*, 206.

PART 4

From the Social Awakening
to Social Service,
1912–1917

CHAPTER 13

Bringing the Denominational Forces to Work Together

The whole work of the Commission [on the Church and Social Service of the Federal Council of Churches] is proceeding in this way, conceiving its function to be that of bringing the denominational forces to work together, rather than considering itself as an independent body.

(Harry F. Ward, A Year Book of the Church and Social Service in the United States, *1914)*

HAVING AWAKENED THE CHURCHES to their Christian responsibilities for the needs of the social order did not mean that social-gospel advocates could relax in their task. It was necessary to build functional structures and activities for their newly recognized status in denominational life. That involved learning how to develop their leadership effectively in their own churches. Working within organizational channels, making use of lines of communication and education, designing workable programs, and finding ways to work cooperatively with other denominational and interdenominational resources for social change and ministry required patience and effort. Between December 1912 and December 1917 leaders of social Christianity labored successfully to make social service an integral part of the life of the socially active Protestant bodies and of the Federal Council of Churches.

Responses to their efforts usually were favorable, but in some instances criticism and direct attack challenged them. When confronted by apathy and opposition, social-gospel leaders sometimes had to clarify their purposes, modify their goals, and find ways to work together to make social service a secure part of Protestant church life and a contributing part of American social welfare and reform. Their goal was to stabilize the social gospel within institutional Protestantism by erecting a permanent program of social service in place of the temporary enthusiasm of the social awakening. To achieve their larger goals also necessitated cooperation with a number of voluntary and governmental agencies. By the time the nation's entry into the First World War intruded with new demands upon the social gospel early in 1917, the natural dynamics of the movement were strong enough to endure the impact, although that international event would affect its life. As social activists shifted gears into a new context in which they were an acknowledged part of institutional Protestantism, the movement evolved from the social awakening to the establishment of a firm foundation for social service in the churches and the nation, which distinguished this five-year period as a fourth stage of social-gospel development.

One of the difficulties that affected Protestant social activists was the lack of clarity concerning their understanding of the church. As noted earlier, several leaders of the movement encountered opposition and rejection within the church when they espoused the cause of social Christianity. In January 1913 Walter Rauschenbusch related on two occasions how the church stood in the way of his social interest. His personal testimony provided evidence that organized Christianity had little part in his emerging social ideas and values.[1] Consequently, his article "The True American Church," which appeared in *The Congregationalist* in October of that year, was a surprising treatment of the subject. This piece revealed that his theological perception was more low church than high, but that view was popular at the time, especially among evangelical social reformers.

"It has long been my conviction that there is a true American church in existence among us," he declared in that article. That church is powerful numerically, exerts great influence, and is "a native product of American life." But "this true American Church has not yet come to a conscious and organized existence. It is still embryonic, lying half-formed in the womb of time." By looking at the religious bodies that decisively influenced the spiritual life in local communities, he determined that the Methodists,

---

[1]Walter Rauschenbusch, "The Kingdom of God," *Cleveland's Young Men* 27 (9 January 1913) unpaginated, reprinted in Robert T. Handy, ed., *The Social Gospel in America, 1870–1920: Gladden, Ely, Rauschenbusch* (New York: Oxford University Press, 1966) 264-67; *Rochester Democrat and Chronicle*, 25 January 1913; quoted in Dores Robinson Sharpe, *Walter Rauschenbusch* (New York: Macmillan Co., 1942) 232-34. These recollections are incorporated in chs. 1 and 4 above.

Baptists, Presbyterians, Congregationalists, and Disciples of Christ comprised that true church. Although they existed as separate denominations, Rauschenbusch believed that "in all religious essentials they are one. . . . God and America have molded them toward a common type." Together they constituted "the fullest expression we have of native American religious life." In turn, by their combined efforts "they have formed the moral and spiritual life of our nation."[2]

Whether or not one agrees with Rauschenbusch's specific exclusion of Episcopalians, Lutherans, Roman Catholics, and others from the ranks of this embryonic American church, his description almost fit the working concept of the church that animated most Protestant leaders of social Christianity. Four of the five socially active denominations were on his list. The primary exception was the Protestant Episcopal Church, and that body would soon withdraw from much of ecumenical participation, as we shall see. Thus, it was not unusual that the socially active denominations easily cooperated in developing social ministry through the Federal Council of Churches. This cooperative planning and action facilitated the development of the social gospel during this five-year period and virtually exemplified Rauschenbusch's theory of the true American church.

Armed with the inspired mood that climaxed the Chicago meeting of the Federal Council, and with enabling legislation that permitted new activities approved by that body, Charles Macfarland quickly took the initiative concerning social ministry in the following months. Although he served as acting general secretary of the Federal Council, he also continued to function as secretary of its Commission on the Church and Social Service. His own social commitment was augmented by a triumvirate of recognized social-gospel leaders who filled important offices in the organization: Shailer Mathews was president of the council, Frank Mason North was chairman of the Executive Committee, and Josiah Strong was chairman of the Church and Social Service Commission. With four champions of social Christianity as leaders, it was not surprising that the Federal Council of Churches functioned as a catalyst in the social-gospel movement during the next several years.

A central organism in Macfarland's strategy was the Council of Social Service Secretaries. At the 1912 meeting of the council he cited it as the prime example of interdenominational cooperation and affirmed that "practically all of the National Assemblies of the denominational bodies have approved this cooperative relationship with each other through the Federal Council

---

[2]*The Congregationalist* (Boston), 23 October 1913; quoted in full in the *Rochester Theological Seminary Bulletin* (November 1918): 64-66.

Commission."[3] Since three of the five denominational secretaries began their full-time work on 1 October 1912, the major achievements of the group began in 1913. According to Harry F. Ward, the Social Service Commission conceived "its function to be that of bringing the denominational forces to work together, rather than considering itself as an independent body." Each secretary made his work interdenominational unless it interfered with denominational interests. In this way the Secretarial Council planned how to divide the work, issue their literature in common, and publicly cooperate at every possible point. Appropriately, each denominational secretary was designated an associate secretary of the Federal Council Commission on the Church and Social Service.[4] In 1915 Ward told the Executive Committee of the Methodist Federation for Social Service that the secretaries met more frequently so that "a unity of impression is being created throughout the country."[5] Macfarland acknowledged the close, free- hearted, and dedicated camaraderie of the secretaries in these early years. While working collegially, they granted him an "administrative primacy" that best enabled the group to function within the structure of the Federal Council of Churches.[6] The ability of the group to function as a clearinghouse enabled the ecumenical organization to play a primary role in social-gospel history.

To strengthen the impact of the council's Commission on the Church and Social Service, Macfarland enlarged its membership so that its ranks contained most of the recognized names associated with social Christianity. This produced a roster of nearly 125 men and women who represented the viewpoint of the churches regarding the nation's social problems. The addition of Washington Gladden, for example, provided the prestige of his name to the commission, but he could hardly afford to attend meetings at his own expense, as members had to do. This unwieldy body seldom functioned in full session, but its duties were implemented by sixteen members who comprised its Committee of Direction. Consisting of persons in the New York area and the denominational social-

---

[3]Charles S. Macfarland, "The Kingdoms of This World; The Kingdom of Our Lord," *Christian Unity at Work: The Federal Council of the Churches of Christ in America in Quadrennial Session at Chicago, Illinois, 1912*, ed. Charles S. Macfarland (New York: Federal Council of Churches, 1913) 160.

[4]Harry F. Ward, *A Year Book of the Church and Social Service in the United States. Prepared for the Commission on the Church and Social Service of the Federal Council of the Churches of Christ in America* (New York: Fleming H. Revell Co., 1914) 26.

[5]"Minutes of the Methodist Federation for Social Service, 1907–1930," typescript, Rose Memorial Library, Drew University, Madison NJ, 14 October 1915, 3.

[6]Charles S. Macfarland, *Across the Years* (New York: Macmillan Co., 1936) 301.

service secretaries, the Committee of Direction shaped the policy and strategy that affected the social ministry of the separate churches as well as of the Federal Council.[7]

Harry Ward's *A Year Book of the Church and Social Service in the United States*, published in 1914 and rewritten in 1916, was one of the cooperative publications. As a handbook for persons at all levels of church social action and study, it contained methods, programs, lists of cooperating agencies and publications, and a brief history of the social gospel up to the time the book went to press. By Ward's account it is clear that the Social Service Commission sought to work with and through other agencies. Efforts were made to establish relations with theological seminaries and training schools for social workers so that men and women would receive training in social service with a "distinctively spiritual point of view." Close ties were maintained with a number of national agencies for social reform, such as the National Child Labor Committee, the Playground and Recreation Association, the American Association for Labor Legislation, the National Conference of Charities and Correction, and the Southern Sociological Congress. Cooperative work was carried on with departments dealing with social service in agencies training youth, including the Young Men's Christian Association, the Young Women's Christian Association, and the Christian Endeavor movement.[8]

Beyond general education, the Federal Council sought to achieve specific aims. In connection with the nationwide campaign for one day of rest in seven for industrial workers that was persistently prosecuted in Congress and state legislatures, the council published a pamphlet titled *Continuous Toil and Continuous Toilers; Or One Day in Seven for Industrial Workers* in 1913 and for several following years. Recognizing that legislatures would not enact such legislation for religious reasons, the pamphlet advised readers to urge one day of rest a week for health reasons and then seek to have it on the Christian Sabbath, which was another widespread program of the council.[9] During 1914, for instance, the Committee of Direction secured commission endorsement of bills introduced into the House of Representatives and the Senate to authorize

---

[7]Ward, *A Year Book* (1914), 26-30; Josiah Strong and Charles S. Macfarland to Washington Gladden, 27 March 1913, Washington Gladden Papers, Ohio Historical Society, Columbus OH.

[8]Ward, *A Year Book* (1914), 26-28.

[9]*Continuous Toil and Continuous Toilers; Or One Day in Seven for Industrial Workers?* (New York: Federal Council of Churches, 1913) 19-20; *Annual Reports of the Federal Council of the Churches of Christ in America* (1913), 29.

a Sunday Rest Bill for all government employees. Similar campaigns were waged for old-age retirement benefits and other benefits for workers.[10]

From time to time the social-service secretaries engaged in investigations of industrial conditions, especially in trouble spots such as South Bethlehem, Pennsylvania; Muscatine, Iowa; and Patterson, New Jersey. Other times they prepared reports on prison conditions. At such times they became involved in local incidents, but generally the strategy of the Federal Council was to deal with religious, moral, and church subjects of nationwide or worldwide dimension, leaving state and local problems to state and local ecumenical federations.[11]

One such national campaign that attracted the involvement of the council was the growing agitation for prohibition in these years. The issue was so important that the Federal Council established a separate Commission on Temperance. That commission met in Washington, D.C., on 10 December 1913, the day that a prohibition amendment to the Constitution was introduced in both houses of Congress. The chairman of the commission also appeared before the Judiciary Committee of the House of Representatives to urge its adoption.[12] Although the bill died in committee that time, the agitation continued by the council's Temperance Commission. When the Executive Committee of the Federal Council met in Richmond, Virginia, in December 1914, William Jennings Bryan was alternate delegate of the northern Presbyterians and addressed the meeting on behalf of total abstinence. Later that night Bryan spoke to a throng of 3,500 in the city auditorium, and Shailer Mathews, as president of the Federal Council, also spoke.[13] Bryan's reputation is colored by the Scopes trial in the 1920s, and his general progressive sympathies and efforts are often forgotten.[14]

During 1914 the Federal Council of Churches took a momentous step, which was a logical extension of the approach they had adopted; they employed Henry K. Carroll as associate secretary and stationed him in Washington, D.C. The ability of the interdenominational federation to fund another staff member was a symbol of significant growth. The federation's awareness of the importance of an official presence in the

---

[10]*Annual Reports of the Federal Council* (1914), 124-25, 160.

[11]Ibid. (1913), 97-98.

[12]Ibid., 109.

[13]Ibid. (1914), 93, 94.

[14]For a list of Progressive legislation that he advocated see *The Memoirs of William Jennings Bryan, by Himself and His Wife, Mary Baird Bryan* (N.p., c. 1925) 463.

nation's capital in order to influence national affairs also showed new political insight and strategy. The associate secretary was able to attend national gatherings of organizations meeting in the city, to attend sessions of the Senate and House and their committees, and to visit government agencies on behalf of causes important to the council.[15] Moreover, Carroll was able to use the Washington office to arrange conferences for council officers and representatives to meet with various government officials.[16]

While Harry Ward made no reference to the political influence of the Washington office in his account of the council's social ministry, he did emphasize the significance of its publications. These included a number of reports, investigations, study courses and bibliographies, social-service catechisms, and other materials covering social questions for pastors and church classes. Collaboration with other organizations to publish joint handbooks and with several publishing houses to facilitate the printing of social-gospel books and literature were important aspects of this emphasis. Reflecting the conviction of liberal Protestants that education is a vital means of redemption for those who believe that people know right from wrong and have the inherent good sense to choose rightly when properly informed, the Federal Council leaders stressed the value of publications in their program of social ministry.

In the 1916 edition of *A Year Book of the Church and Social Service*, Harry Ward evaluated what had occurred during the past two years. "During this period," he wrote, "the denominational agencies have perfected their plans." He pointed to three general methods that were developed: first, "to produce and circulate printed matter"; second, "to conduct information bureaus" that make resources available for sermons and talks to be used in local communities; and third, "to carry on a large speaking propaganda." The methods were essentially educational in purpose. He further concluded that "the interdenominational alliance of social service agencies has also been greatly strengthened in the past two years." Regular meetings of the Secretarial Council produced several positive results: "the literature of one denomination is available for all, a common body of printed matter has developed, methods are standardized, and a joint educational scheme is promoted." In his estimation, the period was a time of "seed-sowing" and of preparing educational material. In Ward's view, these social-service activities of the churches bespoke a changed

---

[15]*Annual Reports of the Federal Council* (1914), 76-77.

[16]Ibid. (1915), 44-45.

attitude on the part of many church members: "A social consciousness and a social conscience have been developed within the churches."[17]

Such a positive appraisal of the years from 1913 to 1916 makes the efforts of social-gospel leaders in the Federal Council look good. However, other evidence suggests that everything was not as uniformly positive as Ward stated. His evaluation was not wrong, but it did not include all facets of the situation. The fundamental problem is suggested by a discrepancy between what was proposed in 1913 and what finally resulted in 1915. When the Commission on the Church and Social Service reported to the council's Executive Committee in December 1913, it indicated that "the present admirable social platform . . . adopted in Chicago in 1912," which focused primarily on problems of industry, needed to be broadened to include other pressing social problems such as rural life and immigration.[18] However, when the commission met two years later, Ward reported that the Secretarial Council felt it unwise to revise the council's platform of social standards "at this time."[19] During the interval, unforeseen problems arose that inhibited the easy development of interdenominational social ministry. Since these problems originated in certain denominations, it is necessary to examine the course of social Christianity in the five churches most active in social outreach in the same three years. As the problems become clear, their effect upon the Federal Council of Churches will be studied in the following chapter.

Samuel Zane Batten was one of the social-service secretaries who officially assumed his office on 1 October 1912, but he had been active in social-gospel causes for more than two decades and had chaired the Baptist Convention's Commission on Social Service since it was first created in 1908. During most of his twenty-four years in pastoral ministry and two years as head of the department of social work at Des Moines College, from which he came to the secretaryship, he was active in the Brotherhood of the Kingdom and was a close friend of Baptist advocates of the social gospel. When the American Baptist Publication Society decided to create a Department of Social Service and Brotherhood in September 1912, Batten was a natural choice to assume its leadership. Due to his long involvement in the movement he was familiar with its issues, programs, and personalities, which enabled him quickly to assume leadership initiatives.

---

[17]Harry F. Ward, *A Year Book of The Church and Social Service in the United States. Prepared for the Commission on the Church and Social Service of the Federal Council of the Churches of Christ in America* (New York: Missionary Education Movement of the United States and Canada, 1916) 22-23.

[18]*Annual Reports of the Federal Council* (1913), 90-92.

[19]Ibid. (1915), 110.

The primary hardship he faced was the necessity of carrying the dual portfolio of running both a program for men's work and one for social concern.

In his first report, made in May 1913, Batten indicated his conviction that his employment marked an epoch-making advance in the area of social service and expressed appreciation for the growing support this indicated among Northern Baptists. Henceforth, the commission that he formerly chaired would serve in an advisory capacity in shaping policy and organizing the new ministry. Several basic components in that ministry were described: study courses were being developed for use by churches, brotherhoods, young people, adult classes, and study groups; fundamental principles of social service were being defined and standardized; much of the secretary's time was given to travel in the field, where by addresses and workshops he sought to broaden the extent of the work; and the secretary cooperated with other denominations and the Social Service Commission of the Federal Council of Churches. The latter involvement showed its impact on his address as he stressed Macfarland's threefold conception of the Christian Church as "conscience, interpreter, and guide of all life and all movements." His report for the Social Service Commission also contained a series of resolutions that were approved after they were processed by the Committee on Resolutions. Those resolutions condemned child labor and poor conditions for women workers, supported the Federal Council's efforts for moral purity to be discussed at the approaching Panama Exposition, urged prison reform and arbitration between workers and employers, encouraged the support of Sunday observance and one day off in seven for workers, and strongly endorsed a constitutional amendment on prohibition. Sentiment on the latter issue was sufficiently strong that the convention directed the commission to take added steps on behalf of temperance.[20]

Responding to this directive, Batten reported in 1914 that he now divided his time in three areas: temperance, the brotherhood, and social service. During the year, he had traveled more than 42,000 miles, given 209 addresses, and participated in 41 conferences, concentrating on meetings with local brotherhoods and social-service commissions. The content and activities involved in both areas were detailed in lengthy reports to the convention.[21] Extensive attention was devoted to prohibition in a section entitled "The Temperance Situation and the Churches' Duty," and Batten explained how he and the Baptist Commission related to the

---

[20]*Annual of the Northern Baptist Convention* (1913), 126-40, 196-98, 518-19, 555-58.

[21]Ibid. (1914), 139-63, 164-66, 666-69.

Federal Council and other groups. He worked especially closely with Dr. Henry K. Carroll and the council's Washington office on the temperance issue.[22] Throughout his report, Batten attempted to clarify a unique Baptist role in the social scene, although he admitted, "Baptist interests are very similar to those of most other Protestant churches." Primarily he emphasized the Baptist "passion for democracy" as a unique contribution of the Baptist free-church tradition. "Some great religious body is needed which shall . . . interpret the positive relation of religion to social affairs, and lead men in their efforts to realize the kingdom of God in the social order." He also challenged the Northern Baptist Convention to accept that responsibility.[23]

The following year revealed how important social-gospel leaders had become in the denomination. Shailer Mathews, already president of the Federal Council, was elected as the president of the Northern Baptist Convention, and Walter Rauschenbusch addressed a joint session of the American Foreign Mission Society and the American Baptist Home Mission Society and also spoke to the Baptist Brotherhood during the convention.[24] Batten's report again was extensive and showed the continuity of social-service programming with preceding years. Perhaps the most distinctive feature of the report was his highlighting of two serious dangers that confronted churches. On one side, Christians could develop such a narrow range of interests that they interpreted the purpose of Christ in entirely personal and church terms so that they left social work to "outsiders and unspiritual people." On the other side, persons interested in social action might neglect "evangelism and spiritual work, lose interest in the church, and attempt to carry on the work of community reconstruction and social salvation without any reference to the Christian ideal." Batten's message to Baptists responded to the issue that Presbyterians raised for the Federal Council of Churches, as we shall see, and showed how pervasive that problem had become by 1915. His conclusion on that issue was obvious: "They err seriously who say Christianity is nothing more than philanthropy and Social Service."[25]

In his 1916 account to the Annual Convention, the secretary was pleased to report that "Social Service has now a recognized place in our denominational programs, and is placed on an equality with other forms of Christian effort." Batten likened that achievement to a quiet revolution

---

[22]Ibid., 140-42, 156-63.

[23]Ibid., 144-45.

[24]Ibid. (1915), 196, 204.

[25]Ibid., 177-96, 1061-67.

that had great significance but came as silently as the springtime. "A reformation is upon us which ought to mean a great advance toward the kingdom of God."[26]

Among Congregationalists, Henry A. Atkinson held a dual responsibility for social service and men's brotherhood similar to Batten's. He assumed those responsibilities in January 1911 as the Congregational Brotherhood employed him in response to a directive of the 1910 National Council that assigned matters of labor and social service to the men's organization. In the interval until the National Convention met again in triennial session in October 1913, Atkinson organized work in both areas. Although the two phases of work were carried simultaneously by one executive, two separate committees considered the distinct facets of his portfolio and each submitted recommendations, which in 1913 conflicted. The report of the Brotherhood Committee reviewed the work carried on by Atkinson, which read much like that implemented by Batten for the Baptists. Similar patterns of travel, meetings, issues, and interdenominational cooperation were evident. Significantly, the committee observed that "in the department of labor and social service, the Brotherhood has a service distinctly its own," and it proposed to continue that emphasis.[27]

In contrast, the report of the Industrial Committee sought to rearrange the duties and emphases. Although acknowledging the contributions of the Brotherhood in assuming responsibilities for labor and social service— "thus recognizing social service as a denominational function . . . in line with the advanced movements of the other denominations"— this committee proposed the discontinuance of both the Brotherhood and Industrial Committees. In their place it recommended the creation of a Commission on Social Service and Men's Work to be appointed by the National Council. By this change it was urged that the function and scope of the work give primary emphasis to social and industrial concerns.[28]

Both reports were considered by the National Council on the same day. Eventually a special committee of five was created to consider the conflicting recommendations. A week later that group presented its report, which substantially embodied the changes proposed by the Industrial Committee. Following debate, the report of the special committee was adopted, and the status of social ministry was substantially

---

[26]Ibid. (1916), 166.

[27]*Minutes of the National Council of the Congregational Churches of the United States* (1913), 235-42.

[28]Ibid., 276-78.

upgraded in Congregationalism. The standing committees on Industry and Congregational Brotherhood were discontinued, and in their place a nine-member Commission on Social Service was established, with the authority to employ an executive secretary "who shall serve the National Council as industrial secretary." There were provisions for budget and for the new commission to "cooperate with the Social Service Commission of the Federal Council of Churches in all matters requiring interdenominational expression and action."[29] By these negotiations the roles of the two phases of Atkinson's work were reversed; henceforth, the Brotherhood became part of Social Service.

Since the National Council of the Congregational Churches had changed from a three-year cycle of meetings to a two-year cycle, the next session convened in 1915. The report of the Commission on Social Service related the various activities and diverse work demanded of executive secretary Atkinson. He and the commission served the National Council in six distinct areas: industry, rural life, social service, organized charities, men's work, and social purity. In addition, during the biennium Atkinson was asked to serve half-time as assistant to Dr. Herring, the executive of the National Council, which meant in effect that the six areas of responsibility were handled on a half-time basis. Further dividing the secretary's workload was the Congregational commitment to cooperative social ministry in relationship to the Federal Council and to other agencies committed to social welfare and reform. Thus, Atkinson worked with other denominations, conducted investigations of strikes in Michigan and Colorado, did surveys and special campaigns, and represented the denomination at the National Conference of Charities and Corrections and the Southern Sociological Congress. While reaffirming the entire Social Creed of the Churches, it was clear that Atkinson and the commission regarded industrial problems as the main concern. The report affirmed that "the solution of our deepest problems is a matter of ideals, and the churches alone can create the faith, remold the consciences and bring about the spirit of co-operation that will result in social adjustment both by means of better legislation and by voluntary outworkings of a new spirit of good will." In this huge task the commission was convinced that "it is much better for the church to co-operate with the organized charity organizations of the community than to do the work itself." At their request the National Council approved their continued work in the six areas, agreed to urge local congregations to become active in those areas in a minimal program, and made the rural church a special emphasis.[30]

---

[29]Ibid., 383, 385, 396-97.

[30]Ibid. (1915), 284-314.

Contrasting with the cool reception that Washington Gladden experienced in 1907 when he spoke about the church and the social crisis, two addresses that centered on social problems were appreciatively received at this National Council session. In his speech entitled "The Spirit of Christ in the Institutions of Our Nation," Raymond Robins affirmed, "we are living in a changing social order," one in which "the old individual control has broken down . . . and the new social control is not yet wholly born." He asserted that every person was now "more concerned about social control through government than ever before" because "the law reaches out to the ideals, the sanitation, the food, the education, the morals, the industry, and the whole life of man." In short, because of Progressive legislation and regulation, former class control had broadened to democratic control.[31] In a similar vein, the moderator's address by Charles Reynolds Brown, dean of the Yale University Divinity School, declared that "the huge task of Christianizing our social order means the introduction of a more democratic spirit" into control of the forces that shape lives. Bemoaning the outbreak of war in Europe as the coming not of a new heaven but of a new earth dressed in a coat of mail, he summoned Congregationalists "to a struggle where the lamb makes war with the beast." At home he stressed that "the social emphasis in religion grows firmer year by year," but he urged Christians to express their faith in all aspects of daily life.[32] The voice of the prophets was still being heard when Congregationalists assembled, and there was still more for the Commission on Social Service to do.

The affinity of men's brotherhood work and social service that was evident with both Northern Baptists and Congregationalists was a general phenomenon of the time. It was a latent potential that provided one of the pleasant surprises of the Men and Religion Forward Movement campaign. Also, it was evident in denominations that did not create the obvious structural alliance of the two causes that we have just noted. Northern Methodists authorized a separate Methodist Brotherhood, which also showed interest in social concerns. When the first convention of men met in May 1910, social service was one of the emphases. Perhaps that was not surprising since the first president was Fred E. Tasker, who served as treasurer of the National City Evangelization Society, which was closely related to the formation of the Methodist Federation for Social Service. Other members of the Brotherhood's Managing Board included the veteran Frank Mason North and the newcomer Harris Franklin Rall, a leader with social sympathies who was beginning to appear on the

---

[31]Ibid., 144-62.

[32]Ibid., 77-96.

national scene. By 1912 Rall was the treasurer of the Federation for Social Service.[33] When 2,500 Methodist men met at the national convention at Indianapolis, Indiana, in October 1913, the social emphasis was again evident in the program. Harry Ward was present to tell about the Methodist Federation for Social Service, Herbert Welch spoke on "The New Day and Social Reform," and Francis J. McConnell challenged with "The Call to Social Service."[34]

In a similar way, the Methodist Episcopal Church was vitally committed to the temperance cause, but it did not assign that responsibility to the Methodist Federation for Social Service. Methodism's enthusiasm for prohibition long antedated its interest in social concerns generally, with a Permanent Committee on Temperance and Prohibition already established by the General Conference in 1888. As more concerted political efforts were mounted in 1912, the General Conference authorized the creation of the Temperance Society of the Methodist Episcopal Church and " 'loosed and let it go.' " During the following quadrennium, phenomenal progress was reported, and the 1916 General Conference voted to double its budget from $50,000 to $100,000 annually. The Committee on Temperance, Prohibition, and Public Morals also recommended asking that all political party platforms include prohibition planks and urged that the Methodist Temperance Society headquarters be moved from Topeka, Kansas, to Washington, D.C., to improve its effectiveness. The denomination's firm stand against liquor was evident in a statement of principles that said in part, "The expansion of religion and the preservation of civilization require its overthrow,—its complete and utter annihilation." The contemporary campaign to enact a prohibition amendment to the Constitution offered that promise and motivated the enthusiastic support of the 1916 General Conference.[35]

Since temperance, brotherhood, and other responsibilities were not assigned to the Methodist Federation for Social Service, the organization was able to devote its total energies to other social problems. Under the zealous leadership of Harry F. Ward, the federation reported considerable progress between 1912 and 1916, although its recommendations were received with less enthusiasm than was shown for temperance. Ward told

---

[33]*The Methodist Year Book* (1912), 147-49, 151, 153.

[34]*Militant Methodism: The Story of the First National Convention of Methodist Men, Held at Indianapolis, Indiana, October Twenty-Eight to Thirty-One, Nineteen Hundred and Thirteen*, ed. David G. Downey, E. W. Halford, Ralph Welles Keeler (Cincinnati: The Methodist Book Concern, n.d.) 238-41, 256-62, 182-89.

[35]*Journal of the General Conference of the Methodist Episcopal Church* (1916), 677-85, 1441.

of his extensive travel and speaking engagements, which averaged more than 300 annually. His correspondence averaged 250 letters monthly. He actively cooperated with other agencies, both denominational and interdenominational. Especially he sought to strengthen and encourage the work of the Social Service Commissions in the various annual conferences of Methodism, so that social ministry might reach local levels of the denomination more quickly and effectively.[36]

With the focus of the federation's work aimed at educational and inspirational activities, Ward concentrated on a program of publication to provide written resource materials that could be utilized throughout the church. These efforts ranged from furnishing social interpretations of the weekly lessons printed in the *Sunday School Journal*, to articles submitted to denominational periodicals, to pamphlets, to the *Social Service Bulletin* he edited and wrote every other month for those committed to the social cause. Social-service programs were developed for the Brotherhood, the Epworth League, the women's societies, and adult Bible classes. His publication efforts also assumed more serious dimensions as he wrote and published several books. Some of these were published by the Federal Council of Churches, where Ward served on the Publication Committee of the Commission on the Church and Social Service: two editions of *The Social Creed of the Churches* (1912 and 1914) and two editions of *A Year Book of the Churches and Social Service* (1914 and 1916). He also published *Poverty and Wealth* and *Social Evangelism* in 1915.[37]

For three of the four years of the quadrennium, Ward reported that he had engaged in seminary teaching. Four months of each year he taught courses in social service at the Boston University School of Theology, and he lectured regularly at two seminaries in the Chicago area as well. Rather than distract from his social ministry through the federation, these teaching occasions stimulated him to develop his ideas more carefully, which fed into his publications. For example, one of his primary interests at the time was the bad conditions affecting the common worker. Ward's book *Poverty and Wealth* was one aspect of his study of that topic, and he wrote it as an elective study course for the adult Bible classes in the Sunday school curriculum.[38] Early in 1915 he lectured on the labor movement in Ford Hall, Boston, which was crowded with a mixture of ministers and laity, employers and employees, professors and union leaders. Two years

---

[36]Ibid., 1427, 1429-31.

[37]Ibid., 1428; Ward, *A Year Book* (1914), 45.

[38]Harry F. Ward, *Poverty and Wealth: From the Viewpoint of the Kingdom of God* (New York and Cincinnati: The Methodist Book Concern, 1915).

later these lectures, which Ward regarded as the best statement of his views on the subject in this period, were published in a book titled *The Labor Movement*.[39]

Ward's preoccupation with labor concerns during the period also was evident in other ways. His report to the 1916 General Conference indicated his role in labor disputes in Iowa and Pennsylvania and related his efforts to mediate between the printers' union and the western branch of the Methodist Book Concern in Cincinnati. In the latter negotiations he tried to get the church institution to pay just wages both in fairness to those workers and to set an example of Christian conduct in relation to labor, which he was convinced was justified in attacking the church for unfair practices.[40] The antagonism that situation created surfaced elsewhere in the General Conference agenda when the Methodist Federation for Social Service recommendation to amplify the Social Creed statement by adding interpretive sections was considered. The majority of those new sections dealt with labor issues and a paragraph of the section titled "Industrial Democracy," which dealt with the church's role as an employer of labor and the recommendation that it engage in collective bargaining, provoked controversial debate.[41] Another consequence of his attack occurred in 1915 when the Book Concern "declined to print" Ward's *Social Evangelism* volume, which finally was published by the Missionary Education Movement.[42]

The recommendation of the Methodist Federation for Social Service to supplement the Social Creed by more than eleven pages of interpretive comments was an interesting development. Previously it was noted that Harry Ward, speaking in behalf of the Secretarial Council, urged that the Federal Council make no changes in the Social Creed in 1916. Yet five months later his own federation proposed that a significant addition be made to the platform by way of interpretation. Since Charles Macfarland prevailed upon the Church of the United Brethren in Christ in 1917 not

---

[39]Harry F. Ward, *The Labor Movement: From the Standpoint of Religious Values* (New York: Macmillan Co., 1919) pref.; Robert H. Craig, "An Introduction to the Life and Thought of Harry F. Ward," *Union Seminary Quarterly Review* 24 (Summer 1969): 337.

[40]*Journal of the General Conference of the Methodist Episcopal Church* (1916), 1433-35; Eugene P. Link, *Labor-Religion Prophet: The Times and Life of Harry F. Ward* (Boulder CO: Westview Press, 1984) 61-63.

[41]*Journal of the General Conference of the Methodist Episcopal Church* (1916), 359-63.

[42]"Minutes of the Methodist Federation for Social Service," 14 October 1915, 2.

to break ecumenical uniformity by changing the Social Creed unilaterally,[43] keeping the declaration's basic wording unaltered obviously was the general position of the Secretarial Council. Ward's recommended additions seemed to be unilateral and contradicted his own statement to the federation's annual meeting in October 1915 that its request to the General Conference would be "largely in the form of the statement to be recommended to the Federal Council of Churches."[44] The wording of the Creed itself remained unchanged, but the Methodist addendum was a modification by one denomination. In printing the 1916 *Discipline of the Methodist Episcopal Church*, the Methodist Book Concern reduced the eleven-page interpretation to two and a half pages.[45]

When the General Conference Committee on the State of the Church reviewed the work of Ward and the Methodist Federation for Social Service it was impressed, but nevertheless modified several of the recommendations. Its primary commendation was that all the work had been accomplished the preceding year for a total cost of $6,092, which led the committee to remark that "no other organization in the church has a stronger influence and is doing a more valuable work at anything near the cost." Authorization of a new budget of $10,000 annually was a notable increase, but hardly comparable to the doubled budget of $100,000 that the Temperance Society received. However, the budget allocations fairly represented the relative importance of the two causes in Methodism at the time. A federation request for an additional $5,000 for publications was ignored, and another for the support of a program for industrial evangelists was watered down. Perhaps the most significant limitation was imposed on the federation's request for general approval as "the executive agency to rally the forces of the Church in support of the measures and principles concerning the relation of the Church to the social question." This recognition was amended so that only those "measures specifically approved as our program of social service" were authorized, which sought to limit more narrowly the autonomy of the federation.[46]

Implicit in this latter action was a lack of clarity concerning the relationship of the Methodist Federation for Social Service to the Methodist Episcopal Church. The federation was the only social-service agency

---

[43]*Proceedings of the General Conference of the United Brethren in Christ (1917), 560.*

[44]"Minutes of the Methodist Federation for Social Service," 14 October 1915, 3.

[45]*The Doctrines and Discipline of the Methodist Episcopal Church (1916), 528-31; cf. Journal of the General Conference of the Methodist Episcopal Church (1916), 602-14.*

[46]*Journal of the General Conference of the Methodist Episcopal Church (1916), 616, 1435-37.*

involved in the Federal Council's Secretarial Council that enjoyed an independent existence; all the others existed at the will of the parent denominations. From its inception in Washington in December 1907, the federation declared its intention to remain "wholly unofficial in its relation to the General Conference, and to the other official societies of Methodism."[47] However, this commitment was clouded by the agency's recurring requests to be recognized as "the executive agency" of Northern Methodism in the area of social concerns.

During the years 1913–1916 a fundamental question was raised concerning whether a department of social service should be organized by the Methodist Board of Home Missions. Faced with this prospect, Ward prepared a document for the Executive Committee of the federation to consider in 1914. In it he identified three groups that continually required attention—the industrial, the immigrant, and the rural groups— and he stated that it might be more effective if departments for each were created in the Home Mission Board. "This is the next forward step for Methodism—to organize the entire outgoing activities in the home land for a more effective attack upon those territories where the church is weakest and the community life the most hostile to Christianity." In this light, there clearly was a need in the realm of home missions, and Ward declared that there was good reason to organize such departments within that board.[48] When the Executive Committee discussed the matter again on 14 October 1915, they insisted that any action concerning the Home Mission Board "should not involve the discontinuance" of the federation. They differentiated between two kinds of social ministry: that for the practical guidance of community-service activities and that related to "aggressive educational propaganda of the social principles of the gospel." It was their conviction that the Board of Home Missions could do the former, but "the inspirational and educational campaigns for the Christianizing of the Social Order is distinctively the function of an organization which is not a collector and distributor of funds."[49] Despite two years of discussion, neither the Board of Home Missions nor the Methodist Federation for Social Service mentioned the issue in their

---

[47]"Minutes of the Methodist Federation for Social Service," 3 December 1907, 12.

[48]Ibid., 26 October 1914, 2; "An Appeal to the Church" by H. F. W., mimeographed document in the Worth Tippy Papers for 1913–1914, Archives of DePauw University and Indiana Methodism, Greencastle IN, Box DC616, Folder 21.

[49]"Minutes of the Methodist Federation for Social Service," 14 October 1915, 5.

reports to the 1916 General Conference, and the precise relationship of social service in the denomination remained an enigma. In the future this lack of clarity would prove bothersome to the federation and the church, but in May 1916 the organization could take pride in its accomplishments and their generally favorable reception. And Harry Ward could bask in the acclaim that came to him when Charles Macfarland told the General Conference that he was "the man regarded by the denominations of the Federal Council as the greatest social prophet to-day, in our Christian Churches, of our social order."[50]

Compared to the expanding social interests of the Baptists, Congregationalists, and Methodists, the Protestant Episcopal Church in 1913 retreated from the pioneering role that it had expressed in the early years of social Christianity. Through its ability to raise funds independently, the Joint Commission on Social Service that was authorized by the 1910 General Convention succeeded in hiring Frank M. Crouch as full-time field secretary beginning 1 October 1912. By virtue of that position, Crouch not only became part of the Federal Council's Secretarial Council but also had the opportunity to establish a social-service program for the denomination. An office was established in New York City, and through extensive correspondence and travel Crouch made contacts by which he hoped to develop further ventures. He delivered numerous addresses to diocesan social-service commissions, departmental missionary councils, local parishes, and theological schools. He and the Joint Commission believed they could make their most useful contribution to their own constituency, but this strategy limited his direct access to local parishes, unless in response to special inquiry, and concentrated more on national and diocesan levels initially.[51]

At the opening session of the General Convention in October 1913, Bishop William Lawrence, long active on the former Joint Commission on Capital and Labor, preached a sermon on "The Challenge to the Church." Primarily he stressed an educational ideal to arouse the church's membership. On the basis of an educated constituency, he held forth three visions: that Episcopalians could live and work together within their own church in peace, that they could hold to the ideal of unity through God's spirit, and that society may be "redeemed and purified by the Power of Christ through His Church." This would result in a brotherhood of man, a united church, and redeemed society, he insisted. "In the turmoil of

---

[50]*Journal of the General Conference of the Methodist Episcopal Church* (1916), 803; *Daily Christian Advocate*, 11 May 1916, p. 170.

[51]Ward, *A Year Book* (1914), 56-58.

industrialism . . . let the Church's voice be strong and full of love."[52] A resolution on social justice, which had been approved by the Lambeth Conference of Anglican churches in 1908, was adopted by both the House of Deputies and House of Bishops.[53] It was more general in nature than the Social Creed of the churches, which was not affirmed by either house, although three of its measures and other resolutions were endorsed individually.[54] Both the House of Deputies and House of Bishops also adopted a resolution that made the Joint Commission on Social Service a permanent commission of the General Convention.[55]

Nevertheless, there were signs of latent problems for the Joint Commission. One sign was the absence of an official report from the organization and the fact that information concerning its work had to be pieced together from a number of smaller reports and resolutions. Another sign was the major conflict that developed during the convention between the House of Deputies and the House of Bishops concerning the denomination's participation in the Federal Council of Churches. The laity in the House of Deputies adopted a resolution approving the aims and purposes of the council and authorizing the Commissions on Christian Unity and on Social Service to send delegates to council meetings. However, the House of Bishops disapproved of this action and proposed a substitute resolution that stated that the Protestant Episcopal church was convinced that the ideal of Christ was organic unity rather than federation; therefore, it should not participate in the Federal Council. However, "when practical without the sacrifice of principle, this convention expresses [the] opinion that the Commissions on Christian Unity and on Social Service may appoint representatives to take part in the Federal Council." When the other house refused to concur with this substitute resolution, a conference committee was created to try to find a compromise. That committee was unable to reach an agreement and was discharged, whereupon the layman who made the original motion asked the House of Deputies to rescind its former approval and concur with the House of Bishops, which they did in the end. In this way, the church's Commission on Social Service continued to relate to the Federal Council, while the Protestant Episcopal church itself did not.[56]

---

[52]*Journal of the General Convention of the Protestant Episcopal Church in the U.S.A.* (1913), 388-91.

[53]Ibid., 122-23, 150, 308-309, 347.

[54]Ibid., 321, 322, 331, 349.

[55]Ibid., 83-84, 100, 230-37, 283, 312.

[56]Ibid., 279, 316-17, 341, 342, 351, 352.

Three years later, when the General Convention met in triennial session, there was again no formal report from the Joint Commission on Social Service. A number of resolutions assigning tasks to the commission appeared throughout the official record, and it was clear that the convention was making use of the permanent commission, but without a report it was difficult to picture its fully developed program. One helpful statement by the Committee on the State of the Church declared that the Joint Commission on Social Service "had marked effect upon the activities of the Church. Her members are now appreciative of the fact that the Christian ideal of human life includes both the salvation of the individual and the salvation of society." It noted also that the number of Diocesan Social Service Commissions had increased to eighty-one, and many local parishes had similar bodies functioning. These combined efforts were "bringing the influence of the Church to bear directly upon social problems," concluded the report.[57]

The absence of reports and recommendations from either the Joint Commission or the General Secretary suggested that they had less initiative in Episcopalian ranks than in Methodist, Congregational, or Baptist bodies, but it was apparent that Frank Crouch was establishing a functional rather than flamboyant program of social service for the Protestant Episcopal church in this period. Moreover, his modest style and approach enabled him to continue to participate in the broader social ministry carried on by the Secretarial Council of the Federal Council, despite his denomination's theological differences with federated Protestantism. Although Episcopalian efforts were less enthusiastic than those of Methodists, Congregationalists, and Baptists, they were essentially positive. Fundamentally, Protestant Episcopal differences with the Federal Council were grounded in the doctrine of the church and not in commitment to social ministry.

During the years from 1913 to 1916 the social-service secretaries of four denominations worked effectively at several levels to establish program and organization. In the Secretarial Council and other agencies of the hospitable Federal Council of Churches, the secretaries enjoyed their greatest achievements and found the most camaraderie. As Harry Ward said, they were "bringing the denominational forces to work together." When each full-time secretary left the area of ecumenical cooperation to function in his own denomination, however, the experiences differed noticeably. Some social-service programs were more officially sponsored than others. Some secretaries were able to concentrate their energies on social projects, while others had to provide leadership for social service

---

[57]Ibid. (1916), 79-80, 139, 162, 251, 262, 263, 278, 279, 407.

in addition to carrying other major responsibilities. Despite this variety, substantial progress was achieved in four of the five socially active denominations, and social service received growing recognition, appreciation, and support during this period.

In contrast to these four was the experience of the Northern Presbyterians, which followed an entirely different course and produced consequences that affected the other social-gospel organizations. Since the Presbyterian episode caused controversies internally for the denomination and externally for the Federal Council, tested the permanence of social Christianity, and resulted in new statements defining Protestant social action, it will be examined more extensively in the next chapter.

CHAPTER 14

A Statement of Principles

[If the Federal Council is precluded from uttering] the voice of the churches upon matters in regard to which the consciousness and the conscience of Christianity are practically unanimous, the Federal Council would be shorn of the power given it by the constituent bodies when they adopted as one of its objects: "To secure a larger combined influence for the churches of Christ in all matters affecting the moral and social condition of the people, so as to promote the application of the law of Christ in every relation of human life."

(A Statement of Principles
Underlying and Guiding the Development and Work
of the Federal Council of the Churches of Christ in America, *1914*)

WHILE CHAMPIONS OF THE SOCIAL GOSPEL were generally rejoicing over the social awakening of the churches in 1912, militant critics began to attack Presbyterian social ministry. The focus of their criticism was Charles Stelzle and his Bureau of Social Service, but soon the conflict involved the Federal Council of Churches and affected the program of all Protestant agencies of social Christianity. As the battle progressed, the ecumenical organization found it expedient to clarify its principles concerning social service more thoroughly. This early encounter between conservative and liberal Protestants indicated that the social gospel was not going to develop without opposition, and it identified some of the basic points of contention. Moreover, the controversy fulfilled Walter Rauschenbusch's 1912 prediction that soon a reactionary movement would occur because older men who cared for older ideas would not permit new ideas to force their way into the church without a fight.

At the time of the second quadrennial meeting of the Federal Council in December 1912, Charles Stelzle was the most respected leader of a denominational social-service program. Presbyterian efforts among urban workers were the model for other churches and had expanded to initiate ministry among immigrants and rural churches also. Although Stelzle's three-person staff was the largest employed by Protestant churches, his interests were broadly ecumenical and widely acclaimed. Thus, many persons were surprised when he abruptly terminated his work as secretary of the Bureau of Social Service in the autumn of 1913, after ten productive years.

Apparently Presbyterian criticism of social Christianity began in the southern Presbyterian church, which "went so far as to say that the Church had nothing whatever to do with social or political questions," according to Stelzle.[1] Through contacts established during church-consolidation discussions among three Presbyterian bodies, conservative Northern Presbyterians also joined the attack. Although it was not widely known, in the summer of 1912 the Executive Commission of the General Assembly in the North authorized a study of charges that utterances by Stelzle were socialistic. That October, however, a review committee recommended that "in view of the information received, the whole inquiry be dropped."[2]

Instead of quieting the critics, the decision motivated them to more militant action. When the General Assembly met in May 1913, the entire Board of Home Missions was under attack, but especially its Bureau of Social Service. It was accused of misappropriation of funds, malfeasance, and mismanagement. An investigating committee found these charges to be ungrounded and suggested that the problem resulted from a difference with regard to methods rather than expenditures.[3] In Stelzle's opinion, the attack resulted from a group of conservatives in the Pittsburgh area who sought to curtail his budget and staff. They appealed to growing feelings that there were too many special departments and experts employed by the Home Mission Board, that Labor Temple was too specialized a ministry for the general church to sponsor, and that the denomination was moving too "rapidly toward a sympathetic attitude with relation to social problems."[4] After considering every facet of the board's work, including the Bureau of Social Service, the Executive Commission of the General Assembly presented a series of

----

[1]Charles Stelzle, *A Son of the Bowery: The Life Story of an East Side American* (New York: George H. Doran Co., 1926) 167.

[2]*Minutes of the General Assembly of the Presbyterian Church in the United States of America* n.s. (1915), 168-69.

[3]Ibid. (1913), 178-79.

[4]Stelzle, *Son of the Bowery*, 167-68.

recommendations that was approved by the delegates. Four of its recommendations directly affected the bureau. One called for the discontinuance of the Department of Church and Country Life. Another urged the need to continue the Immigration Department. A third stated that "although considerable criticism is made of the Bureau of Social Service, these criticisms seem to relate to methods rather than functions"; therefore, they thought the bureau should be maintained. A fourth recommendation transferred full support and supervision of Labor Temple from the Bureau to the New York Presbytery.[5]

In the midst of these attacks on Stelzle and his bureau, Charles Macfarland brought a four-page, printed report from the Federal Council's Executive Committee to distribute to the Northern Presbyterian General Assembly. That document asserted that it was part of the council's work to give "moral guidance and direction" where it did not duplicate efforts by member constituencies. Functioning as a representative body rather than as a voluntary association, the council "upon appropriate and warrantable occasions . . . has voiced the common consciousness of the churches in the life of the nation." Pointing to the work of its Commission on the Church and Social Service, the report commented that in light of problems in the social order, "various denominations are facing our social mission with a common program and united action." In such activities the commission's endeavors were "written through and through with spiritual implications and its deep religious and evangelical spirit," which indicated that the council was "in no danger of losing its spiritual grasp as it [entered] more largely into the religious treatment of social problems."[6] The social-action portions of Macfarland's report showed an affinity for the type of work Stelzle advocated.

Before adjourning, the 1913 General Assembly took other action that revealed a more favorable reading concerning social concerns. Two portions of the report of the Special Committee on Christian Life and Work repudiated the suggestion that social service should be divorced completely from the church and insisted that various voluntary societies needed to have the guidance of the churches in their work. Since the problems in society were too vast for any single denomination, it was imperative that federations of churches function to meet these needs.[7] These recommendations also were in accord with Stelzle's social ministry.

---

[5]*Minutes of the General Assembly* (1913), 297-98.

[6]"Report of the Executive Committee of the Federal Council of the Churches of Christ in America to the General Assembly of the Presbyterian Church in the U.S.A. in Session at Atlanta, Georgia, May 15, 1913" (N.p., n.d. [1913]) 1-2.

[7]*Minutes of the General Assembly* (1913), 295, 297-98.

Potentially the most threatening action taken by the General Assembly was the vote to create a Committee on Social Reform and Church Federation, which was to meet with similar groups from the Southern Presbyterian and United Presbyterian churches to draw up "A United Declaration on Christian Faith and Social Service." The statement was to be presented to the 1914 General Assembly. Since the assemblies of all three Presbyterian bodies were to meet simultaneously in Atlanta because of a church-union proposal, the measure was easy to implement and difficult to oppose. The committee of five appointed by the Northern Presbyterian moderator consisted of three clergy and two laity, all of whom were conservatives.[8]

Stelzle's reasons for submitting his resignation in the autumn of 1913, according to his autobiography, were to save the Board of Home Missions further embarrassment and to avoid damaging their fund raising campaign.[9] His other reasons have been presented, along with the reports and actions of the General Assembly of 1913. Obviously, the legislation curtailed and altered responsibilities for some of the programs he had developed over the years, but his Bureau of Social Service survived. Perhaps he correctly anticipated the negative impact the critics would have on the work he had developed and felt it impossible to stem the new momentum. Or perhaps he believed that he was unjustly accused, for he appealed his treatment during 1912 and sought an apology, which said no more than "we can only regret that the initiative and not the final action was reported in the public press," when the matter was reviewed at the 1915 General Assembly.[10] By that time, however, the United Declaration had been received, the Board of Home Missions was reorganized, and there was no reference to social service in the Home Missions report.

Before proceeding further with Presbyterian developments, it is important to notice that the Federal Council of Churches sought to clarify its own position concerning interdenominational federation and social ministry at the same time as this controversy. On 1 December 1913 it published a four-page bulletin entitled *A Statement of Its Plan, Purpose and Work*. While stating that its general functions needed to be coordinated with the variety of church polities represented in the council, the statement declared that denominations conceded that the council "should represent and declare the common conscience of the Christian churches upon important questions with regard to which the common consciousness of

---

[8]Ibid., 56, 170-71, 281, 448[48].

[9]Stelzle, *Son of the Bowery*, 168-69.

[10]Ibid., 96-97; *Minutes of the General Assembly* (1915), 168-69.

Christianity is practically unanimous." The best illustrations were its "declarations on the problems of the social order and concerning the moral life of the nation."[11]

In hindsight the publication of this small bulletin on 1 December seems unusual because a few days later the Executive Committee of the Federal Council adopted a more comprehensive statement of principles. If anything, the timing of the little pamphlet evidenced Charles Macfarland's anxious concern to clarify the relationship of the Federal Council of Churches to its constituent denominations. As he stated in his report to the Executive Committee, it was a "sense of the necessity for a real and not only a formal co-operation which led the Secretary, as the result of his visits to the constituent bodies, to recommend the appointment of a committee to prepare a statement of the policy of the Council relative to its constituent bodies."[12] While our primary concern has been to trace the development of Protestant social ministry, there were a number of other concerns that confronted Macfarland and the council during 1913, such as the decision of the Protestant Episcopal Church not to participate fully in the council because of its conviction that God wanted organic unity and not federation, reservations by the Moravians, and the withdrawal of the Primitive Methodists from further participation.[13] The context of the council's statements concerning social service were made in a time of overall concern about ecumenism as well as social action.

"A Statement of Principles Underlying and Guiding the Development and Work of the Federal Council of the Churches of Christ in America" was presented to the organization's Executive Committee on 3 December 1913 and was officially adopted. Beginning with provisions of the original plan of federation endorsed in 1908, the statement made it clear that the Federal Council differed from similar groups because it was not a voluntary agency or an interdenominational fellowship but rather was "a body constituted by the Churches." Another differentiation was that it brought together "the various denominations for union in service rather than in polity or doctrinal statement." Essentially, the council was conceived to be "the sum of all its parts." As such, its function was to be representative in nature, "expressing the will of its constituent bodies" rather than legislating for them. A number of safeguards were built into

---

[11]Federal Council of the Churches of Christ in America, "A Statement of Its Plan, Purpose and Work," Bulletin No. 6, 1 December 1913 (New York: National Office, 1913) 1-2.

[12]*Annual Reports of the Federal Council of the Churches of Christ in America* (1913), 27.

[13]Ibid., 24-27, 51.

its constitution so that no action of the Federal Council could be "legally imposed upon those constituent bodies," thus guaranteeing the autonomy of each member church. Instead of being an independent entity, its duty was "to represent the churches upon important matters of common concern" and "to exercise a genuine leadership" within its proper sphere. That limited sphere was not "so much to do things, as to get the denominational bodies and the interdenominational movements to do the work of the churches in co-operation." Its function was that of correlation and coordination, not that of overseer and director.[14]

With regard to local and state federative agencies, however, the Federal Council envisioned a more aggressive leadership role, "as the initiator, creator, inspirer, and so far as possible, the directing agency." As for its own commissions, it was understood that "they act always as agents of the Council" and were subject to its Executive Committee. Functionally, the council indicated that it desired "to find the will of the constituent bodies and their departments and to interpret and express it in common terms." Such cooperation, however, "does not require any one of the constituent bodies to participate in such co-operative movements as may not be approved by it or for which its methods of organization and work may not be adapted." Only in one realm was there an expressed disclaimer.

> Were this . . . to be construed as precluding the utterance of the voice of the churches upon matters in regard to which the consciousness and the conscience of Christianity are practically unanimous, the Federal Council would be shorn of the power given it by the constituent bodies when they adopted as one of its objects: "To secure a larger combined influence for the churches of Christ in all matters affecting the moral and social condition of the people, so as to promote the application of the law of Christ to every relation of human life."[15]

This policy statement, hammered out in a troubled year when some denominations were having second thoughts about the council and some conservative factions were militantly attacking some of its most dynamic leaders and social programs, represented a serious attempt to soothe and reassure those who were aroused to criticism. As such, it put the policy of the Federal Council in the most favorable and least threatening light.

---

[14]Ibid., 56, 66-68.

[15]Ibid., 56, 68-69; "A Statement of Principles Underlying and Guiding the Development and Work of the Federal Council of the Churches of Christ in America," Bulletin No. 7, 15 January 1914 (New York: United Charities Building, 1914) 2.

To make the policies known, members of the council sent the principles to denominational papers and also had them printed as a small bulletin for broad distribution.

While the statement sought to mollify, other actions of the Executive Committee and staff late in 1913 did not show signs of retreat. H. K. Carroll was confirmed as associate secretary with responsibilities for running the new Washington office of the council, and Charles O. Gill was appointed as field investigator for the Committee on Church and Country Life, which was suddenly energized to build on the work already initiated by Warren H. Wilson of the Presbyterian Church before his department was dissolved.[16] Both appointments strengthened the social ministry of the Federal Council, as did the creation of a new Joint Commission on Theological Education, which was to improve the study of social and industrial questions in Protestant seminaries. The eleven-member commission included such familiar social-gospel leaders as Shailer Mathews, Walter Rauschenbusch, Josiah Strong, Washington Gladden, and Charles Macfarland.[17] Clearly, in the Federal Council of Churches there was no desire to curtail social ministry, even though there was a genuine desire to quiet dissension among constituent bodies.

A year later Macfarland was able to report that "the Statement of Principles adopted last year at Baltimore has received the approval of all the bodies which have met during this year." He noted at length that the southern Presbyterian General Assembly received him more sympathetically and adopted a resolution that declared, "We have given most careful attention to this statement of principles underlying and guiding the development of the work of the Council, and find such safeguards and limitations as to denominational autonomy of the constituent bodies, that we can and do most heartily recommend their approval." At the Northern Presbyterian General Assembly, the principles were also affirmed, but cautious actions indicated less than full accord with the Federal Council's social activities. The assembly warned its representatives to the council to watch carefully "lest there should be intrusion by the Church into the sphere of duty of the civil magistrate" and advised the council of the General Assembly's conviction "that the power of the Gospel as the true source of all true social progress should be increasingly recognized by the Council in its advocacy of social service."[18]

----

[16]*Annual Reports of the Federal Council* (1913), 28-29, 53-54, 65.

[17]Ibid., 34-35, 142.

[18]Ibid. (1914), 22-24, 29.

As requested, the Joint Committee of the Presbyterian Church in the United States, the Presbyterian Church in the United States of America, the United Presbyterian Church of North America, plus the Associate Reformed Presbyterian Synod that joined them, presented a United Declaration on Christian Faith and Social Service to their parent bodies in 1914. Defining their task as a declaration of the four churches concerning "their common faith in the great truths of the Gospel in relation to what has come to be known as Social Service," they identified social service as "the practice of the principles set forth in God's holy law which regulate the relations by which men are bound together in the social order, this practice being a part of those good works of which our Confession of Faith teaches." By that definition it was inevitable that the declaration was largely propositional in substance. And, being Presbyterian, the first proposition was the assertion that "man's chief end is to glorify God and to enjoy Him forever." Those social relationships that give glory to God and happiness and usefulness to humanity were put in the hearts of humans, but those principles were obscured by sin until revealed anew in the Bible. "Inasmuch as all evils, social and individual, have their source in human sin and selfishness, they can be remedied only by the divinely appointed plan for salvation from sin," which is the love put in human hearts through God's redemptive gift of Christ. Such love can only be gotten through the church, which is "the appointed means to salvation." Along with the state and the family, which also are ordained by God, the church has a distinctive work to do "in bettering the social relations of men in this present world." That work is primarily "spiritual, ministerial and declarative," and it consists of inculcating and applying the principles in order "to quicken those motives which are essential to all true and lasting reform." With such a biblical and doctrinal foundation undergirding their principles, the Presbyterians began with a different basis than the Federal Council principles, which avoided doctrinal and polity issues and emphasized service as the basis for cooperation.[19]

The two statements of principles found common ground when they agreed that the social conditions of the time required Christian attention. The Presbyterian Declaration noted the vast but uneven and unjust distribution of wealth that had developed in commercial and industrial enterprises, and it recognized that the exploitative privileges of the few weakened the sense of individual responsibility for social wrongs. Also the document indicated that vice was used as an instrument of private gain and the means to "selfish ambition for place and power," while large

[19]*Minutes of the General Assembly* (1914), 52-56. The report also was printed in the *Annual Reports of the Federal Council* (1914), 186-90.

classes of people were submerged in such poverty and ignorance that it was difficult to proclaim the message of Christ to them.[20]

Amid such conditions it was necessary for the church to take "its stand as Christ did against the sins of social injustice and tyranny." Thus, the United Declaration emphasized the duty of individuals on behalf of other persons and toward society. It was "the duty of men to put into practice the Christian principles of love, justice and truth in all their social relations, economic, industrial or political," whether they were employers or employees, officials or citizens. Likewise, all persons were responsible "for the manner in which they acquire positions, possessions and power in their social relations," lest at the judgment day they be found unfaithful. And individuals were obligated to learn that they were responsible not only for social wrongs they committed but also for those they could have helped to abolish by their efforts and prayers. Moreover, Christian citizens were to do their "full share of the world's work," to lead others to live self-respecting and God-fearing lives, and to share in movements "to secure childhood against forced labor and women against conditions degrading to womanhood." Above all, persons had the duty "to accept Jesus Christ and obey His teachings as the only cure for the injustice, tyranny and sins now looming so large upon the world's horizon."[21]

Since these evils were rooted in the past and were deeply ingrained in civilization, they could be cured only by the organized effort of all good citizens. "Our Churches, therefore, should always encourage voluntary organizations for the betterment of social conditions and urge their members to cooperate in them, leaving private judgment to decide what means or methods or what organizations are best adapted to the promotion of these desirable ends." Although there was agreement on many of the social problems, the United Declaration of the four Presbyterian bodies differed in methods from the Federal Council's Statement of Principles. The stress of the declaration upon working only through voluntary agencies on the basis of individual judgment and action was not the same responsibility that the council's statement asserted to shape the consciousness and conscience of the nation.[22]

While the years 1913 and 1914 were a time for formal statements of principles, the official proclamations by the Presbyterian churches and the Federal Council of Churches unfortunately worked from differing presuppositions. Although they chose not to make a major issue of it at

---

[20]*Minutes of the General Assembly* (1914), 54.

[21]Ibid., 54-55.

[22]Ibid., 55; Cf. Federal Council argument at n. 15 above.

the time, the United Declaration of the Presbyterians recognized the difference and urged its representatives to the Federal Council to seek to change the basic premise of that organization's social ministry. It acknowledged that the Federal Council afforded "a common ground where all who love and serve our Lord Jesus Christ may meet for conference and cooperation in the vast and holy enterprise of Christian Social Service." Nevertheless, to be certain that such conferences continued "to be truly Christian and this cooperation really effective," Presbyterian delegates were "directed to endeavor at all times to have the Federal Council distinctly recognize the great truths of the Christian Faith held in common by the Evangelical Churches and thus avoid and allay misunderstandings." In fact, the Presbyterians not only recognized the difference in principles, they advised how to overcome the diversity. At the same time, as noted earlier, Charles Macfarland chose to play down the differences in his report to the Federal Council at the end of the year.[23]

The significance of the difference in principles was evident in what happened to social service in the Northern Presbyterian Church. When the Board of Home Missions presented its annual report to the General Assembly in May 1914, it remarked that the work of the Bureau of Social Service "was seriously crippled last fall, when . . . Charles Stelzle felt obliged to resign in order that he might take up a broader social ministry." It was noted that in compliance with General Assembly action in 1913, the Church and Country Life department was being closed out and the Immigration department was being continued. Otherwise, the only reported activity consisted of surveys, research, and statistics. In the report of the Assembly's Standing Committee on Home Missions, a plan of reorganization of the Board of Home Missions was described and permission was requested to implement it. The board was to be divided into four general departments, one of which was designated the Department of Immigration and Social Service. Thus, in implementing the actions of 1913 the reorganization placed social service under immigration, the opposite of their previous relationship. The description of the work of the new department indicated that it "shall deal with the special problems centering in the country and city, and . . . shall magnify the relation of the Gospel to all the questions bearing upon social righteousness and moral and spiritual progress."[24]

By the time the General Assembly convened again in 1915, there were no references to social service in reports of the Board of Home Missions, the Narrative of the State of Religion, or its Special Committee on Christian

---

[23]*Minutes of the General Assembly* (1914), 55-56.

[24]Ibid., 133-34, 136-37, 375-76.

Life and Work. At least part of the reason was expressed in the report of the Standing Committee on Home Missions by its chairman, Charles R. Erdman. He indicated that the reorganization of the board had been accomplished despite the fact that much criticism had been directed at the board during the year. One recommendation of the committee recognized "the pioneer character of the work done by the Board in connection with the problem of immigration, of social service and of the needs of rural communities" and stated that such work would be managed "with due consideration of the wider aim of the Board," which was to permeate all its departments "with a fervent evangelical spirit" and to conduct all its work "with a definite evangelistic aim."[25]

Charles R. Erdman's impact upon these changes in Presbyterian social ministry was significant. He was a professor at Princeton Theological Seminary, one of the five members of the Northern General Assembly who wrote the United Declaration on Social Service, and chaired the influential Standing Committee on Home Missions during these crucial years. His father's long association with "The Fundamentals of the Faith" adopted by the Niagara Bible Conference a quarter century earlier, which were reprinted in pamphlet form in 1914,[26] as well as his own contribution to the last of the twelve-volume edition of *The Fundamentals*, which appeared in 1915, evidenced the basis of his biblical and theological conservatism. Since the latter article was titled "The Church and Socialism," and since it clearly revealed his views of the social gospel and was not limited to socialism as such, it provides a contemporary statement of his ideas that disclosed his perspective on social service.

In his article in *The Fundamentals*, Erdman explained that socialism was really several things. It was a scientific economic theory, a popular materialistic philosophy, and a protest against the wrongs and cruelties of modern society. He discharged Christianity from any relationship to the economic theory, just as he said the church was distinct from political socialism. However, popular socialism was a more serious problem. "It is a social creed, offered as a substitute for religion, promising material benefits for all mankind, and bitterly opposed to Christianity and the Church." For Erdman, popular socialism was defective because it placed human physical needs above spiritual needs and maintained that improved social conditions would produce better persons. Central to his argument was this distinction: "Socialism endeavors to elevate individuals

---

[25]Ibid. (1915), 172-74, 306-28, 389-91.

[26]Great Commission Prayer League, *The Fundamentals of the Faith; As Expressed in the Articles of Belief of the Niagara Bible Conference* (Chicago: Great Commission Prayer League, n.d. [1914]).

by elevating society; Christianity contends that society can be elevated only by the regeneration of the individuals." And the solution lay in his affirmation that "such regeneration is the supreme effort and function of the Church."[27]

When Erdman dealt with socialism as a protest against special privilege, injustice, and widespread poverty, hunger, and despair, he recognized its attraction to the discontented masses because it expressed the social unrest of the day. "This protest of Socialism is a call to the Church to proclaim more insistently the social principles of Jesus," he asserted. However, that did not mean "the adoption of a so- called 'social gospel' which discards the fundamental doctrines of Christianity and substitutes a religion of good works." Since Christian doctrine cannot be divorced from Christian duties, "a true Gospel of grace is inseparable from a Gospel of good works." What was needed was a new emphasis on essential Christianity, not the substitution of "some modern social creed" for genuine religion.[28]

Socialism's protest should serve as "a distinct call to the Church to define anew to herself her function." In the name of Christianity, many "have been promising a new social order, a kingdom of God, which they declare the Church will introduce." It was the continued failure to deliver these promises that subjected the church to undeserved criticisms by socialists. Despite the assertions of Christian social activists, the church had wrongly arrogated functions that belonged to the state, which also was divinely instituted and had its own sphere of duties. The church was not responsible for social sins and injustice; that was the work of the state. The abolition of abuses, establishment of justice, and securing of social reconstruction were for the state to implement. "When the Church assumes functions belonging to the state, she involves herself in needless difficulties and places herself in a false position before the world." Instead, the church should concentrate on "her supreme function" of proclaiming the gospel of Christ and securing the faith and allegiance of individuals to it. Erdman concluded his article with genuine millennial expectation: "The real blessedness of the Church and of the world is not in a new social order instituted by unregenerate men; not a millennium made by man; not a commonwealth of humanity organized as a Socialistic state; but a kingdom established by Christ which will fill the earth with glory at the coming of the King."[29]

---

[27]Charles R. Erdman, "The Church and Socialism," ch. 7 of vol. 12 of *The Fundamentals: A Testimony to the Truth*, 12 vols., published in 2 bound vols. (Chicago: Testimony Publishing Co., n.d. [1910–1915]) 2:108-15.

[28]Ibid., 2:115-16.

[29]Ibid., 2:117-19.

His words reiterated the essence of Article 14 of "The Fundamentals" adopted by the Niagara Bible Conference, which was a primary point that polarized millenarian fundamentalists from proponents of social Christianity. On the basis of his "The Church and Socialism" treatise, Erdman's viewpoint in the Northern Presbyterian actions concerning social service and in the United Declaration on Christian Faith and Social Service becomes clearer and amplifies our understanding of the differences in principles that emerged between contending groups in the years 1913 to 1915.

Another point of difference between the groups was evangelism. As Charles Erdman stated clearly, fundamentalists believed the primary task of the church was to proclaim salvation to individuals and leave the problems of society to the state. For social activists, the church was responsible for both an individual and a social gospel. Although this dual task had been evident in social-gospel literature since at least the turn of the century, it found new expression in the years when Erdman and his associates drastically altered Presbyterian social ministry. In 1914 Shailer Mathews published a study book for the Missionary Education Movement titled *The Individual and the Social Gospel*. The dean of the University of Chicago Divinity School and president of the Federal Council of Churches already had noted the two types of gospel when he wrote his earlier volume *The Social Gospel* in 1910. But at the conclusion of this little volume, he made both the distinction and the interaction quite obvious.

> And this is the social gospel: the joyful message that the power of Jesus Christ . . . is sufficient to regenerate the social order which tends to express itself in individuals; that the gospel is the power of God unto salvation not to the individual *or* society, but to the individual *in* society. And thus the individual gospel and the social gospel are seen to be the same glad news of the saving power of God in Christ.[30]

Two more social activists who were leaders in the Federal Council published books in 1915 that also discussed evangelism from a social-gospel point of view. Harry F. Ward's *Social Evangelism* was a serious study of the subject that reflected the controversies of the period, although he had spoken on the subject at the National City Evangelization Union eight years earlier.[31] In his new volume Ward mentioned that recent events tended to contrast social service and evangelism as if they were "inherently antagonistic or mutually exclusive." While admitting that the

---

[30]Shailer Mathews, *The Individual and the Social Gospel* (New York: Missionary Education Movement of the United States and Canada, 1914) 83, passim.

[31]*Western Christian Advocate* (Cincinnati), 18 December 1907, p. 21.

social movement had left its faintest trail in the field of evangelism, he maintained that the tasks were really so interdependent that the term *social evangelism* best described their relationship. To him the church was not "a mere agent for social reform"; rather, it existed for the "regeneration of the social order" and only promoted reforms as a means to achieve social salvation. In that task evangelism and social service were so closely related that "one is the inseparable complement of the other." On the other hand, to conceive of evangelism as limited to individuals alone was a distortion to be avoided: "An evangelism that is true to its gospel must be both individual and social." For Ward, it was necessary to insist upon an evangelism that was directed at the group life of humans, as well as at individuals, so that the social conscience could be "quickened with the righteousness of God" and the social will created "in harmony with the eternal purpose of God." That was the way to transform an unregenerated social order into the Christian social order. However, those pietists who ignore organized community life and "keep the church apart from the other human activities in which God is working" will only succeed in shutting themselves off from God.[32]

Apparently with his mind on the conflicting statements of principles concerning social service, Harry Ward stated that "all declarations of the social function of the Church that do not marshal its forces for social action around the conviction of social sin and the desire for social righteousness are futile." Furthermore, he said that expounding the social principles of the gospel while holding the church back from methods of social reform evaded the real task of religion. For him the task of social evangelism was not simply to proclaim the needs and the laws of the kingdom; it was also to use such power and charm that persons will not only see the social ideal but rise up and follow it.[33]

The other leader of the Federal Council who provided insight concerning the relationship of evangelism and social service was Charles Macfarland. In an address that he gave at seminaries and on other occasions during 1913 and 1914, Macfarland asked why it had taken Christians so long to get involved with the urgent problems of social regeneration. He answered his question by saying that the delay was caused by discussing "our alleged differences which do not exist except in our discussion" and then went on to state boldly, "The specious differentiation between personal regeneration and social salvation is a divergence purely in philosophy and not in fact." While many have

---

[32]Harry F. Ward, *Social Evangelism* (New York: Missionary Education Movement of the United States and Canada, 1915) 1-24, 35.

[33]Ibid., 102, 112.

discovered "that evangelism and social service are not only inseparable now and forever, but are one and the same," he contended that a few have not. He believed that while Christians were praying for a revival of religion, they were "in the midst of what promises to be one of the greatest revivals that this world has ever known." In an analogy to former revival techniques, Macfarland suggested that the only difference between true social evangelism and the full mourners' bench and mercy seat is that "we come, not one by one, but all are kept on our knees together. True social service is simply evangelism a hundred or a thousand fold."[34]

Dissension among those who disagreed concerning evangelism and social service limited the effectiveness of church unity, insisted Macfarland. On the basis of his experience, he found that the way to have a conference that was harmonious rather than bitter was to get everyone together to face a common task. He found more divisiveness among persons of one denomination meeting together than when men and women met interdenominationally. Thus, he concluded that "the differentiation and distance between the two remotest constituent bodies of the Federal Council are less than the variance between the two wings of any one of them." When such divisiveness can be overcome by unity, then the church can get on with its task to be "the conscience, the interpreter, and the guide of the social order." If the church hoped to meet its social obligation and opportunity, she "must unite her scattered forces."[35]

One way that Macfarland attempted to avoid dissension and emphasize unity during these controversial years was to invite prominent Presbyterian laymen to give addresses at the meetings of the Executive Committee of the Federal Council. William Jennings Bryan spoke on temperance in 1914, and President Woodrow Wilson spoke on "The Rural Church, the Center of the Rural Community" in 1915.[36] In addition, the council's Annual Meeting in 1914 met at Richmond, a year after assembling in Atlanta, suggesting an attempt to placate Southern Presbyterians since there normally was more regional alternation of the business sessions. Moreover, at Richmond the Executive Committee expressed gratitude to the four Presbyterian bodies that prepared the

---

[34]Charles Macfarland, "The Federal Unity of the Churches a Social Obligation," in *Christian Service and the Modern World* (New York: Fleming H. Revell Co., 1915) 99, 105-107.

[35]Ibid., 111-13.

[36]*Annual Reports of the Federal Council* (1914), 93; (1915), 95.

United Declaration "in view of its clear statements in harmony with the past action of the Federal Council."[37]

Another way was for the council to avoid altering the Social Creed, since it was a divisive influence for some. Some, like Charles Erdman, tended to identify modern social statements as social creeds, as when he referred to socialism as a social creed. They found the creedal reference bothersome too because the council's Social Creed was not like the historic ecumenical creeds of early Christianity. The strength of those historic statements was in their unchangeable language, and proposals to change the Social Creed to keep it relevant suggested its different nature. Some denominations preferred to regard the social platform as ideals for which the church ought to strive rather than be confused by the customary interpretation of creeds as unchangeable truths. For example, the Northern Baptist Convention published a pamphlet entitled "Social Service Ideals" in 1915, which was a loose paraphrase and interpretation of the 1912 Social Creed of the Churches.[38] While no reason was given, the 1915 *Annual Report* of the Federal Council stated that "Mr. Ward reported concerning the matter of the revision of the platform of social standards, that it was felt unwise by the Secretarial Council to make any changes in this platform at this time."[39] This action rescinded the expansion of the Social Creed to include more than industrial concerns that the council's Executive Committee had approved the preceding two years.[40]

During the 1915 meeting of the council's Executive Committee at Columbus, Ohio, there were other evidences of Macfarland's desire to defuse the Presbyterian protest. In his own Annual Report he specifically noted the Northern General Assembly's warning about dealing with "subjects upon the border line of the State and the Church" and in the realm of doctrinal discussion. Identifying the problem as one of constitutional principles, Macfarland declared that "the Federal Council should take no action which would violate the constitutional principles of any one of its constituent bodies." Obviously attempting to avoid any danger of the council "dividing into wings and elements," he said that he did not think it had ever taken such action "when its procedure has been rightly construed . . . although it may be that at times the wording

---

37Ibid. (1914), 99, 100-101.

38"Social Service Ideals," issued by the Social Service Commission of the Northern Baptist Convention, 1915 (N.p., n.d.), in file entitled "Commission on Social Service, 1916," in the Worth M. Tippy Papers, Archives of DePauw University and Indiana Methodism, Greencastle IN, Box DC 618, Folder 2.

39*Annual Reports of the Federal Council* (1915), 110.

40Ibid. (1913), 92; (1914), 103, 122.

of a resolution has been faulty."[41] When the Commission on the Church and Social Service reported, it indicated little that was new. Remarking that the commission's general policies had been "pretty well defined" for several years, it consequently was able to proceed in established patterns. Primarily, it sought to bring its work into "closer unification" with that of the denominational departments.[42]

Avoiding controversy at the time was not easy, despite all of Macfarland's efforts. Probably to his surprise, even the ranks of social-gospel proponents were divided unexpectedly by remarks that Charles Stelzle made to the Social Service Commission at Columbus on 9 December 1915. Stelzle, who was still a member of the commission during the quadrennium, not only attended the meeting but brought a paper that he presented. The paper proposed that the Federal Council initiate a program to be known as the Conservation of Human Life, and it should be implemented by the commission. A summary of the general nature of the proposal was included in the official minutes, since it was endorsed and referred to the Secretarial Council to be made part of its immediate program.[43] From other accounts, however, the former superintendent of the Presbyterian Bureau of Social Service used the occasion to criticize caustically the Federal Council's commission for not doing more to make operative the social platform adopted in 1908. His remarks condemned most of the commission's work as a failure. So strong were his feelings that he also expressed them publicly in an article in *The Independent*. According to Macfarland, several on the commission felt that both the article and the address would "prove seriously injurious."[44] With reference to Stelzle's actions, Frank Mason North told Worth Tippy that he felt it was unwise to "discourage the ardor of that growing company in the Christian churches who are awakening . . . to the social conditions and the social conscience . . . by assuring them, point blank, that the persons and agencies which have been central to the agitation are back numbers and essentially no-good conservatives." He believed it was poor strategy to seek advance by denouncing the progress already made.[45]

Stelzle's discontent was not limited to denunciation, however. By the end of December he had convened the first of two meetings of thirty

---

[41]Ibid. (1915), 15-16.

[42]Ibid. 105-108.

[43]Ibid., 93, 108-11.

[44]Charles S. Macfarland, *Across the Years* (New York: Macmillan Co., 1936) 191-92.

[45]Frank Mason North to Worth M. Tippy, 29 January 1916, Tippy Papers.

selected specialists in all phases of social work to discuss frankly what direction the church should take toward social problems. At that meeting fundamental principles were considered and the organization of the National Committee on Church and Social Problems was proposed. A month later a second meeting closed without taking any further action because those present felt the purpose of the conference had been fulfilled by eliciting frank discussion of the matter. Among the agreements noted by Stelzle were two that related to the Federal Council. One was the recognition that the council began social ministry "with a strong set of resolutions and with excellent purposes," but the lack of staff and funds made it impossible to "carry out an aggressive social service program." In light of the condition that developed, a second agreement said, "There is imperative need for the Federal Council of Churches and the denominational groups either to engage in a more sincere and earnest effort to make practical their generally announced social programs, or to permit some other religious agency or group to enter this field without prejudice."[46]

When the Commission on the Church and Social Service met in New York on 1 March 1916, it undoubtedly discussed these matters because Worth Tippy, who had replaced Josiah Strong as chairman because of the latter's long, painful, and ultimately fatal illness, was among those whom Stelzle had involved in the two conferences and also in informal contacts by phone and letter in between conferences. One direct result of the meeting was an immediate effort to activate the often-stated need for a full-time executive in social service for the Federal Council.[47] Letters were sent out to elicit nominations for such a person, but Harry F. Ward apparently was Macfarland's choice.[48] When Ward learned of this, however, he withdrew his name from consideraton.[49] At that point, it occurred to Macfarland to transpose Stelzle's criticisms into constructiveness. Going to Stelzle directly, he challenged him to go beyond his criticisms by returning to work with the churches through the

---

[46]Charles Stelzle, "Report on Conferences on the Church and Social Problems," 7 February 1916, in "Stelzle Committee" file in Tippy Papers, Box DC 618, Folder 1.

[47]See "Stelzle Committee" file in Tippy Papers; "Report of the Commission on the Church and Social Service," *Christian Cooperation and World Redemption*, ed. Charles S. Macfarland, vol. 5 of Library of Christian Cooperation, 6 vols. (New York: Published for the Federal Council of Churches by the Missionary Education Movement, 1917) 44.

[48]J. W. Magruder to Tippy, 20 March 1916, Tippy Papers.

[49]Harry F. Ward to Tippy, 21 March 1916, Tippy Papers.

Federal Council if funds could be secured. Stelzle admired the daring proposal and agreed to accept the new position of Field Secretary for Special Service, which was all that could be funded then, with the hope that his relationship would become permanent when the council met in quadrennial session in December 1916. Initially, his major work was to be with the economic phases of the liquor problem and the church and labor.[50] By September Stelzle had drafted a general social-service program that incorporated these interests as well as his campaign for the conservation of human life.[51] When Tippy submitted the report of the commission to the quadrennial meeting, the work of social service was being carried on jointly by Stelzle and Macfarland, and many of Stelzle's ideas were embodied in the report.

Thus, by the fall of 1916 Charles Stelzle had returned to a leadership role in social service, three years after resigning from such a position in the Northern Presbyterian Church. This time he labored in the larger field occupied by the Federal Council of Churches. There seemed to be little reason for regret that he was no longer part of the Presbyterian program because there was only one brief, general statement about social service in the General Assembly minutes that year.[52] More explanation of the situation was expressed in the annual report of the Board of Home Missions, where it was obvious that the social-service work had become so diversified through the board that a centralized department was hardly needed. Even worse, during the preceding year the social-service work had been seriously curtailed due to a 25 percent budget cut, which the report admitted "fell relatively most heavily of all upon the social offices and programs."[53] Somehow Warren H. Wilson, who formerly headed the Country Life department, survived the continuing assault against social service by serving quietly within the board and as a Presbyterian representative on the Secretarial Council of the Federal Council. When

---

[50]"Minutes of the Meeting of the Commission on the Church and Social Service, Held at the National Office of the Federal Council of the Churches of Christ in America, June 24, 1916," mimeographed minutes in "Commission on Social Service, 1916" file in Tippy Papers, Box DC 618, Folder 2; Macfarland, *Across the Years*, 192.

[51]Charles Stelzle to Tippy, 21 September 1916, plus six pages of program ideas attached, in "Commission on Social Service, 1916" file, Tippy Papers, Box DC 618, Folder 2.

[52]*Minutes of the General Assembly* (1916), 365.

[53]Presbyterian Church in the United States of America, Board of Home Missions, *Annual Report of the Board of Home Missions . . . 1916* (New York: Presbyterian Building, 1916) 118.

the political winds changed, he was in a position to rebuild the social ministry of the Northern Presbyterians. In 1916 his former colleague, Stelzle, returned to leadership with the council, and they were able to work together again.

The arrival of Stelzle on the Federal Council staff was part of a new vigor in the organization's social-service program. Macfarland's report as general secretary indicated that the Social Service Commission had pursued "only a normal work during the first three years of the quadrennium, but during the past year had greatly increased its resources and its effectiveness."[54] The commission's own extensive report confirmed that appraisal.[55] Admitting that the commission's work suffered because it received only partial attention from the general secretary and the voluntary efforts of the denominational associate secretaries, the report's writers believed the hiring of Stelzle and efforts to employ a full-time secretary for the commission showed that the commission "was now ready for the consummation of the plans and program" latent since 1908.[56]

Part three of the Social Service Commission report was titled "Statement of Principles" and brought to culmination the statements of principles affecting social service in the years from 1913 to 1916. It differed from the earlier Statement of Principles adopted for the entire Federal Council in 1913 by focusing only on the area of social service. Consequently, it amounts to the fullest expression of social-service theory developed by Protestantism to this point.[57]

The work of the commission was "the realization of clearly discerned fundamental principles" that were expressed in the Statement. Underlying all else was a deepening conviction that both the scope of the gospel and the program of the churches "must include the creation on earth of a Christian civilization" based on the ethical teachings of Jesus and guided by his spirit. In addition to the recognized mission of the church to individuals, there was also a mission that involved "certain great social accomplishments." A list of ten was presented that ranged from the abolishment of war to the extension of democracy throughout the world. It included equality and justice for capitalists, employers, and workers, urged the destruction of "the curse of strong drink," and sought the

---

[54]*The Churches of Christ in Council*, ed. Charles S. Macfarland, vol. 1 of Library of Christian Cooperation, 6 vols. (New York: Published for the Federal Council of Churches by the Missionary Education Movement, 1917) 184.

[55]*Christian Cooperation and World Redemption*, 35-69.

[56]Ibid., 44-45.

[57]Ibid., 48-50.

control of vice as well as infectious diseases. In addition to such general objectives, it listed sixteen particular and immediate goals for which the Federal Council stood, which was the Social Creed of the Churches adopted in 1912, although the Statement made no use of that terminology.[58]

To attain these objectives, the Federal Council urged "the unselfish cooperation of the churches with what is being done for the welfare of every community." Nationally, it encouraged churches to support efforts for "a free church in a free state" and for social progress, without seeking special privileges for themselves. Moreover, the church as an organized body should not attempt to dominate the state politically or "to control specific legislative action." Instead, the church should "set forth and interpret the principles of the gospel of the kingdom of God so clearly to the entire life of the nation" that citizens would be motivated to achieve those principles in the politics and legislation of the state by various methods.[59]

Before and after its pronouncement of these social standards, the Statement of Principles indicated certain practical matters concerning their implementation. For instance, there was recognition that different denominations "vary in the directness of their social action," and there was no insistence on the ways that Christian principles should be facilitated. Whether ecclesiastical bodies or voluntary groups of Christian men and women sought to address particular issues was a matter of method left to each constituent body, but the obligation to make Christian principles prevail was stressed. To help Christians achieve this goal, the commission recommended that its own report would be useful because its task was to make the social mission of the church specific and concrete. In addition, the Statement recognized that the social standards needed to be "extended or modified from quadrennium to quadrennium, to express the living social faith of the churches of Christ in America."[60]

Shailer Mathews's presidential address to the quadrennial meeting of the Federal Council of Churches in December 1916 summarized the social activist's view of the current status of the ecumenical organization. While he believed that the church could not "build into its message any definite scheme for reorganizing society," he was convinced that "Christian principles must be put into society" through Christian people who would be the leaven in the social order. Recognizing that more work

---

[58]Ibid.

[59]Ibid., 50.

[60]Ibid., 48, 50.

needed yet to be done, he concluded, "Just how our churches bring to bear upon national life the ideals of Jesus is not yet altogether clear, but, after all, that is a matter of method rather than purpose."[61]

By the end of 1916 the various conflicts that had arisen with regard to social Christianity since 1913 had been resolved to matters of method rather than of purpose in the understanding of social-gospel advocates. However, differences of purpose and principle had clearly emerged within the ranks of the Federal Council and the Northern Presbyterians. Among the latter, the differences had almost destroyed an effective and well-developed social ministry, which barely survived a concerted attack by conservatives in the denomination. In the Federal Council, the issues were both social and ecumenical, and the interdenominational body sought to settle the problems through several statements of principles. As negotiated documents, these declarations contained conciliatory views, but they expressed unequivocal support of social service while admitting there was no uniformity of implementation. Thus, the various conflicts between 1913 and 1916 resulted in greater clarification of purpose and narrowed existing differences to methods of implementation and program rather than principles.

Nevertheless, the differences that were articulated evidenced basic problems that social activists could not ignore. The underlying presuppositions of Charles Erdman and Charles Stelzle were essentially different. While Macfarland could challenge Stelzle to turn his criticisms into constructive programs because the two agreed on primary purposes, that approach would not work with committed conservatives who had entirely different goals and methods in mind. In this public skirmish between contending ideologies that were becoming increasingly divisive among evangelical Protestants, the conservatives could not at this time hold their ground and had to retreat, but the issues remained. Shailer Mathews could say in his presidential address that "the Commission on the Church and Social Service may well strike hands with the Commission on Evangelism, and the two together work toward the bringing in of the kingdom of God," but that really did not settle the diversity of principles between liberals and conservatives. At best, conservatives in these years forced the Federal Council to moderate its social service and to clarify its social principles.

One unexpected consequence of the conservative attack resulted when Stelzle concluded that none of the church's social-service programs was sufficient to meet the needs of the time and launched a militant

---

[61]Shailer Mathews, "The Present Outlook for Cooperative Action by the Churches," *The Churches of Christ in Council*, 54-68.

critique of his own against his liberal coworkers for not being aggressive enough. Charles Macfarland gambled that Stelzle was right, added him to the Federal Council staff, and in the process initiated a new vitality in the social-service cause.

Amid conflict as well as cooperation, social Christianity made progress during these four years. Clarification of principles strengthened the social-service cause and helped it build a firmer foundation for the movement in both denominational and ecumenical Protestantism. And the fact that the social-gospel forces could withstand direct assaults on its strongholds showed that now it enjoyed more status in the corridors of power in Protestantism than earlier. As the critiques were handled responsibly, the initiatives of Stelzle and Macfarland revealed a new dynamic in institutional social Christianity. The social movement was finding a permanent place in the socially active denominations. Also the movement was finding more solid standing in relationship to the other movements concerned about social reform in the Wilsonian phase of the Progressive Era, with which, by principle, they were committed to function as partners.

CHAPTER 15

Our Problem
Requires Cooperation

Our problem requires co-operation between the public school, the home, the churches, agencies of philanthropy and reform like the National Child-Labor Committee, the civic authorities, and right-minded individuals.

("Declarations of the Religious Education Association,
March 5, 1915")

ALL THE WORK OF SOCIAL ACTIVISTS in relation to the social order was not limited to the Federal Council of Churches and five denominations. Much of it was channeled into a number of voluntary organizations that fought for social welfare and reform, improved conditions for workers, and shaped values through moral education. Although each agency had its distinctive purpose, persons frequently were active in several groups and a spirit of cooperation led to interaction among the agencies in order to achieve common goals. As a matter of strategy, social-gospel leaders in the churches shared in this cooperative activity.

One organization in which advocates of social Christianity continued to participate was the Religious Education Association. Shailer Mathews, George Albert Coe, and Francis Greenwood Peabody continued to serve on its Executive Board, and the general secretary, Henry F. Cope, was committed to the social-gospel movement. Moreover, it was not unusual to find social-service leaders from the Federal Council and the denominations speaking at its annual meetings.

Charles S. Macfarland, in one of his first exposures outside church circles after assuming his duties with the Federal Council, spoke at the annual meeting of the Religious Education Association in March 1912. Addressing the theme of training religious leaders, he presented a paper entitled "The World of Toil as a Field of Religious Leadership." With his basic conviction that "the Church should be the conscience, the interpreter, the guide of our Democracy," he argued that either directly or indirectly the church should be "the leader, the inspirer, the supporter of philanthropy, charity and social uplift." Macfarland maintained that at that time "the conscience of the Church and what we call the public conscience [were] becoming one and the same," and in the process the church was "assuming a moral responsibility for the public welfare."[1]

Applying these presuppositions to society, he found that modern industry was behind all social wrongs. Related to the problem of getting workers into the church was the larger issue "of getting the Christian gospel into industry." Neither employees nor employers could settle for self-interest and accusations against the other because underneath both was "the whole public welfare." Consequently, the church should cooperate with the state to solve the problems of modern industry. In this joint enterprise, the church ought not entangle herself in economic machinery but should concentrate on infusing society with the idealism of the gospel. In turn, the state should create the economic conditions and environment where that idealism can be fulfilled. Thus, in solving the problems of industry, the church should provide "the moral leadership of the nation" while the state should provide "the economic leadership." Although the leaders of government, industry, and labor had not yet understood that the solution of their problems lay in the moral leadership of the church, Macfarland used this occasion to speak in the name of the churches of the nation "to proclaim the moral and spiritual leadership of the Church, inspiring the State, inspiring Industry, inspiring Labor."[2]

Despite this triumphalist tone in Macfarland's address, the church did not provide as much moral leadership or exercise as much moral responsibility as he had proclaimed. In more realistic terms, Chancellor James Hampton Kirkland of Vanderbilt University in his presidential address recognized that the churches were "extending their sweep and sway" but admitted that they lacked power. "The Church does not hold the commanding position today that it once did." Moreover, the Religious Education Association was not an agency for correcting social ills; it existed to strive for fundamental principles and high ideals. "Our work has been to secure better schools, better colleges, better seminaries, better theology, better churches, better homes, better society, better government, better

---

[1]Charles Macfarland, "The World of Toil as a Field of Religious Leadership," *Religious Education* 7 (June 1912): 146-47.

[2]Ibid., 148-56.

men and women." In the quest for such general uplift, "Our mission has been one of helpful co-operation with all existing agencies."[3]

Kirkland's idealism was similar to Macfarland's, but his recognition of the need for cooperation to achieve the goals was more apparent. The veracity of his description of the association's role was borne out by a report of a conference of social workers that met concurrently as part of the association's program. Samuel Zane Batten chaired the sessions and reported that after discussing whether or not to create a department of social service within the Religious Education Association, the social workers accepted General Secretary Cope's recommendation not to organize one at that time. Instead, it was urged that social ideals should permeate all the departments of the association and that cooperative relationships should be established with the social-service commissions of the denominations. This cooperative relationship was approved.[4]

That action did not mean that the social commitment of the Religious Education Association had waned, for the theme of the next meeting was "Religious Education and Civic Progress." Meeting at Cleveland in March 1913, the organization celebrated its first decade of existence. Henry Cope's report "Ten Years Progress in Religious Education" set those years in the context of national developments. Not only did he find growth in religion and education generally but also in "the general social organizations and movements of our times," such as social settlements, civic leagues, recreation centers, playgrounds, and rural betterment movements. "In the past ten years the emphasis has passed from charitable relief to constructive social welfare. The phrase 'social service' has become generally current, and social service has received an educational emphasis." Welfare no longer was limited to physical needs but regarded human personality and the soul as important. Furthermore, the religious spirit had entered political life, and moral values and social responsibility had turned people's attention "to the cry of the man lower down." The religious spirit evident in social settlements and among social workers also influenced the thinking of educators and increasingly dominated the churches. Thus, "a similar movement in the development of social responsibility has brought the churches and the schools into the same field of endeavor."[5] Cooperation, consequently, was not difficult.

---

[3]James Hampton Kirkland, "President's Annual Address," ibid. 7 (April 1912): 1-6. His assessment that the church had lost ground and exerted less influence at the time than one hundred years earlier also was emphasized by historian Williston Walker of Yale, ibid., 7:11.

[4]Ibid. 7 (August 1912): 280-81.

[5]Henry F. Cope, "Ten Years Progress in Religious Education," *Religious Education* 8 (June 1913): 146-49.

Consideration of the question "What is the dominant function of the church in the life of today?" was a special theme for one afternoon of the convention. The topic was addressed by an educator, a social worker, and a leading pastor. Washington Gladden accepted Cope's invitation to speak to the question as "the pastor with the social view point in the country,"[6] and Gladden presented one of his last important interpretations of the purpose of the social gospel. His address concurred with Cope's assessment that change had occurred recently. "It is not too many years ago that the possibility of social regeneration began to get some hold on the thought of the church, and that the gospel of the Kingdom began to be preached with conviction." For the previous century, however, the church had thought that its great task was "the conversion and salvation of individual souls, in preparation for a future state of existence." But "its business is to leaven human society with Christian ideas and Christian motives; to organize society under the Christian law." According to Gladden, "the dominant function of the church in the life of today . . . is the Christianization of society, or the establishment, in the world, of the Kingdom of Heaven." While recognizing that the conversion of individuals was important because "society cannot be Christianized without the Christianization of the individuals composing it," the patriarch of the social gospel felt that too much emphasis on "self-centered saints" was not the way to construct a Christianized community devoted to the well-being of others.[7]

If Gladden was critical of those in the church who emphasized individual salvation, he also was critical of those who overly stressed reform. Reform had a political connotation, he feared, and if it meant that the work of the church consisted primarily of opposition, antagonism, and prohibition in order to repress evil, then he objected. "After all the main business of the Christian church is positive rather than negative." It was more imperative to "reveal the principles on which God is organizing the Kingdom in the world" so that people could "find the way of Jesus and follow it." The church was in the world to lead the world into that way. "She isn't here to teach sociology. . . . She is not here to substitute social service for religion. . . . She is here to Christianize society." That Christianization of society was partly an educational task because "cogent and convincing teaching of vital and fundamental truth" was essential if the minds of the people were to be influenced and lives were to be

---

[6]Henry F. Cope to Washington Gladden, 3 December 1912, Washington Gladden Papers, Ohio Historical Society, Columbus OH.

[7]Washington Gladden, "The Dominant Function of the Church," *Religious Education* 8 (June 1913): 149-51.

changed. In large measure, the Christianization of society depended on effective religious education.[8]

It was not surprising at a convention of religious educators that other speakers agreed with Gladden's conclusion. Henry Churchill King, president of Oberlin College, asserted that religious education was the only means to create a deep sense of meaning and value in one's life. Given the transitional state of the times, he believed that guidance in morals and religion could not be provided adequately by the home and church unless educators improved their methods.[9] According to George Albert Coe, who was then a professor of religious education at Union Theological Seminary in New York City, "The cause of social existence requires of us something vastly more difficult than the reconstruction of a law, or a court, or an economic procedure; it requires the production of men and women whose thinking has been socialized, and whose motives have been brought into willing obedience to the social ideal of a family of God here upon earth." To create such thought and motivation, the church should rely on the Christian home and Sunday school. "Into the Sunday school then must go the social issue," he concluded. "We must see to it that the Sunday school consciously assumes the function of moral education."[10] The motivation of conscience, agreed President Harry Pratt Judson of the University of Chicago, was the fundamental concern for religious education. "Right conduct is the child of conscience, and conscience is ruled by religion," he insisted. The future of the nation was at stake because its existence depended on "law abiding citizenship." For Judson, upright citizens were the product of individual conscience, and "the most effective motive of the individual conscience [was] found in religion."[11] Therefore, concluded the annual meeting, the emphasis should be upon "the moral aspects of education" so that education in religion might most effectively be "secured as part of our national life."[12]

Plans for the 1914 convention consistently followed the previous line of argument by adopting the theme "Education and Social Life." There were general sessions entitled "Making Social Citizens," "The College in Relation

---

[8]Ibid., 154-58.

[9]Henry Churchill King, "The Challenge of Religious Education," ibid. 8 (August 1913): 241-43.

[10]George Albert Coe, "Moral Education in the Sunday School," ibid. 8 (October 1913): 314-16.

[11]Harry Pratt Judson, "Religious Education and Civic Progress," ibid. 8 (June 1913): 114-16.

[12]"Report of the Convention," ibid. 8 (April 1913): 101.

to Citizenship and Character," and "The College and the New Social Order."[13] In its "Declaration of Principles" that year, the Religious Education Association reaffirmed "the possibility and the necessity of permeating all the educational life of the modern world with the religious ideal and all the religious life with the educational ideal." Additionally, the association declared that "the age of sheer individualism is past and the age of social responsibility has arrived." As a consequence, the members believed that they had abandoned none of the educational ideals of their predecessors when they announced, "We must now exalt the newer ideals of social justice, social service, social responsibility."[14] Through these assertions in its "Declaration of Principles" for 1914, the Religious Education Association recognized the importance that social responsibility had achieved through the application of religion to social problems.

At the association's 1915 General Convention the customary annual survey of progress in religious and moral education became a biennial survey. Reviewing the past two years led to an awareness that there had been a growing emphasis on "the necessity of religion for civic life." Educators increasingly recognized the value of religion for good citizenship, and this was as true of the National Education Association as it was for the Religious Education Association.[15] Although the theme— "The Rights of the Child"—seemed narrowly focused, that central interest enabled the association's Declarations to be quite specific.

To assure that children had rights to family life, health, education, religious heritage, and other things was so inclusive that it caused a problem for those who desired to guarantee such prerogatives. The size of the task led to Declarations which affirmed that "our problem requires co- operation between the public school, the home, the churches, agencies of philanthropy and reform like the National Child-Labor Committee, the civic authorities, and right-minded individuals."[16] Recognition of the larger dimensions of one problem led the religious educators to express once again the need to cooperate with other institutions and agencies in society in order to achieve the goal, which was what their association had been saying repeatedly for several years.

Among the speakers at the Religious Education Association Convention was Walter Rauschenbusch. His address entitled "The Rights

---

[13]Program of the Eleventh Annual Convention, ibid. 9 (February 1914): 88-89, 93-94, 95.

[14]"Declaration of Principles," March 1914, ibid. 8 (April 1914): 98.

[15]Ibid., 10 (April 1915): 114-15.

[16]"Declarations of the Religious Education Association, March 5, 1915," ibid., 203-205.

of the Child in the Community" asserted that children not only had a right to an education but also to an education that should include religion and morals. He criticized the exclusion of religion from public schools and claimed that such a restriction helped create the moral and cultural chaos in society.[17]

With regard to the role of religion in public education, Rauschenbusch expressed ideas that were receiving increasing sympathy among secular educators at the time. On the basis of a financial gift that offered a $1,000 prize for the best essay on "The Essential Place of Religion in Education," the Executive Committee of the National Education Association authorized a contest during 1915. By the 1 June deadline, 432 essays had been received and evaluated, although nationwide interest ultimately led 1,381 persons to submit entries. A winner was selected by a panel of five judges, who also gave special mention to four other essayists. The five essays and a synopsis of the ideas in all the legitimate entries were published as a book in January 1916. The synopsis noted a wide and increasing sentiment for the restoration of religious teaching in the public schools, which was a significant change from the opinion of the National Council of Education in 1895 that religious instruction should be limited to the home and the church. Just within the preceding year the recognition developed that morality found its sanction and motivation in religion. Since "the state must safeguard its own existence by upholding the highest standards of morality," said the synopsis, "it has the right and therefore the duty to demand righteousness in the nation, in private life, in business affairs, in government and international transactions." "To instill these high ideals what agency can serve but the public schools?" concluded the synopsis. During the summary it was observed that the Religious Education Association, the Federal Council of Churches, and many organizations other than the National Education Association favored the improvement of moral instruction in the public schools, and cooperation was encouraged.[18]

When the Religious Education Association met on 28 February 1916 its theme, "Religious Instruction and Public Education," was directly related to the growing national concern. After addressing the subject, the association adopted five affirmations as its "Declaration of Principles." First, the church and the state were "regarded as distinct institutions,

---

[17]Walter Rauschenbusch, "The Rights of the Child in the Community," *Religious Education* 10 (June 1915): 219-25.

[18]National Education Association, *The Essential Place of Religion in Education* (Ann Arbor MI: Monograph published by the National Education Association, 1916) 3-4, 94-102.

which, as far as possible, co-operate through the agency of their common constituents in their capacity as individual citizens." Second, all children should have "an organic program of education" that should include religious as well as general instruction. Third, arrangements for children to have the opportunity for religious instruction should be negotiated by parents with public-school authorities rather than by a formal agreement between the church and the state as institutions. The fourth principle was surprisingly different from earlier proposals: "The work of religious instruction and training should be done by such institutions as the home, the church, and the private school, and not by the public school nor in official connection with the public school." And, last, religious education should "depend for dignity, interest and stimulus upon the recognition of its worth," not only by public-school authorities but also by all people in the community.[19] Thus, the Religious Education Association was firmly committed to the necessity of religious instruction as part of the education of all children, but the association believed this instruction should not occur in public schools because of the separation of church and state as institutions. Although public educators and religious educators both recognized the value of moral and religious instruction, they differed over the location for such training. Fortunately, the prevailing mood of cooperation among institutions at the time made it possible to work together despite a lack of agreement on this point.

Through cooperative interaction with educators, social-gospel advocates stimulated professional teachers to work out some of the implications inherent in the concept of Christianizing the social order. This work involved theoretical assumptions concerning the relation of church and state and practical considerations about whether to use the public schools for moral and religious training. Although the answers of secular and religious educators were not uniform by 1916, at least educators generally were confronting problems raised by basic social-gospel teaching. Closely related to those concerns were the theoretical and theological bases of democracy and the nation, with their ethical connotations for the morality of both. (This issue will be considered later when these matters come into focus more sharply.) Regarding these issues, as well as those just examined, the Religious Education Association was sensitive to current thought, and its consideration of topics served as a barometer of Protestant social Christianity.

As the problem of education required cooperation, the problem of labor produced the same need. In spite of the negative tone of the

---

[19]"Declaration of Principles," (February 1916), *Religious Education* 11 (April 1916): 181-82.

conservative attack upon the Presbyterian Bureau of Social Service, and particularly against Charles Stelzle's ministry to workers, other leaders of denominational and interdenominational social ministry continued to regard labor as a major emphasis in their planning. As noted earlier, Charles Macfarland and the secretaries for social service of the other denominations active in the work devoted a large amount of personal time and energy to church literature and declarations dealing with this concern. But they also committed themselves to cooperation with other organizations that sought similar goals with regard to labor. Important as it was to arouse Christian sentiment in support of workers, much of the needed work was being implemented through unions and other organizations, and collaboration with those efforts also was valuable.

The report of the Commission on the Church and Social Service to the quadrennial meeting of the Federal Council of Churches in December 1916 evidenced the extent and nature of its cooperation in the area of industrial relations during the past four years. Through cooperative action with the American Association for Labor Legislation, the commission had a part in getting laws passed in New York and Massachusetts that provided one day's rest in seven for workers, and similar acts were pending in several other state legislatures. "In cooperation with the Lord's Day Alliance," the report states, "effective help was rendered the New York Letter Carriers' Association and the Letter Carriers' Association of Washington, D.C., in securing Sunday rest." Moreover, the Washington office of the council actively assisted efforts to achieve "retirement measures for aged and infirm federal employees."[20]

Annual sessions of the American Federation of Labor were attended by Macfarland, Stelzle, Samuel Batten, Shailer Mathews, and three other representatives during the quadrennium. Some of the workers questioned the advisability of receiving fraternal delegates from religious bodies. The council's delegates explained that "the purpose of the churches through this commission [was] to express sympathy and offer cooperation for bettering the moral, religious, and industrial conditions of working men." An officer of the labor union defended the religious leaders' presence by stating that the "moral effect" of their representation "cannot be overestimated." The mingling of religious leaders with laborers created feelings of "fraternity and brotherhood" that were mutually beneficial, he maintained. Women representatives of the commission also attended meetings of the National Women's Trade Union.[21]

---

[20]*Christian Cooperation and World Redemption*, ed. Charles S. Macfarland, vol. 5 of Library of Christian Cooperation, 6 vols. (New York: Published for the Federal Council of Churches by the Missionary Education Movement, 1917) 35-36.

[21]Ibid., 36-37.

Through the associate secretaries of the commission and other members, investigations of industrial problems in five states were implemented and reported so that citizens could learn "the moral aspects of these industrial strifes." Later in the commission's report, major sections were devoted to unemployment, overwork, a living wage, unequal distribution of wealth, and industrial democracy. Member churches of the Federal Council were urged to study these concerns and the general field of social welfare during the next four years.[22]

While industrial problems were developed more extensively than other social concerns, the Federal Council had a clear understanding of cooperative relationships with other organizations striving to resolve problems in society. Full cooperation "with other bodies upon matters of general religious and moral interest" was the goal, as long as the relationships were not "confusing the mind of our constituency." Questions had been raised by member churches about actions of some of the council's commissions, which seemed to take on tasks that properly belonged to legislative bodies and should have been promoted more properly by voluntary organizations. General Secretary Macfarland preferred that the council's commissions "should keep clearly within their own appropriate spheres," but believed that some moral-reform societies were dangerously close to "assuming functions which belong to the Council," such as assigning special Sundays for observance by churches.

Concerned to preserve the "distinctiveness of the constituency and work of the Council," Macfarland nevertheless desired appropriate cooperation with other organizations. He preferred that the council relate to such groups as the Southern Sociological Congress and the National Conference of Charities and Correction in unofficial ways and on specific matters. It should be clearly understood, said Macfarland, "that these matters of cooperation are entirely in relation to particular objects and movements and that they do not involve any further relationship or responsibility in connection with such bodies." With such understanding, he gladly made the council office available to denominational agencies that desired to reach general as well as denominational constituencies, "especially in relation to social service." In the same way he also made the council's mailing lists and multigraphing machinery available to important organizations seeking to reach Christian constituencies for good causes. During the preceding two years he had done so for at least fourteen organizations whose interests ranged from peace to temperance to labor legislation. "I regard this as a very important function of our national office," wrote the general secretary, "and it is doing much to create among

---

[22]Ibid., 37, 54-56, 61-68.

our leaders of social movements a cordial sense of appreciation of the churches and their efficiency."[23]

An examination of the quadrennial and annual reports of the Federal Council of Churches as well as two volumes of *A Year Book of the Churches and Social Service* between 1912 and 1916 provides a composite picture of the organizations with which the ecumenical body maintained cooperative relationships. Fraternal visitors from the council were sent to twenty-four organizations, which covered a wide range of the social movement: Academy of Political and Social Science, American Association for Labor Legislation, American Federation of Labor, American Prison Association, American Public Health Association, American Sociological Society, Charities Publication Committee, Child Welfare Committee, Committee on Peace and Arbitration, Consumer's League, Institute of Criminal Law and Criminology, National Association for the Study and Prevention of Tuberculosis, National Child Labor Committee, National Civic Federation, National Conference of Charities and Correction, National Municipal League, National Prison Committee, National Purity Committee, New York Association for Labor Legislation, Playground and Recreation Association of America, Russell Sage Foundation, Sagamore Conference, Southern Sociological Congress, and Women's Trade Union League.[24]

During 1917 the Federal Council published *The Manual of Inter-Church Work*, which included a clear statement of its policy with regard to cooperation. Having no desire to modify any existing agencies because its approach was inclusive rather than exclusive, the *Manual* stated that "every ecclesiastical, missionary, philanthropic, educational, and social agency that has demonstrated its worthfulness, is gladly welcomed into

---

[23]"Report of the General Secretary for 1912–1916," *The Churches of Christ in Council*, ed. Charles S. Macfarland, vol. 1 of Library of Christian Cooperation, 6 vols. (New York: Published for the Federal Council of Churches by the Missionary Education Movement, 1917) 184.

[24]Charles S. Macfarland, "The Kingdoms of This World; The Kingdom of Our Lord," *Christian Unity at Work: The Federal Council of the Churches of Christ in America in Quadrennial Session at Chicago, Illinois, 1912*, ed. Charles S. Macfarland (New York: Federal Council of Churches, 1913) 164-65; Harry F. Ward, *A Year Book of the Churches and Social Service in the United States. Prepared for the Commission on the Church and Social Service of the Federal Council of the Churches of Christ in America* (New York: Fleming H. Revell Co., 1914) 26-28; Harry F. Ward, *A Year Book of the Churches and Social Service in the United States . . .* (New York: Missionary Education Movement of the United States and Canada, 1916) 134-47; *Annual Reports of the Federal Council of Churches* (1914), 50; (1915), 21-22, 107; Macfarland, *The Churches of Christ in Council*, 185-87; Macfarland *Christian Cooperation and World Redemption*, 37, 51, 54-55.

the combination of forces that seek to glorify God by the enthronement of the spirit of Christ in human life." The Federal Council had no desire to take credit for work it did not do and no desire to duplicate existing machinery. Rather, it desired "to promote the spirit of cooperation between organizations" and to correlate productive forces in order to prevent wasted time, money, and energy. Its goal was "to unify existing Christian forces for the service of the Kingdom of God."[25]

In the *Manual* was a chapter on social service written by Worth M. Tippy that described ways to organize a Department of Social Service at the local level. For churches in cities he suggested the formation of three committees and provided job descriptions for each. A Social Betterment Committee should work with charities and welfare work, and it should cooperate with community agencies and government departments dealing with such problems as public health, recreation, and juvenile courts. The Civic Relations Committee should deal with law enforcement, education in citizenship, municipal efficiency, temperance, social hygiene, and all relations with local government other than welfare. An Industrial Relations Committee should work with such problems as one day of rest in seven, shorter working hours, unemployment, industrial welfare of women and girls, health and safety of workers, legislation affecting working conditions, and cooperation between employers and employees. Tippy pointed to the importance of cooperation at all levels in carrying out these multiple responsibilities. Furthermore, he stated a fundamental working principle for churches: do not promote work that is being done adequately by other organizations, but cooperate with them, and any work undertaken should be given over to other organizations if they are better able to do it. Also, all social work undertaken should depend largely on local needs and circumstances.[26]

Almost as if he were accounting for the wide range of social organizations listed above, Tippy proceeded to recommend a number of forms that social work might take: joint service with social agencies, civic relations, industrial conditions and relations, public recreation, prison reform and juvenile delinquents, social hygiene, public health, housing, community forums, and institutional churches.[27] Even his inclusive topical approach to cooperation did not easily contain all of the twenty-four organizations listed previously. Nevertheless, Tippy's approach indicated

---

[25]Roy B. Guild, ed., *The Manual of Inter-Church Work* (New York: The Commission on Inter-Church Federations of the Federal Council of the Churches of Christ in America, 1917) 7.

[26]Ibid., 91-97; *Annual Reports of the Federal Council of Churches* (1917), 151.

[27]Guild, *Manual*, 97-110.

the vast range of interests that should be met by churches if they were responsible and desired to Christianize the social order. Moreover, his lists revealed the vast field of need and the reason why the social task of the churches required cooperation.

Tippy's advice had the advantage of personal experience, since he had been involved in the kinds of cooperative social work that he urged upon his readers. During his ten years as the pastor of Epworth Memorial Church in Cleveland, he was active in just the type of ministry he recommended. Because of his personal success in that ministry, the editors of the Missionary Education Movement asked him to write a simple, brief account of the development of the community relations of Epworth Church as a model for others. Finally, Tippy wrote a little volume entitled *The Church: A Community Force* that was published in 1914. The suggestions noted above were based on the practical experience described in that book.

Starting with a church on the edge of downtown Cleveland that had a community outlook but no community relations, Tippy recounted how his congregation gradually was transformed into a congregation "thoroughly permeated by the community spirit." He began with his basic convictions that community relations were part of a church's work and that the pastor must be the leader if his church was to be a community force. Such feelings had motivated him to become involved in the social movement of the city. He became active in Associated Charities, Chamber of Commerce, City Club, Humane Society, Church Federation, and Ministerial Association. These memberships led to his being invited to serve on several mayor's committees dealing with general city problems. Although these activities involved heavy responsibilities, Tippy found them fulfilling: "Such work is an inspiring religious duty and an obligation involved in my citizenship." However, personal gratification was not enough; he had to educate the congregation so that others shared in community life. That educational campaign was not accomplished primarily from the pulpit as much as within church organizations such as the Men's Club, young people's societies, and Sunday school classes. As individuals became interested, he urged them to join social organizations outside the church. After nine years, he found that his parishioners were active in forty-one civic and charitable groups. Sending a steady stream of morally instructed citizens into the city was "one of the church's highest community functions," and that was what made the church a community force, according to Tippy.[28]

---

[28]Worth M. Tippy, *The Church a Community Force: A Story of the Development of the Community Relations of Epworth Memorial Church, Cleveland, Ohio* (New York: Missionary Education Movement of the United States and Canada, 1914) 8, 13-18, 22-23, 27, 30-34, 72, passim.

When he moved from Cleveland to New York in 1915 to become pastor of the Madison Avenue Methodist Episcopal Church, Tippy learned in a short time that his previous succesful ways did not work under new conditions. By the third year there was dissatisfaction in the congregation when he urged them to carry the city in their hearts and when he preached social-gospel and liberal theology.[29] Although his own experience was unhappy, he did not lose his commitment to social ministry. During those years he wrote the chapter for *The Manual of Inter-Church Work*, which ended with his description of the distinctive function of the church in social work. That function was "to endeavor to lift all social effort to the plane of spiritual ministry." For him, social service was "love in action guided by social experience." Unless social service was impassioned by the love of God and love of humanity, it lacked spiritual vitality and tended "to become mechanical and lifeless."[30]

Two years earlier Walter Rauschenbusch had expressed similar ideas when he addressed the Northern Baptist Convention. Christianity, he said, "must be the inspirational prophetic power inside our commonwealth." Churches should "study their communities and link up their own work with the other constructive institutions of social life." Only by a conscious and determined mission to organized community life could Christianity fulfill its task with regard to national life. Concentration on building up only one organization in the community would not result in the general welfare that was needed for social redemption.[31]

Evaluating the effectiveness of social-gospel cooperation with other social organizations is difficult, but certainly it was part of the progressivism of Wilson's first term. Writing in 1915, Benjamin Parke DeWitt believed that the Progressive Movement was in its third and final phase. It had attained its first goal of controlling abuses by the railroads and its second purpose of modifying the machinery of government in order to remove corruption. What still needed to be achieved was to relieve "the distress caused by social and economic conditions," which Progressives hoped was to be accomplished by social legislation. Progressives in all parties proposed to regulate conditions of employment for women and children in factories, to set maximum hours of work each day for men, to provide old-age benefits for workers, to lower the tariff

<hr>

[29]Worth M. Tippy, "Autobiography," unpublished manuscript, Worth M. Tippy Papers, Archives of DePauw University and Indiana Methodism, Greencastle IN, Box DC 627, pp. 5-6.

[30]Guild, *Manual*, 120.

[31]Walter Rauschenbusch, "American Christianity and National Life," *The Standard* (Chicago), 19 June 1915, pp. 1303-305.

and replace it with a graduated system of taxation, to adopt a minimum-wage law, and to seek the alleviation of poverty, disease, and crime.[32]

After Woodrow Wilson's victory in 1912, a Congress controlled by Democrats under the new president's leadership had revised the tariff, authorized the creation of the Federal Reserve System, and strengthened provisions to regulate trusts and monopolies. DeWitt doubted that the Democrats could adopt much more of the program of Progressive legislation.[33] According to historian Arthur S. Link, by 1914 President Wilson believed that his program to reorganize American economic life by government regulation was complete and that the mission of the Progressive Movement had been fulfilled because he had not run on a program of social reform. Compared to Theodore Roosevelt, Wilson's Progressivism was not inclined toward social welfare and reform, and he did not proclaim that message as openly. As Progressives began to understand the situation, a negative reaction slowly emerged. Herbert Croly concluded that Wilson's Progressivism was superficial. One evidence of the president's lack of commitment to social reform was obvious when he refused to support a model child-labor bill prepared by the National Child Labor Committee that was introduced in the House of Representatives in January 1914. Without his support, the bill received no serious consideration in Congress at the time.[34]

Only when it became apparent to political analysts in 1916 that Wilson and the Democrats faced certain defeat in the fall election unless they could win over the Progressive vote did a noticeable change occur. To achieve that end, said Link, the Democratic Congress "enacted the most sweeping and significant progressive legislation in the history of the country up to that time." Before 17 July Wilson had done nothing on behalf of the Keating-Owen child-labor bill, but when informed that independent Progressives regarded that legislation as a test of the administration's Progressivism he pleaded with Democrats to pass it. On 1 September that bill, which excluded the products of child labor from interstate commerce, was adopted.[35]

---

[32]Benjamin Parke DeWitt, *The Progressive Movement: A Nonpartisan, Comprehensive Discussion of Current Tendencies in American Politics* (New York: Macmillan Co., 1915) 15-25.

[33]Ibid., 44.

[34]Arthur S. Link, *Woodrow Wilson and the Progressive Era, 1910–1917*, The New American Nation Series, ed. Henry Steele Commager and Richard B. Morris (New York: Harper & Row, 1954; Harper Torchbooks, 1963) 78-80.

[35]In June 1918 the U.S. Supreme Court declared the act an unconstitutional encroachment upon states' rights. Ibid., 227 and note.

In similar fashion, a model workers' compensation measure for federal employees, which had been drafted by the American Association for Labor Legislation, was resurrected and passed on 19 August. In mid-July the Federal Farm Loan Act was approved, although virtually the same law had been defeated in 1914. Early in September the Adamson bill, which provided an eight-hour day and time and a half for overtime on interstate railroads, was signed by Wilson just in time to avoid a national strike. A few days later a workers'-compensation act that brought 500,000 federal employees into the system was enacted. With this rash of legislation, the Democratic Congress had adopted "almost every important plank in the Progressive Party platform of 1912" by October 1916, and Wilson could correctly proclaim that Democrats also were Progressives.[36] However, Wilson's efforts to that end seemed to be inspired more by political pragmatism than by conscientious conviction.

The role of the National Child Labor Committee and the American Association for Labor Legislation in this political maneuvering indicated the influence of at least some of the organizations with which the Federal Council of Churches allied itself. Professor Link identified both groups, along with the Consumers' League and organized labor, as among "the more radical progressives" in the cause of social justice.[37] Most of the bodies associated with the Federal Council were more moderate in their desire for welfare and reform, but these single-cause organizations often relied on political lobbying as a legitimate means to achieve change in the social order. Cooperating with such agencies was a legitimate function of the church according to social-gospel proponents; indeed, it was a wise and necessary way to achieve the Christianization of the social order as well as to solve particular problems. The assertion of the Religious Education Association that "our problem requires co-operation" was true of other agencies as well because social redemption was a large task.

In these cooperative activities, the churches and the Federal Council sent representatives who demonstrated the interest of the churches, maintained liaison, and kept abreast of the programs and emphases of the organizations. At times the representatives participated on committees of the other bodies for limited periods. Also the council serviced many of the groups by providing mailing lists. In the interchange, religious social activists clarified the distinctive role of the church in relation to social welfare and reform, and they used the knowledge learned in their collaborative relationships when writing their own literature for the denominations.

------

[36]Ibid., 57, 225-30.

[37]Ibid., 54n.

Such cooperation between the social and church agencies for welfare and reform was a hopeful sign that "the age of social responsibility" had arrived. The cooperative endeavors evidenced progress in attaining the ideal, although the strategies employed by social-gospel forces suggested that the achievement of the ideal was still in the future. Working with limited funds and personnel, church social activists saw the wisdom of functioning with other persons and groups who shared their motivation to improve society and the nation. At the same time, social-gospel advocates came to realize that the church had a distinctive function in this social ministry. Its unique purpose was primarily motivational and educational, and the church sought to provide those qualities for the other social organizations as they worked together for the growth of social responsibility. As Macfarland noted early in the period, two things were happening in these years: "The conscience of the Church and what we call the public conscience were becoming one and the same," and in the process the church was "assuming responsibility for the public welfare."[38]

---

[38]Macfarland, "The World of Toil as a Field of Religious Leadership," *Religious Education* 7 (June 1912): 146-47.

CHAPTER 16

The Social Gospel
Is a Permanent Addition

The argument of this book is built on the conviction that the social gospel is a permanent addition to our spiritual outlook and that its arrival constitutes a stage in the development of the Christian religion.

(Walter Rauschenbusch,
A Theology for the Social Gospel, *1917)*

DURING THE YEAR 1917 there were several indications that social Christianity was being taken seriously by the socially active denominations and had become a lasting part of their ministry. One of the signs occurred on 15 February, when the staff of the Federal Council of Churches and other social-gospel leaders rejoiced at what had happened in their movement. On that day Worth M. Tippy assumed the duties of executive secretary of the council's Commission on the Church and Social Service and of associate secretary of the Federal Council. After years without a full-time leader, the social-service program anticipated the opportunity to proceed at a more rapid pace. The occasion was a victory for social Christianity, an evidence that the social gospel had achieved full status in institutional Protestantism.

When Tippy moved from Cleveland to New York in 1915 he became increasingly involved in the affairs of the Federal Council. After Josiah Strong was stricken by a debilitating sickness, from which he died on 28 April 1916, Tippy took up many of the duties that his renowned colleague had carried in the council. He chaired the Church and Social Service Commission and headed the committee to select a full-time executive secretary for the commission. In those capacities he was active in the previously noted events associated with Charles Stelzle's criticism of the council and his subsequent hiring by the organization.[1] Also, he prepared the extensive report that the commission submitted to the quadrennial meeting of the council in December 1916. That meeting empowered Charles Macfarland to fill the authorized secretaryship, and in the following weeks he convinced Tippy to accept the position. Since Tippy had become disillusioned with his ministry at the Madison Avenue Methodist Episcopal Church, he was ready to receive the invitation and began his work with the Federal Council of Churches before his final Sunday in the pulpit of that congregation. Subsequently, an assistant secretary, the Reverend Clyde F. Armitage, and an office secretary were employed to aid Tippy in his new duties.[2]

With the selection of a full-time Secretary for Social Service, the prospects for social Christianity looked extremely good at the Federal Council early in 1917. Frank Mason North had been elected as its new president at the quadrennial meeting, succeeding Shailer Mathews. Since North had chaired the Executive Committee the preceding four years, he provided continuity both of administrative knowledge and social-gospel sympathy in the leadership of the national federation. Such leadership, combined with the social interests demonstrated by members of the staff such as Macfarland, Stelzle, and Tippy, made it clear that the social gospel would continue to receive genuine concern in the Federal Council.

By 1917 the Federal Council of Churches had attained considerable stability and stature in American Protestantism. This standing was clearly evident in Macfarland's *The Progress of Church Federation*, which was published that year.[3] This book was written in popular language to provide a brief interpretation of the six voluminous books that formed the official record of the previous quadrennium. One of the tendencies of the council in this period was to produce an extensive written record, printed in its own publication office, which even one of its own committees thought "might seem excessive, were it not for the fact that we are developing in the Council a new religious movement, . . . of which our constituency has known little, thus requiring much informational material in detail."[4]

----

[1]See pp. 236-37 above.

[2]Worth M. Tippy, "Autobiography," unpublished manuscript, Worth M. Tippy Papers, Archives of DePauw University and Indiana Methodism, Greencastle IN, Box DC 627, pp. 6-7.

[3]Charles S. Macfarland, *The Progress of Church Federation* (New York: Fleming H. Revell Co., 1917) preface, 3-4.

[4]*The Churches of Christ in Council*, ed. Charles S. Macfarland, vol. 1 of Library of Christian Cooperation, 6 vols. (New York: Published for the Federal Council of Churches by the Missionary Education Movement, 1917) 16, 78-79.

In the total scope of its work, the Federal Council had enlarged substantially by 1917. Its national offices in New York City occupied an entire floor of thirty offices in the United Charities Building. There was a branch office of the council in the Woodward Building in Washington, D.C., a branch office of the Commission on the Church and Country Life in Columbus, Ohio, and branch quarters of the Commission on Evangelism in Chicago. The council's secretarial force consisted of General Secretary Macfarland, Field Secretary Stelzle, Associate Secretary Tippy—who also served as secretary of the Commission on the Church and Social Service—plus the secretary of the Commission on the Church and Country Life, the executive secretary and field secretary for the Commission on Inter-Church Federation, the secretary of the Commission on International Justice and Goodwill, the secretary for Temperance Work, three secretaries at the War Commission, an assistant secretary at the New York office, an assistant secretary at the Washington office, a general office director, a director of the Publication and Printing department, an assistant to the treasurer, and a support staff of about forty secretaries, stenographers, clerks, and assistants.[5]

At the New York office there was a Library of Social Service and Missions that contained 3,000 volumes and about 500 current social, religious, and labor papers and magazines. Its publication department had published fourteen books during the quadrennium; its multigraphing staff averaged about 225,000 letters a year for the council and another 500,000 letters annually for cooperating organizations and also distributed about 2,000,000 pamphlets and leaflets in 1916 alone.[6]

Also during that year, according to Macfarland, the treasurer's office handled nearly $300,000. At the end of the 1916–1920 quadrennium, the report of the treasurer showed the proportional growth of the council's finances by four-year periods: average expenses for 1908–1912 were $22,000 each year; for 1912–1916 they averaged $68,000 each year; and for 1916–1920 they averaged $181,000 each year. In addition, there were additional receipts for special projects that totaled $205,000 for the three quadrenniums.[7]

Along with the remarkable increases in staff and finances came a growing conviction about the stability of the church federation that was

[5]Ibid., 358-59; Macfarland, *The Progress of Church Federation*, 69-70.

[6]Macfarland, *The Progress of Church Federation*, 70- 71.

[7]Ibid., 73; "Report of the Treasurer," *The Churches Allied for Common Tasks: Report of the Third Quadrennium of the Federal Council of the Churches of Christ in America, 1916–1920*, ed. Samuel McCrea Cavert (New York: Federal Council of Churches, 1921) 365.

evident in the attitude of council leaders. Previously, matters of social action that troubled several Presbyterian bodies concerning the possible overlap of church and state responsibilities had led to complications for the church federation. However, when these matters continued to bother Southern Presbyterians during 1916 their communication to the council was acknowledged, but the Executive Committee refused to carry the matter any further than continuing discussion for clarification. The problem of relating to constituent bodies led the Executive Committee to conclude its report to the quadrennial meeting with an extended statement, which indicated that council leaders felt that the churches had learned to work together through a number of "tests and discoveries." Given great diversities represented in the federated organization, it was admitted that there would not be "perfect agreement in opinion" or "placid uniformity in expression and method," and the quest for either would be a waste of energy. In the end, it was the conviction of the Executive Committee that "the period of experiment is past." While the Council of Churches mechanism might be repaired and adjusted in some ways, it was their conclusion that "this fellowship of great churches in America expresses in some large measure the mind of our common Lord." A number of amendments were enacted by the 1916 meeting to perfect the constitution, which firmly established the primary organizational design of the Federal Council of Churches. Despite its length, Macfarland emphasized the importance of this concluding statement in his thinking by quoting it completely in *The Progress of Church Federation*.[8] Obviously, he concurred that "the period of experiment" had ended for the Federal Council.

With the extent of the council's growth evident in staff, finances, and conviction, it was obvious that Charles Macfarland had many concerns other than social service. Thus, the selection of an additional person was needed if that interest was to continue to grow. In his popular book about the Federal Council, Macfarland summarized the main developments of social service in the ecumenical organization from 1908–1917. The election of Worth M. Tippy was presented as the culmination of that evolving social ministry. Although social service was treated directly in certain locations, the volume also revealed that social concern was a motivating purpose in many other facets of the work of the Federal Council of Churches, such as temperance, Christian education, morality at the Panama Pacific Exposition, and international relations. According to Macfarland, "Social regeneration must have a social approach. The social tasks and problems

---

[8]Macfarland, *The Churches of Christ in Council*, 26-29, 100-103, 146-49, 174-81; Macfarland, *The Progress of Church Federation*, 62-64.

of a city cannot be met by any Church except in common conference with every other Church."[9]

When two of the constituent denominations met in May, it was apparent that social service also had achieved more permanent status in those bodies as well. Samuel Z. Batten's report on social service to the Northern Baptist Convention declared that "the year has been marked by a widening and deepening interest in social work on the part of our people." Acknowledging that for years many Baptists showed "indifference" to his program of social mission, he was delighted to find that "our people are giving social work a place in their thought and plans."[10] And after years of criticism and open attack upon social service among Northern Presbyterians, the General Assembly in 1917 showed that the pendulum had begun to swing back to a more favorable position. That legislative body authorized the creation of a new Social Service Commission that was to report directly to the assembly. Moreover, Charles Stelzle was among those elected to it, and he was one of nine persons to serve on its Executive Committee.[11] Like the faithful remnant of Israel who survived exile in Babylon, social-gospel advocates were permitted to return to a visible place in the power center of Presbyterianism.

Thus, in denominations where indifference and hostility had negatively affected social ministry, important shifts were noticeable in 1917. Indeed, when these changes are evaluated in relationship to developments in the Federal Council of Churches, the year 1917 marked a high point for the social- gospel movement. Forces that were activated a decade earlier had progressed by their own momentum to levels that indicated that social Christianity had achieved recognized status in institutional Protestantism. Furthermore, such accomplishments were accompanied by influences of the social gospel upon Protestant theology and Christian education in that same year.

In April 1917 Walter Rauschenbusch presented the Nathaniel Taylor lectures at Yale University, which were published in expanded form in November as *A Theology for the Social Gospel*. Although the Taylor endowment provided for lectures dealing with doctrinal theology, Rauschenbusch disavowed that he was a doctrinal or systematic theologian and claimed to be only a church historian whose life and

---

[9]Macfarland, *The Progress of Church Federation*, 20, 83-89, passim.

[10]*Annual of the Northern Baptist Convention*, (1917), 265.

[11]*Minutes of the General Assembly of the Presbyterian Church in the U.S.A.* n.s. (1917), 183-84, 448⁵⁰-448⁵¹ .

religious experience "laid social problems on my mind." It was the Yale faculty's invitation to him to discuss "some phase of the social problem" that led him to undertake a task that he believed needed to be done because nobody had yet attempted it. In his words, "The social gospel needs a theology to make it effective; but theology needs the social gospel to vitalize it." His lectures and book dealt with both dimensions, but concentrated on the latter.[12]

"The argument of this book," Rauschenbusch declared at the outset, "is built on the conviction that the social gospel is a permanent addition to our spiritual outlook and that its arrival constitutes a stage in the development of the Christian religion." Social Christianity was "no longer a prophetic and occasional note." It was preached in pulpits, proclaimed in religious literature, and accepted by denominational leaders. It inspired interdenominational organizations and influenced American politics. Workers, college students, and ministerial candidates craved a social application of Christianity because they recognized that it was motivated by "religious compulsion" rather than by "prudent adjustment." Even conservative denominations "formally committed themselves to the fundamental ideas of the social gospel and their practical application." This evidence convinced him that "the social gospel has become orthodox."[13]

For Rauschenbusch, the social movement was "the most important ethical and spiritual movement in the modern world, and the social gospel is the response of the Christian consciousness to it." The social gospel, he said, was an "enlarged and intensified" expression of "the old message of salvation" that convinced people of their "collective sins" and created "a more sensitive and more modern conscience." Nevertheless, he admitted that "the pioneers of the social gospel have had a hard time trying to consolidate their old faith and their new aim." The problem was caused by systematic theology, which proved to be a hindrance rather than an aid for those trying to understand the relevance of Christianity to the regeneration of the social order. Persons who struggled to find "a clear faith in the social gospel" usually found that formulations of doctrinal theology produced a spiritual crisis rather than resolving it. The weight of traditional beliefs shaped in earlier eras overtaxed mental energies and seemed to provide no real nurture for those seeking a dynamic faith amid a world in flux. As the Nicene theology of the fourth century and the

---

[12]Walter Rauschenbusch, *A Theology for the Social Gospel* (New York: Macmillan Co., 1917) foreword, 1.

[13]Ibid., 2-5.

Reformation theology of the sixteenth century showed, "Theology needs periodical rejuvenation."[14]

"Can we not justly expect that the increasing influence of the social gospel and all that it stands for, will have a salutary influence on theology?" Rauschenbusch asked. Assuring readers that it would, he anticipated the constructive renewal "in a great epoch of change like ours." In his judgment, the social gospel introduced "nothing alien or novel." It had its roots in the Bible, developed doctrines already in Christian tradition, and emphasized some central ingredients that had been forgotten by "individualistic theology." Such essential ideas as the redemption of the social organism and the kingdom of God were rooted in the tradition of the apostles and the prophets and were not temporary interests. In light of "the neglect of the social contents of Christianity in former generations," he believed that the social gospel was "bound to become one of the permanent and commanding ingredients of theology." These convictions formed the basis for his review of several traditional doctrines that would be affected by the social gospel.[15]

Rauschenbusch's purpose in *A Theology for the Social Gospel* was threefold. First, he wanted "to show that the social gospel is a vital part of the Christian conception of sin and salvation." Second, he insisted that teaching concerning the sinful condition of humanity and its redemption from evil that failed "to do justice to the social factor and processes in sin and redemption" was "incomplete, unreal and misleading." And third, he argued that since the social gospel hereafter was an important part of the Christian message, "its chief convictions must be embodied in these doctrines in some organic form." He regarded the doctrine of sin as the starting point and the doctrine of salvation as the goal of Christian theology. Other doctrines were discussed more briefly in light of the impact he believed the social gospel might have upon them.[16]

Boldly, he began with the doctrine of sin because one of the primary criticisms of the social gospel was its failure to appreciate the power and guilt of sin by placing too much emphasis on environment. In defense, he maintained that the social gospel did not avoid sin but tried to shift the emphasis from individual sin to the consideration of public morality, wrongs done to entire classes of people and sins that "submerge[d] entire mill towns or agricultural states."[17] He desired to get theology to

---

[14]Ibid., 4-13.

[15]Ibid., 21-30.

[16]Ibid., 167.

[17]Ibid., 31-37.

concentrate on "the present and active sources of evil" rather than devoting inordinate attention to such speculative matters as the origin of sin in the fall of humanity.[18]

In agreement with traditional theology, the social gospel accepted as normative the definition of sin as selfishness, but it preferred to use "impressive examples of high-power selfishness" from contemporary society that usually were overlooked. By emphasizing the biological transmission of evil, doctrinal theology seemed to forget that sin also was passed on by social tradition. "One generation corrupts the next" socially as well as biologically. Individuals absorb sin through social customs, groups, and institutions, not just through the doctrine of original sin, Rauschenbusch insisted. Moreover, it was unfortunate that traditional theology had lost all vision of the kingdom of God, which was central in the teaching of Jesus, because "a clear realization of the nature of sin depends on a clear vision of the Kingdom of God." Thus, the social gospel sought to revive that vision in Christian theology.[19]

Without denying the importance of the salvation of individuals, Rauschenbusch argued that the chief interest of the social gospel was to concentrate "on those manifestations of sin and redemption that lie beyond the individual soul." If sin was selfishness, then salvation had to turn an individual from self to God and humanity. "A Christian regeneration must have an outlook toward humanity and result in a higher social consciousness." The trouble was that doctrinal theology so emphasized individual religious experience that it failed to prepare Christians adequately to achieve salvation from the superpersonal forces in the world that get in the way of establishing the kingdom of God.[20]

Providing new vitality and importance to the doctrine of the kingdom of God was "the chief contribution which the social gospel has made and will make to theology," according to Rauschenbusch. His description of the kingdom of God in this book has become a classic. "The Kingdom of God is humanity organized according to the will of God," he declared. Moreover, "since the Kingdom is the supreme end of God, it must be the purpose for which the Church exists." On that basis all the activities, worship, organizations, and theology of the church must be tested for their "effectiveness in creating the Kingdom of God." Furthermore, all problems of personal salvation should be examined anew from the point of view of the kingdom. But the kingdom was not limited to the church

---

[18]Ibid., 38-68.

[19]Ibid.

[20]Ibid., 95-117.

and its activities. "It embraces the whole of human life. It is the Christian transfiguration of the social order. The Church is one institution alongside of the family, the industrial organization of society, and the State. The Kingdom of God is all of these, and realizes itself through them all." Since the kingdom was more inclusive than the church, institutional Christianity not only had the indispensable responsibility for the religious education of humanity and the conservation of religion, but also for carrying religion into "the public life of humanity."[21]

The perspective of the social gospel focused on the present and the future, although as a historian Rauschenbusch made use of the past to understand the other two. "The social gospel," he said, "is not a doctrine turned backward to the sources of authority, but a faith turned forward to its task." That task was to overcome the kingdom of evil and to establish the kingdom of God. Those goals involved both the future of individuals and the destiny of humanity, which made the doctrine of eschatology an important consideration. But eschatology hampered social Christianity at the time because the apocalyptic ideas of premillennial Christians conflicted with the social-gospel vision. Whereas social Christianity looked for righteousness and salvation in the social order, premillennialists were delighted when humanity was "defeated and collapsing" and Christ could be expected to return again to intervene in the human order. In contrast to such a cataclysmic intrusion, social-gospel advocates believed that human effort on behalf of the kingdom of God on earth would affect the life of heaven. Life in God had continuity, and "heaven and earth are to be parts of the same realm." The social gospel was concerned about "a progressive social incarnation of God."[22]

Several other doctrines were examined by Rauschenbusch in light of the social gospel, but his primary emphases were sin, salvation, and the kingdom of God. Despite his denials that he was a systematic theologian, *A Theology for the Social Gospel* was the first major theological interpretation of social-gospel ideas. It became an immediate best-seller and had to be reprinted within three months. Over the years it continued to be reprinted periodically because it best expressed the essence of social-gospel theology.

This volume by Rauschenbusch in 1917 was important in its own right, but when viewed in relation to his other two major books in 1907 and 1912 it revealed how much progress had occurred in social Christianity in a decade. When he wrote *Christianity and the Social Crisis* he attempted to arouse Christians to do something about a social order in trouble. Five

---

[21]Ibid., 131-45.

[22]Ibid., 196, 208-39, 148.

years later he happily reported in *Christianizing the Social Order* that a social awakening had occurred. After only five more years he was able to announce in *A Theology for the Social Gospel* that "the social gospel is a permanent addition."[23] The accuracy of Rauschenbusch's understanding of precisely where the social-gospel movement stood at crucial times of its development was a talent that has been scarcely noticed, but it may have been a factor in the immediate popularity of his major books. At the same time, the quality of his theological analysis in this volume made an important contribution to the permanence of social Christianity in institutional Protestantism.

Another example of the stability of the social-gospel movement in 1917 was George Albert Coe's *Social Theory of Religious Education*. Completed in May and published in October, this major study showed how religious education was influenced by the social gospel. A distinctive feature of the book was its dedication: "To Harry F. Ward, who sees and makes others see." It is not often that a teacher dedicates a volume to a former student, yet that was the case in this instance. Ward did his major work at Northwestern University under the tutelage of Coe, who was a professor of philosophy. Later Ward indicated that Coe was one of two persons who most influenced his thought.[24] When the Methodist Federation for Social Service was first organized, Coe was a member of its General Council, while Ward was a vice-president and editorial secretary.[25] Coe continued to function in an advisory capacity with the federation even as he became an active leader in the Religious Education Association, where his social interests frequently found expression.[26] He served as its president during 1909–1910 and was on its Executive Committee for years. In 1909 he moved to New York City to become Professor of Religious Education at Union Theological Seminary. Through his work there he developed a close friendship with John Dewey, whose social and educational ideas he valued.[27]

---

[23]Ibid., 2.

[24]Ward to Coe, 6 January 1946; quoted in Robert H. Craig, "An Introduction to the Life and Thought of Harry F. Ward," *Union Seminary Quarterly Review* 24 (Summer 1969): 332-33.

[25]Methodist Federation for Social Service, "The Church and Social Problems; Including the Statement of the General Conference of 1908 and the Social Problem in the Episcopal Address," Federation Publications no. 5 (N.p., n.d. [1908]) 1.

[26]For example, see his "Annual Survey of Progress in Religious and Moral Education," *Religious Education* 4 (April 1909): 7-22, and his presidential address titled "New Reasons for Old Duties," ibid., 5 (April 1910): 1-5.

[27]George Albert Coe, *A Social Theory of Religious Education* (New York: Charles Scribner's Sons, 1917) x.

Coe's interest in social education had been evident as early as 1904 when he wrote *Education in Religion and Morals*,[28] but by 1917 he recognized that his earlier views were based on prevailing ideas of character and how character was formed that were no longer valid. "When the purposes of society are transformed, education must be made over," he announced in *A Social Theory of Religious Education*. Consequently, his purpose for the book stated, "This is the first attempt to work out in a systematic way the consequences that will follow for religious education when it is controlled by a fully social interpretation of the Christian message." In his estimation, it was necessary to revise policies affecting adults as well as children, in both public and religious education. "There must be a theory and a practice in which the love of God to us and our love to him are not separated from, but realized in, our efforts toward ideal society, the family or kingdom of God." Such a theory of Christian education did not yet exist, and the intent of his book was to propose a fresh approach to an entire curriculum based on social issues and ideals.[29]

In Coe's view, the social idealism of Christianity prescribed that the ultimate goal of religious education should be "the transformation of a social order that is largely unjust into one that shall be wholly just." To achieve that end, religious education needed to enter directly "into the social struggles of the present." As an example, Coe listed several points of the Social Creed of the Churches, such as abolishing child labor, shortening the hours of work, and improving sanitary conditions, and then he indicated ways such goals might be communicated and achieved. Religious education in the Sunday school could include participation in the problems as well as discussions about them. Moreover, a Christian family could support the Sunday school effort by both confronting the concerns at home during the week and taking local social problems to the teachers to provide relevant data. And ministers and adult members could identify families depressed by conditions through pastoral calls or community surveys and could engage children in analyzing and meeting the needs. Coe's plan called for involving children in the problems and not just transmitting information about the concerns or drilling the learners in memorized teachings that were supposed to resolve the issues without direct action. "In moral instruction," he concluded, "nothing so effectively shakes pupil and teacher out of moral conventionality as to face the actual, present struggle of men for justice, and especially to take some part in it."[30]

[28]George Albert Coe, *Education in Religion and Morals* (Chicago: Fleming H. Revell Co., 1904).

[29]Coe, *Social Theory of Religious Education*, vii-ix, 7-9.

[30]Ibid., 64, 220-21, 281, 342.

For Coe, this task of religious education was as much a matter of concern for the public school as for the Sunday school. "The interest of a socialized religious education in the public schools is not that they should teach religion in addition to reading, writing, and arithmetic, but that they should teach democracy." If instructors thoroughly taught democracy, they would develop democratic activities, attitudes, habits, and purposes—in short, they would enable the children to live democratically. To Professor Coe, this would be the democracy of God, which was the socially unifying aim that brought public education and Christian education into one curriculum of national and religious education. "The problem of morals in the schools melts into the problem of creating ambition for a sort of society" that is prefigured in both American and Christian ideals.[31]

To implement his theory, Coe suggested that a common social purpose would break down denominational divisions. The task of social justice required an "interdenominational union of effort." The Federal Council of Churches might be such an agency, but while its delegates could agree to work for a weekly rest day, they would be unable to "agree on a scriptural basis for Sunday observance." For that reason, he was more impressed by the unity of social purpose evident in the Religious Education Association. In that organization educators understood education "in more social terms than those of dogma or of ecclesiasticism, even in terms of the needs of modern society." Thus, when the association met, problems of social advance were placed side by side with problems of educational methods, materials, and organization. Through that process, Coe believed the association was "the forerunner of a unified educational consciousness among the Protestant bodies."[32]

Coe's extensive analysis included organizational plans for the family and the church school as well as for the denomination. It included not only the general learning process but also evaluated existing styles of Christian education in Roman Catholic and Protestant churches, clearly preferring Liberalism to dogmatic, ritualistic, or evangelical Protestantism.[33] This volume was one major contribution in Coe's lifelong dedication to identifying social values and enabling persons to achieve self-realization in society. As he said later, "The theory of Christian education had to be a social theory, and the practice of Christian education had to be a present exercise of ethical

---

[31]Ibid., 262-65.

[32]Ibid., 284-85.

[33]Ibid., 207-94, 295-342.

love."[34] By his own admission, that type of education did not exist in 1917, but social-gospel ideas and values enabled him to formulate the theory that motivated the rest of his influential career. Also, his volume revealed the impact the social gospel could have on a scholarly discipline if taken seriously, which in itself indicated that social Christianity had more substantial status than ten years earlier.

About the time Coe's volume reached bookstores in the fall of 1917, the Congregational churches showed that the interaction of social service and Christian education was close enough that the two areas could be combined structurally in a denominational reorganization. In the realignment of general agencies, the Commission on Social Service was changed to a department within the Education Society. Henry A. Atkinson, who had headed the commission, became secretary of the Social Service Department within the Educational Society. Meanwhile, the commission continued within the National Council, but in an advisory relationship to the department. Work areas assigned to the Social Service department showed that it performed all the tasks previously assigned to the commission— men's work, industry, rural life, organized charity, and social purity—plus assuming additional responsibilities for the welfare of enlisted men in the army and navy, which formerly had been delegated to a separate commission.[35]

The rationale for including social service in the Education Society was clearly stated in the biennial report: "Teaching is a primary function of the church. Not only is the church under obligations to educate its own members—it must educate the community and the world to think of all life and life-relations in terms of Christian ideals." In order to do so, the church "must cooperate with all other churches and social agencies." This task of maintaining broad relationships and multiple assigned responsibilities caused difficult problems for Secretary Atkinson. He was a member of three commissions of the Federal Council and one of its associate secretaries, as well as on the staff of the Education Society. His summary of the program of the Social Service department revealed how overworked he was, especially with the addition of war work to his portfolio, which also put him on the War Work Council of the Federal Council.[36] During the session when the social-service report was presented, Atkinson gave an address. Then he introduced Washington

---

[34]George A. Coe, "My Own Little Theatre," *Religion in Transition*, ed. Vergilius Ferm (New York: Macmillan Co., 1937) 109-13.

[35]*Minutes of the National Council of the Congregational Churches of the United States* (1917), 221.

[36]Ibid., 223-38.

Gladden, whose speech "The Range of the Social Demand of the Gospel" was his last official word to the National Council of the Congregational Churches.[37]

Atkinson's reference to the new responsibilities he had to assume for war work was only one instance of a dissonant note that intruded on an otherwise harmonious score for the social-gospel movement in 1917. George Coe remarked in the foreword of his book that even as he wrote about educating children in an ethic of love, the United States had gone to war and intertwined the moral destiny of Americans with "neighbors beyond our national boundaries."[38] Looking at the social-gospel movement more explicitly, Walter Rauschenbusch remarked in his book that "the Great War has dwarfed and submerged all other issues, including our social problems." He regarded the social problem and the war problem as one problem fundamentally and he believed that the social gospel could serve both. But he recognized that the war would dominate all phases of American life until peace was restored. "After the War," he concluded, "the social gospel will 'come back' with pent-up energy and clearer knowledge."[39]

Looking at social Christianity from 1913 through 1917, it is obvious that the movement had made significant progress. Denominations that created full-time departments to solve social problems developed substantial social-service programs for their separate churches during this period. As a result, Protestants who were sensitive to society's needs were able to do social service and not just urge it upon people. Although these programs were formed in various denominations, much of the creativity resulted from working together interdenominationally. In that way Protestants as a whole accomplished more than the sum of their individual efforts. Through the Secretarial Council of the Federal Council of Churches there was a pooling of ideas and resources that achieved much with limited funds. Despite an attack against Charles Stelzle and social service in Northern Presbyterian circles, the social-gospel forces survived the battle. Indeed, by diplomacy and slowly unfolding ideology, the unified social-service programs evolved statements of principles that provided more clarity in theory and practice than existed before the critical assault. This benefited both ecumenism and social action.

Coordination was not limited to interchurch relationships in this era. It also was the conviction of socially active Protestants that cooperation

---

[37]Ibid., 52.

[38]Coe, *Social Theory of Religious Education*, ix.

[39]Rauschenbusch, *Theology for the Social Gospel*, 4.

was necessary in order to solve the many problems of society. Collaboration with religious and secular educators in order to shape the conscience and values of citizens motivated the social-service secretaries. Combining efforts with a wide range of social-welfare and reform groups helped to achieve desired progressive legislation, although the motives of the various parties were not always the same. And mutual interchange of fraternal delegates with such organizations and with labor unions provided better understanding and trust because persons were mutually aroused to effect social improvement. Through such shared endeavors the age of social responsibility had emerged.

By 1917 the forces that had been set in motion ten years earlier had produced significant levels of accomplishment through their latent energy and the resourcefulness of Protestant social activists. The social gospel was firmly established in the Federal Council and in four denominations, and even the Northern Presbyterians revived their Social Service Commission. In addition to such organizational stability, Rauschenbusch's *Theology for the Social Gospel* provided a substantial theological basis for the movement, and Coe's *Social Theory of Religious Education* showed how social thought could affect the instruction and involvement of Christians. From the viewpoint of the natural development of social-gospel ideas, values, and practices, the year 1917 was a time of achievement that indicated the permanence of social Christianity in American Protestantism. Unfortunately, the nation's involvement in the First World War that year overshadowed these victories and distracted the moral energies of citizens from social service to a holy crusade. Nevertheless, that hiatus should not obscure the remarkable development that enabled Protestantism to advance from a rousing but nebulous social awakening to a durable and productive social-service ministry. That attainment signified the close of the fourth phase of growth for the social gospel between 1900 and 1920.

PART 5

From Social Service
to Social Reconstruction,
1917–1920

CHAPTER 17

Wartime Service

The staff of the Commission organized the Interchurch Committee on War Work, . . . studied training camps in the United States and Canada in order to determine a program, and did initial work on the problem of the effective organization of the churches for national and community war-time service.

("Report of the Commission
on the Church and Social Service," 1920)

FURTHER DEVELOPMENT OF THE SOCIAL GOSPEL was impeded by America's involvement in the Great War in Europe. While it did not entirely undo the work of social Christianity, the war effort diverted the energies of the movement into other channels and affected its ideas and pattern of growth. The total mobilization required by a nation engaged in a world war led the churches into new areas of need, but the previous experience of the social-service forces in solving local and national problems enabled them to assume leadership roles in the wartime work of the denominations. Gradually, the world conflict broadened the perspective of Protestant social activists, which produced modifications in ideology that both enriched and threatened the thought and organization of social Christianity. In various ways the war and its aftermath directly affected the evolution of the social gospel in America. Consequently, the years from 1917 through 1920 constitute another distinct stage of its growth.

Prior to the official involvement of the United States in the hostilities, the strife in Europe influenced the nation and the churches. A month after the assassination of Archduke Franz Ferdinand at Sarajevo on 28 June 1914, Austria-Hungary declared war on Serbia. During the following week the warfare escalated to include Germany, Russia, France, Belgium, and Great Britain. On 5 August, America proclaimed neutrality and sought to stay uninvolved for the next two and a half years. Owing to many factors, including submarines sinking ships, blockades of European ports, and loans to Britain and France by the nation's bankers, it became increasingly difficult for the United States to maintain a neutral stance. Finally, on 2 April 1917 President Woodrow Wilson asked Congress to declare war against Germany, pleading that it was necessary because "the world must be made safe for democracy." Four days later he signed the Proclamation of War approved by both houses of Congress.

Since the primary focus of social-gospel advocates was on social problems in America, there were few references in its literature to the fighting in Europe prior to the declaration of war. Although the impact of the hostilities was evident in the Northern Baptist Social Service Committee report in 1916, there was little evidence that the situation abroad was a major concern in the other socially active denominations.[1] That is not to say that these denominations had no interest, but when they did, it was expressed by other official groups in their structures. Until the United States took an active role in the war, the outlook of social-service agencies and leaders centered on the role of the church in the nation; a world dimension was not generally characteristic of the social gospel during the years it achieved official recognition and status.

Although the Social Service Commission of the Federal Council of Churches similarly had little to do with international affairs, Charles Macfarland was keenly aware of events in Europe from the start of the bloodshed. In his quadrennial report of 1916 he wrote, "Since the beginning of the war, constant correspondence has been carried on with representative leaders of the churches of both the neutral and warring nations in Europe." At his suggestion, by the fall and winter of 1914, the Administrative and Executive Committees of the council had authorized the treasurer "to receive and transmit funds for legitimate specified objects in connection with the war." During 1915 and 1916 he diligently organized a fund-raising effort in the United States for war relief overseas. From December 1915 through January 1916, Macfarland traveled to Europe "on a mission of fraternity and goodwill to the churches and Christians of the belligerent nations," with the approval and advice of President Wilson. He visited Germany as well as the Allied nations and garnered firsthand experience of the devastation and need for relief.[2]

---

[1]*Annual of the Northern Baptist Convention (1916)*, 169-72.

[2]*The Churches of Christ in Council*, ed. Charles S. Macfarland, vol. 1 of Library of Christian Cooperation, 6 vols. (New York: Published for the Federal Council of Churches by the Missionary Education Movement, 1917) 133, 138-41, 187, 191-231; Charles S. Macfarland, *Across the Years* (New York: Macmillan Co., 1936) 101-11; *Christian Cooperation and World Redemption*, ed. Charles S. Macfarland, vol. 5 of Library of Christian Cooperation, 6 vols. (New York: Published for the Federal Council of Churches by the Missionary Education Movement, 1917) 35-69.

Macfarland's interest in both peace and war had long been evident. Before the war started, in 1913 he had urged the Federal Council to create a commission to improve relations between the United States and Japan. He had also encouraged the formation of a Commission on Peace and Arbitration prior to the assassination at Serajevo. At the same time he had initiated efforts to improve the number and status of chaplains in the army and navy by conferring with the Secretary of the Navy and the Secretary of War. This interest was further implemented by H. K. Carroll when he was selected to head the Washington office of the Federal Council. Thus, through the initiative of Macfarland, the interdenominational agency had a vision that was both international and national in scope.[3] That larger perspective was channeled through commissions of the council other than Social Service and did not directly affect that group until the United States officially joined the battle against Germany in April 1917.

A second organization that reflected the impact of the war in Europe before America entered the action was the interdenominational Religious Education Association. At its annual meeting 28 February–1 March 1916, General Secretary Henry F. Cope reported that the conflict had cut off the "entire foreign membership" of the agency, and the loss of this group was enough to create "the severest financial strain" the association had experienced. At the same meeting, the president's Annual Address declared that "one of the impressive results of the present war is the compelling power it has for making men think in world terms." As a result, the strife was "creating a new era," and he asserted that the churches had to "supply moral motive power suitable to the new era."[4]

The next year the association's theme was "Religious Education and the Coming World Order." The association met late in February 1917, before the nation officially joined in the struggle, and war was part of the agenda. Bishop Francis J. McConnell's presidential address stated that "the world cannot emerge from its present stress unchanged." He admitted that "religion was caught unawares by the outbreak of the terrific world tempest" but saw no reason why religion should be surprised by the problems that would follow it. The "Declaration of Principles" that year maintained that the war pointed to the moral inadequacy of the social order and called for "a rigorous scrutiny of the underlying premises of our civilization." A new and better social order would result from the agony of the hostilities. Arguing that a new education was necessary in

---

[3] *Annual Reports of the Federal Council of Churches* (1913), 7-11, 12-16, 32-33; (1914), 9-19, 29-43, 71-73.

[4] George B. Stewart, "Religious Education and the Present World Situation," *Religious Education* 11 (April 1916): 141-47, 150.

order to achieve that goal, the Declaration further asserted, "The building of the new social order calls for the earnest co-operation and effective organization of all social and educational agencies, in the community, in the nation and in the world."[5]

Although the Religious Education Association felt the impact of the war and perceived its general implications for the churches, it lacked the continuing organization and staff that enabled the Federal Council of Churches to act. Consequently, it was limited to words, while the council was able to initiate action. By his own convictions, as well as with the encouragement he received from church leaders in Europe, Charles Macfarland came to believe that the interdenominational Federal Council of Churches was the proper body to act for Protestantism in the war effort. European Christians of both neutral and warring nations were divided by the fighting and were unable to take any united action, but they were impressed by the potential role of the federated and representative structure of the council. Moreover, Macfarland felt that his organization best reflected the largest dimension of Protestantism and, therefore, was best qualified to work both with the government and with Roman Catholics and Jews.[6] With war imminent, the previous agonizing conflicts concerning church federation and social service that had produced statements of principles and functional commissions within the council enabled Macfarland to act quickly.

On 27 March 1917 Macfarland asked Worth Tippy to move to the Washington office to reorganize the work with army and navy chaplains. Ten days later Congress approved the Declaration of War against Germany. Thus, little more than six weeks after assuming responsibilities as secretary of the Commission on Church and Social Service, the war caused Tippy to change his plans and activities drastically. Until peace was restored, his life, and the life of the commission, was dominated by the wartime needs of the nation.[7]

Over the signatures of President Frank Mason North and General Secretary Charles Macfarland, a call was sent to all members on 20 April 1917, summoning them to a special meeting of the Federal Council in Washington, D.C., on 8 and 9 May. The announced purposes were:

To prepare a suitable message for the hour;
To plan and provide for works of mercy;

---

[5]Francis J. McConnell, "Instruments and Ends in Spiritual World Conquest"; "Declaration of Principles," 1 March 1917, ibid. 12 (April 1917): 82, 83.

[6]"Report of the General Secretary," *The Churches of Christ in Council*, 214-18.

[7]*Annual Reports of the Federal Council of Churches* (1917), 77-80, 151-58.

To plan and provide for the moral and religious welfare of the army and navy;
To formulate Christian duties relative to conserving the economic, social, moral and spiritual forces of the nation.[8]

Also invited to attend were persons from a number of cooperating organizations, such as the American Bible Society, Home Missions Council, Council of Women for Home Missions, and the Young Men's and Women's Christian Associations. According to Tippy, "The thinking of the church was largely crystallized in the Washington Conference . . . and at the same time a beginning was made at the program of action, and at organization."[9]

Following the May meeting the message was sent to the churches and the public, representatives returned to their constituencies to create denominational war commissions, and the Federal Council sought to find ways to implement the diverse suggestions. "The Message to the Churches" contained two parts, one a general statement of spirit and purpose and the other a list of practical duties. In the former the council stated the dual responsibility felt by citizens who were both Americans and Christians, persons struggling to balance their national heritage of freedom and democracy with the obligations of their universal faith in Jesus Christ. Thus, the mission of the church in this time of crisis was "to bring all that is done or planned in the nation's name to the test of the mind of Christ."[10]

Although admitting that not all Christians interpreted that mind the same way, the message nevertheless suggested a number of practical duties that were felt to be appropriate. The list included a primary responsibility for the moral and spiritual welfare of the army and navy. It urged churches "to secure national prohibition as a war measure" and to guard against lowering "the sexual standards of the community." In light of the increased suffering caused in wartime, churches and members were encouraged to increase "gifts and service," especially to

---

[8]Charles S. Macfarland, ed., *The Churches of Christ in Time of War* (New York: Published for the Federal Council of Churches by the Missionary Education Movement, 1917) iii-iv.

[9]Worth Marion Tippy, *The Church and the Great War* (New York: Fleming H. Revell Co., 1918) 24. See John F. Piper, Jr., *The American Churches in World War I* (Athens OH: Ohio University Press, 1985) 14-18, passim, for an excellent study of Protestant and Roman Catholic ministries during the war. His interpretation, like mine, focuses on the role of the Federal Council and sets Protestant social service in the larger religious context of the time in greater detail.

[10]Tippy, *The Church and the Great War*, 24-25; Macfarland, *Churches in Time of War*, 129-33.

organizations like the American Red Cross. Proper provision for child welfare and maintenance of industrial standards were affirmed. Increased production of food was advocated as "an urgent national duty." Prevention of waste, justice in distribution, and evenly bearing the burden of war costs were emphasized. And safeguarding democracy in industry as well as government was proclaimed as a present necessity and the beginning of world democracy. If several of the duties sounded familiar to social activists, it may have been due to the contributions of Henry Atkinson, Samuel Batten, Bishop McConnell, Charles Stelzle, Worth Tippy, and Harry Ward, who served on the committees that shaped the message.[11]

Moving beyond words to action was more demanding. Correct deeds and organizational forms were uncertain in a realm where church leaders had no experience. Tippy confessed that Protestant churches were not prepared for the emergency of the war, and it took seven months "to know thoroughly what to do and to get together for action." After the Washington meeting he organized a temporary Committee of the Churches on War Work, which had its headquarters in the office of the Social Service Commission. Finally, on 20 September 1917, the General War-Time Commission of the Churches was created by the Federal Council to serve as the central coordinating agency for Protestant denominations in the war effort. Similarly, Tippy created the Committee on War-Time Work in the Local Church and Cooperation with the American Red Cross and administered it. However, when Tippy returned to the New York office in the autumn of 1917 Stelzle took over the work with the Red Cross.[12]

Under the leadership of William Adams Brown, the General War-Time Commission of the Churches became the umbrella agency for a vast array of committees, which freed Tippy to create new organizations as needs emerged. While the General War-Time Commission worked with comparable Catholic and Jewish agencies and the government, Tippy and the Social Service Commission cooperated with the New York State Woman Suffrage Party, the National Child Labor Committee, the Department of Agriculture, the American Committee for Armenian and

---

[11]Macfarland, *The Churches in Time of War*, 133-37; Federal Council of the Churches of Christ in America, *Report of Special Meeting, Washington, D.C., May 7, 8, 9, 1917* (New York: National Office, [1917]) 11-12.

[12]Tippy, *The Church and the Great War*, 88; Margaret Renton, ed., *War-Time Agencies of the Churches: Directory and Handbook* (New York: General Wartime Commission of the Churches [FCCCA], 1919) 152-53, 179; *Annual Reports of the Federal Council of Churches* (1918), 24.

Syrian Relief, the National Organization for Public Health Nursing, and the United States Public Health Service.[13] Although the agenda was now oriented to war needs, Tippy and his commission staff used the same principle of cooperating with other agencies to solve problems that the social-service secretaries had developed prior to the international struggle.

In collaboration with the Public Health Service, Tippy formed a Joint Committee on Social Hygiene that brought the churches into a "new national movement for the control of venereal diseases." Leadership of this program remained with the Social Service Commission, but eventually Paul Moore Strayer, chairman of the Commission on Social Service of the northern Presbyterians, became its leader. That enabled Tippy to undertake his "heaviest work for the year" (1918) as executive secretary of the Joint Committee on War Production Communities. Initially conducting surveys in nearly one hundred local communities that suddenly became centers for shipbuilding, manufacturing airplanes, or producing other war supplies, he then had to negotiate extensively with several large denominational boards and war councils to induce them to finance a new pattern of ministry by Protestants where no local congregations existed. This led to the formation of interdenominational Liberty Churches, which provided a model for future cooperative endeavors in unchurched communities when the war ended.[14]

Through the Joint Committee on War Production Communities, work in rural communities, in behalf of women in industries, and for "the industrial and social welfare of the Negro population" was implemented. These activities were carried out by persons assigned to Tippy's staff in the Commission on the Church and Social Service by the Mennonites, Congregationalists, and Council of Women for Home Missions. He reported that approximately seventy-five full-time and part-time workers were engaged in the War Production Communities project during a period of a year and a half. In addition to the staff increases necessitated by this project, the staff of the Commission on the Church and Social Service had to enlarge its own ranks to maintain the workload assigned to it. F. Ernest Johnson was employed as research secretary and assumed much of the "burden of detail involved in the Commission work." Since the commission already employed Clyde Armitage as assistant secretary to manage the Washington office and depended on the efforts of Henry Atkinson and Samuel Batten, who were assigned by their denominations to work closely with the Federal Council on the wartime activities, the

---

[13]Renton, *Wartime Agencies of the Churches*, 149-76, 180-81.

[14]Ibid., 181, 193-99; *Annual Reports of the Federal Council of Churches* (1918), 24-27.

number of persons serving the organization far exceeded any previous time. Furthermore, the efforts of Field Secretary Charles Stelzle with regard to prohibition, labor, publicity, and the Strengthen America Campaign were closely related to the commission's work.[15]

During the wartime months the crusade to make the world safe from democracy clearly dwarfed the Social Gospel movement. But at the same time it so engulfed social activists in its needs that they probably worked together more than they had previously. The 1917 and 1918 reports of the Federal Council's Commission on the Church and Social Service and of its executive secretary and assistant secretary were almost totally devoted to wartime work. In 1919 the proportion allotted to that subject in the commission's report quickly diminished to a quarter, and by 1920 only 20 percent of the commission's quadrennial report described such activities. The latter document indicated that the commission had determined a program for and created an effective organization of the churches "for national and community war-time service." Of the varied duties that were fulfilled, they called attention to the Social Service staff's contributions to the Interchurch Committee on War Work, the General War-Time Commission of the Churches, efforts in behalf of the American Red Cross, joint activities regarding social hygiene, and the management of the Joint Committee on War Production Communities, which was described as "probably the greatest single service of the Commission during the war." According to the report, three valuable lessons resulted from this wartime service: "the war brought the churches powerfully into community and national service," Protestants established good cooperation with Catholics and Jews, and the idea of the Liberty Church "might well be applied to most small communities."[16]

Since only one of the three lessons related directly to the social-service responsibilities of the commission, it appears that the long-range impact of the wartime work was not as significant as it seemed when the needs faced the staff. However, if one reads Tippy's remarks in his *Church and the Great War* concerning the spirit of the churches when America entered the hostilities, there were clear echoes of social-gospel motivation. In the

---

[15]*Annual Reports of the Federal Council of Churches* (1918), 26-27; "Report of the Commission on the Church and Social Service," *The Churches Allied for Common Tasks: Report of the Third Quadrennium of the Federal Council of the Churches of Christ in America, 1916–1920,* ed. Samuel McCrea Cavert (New York: Federal Council of Churches, 1921) 106-108; Renton, *Wartime Agencies of the Churches,* 30-31, 156, 158, 160, 161, 162, 167, 169, 173, 174, 175, 184-85, 200.

[16]*Annual Reports of the Federal Council of Churches* (1917), 151-58; (1918), 96-106; (1919), 99-107; *Churches Allied for Common Tasks,* 104-108.

midst of the conflict, he commented that "the church in war time cannot be other than an inseparable part of the life of the people, strengthening them, comforting them, speaking their highest vision and morality, but not separate from them as a voice thundering from the skies." Reminiscent of social Christianity was his assertion that the church "dare not close its eyes to evil for it is or should be the conscience of the nation, speaking like the conscience of a man's own soul." And that conscience was not human but divine: "Whatever voice it speaks must be the voice of Him who is in the midst of the nation, the Soul of democracy, and not the voice of an institution whose responsibility is in heaven and not in the earth." Consequently, it was not surprising for him to conclude that the church "is to do everything within its power, in ways that are clearly within its province, making fullest use of its organization and equipment, to hasten the victory." These impassioned ideas seemed to fit better with the devotion and action that social-gospel activists brought to wartime service than the rather anemic lessons his report indicated in 1920. By that date the idealism of the wartime crusade had been modified, but the ardor of the war months ought not to be forgotten as a part of the history of the Social Gospel movement. Although his concepts were strongly nationalistic in 1918, Tippy also exposed the kernel of future ideas, as, for example, when he said that the church "is to look ahead to the new brotherhood of the nations which must follow the war."[17]

While the central coordinating agency for Protestant service was the General War-Time Commission of the Churches, created by the Federal Council of Churches, most of the actual ministry of the churches was performed by the war commissions of the various denominations. Those bodies have had little place in this account because most of the war commissions made little direct use of the social-service commissions within their structures. In the official compilation, *War-Time Agencies of the Churches*, the record of each church's war activity was prepared by a representative of the denomination; only in one instance was the Commission on Social Service directly utilized. The National Service Commission of the Congregational churches noted that its Social Service Commission attempted to meet national needs prior to the declaration of war, but after that the work was too large to leave to one special agency. After its creation in October 1917, the National Service Commission requested that "the Social Service Department of the Education Society be requested to loan the services of its Secretary" to the National Commission "for the period of the war." This was done, and Henry Atkinson played an important role in the wartime work of his

---

[17]Tippy, *Church and the Great War*, 16-17.

denomination and of Federal Council agencies.[18] Northern Baptists did not make as clear a statement concerning the involvement of Samuel Batten, but he also was directly involved in much the same way as Atkinson because he was chosen to be the secretary of the denomination's War Commission. Without an explicit explanation, the annual convention in effect coopted Batten's social-service commission as the central agency through which its wartime activities were carried out.[19]

Standing in sharp contrast, the official accounts of the war commissions of the Northern Methodist, Northern Presbyterian, and Protestant Episcopal churches made no reference to their social-service agencies and staff.[20] Nevertheless, the names of Methodist Harry Ward, Presbyterian Paul Moore Strayer, and Episcopalian Frank Crouch appeared in the committees of the Federal Council. A further indication that the official accounts of the denominations were incomplete occurred with the Methodists. Although there was no reference to the work of the Methodist Federation for Social Service in the official report, the *Methodist Year Book* stated that the federation carried out a special wartime program of education and propaganda concerning "Vacant Lot Gardening; Elimination of Waste; Relief, in cooperation with Red Cross and local charities; Americanizing immigrants; Maintaining industrial standards; Fighting the venereal peril; Keeping prices down; National prohibition as a war measure, Social justice in war finance; Spiritual leadership in keeping down hate, defending democracy at home, and creating the international mind."[21] Undoubtedly other denominations had similar programs for local churches that were not included in the brief official summaries. If nothing more, this program of the Methodist Federation evidenced how the practical needs of the initial "Message of the Churches" in May 1917 found their way into denominational life and illustrated the range of activities to which the social- service agencies diverted their energies during the military conflict.

Accustomed to responding to the moral and social needs of the nation in peaceful times, social-gospel advocates responded similarly in time of war. While the normal emphases of social Christianity had to be set aside in order to concentrate on "the duty of the Church in this hour of national need,"[22] advocates approached America's new crisis with the same

---

[18]Renton, *Wartime Agencies of the Churches*, 29-34.

[19]Ibid., 9-17.

[20]Ibid., 66-71, 88-95, 99-101.

[21]*The Methodist Year Book* (1918), 160-61.

[22]This was the title of the "Message to the Churches" in the official minutes, *Report of Special Meeting . . . May 7, 8, 9, 1917*, 22.

devotion to democracy and the same pragmatic energy that characterized other developments in social service. Utilizing such procedures as community surveys and cooperation with secular organizations that they had developed in their social-service programs, Protestant social activists shared the experiences learned in their campaigns to Christianize society. Later looking back at the Federal Council during the war, Shailer Mathews was pleased that the federated organization was "prepared to act as an agent of Protestantism in conditions that had never been experienced." The council took the initiative on behalf of its constituent bodies, and other denominations willingly accepted its coordinating role. "For the first time," said Mathews, "Protestant forces in America were in a position to act cooperatively without the preliminary and time-consuming processes of organization."[23] Moreover, since social service now occupied a respected place in Federal Council circles, social-gospel leaders assumed administrative functions in the war effort. Thus, in the nation's stress, Protestant social leaders were able to translate their achievements in social service to the needs of wartime service.

One of the major consequences of the war was the emergence of new ideas, or the reformulation of old ideas in modified forms. The postwar years were a time of reconstruction, and proponents of social Christianity had a number of their own ideas to share with the churches and the nation. In effect, this also was part of their wartime service.

---

[23]*Twenty Years of Church Federation: Report of the Federal Council of the Churches of Christ in America, 1924–1928,* ed. Samuel McCrea Cavert (New York: Federal Council of Churches, 1929) 27. Charles Macfarland made similar statements in a more defensive way in his report six months after the fighting stopped. "The Work of the Council as Affected by the War," Federal Council of the Churches of Christ in America, *Report of Special Meeting. Cleveland, Ohio. May 6, 7, 8, 1919* (New York: National Office, 1919) 53-54.

CHAPTER 18

The Church
and Social Reconstruction

The most significant document issued by the Commission on the Church and Social Service during the Quadrennium was its statement on "The Church and Social Reconstruction."

("Report of the Commission on the Church and Social Service," 1920)

IN ADDITION TO PROVIDING INSPIRATION, leadership, coordination, and service to the American war effort, Protestant Christianity also furnished ideas to the nation, especially contributing to the religious basis of democracy. Primarily, these ideas were modifications of concepts already generated by social Christianity: the relationship of religion and democracy, the process of Christianization, and the pattern of social reconstruction. The intellectual and theological contributions of social activists may well have produced more lasting influence on the social-gospel movement than their wartime service.

Even before the Declaration of War, the Religious Education Association understood that the struggle in Europe would result in a new world order, which made the formation of new motives imperative. "A religious interpretation of life is the world's great need," said Executive Secretary Henry F. Cope before America entered the battle. "Ultimately the basic issues of this war will be settled for good or ill by success or failure in religious education," insisted an editorial in *Religious Education* after the United States joined the Allied cause. Acknowledging the need to raise armies and crops, the editorial urged educators not to forget the greater "need of a generation guided by righteousness and truth."[1] Although their

---

[1] The theme for its 28 February-1 March 1917 Annual Meeting was "Religious

words suggested that they knew how to do so, other words and actions showed that the members of the association lacked full comprehension of the needs; they relied mainly on general theories, relationships, and pragmatic adaptation. While limited largely to the expression of ideas, the organization under Cope's leadership sought to meet the needs during the war years.

Since President Wilson had called the nation to war to make the world "safe for democracy," it was not surprising that one topic that dominated the addresses at the annual conventions during and after the nation went to battle was the fundamental relationship of religion to democracy. "Faith in democracy" was a basic ingredient in the religious education of an American citizen, insisted Francis Greenwood Peabody in 1917. Despite the imperfections of the institutions of American citizenship, they must be "the instruments of a religious life." The motives of citizenship and of religion were closely related: "If the Kingdom of God is to come in America it must come through the agencies of citizenship."[2] Another speaker maintained that serious world problems could be solved "only through the establishment of a true democracy," which need not be a particular form of government or political organization but "the recognition and practice of the principle of human brotherhood."[3] A third participant declared that a new social order was to emerge, in which "the state is more and more to take over the administration of the details of the brotherly life in a democracy in which justice and love are the chief makers and administrators of its laws." Creating such values was the task of the churches.[4]

While references to the interaction of religion and democracy often were as general in scope as those just noted, the interpretations, when viewed together, covered several facets of the subject and provided evidence for the evolving nature of one aspect of social-gospel thought. The association's "Declaration of Principles" in 1918 reaffirmed its commitment to democracy, asserting that "democracy and religion can be and ought to be two aspects of one and the same life," a life in God. To achieve the "democratization and spiritualization of life," the church should cooperate with other social institutions, because it bore a special

---

Education and the Changing World Order." *Religious Education* 12 (June 1917): 192-93, 179-80.

[2]"The Religious Education of an American Citizen," ibid. 12 (April 1917): 94-102

[3]Herbert Wright Gates, "Religious Education and Human Welfare," ibid. 12 (October 1917): 308.

[4]James L. Kesler, "The Demand of the Coming Social Order," ibid., 12:343.

responsibility to deal with "the ultimate motives of democracy and religion."[5] Professor William Adams Brown of Union Theological Seminary in New York, who served at the time as executive secretary of the General War-Time Commission of the Churches, told the organization's annual convention on 6 March 1918 that the Christian religion was "the unifying element which democracy needs if it is to fulfill its world task." The church's contribution to the democracy of the future was to provide "continuity, reverence, faith." Through these values "let her help the world to find its soul."[6]

At the same meeting the "Annual Survey of Progress" pointed to various community activities for betterment and declared, "If the aim of Christianity is the establishment of the Kingdom of God, or the democracy of God, on earth, there can be no question but that religious leaders should be vitally interested in these significant social endeavors." Having modified the kingdom of God concept to a belief in the democracy of God, the report went on to say that religion's role was to permeate all social activities "with the leavening spirit of Christian neighborliness" and thus perform "a coordinating influence." The writer admitted that this approach bore little resemblance to traditional religious ends, but practical applications of the spirit of Christian brotherhood formed a real part of the development of the democracy of God on earth. "If human associations are thereby rendered more just and more happy, the ends served are identical with the ends of a dynamic Christianity as expressed by Jesus, even though the traditional forms of Christian aims and methods are not in evidence."[7]

During 1918 the Religious Education Association's unfolding understanding of democracy and religion became clearer. At the annual meeting in March, the members voted that the theme of the next convention should be "Training in the New Citizenship." However, by August, in an editorial dealing with the revival of religion that was expected to accompany the war but did not materialize, Henry Cope challenged the church, schools, colleges, and other educational agencies to lead the world to a spiritual understanding of democracy. In October

---

[5]Ibid., 13 (April 1918): 91-92. The dominance of the idea of democracy in the organization during these years is evident in Stephen A. Schmidt's *A History of the Religious Education Association* (Birmingham AL: Religious Education Press, 1983) where ch. 2 is titled "Building the Democracy of God: 1903–1923."

[6]William Adams Brown, "The Contribution of the Church to the Democracy of the Future," ibid. 13 (October 1918): 347.

[7]"The Annual Survey of Progress: Community Cooperation," ibid. 13 (April 1918): 93-106.

an editorial announced that the theme for the next annual meeting would instead be "A Religious Interpretation of Democracy." By the December issue of *Religious Education,* another editorial explained,

> The democracy of tomorrow is not so much a matter of social and political arrangement as it is a matter of ways of thinking, of ideas of life's values and of the rights of others. It calls for new motives in living, new standards of conduct, and a new ethics. In a word, the changes that must come in reconstruction are changes in the wills, ideals and motives of men and women.[8]

In an article in that same issue Cope clarified his interpretation of the church's role in democracy: "The special part which the church plays in relation to the development of democracy is an educational one. This is because the function of the church is essentially educational, it is that of social organization for the growth of lives and the direction of society." Arguing that churches could not afford to be quiet coves separated from the main streams of life in society, he urged churches to teach by demonstration, not by exposition. "If Christianity is a democracy of the spirit its churches must be spiritual democracies. Unless they practice democracy they cannot persuade our world society to spiritual democracy." Cope believed that the church should "cause democracy to become an experience of religion." By revealing the spiritual purpose and work of democracy, the church could change democracy "from a political experiment into a spiritual reality." And, finally, he maintained that "the church exists not alone to give society a religion it has not hitherto possessed but to help it to identify the religion it already has." That was so because "true democracy was not something that may be made religious; it is religious already in that it is devoted to spiritual ends."[9]

During the same months that Cope crystallized his thoughts about religion and democracy, another renowned educator who participated in the Religious Education Association also developed his ideas on the same relationship. Arthur Cushman McGiffert of Union Theological Seminary in New York City dealt with similar ideas in his commencement address at Andover Theological Seminary in June 1918. Speaking on the topic "Christianity and Democracy," McGiffert indicated that the war had rendered a useful service by showing that the fundamental issue was between autocracy and democracy, which he regarded as a moral rather

---

[8]Ibid. 13 (June 1918): 261; (August 1918): 266; (October 1918): 306; (December 1918): 386.

[9]Henry Cope, "Democratic Training through the Church," ibid. 13 (December 1918): 401-11.

than a political matter. Germany's cruelty and ruthlessness made the nations realize how evil autocracy and imperialism could be and, as a result, other nations now looked to democracy for freedom and independence of individuals and nations. Formerly the Christian church had defined brotherhood in terms of benevolence, but now democracy broadened the context so that there was no genuine brotherhood without liberty and love.[10]

By McGiffert's interpretation, the cherished privilege of individuals or nations to regard themselves as peculiarly called to serve others was rendered dubious. "The whole notion of chosen nations is beginning to be looked upon with suspicion," he said. "Democracy is consistent only with the recognition of a universal call." America conceived itself to be a democratic nation, but it had learned that its democracy was sorely limited in many areas by selfishness. Thus, the special duty of Christianity was to serve democracy by promoting the spirit of unselfishness. To Christianize democracy was "to make it human instead of mechanical, to put love and sympathy, and the desire to serve in place of indifference and jealousy and greed of personal gain and power. This is Christianity's great duty to the democracy of today and tomorrow." This posed a twofold duty for Christians: "to democratize Christianity and to Christianize democracy."[11]

McGiffert drew several inferences from this analysis. One said that democracy was "the only state of society worthy to be called the Kingdom of God on earth." Another insisted that God's character had to be consonant with the ideas of liberty and service implicit in democracy; thus, the deity could not act autocratically and had to treat individuals not as puppets but as sacred persons with "liberties too precious to be invaded." A third consequence derived from this: "faith in God divorced from faith in man is no faith for the Christian of today."[12]

Flowing consistently from these ideas were McGiffert's assertions in a paper at the Religious Education Association convention in March 1919, which elected him as its president. Addressing the topic "Democracy and Religion," the professor argued that education in a democracy should be more humanistic than scientific. Moreover, he insisted that democracy should be a religion because its "very essence is idealism." Central tenets of a religion of democracy, said McGiffert, would include "idealism, faith

---

[10]Arthur Cushman McGiffert, "Christianity and Democracy," *Harvard Theological Review* 12 (January 1919): 36-42.

[11]Ibid., 43-48.

[12]Ibid., 48-50.

in man, good will and co-operation for a world-wide cause." "With these," he concluded, "democracy is itself a religion."[13]

Through an unusual intellectual chemistry in the collective mind of Religious Education Association speakers, the image of the relationship of religion and democracy went through a metamorphosis in the war years. Drawing on Protestantism's long-standing interest in American democracy and building upon President Wilson's challenge to fight to make the world safe for democracy, association thinkers altered the relationship. Slowly the religion that had been mobilized to save American democracy from its social crisis was replaced by a democracy that was itself regarded as a religion. The faith that was intended to Christianize the social order of the nation had become the basis for aiding the whole world to find its soul. The conviction that America was a chosen nation was universalized into a faith to make world society into a spiritual democracy. This was to be achieved by placing a greater emphasis on human capacity and less reliance on divine power. And, in the end, democracy itself would be the kingdom of God. How widely these concepts were accepted is impossible to determine, but they expressed ideas that were repeated in succeeding years. At the least, they demonstrated the romantic idealism of social-gospel thinking that at times failed to distinguish rhetoric from reality.

In contrast to the collective development of an idea in one organization, the modification of a second central social-gospel motif, the Christianizing of the social order, was evident in a small study book published in 1917. Harry F. Ward and Richard Henry Edwards collaborated to write *Christianizing Community Life* for the College Voluntary Study Courses of the North American Student Movement. As the secretary for Social Study and Service of the Student Young Men's Christian Association, Edwards was well qualified to work with Ward, who continued to head the Methodist Federation for Social Service and teach at Boston University School of Theology. The volume was paired with Walter Rauschenbusch's *The Social Principles of Jesus* as the fourth-year curriculum of the study course. Although the book emphasized local community life as the best place for students to work out the social principles of Jesus in social living, it also discussed various types of communities all over the world. This world dimension provided the context for the authors to universalize several features of social Christianity that had developed originally in and for an American setting. The book was designed to challenge readers to social action by combining "the great

---

[13]Arthur Cushman McGiffert, "Democracy and Religion," *Religious Education* 14 (June 1919): 156-61.

tasks of social reconstruction" with "immediate concrete measures" that could be used to resolve local problems.[14]

As the authors moved beyond social reform to the "reconstruction and transformation of the community life," they introduced several innovations to what had become accepted social-gospel teaching. Every social reform, they insisted, involved government action. But they demanded government by the people and not just such improvements as direct primaries or city managers. They wanted the church to be willing to sacrifice its own property and privileges, if necessary, "in order to lead the world into the path of economic righteousness and social justice that leads to the Commonwealth of God." "Are we engaged in tinkering with the machinery?" they asked, "Or do we seek the greatest objective possible to human life— the establishment on earth of the Commonwealth of God?" Their explanation of the commonwealth was similar to what others termed the democracy of God.[15]

Challenging Christians to be visionary enough to attain ultimate goals rather than proximate remedies was one of the innovations in these ideas. Another was the substitution of the concept of the commonwealth of God for the kingdom of God. A third was the universalizing of social service on a world scale. Adding to those innovations the belief that the evolution of society was "man-controlled" rather than a "blind process of nature," the authors affirmed that the human mind and will was gaining in "the power to make a world." Though social evolution moved slowly, "it continually accelerated," and humanity had less distance to travel to the ideal of the commonwealth of God than it had already traversed. Uniting the idea of progress to that of human capacity, Ward and Edwards declared, "The Commonwealth of God as the ideal social order has come only as far and as fast as men have consciously joined with the purpose of Jesus." With the expectation of further advance, they concluded that Christianizing community life around the world would create the commonwealth of God.[16] If nothing more, the Great War had lifted the vision and goal of social-gospel thought beyond the nation to the world, which led a growing number of its writers to broaden the movement's concepts. Ward and Edwards were among the first to do so, and Ward went on to express his interpretation more radically in 1919, with significant consequences that will be evident later.

---

[14]Harry F. Ward and Richard Henry Edwards, *Christianizing Community Life* (New York: Association Press, 1917) intro. and other preliminary pages.

[15]Ibid., 13, 121, 130-31, 148-64.

[16]Ibid., 164-75.

Expansion of social-gospel ideology to an international scale affected not only the concepts of the kingdom of God and of Christianization but also the introduction of the theory and program of social reconstruction. Whereas the war gave social Christianity the opportunity to adapt social service to national survival, the peace provided the occasion to expand programs designed to reform America's social ills to the reconstruction of the social order on a worldwide scale. Six months after the armistice was signed on 11 November 1918, such a program was seriously considered at a special meeting of the Federal Council of Churches. General Secretary Charles Macfarland asked the Commission on the Church and Social Service in March 1919 to prepare recommendations for an uncommon session of the council on 6-8 May. Executive Secretary Worth Tippy and Research Secretary F. Ernest Johnson prepared a carefully researched first draft that was taken to the meeting at Cleveland, Ohio. The "Statement on the Church and Social Reconstruction" was studied by the powerful Committee of Fifteen, which recommended that the document be polished editorially and then issued for study and use by the churches. In July it was published as a pamphlet and then it was reprinted as part of the Labor Sunday Message that year.[17]

Apparently the statement was longer than desired by the special meeting in May, for the body issued a shorter message of its own titled "From World War to World Brotherhood." That declaration noted that as Christians turned "from the war behind us to the new age that is waiting to be built," there were "four prime demands of the hour upon the Church of Christ." One was "a new sense of world responsibility animating all departments of church life." Another called for "a resolute effort to understand what a Christian social order in America should be and to secure it." A third urged "a swiftly increasing cooperation among the churches." And the fourth was a general appeal for "effective proclamation of fundamental verities."[18]

Compared to this brief indication of general direction for the constituent denominations after the restoration of peace, "The Church and Social Reconstruction" statement was a more extensive pronouncement of principles and a positive program of action for churches "in the social crisis immediately following the war." Although it paralleled similar statements by religious bodies in Europe, it was set in an American

---

[17]"Minutes of the Meeting," *Report of Special Meeting. Cleveland, Ohio. May 6, 7, 8, 1919* (New York: National Office, 1919) 37, 39; "Report of the Executive Secretary, Commission on the Church and Social Service," *Annual Reports of the Federal Council of Churches* (1919), 104.

[18]*Report of Special Meeting*, 39, 72-76.

context. Its purpose was "to crystallize the thinking of the churches and to erect a platform upon which there may be fairly united action." Tippy's evaluation of the declaration was evident when he told the Federal Council in December 1920 that it was "the most significant document issued by the Commission on the Church and Social Service during the Quadrennium."[19]

Methodologically, this postwar statement's approach was similar to the general analysis and response used by social-gospel proponents when facing the social crisis in 1907 and 1908. "The church finds itself this May of 1919 in the midst of profound unrest and suffering" was the analysis. Nevertheless, the response was expressed with a larger vision than a decade earlier. "The churches today recognize, as they did not a generation ago, that the Kingdom of God is as comprehensive as human life with all its interests and needs, and that they share in a common responsibility for a Christian world order." On the basis of the Social Creed adopted by the Federal Council, the declaration attempted to lay the pattern for social reconstruction. Broadly, and yet specifically, the pronouncement discussed such themes as labor-management relations, wages, unemployment, vocational training, industry as service, rights of women, justice for blacks, housing, immigration, sexual morality, and temperance. Poor attitudes toward workers, women, blacks, immigrants, and freedom of speech were interpreted as denials of fundamental democratic rights.[20]

When addressing these problems, the statement recognized that social reconstruction was so highly technical that most ministers lacked competence to solve the issues. But the problems were also moral issues, and ministers should speak to this dimension. Churches should "study social problems from the point of view of the spirit and teachings of Christ." On this basis they should use their "vast educative influence" and their "institutional organization for human happiness, social justice, and the democratic organization of society." The nature of the church's response was vitally important. "In some respects, the most urgent question before the world at the present time is the method of social

---

[19]Federal Council of the Churches of Christ in America, Commission on the Church and Social Service, *The Church and Social Reconstruction* (New York: Federal Council of Churches, [1919]) 3; "Report of the Commission on the Church and Social Service," *The Churches Allied for Common Tasks: Report of the Third Quadrennium of the Federal Council of the Churches of Christ in America, 1916–1920*, ed. Samuel McCrea Cavert (New York: Federal Council of Churches, 1921) 109. Several major sections are quoted in Tippy's report, 109-13.

[20]*The Church and Social Reconstruction*, 5-16.

reconstruction; shall it be by constitutional and peaceable methods, or by class struggle and violence?" The statement "The Church and Social Reconstruction" clearly favored the process of education and reform to violent struggle. Nevertheless, "The social question cannot be dealt with casually." The challenge was clear: "We are entering upon an era in which the absorbing concern of the world will be for social justice and the greatest well-being of the greatest number." In such a context, the churches needed to see that "the ethical principles of the Gospels are to be applied to industry and to the relations of nations."[21] While their vision had broadened to include the world and not just the nation, the fundamental perspective and approach of social-gospel advocates in the Federal Council continued to be that applied to the earlier social crisis in America. Although expanding in scope, the tenets of social Christianity remained substantially constant in program.

Another evidence of elaborating on ideas in a customary form occurred in the revision of the Social Creed of the Churches by the special meeting of the Federal Council of Churches. At the May 1919 gathering, the sixteen basic affirmations adopted in 1912 were reaffirmed, but four paragraphs were added to assist Christian churches in facing "the social issues involved in reconstruction." The first declared "that the teachings of Jesus are those of essential democracy and express themselves through brotherhood and the cooperation of all groups." This item went on to "deplore class struggle" and to "declare against all class domination, whether of capital or labor." Moreover, this addition indicated that the churches stood "for orderly and progressive social reconstruction instead of revolution by violence." A second addendum announced that "an ordered and constructive democracy in industry is as necessary as political democracy" and could be attained through collective bargaining and sharing shop control and management. The third addition urged industry to provide "a wage sufficient to support an American standard of living." That was possible by a guaranteed minimum wage and control of unemployment through government programs such as public works and social insurance. Fourth of the new elaborations was a claim for "full political and economic equality with equal pay for equal work" for women, who "played no small part in the winning of the war." Not only did these paragraphs provide added commitment, they also included specific suggestions for current problems in the economic, social, and political life of postwar America. The Social Creed with these supplementary resolutions also was adopted by the Young Men's Christian Association in 1919 and the Young Women's Christian Association in 1920. Despite

---

[21]Ibid., 5, 17-21.

the consistent use of the term *Social Creed* in these official references, the Federal Council, when it published the pronouncement as a pamphlet, titled it "Social Ideals of the Churches," revealing a continuing ambiguity in its own understanding.[22]

There were clear indications in 1919 that the meaning of these changes in social-gospel thought and action concerning social reconstruction were understood. Professor John Marshall Barker in his book *The Social Gospel and the New Era,* published in September, recognized that "the reconstruction period has brought an enlarging conception of the kingdom ideal which is leading the modern Church to recast some of its notions and to readjust its methods." At the beginning of his volume he summarized the changed situation.

> The Christian Church is the bearer of a vital and definite social message of world-wide significance. It is nothing less than a new social order in which God is consciously present in the common life of men as a ruling and inspiring power. The social ideal is that of a commonwealth of God. It presents the social vision of a new heaven and a new earth wherein justice, brotherhood, and cooperative service among men became the ruling principle of action. It implies the progressive social incarnation of God in the realm of good will and mutual service. This common objective touches the very heart and center of the world life.[23]

Institutionally, some denominations moved quickly following the special meeting in Cleveland to implement the commitment to social reconstruction. The Board of Bishops of the Methodist Episcopal Church issued a pastoral letter addressed to all ministers and laymen on May 10 calling them "to give most earnest heed to the application of Christian principles to social reconstruction." Recognizing "the inevitability of the application of democracy to industry," the bishops urged equitable wages for workers, collective bargaining, profit sharing, and putting workers on boards of directors. They encouraged tolerance and mutual respect and reminded Methodists to keep in mind "that the richest source of sound idealism is the Gospel of Jesus Christ." A special program dealing with "the problems of social reconstruction after the war" was created in the denomination that year.[24]

---

[22]*Report of Special Meeting,* 37-38. Also the Creed and the additions were included in Tippy's quadrennial report, *Churches Allied for Common Tasks,* 113-14, 109.

[23]John Marshall Barker, *The Social Gospel and the New Era* (New York: Macmillan Co., 1919) v, 1.

[24]*Christian Advocate* (New York), 22 May 1919, p. 642; *The Methodist Year Book* (1919), 160.

When the Northern Baptist Convention assembled late in May the report of its Social Service Committee told delegates that the war was "nothing less than a world revolution" that marked "the close of one age and the opening of a new epoch." It caused the break up of ideas and shattered policies of state. As a result, "Society is now faced with some urgent questions of reconstruction that have to do with the very life of man and the future of the state." Calling attention to "the social unrest that prevails in all lands and the acute industrial situation in our own country," the report called pastors and leaders to study the causes and conditions of discontent and to work for social reconstruction.[25]

Whether expressed in terms of social reconstruction, Christianization, or democracy, the new thinking had a world dimension. In a peculiar way, the tragedy of a world war broadened the scope of social-gospel ideology so that the satisfaction of needs was conceived as an international rather than a national mission. After a decade of American Christians who responded primarily to American problems, the war revived a global sense of mission that earlier had been a part of the thought of social Christianity. Decades before, Josiah Strong had summoned Protestants to world mission, and Washington Gladden and Walter Rauschenbusch had also challenged church people to worldwide perspectives. Apparently the immensity of America's social problems was so great that it dominated not only the energies but also the thought and program of the social gospel so that it became primarily an American response to American social problems, leaving needs in other lands to mission boards. The war and the peace once again enlarged the movement's vision from the nation to the world, and social thinkers applied that wider angle of vision to the needs of the time. Like the United States and other nations, the church was called to enter a new age, and in the process it seemed ready to revive a part of its earlier thought from the days when the Social Question dominated social Christianity.

Unfortunately, just at a time when the earlier ideas of world mission might be revived, the several persons who originally expressed them died. Almost symbolic of the changing of eras were the deaths of three of the most renowned leaders of the social gospel in the Progressive Era. Between July 1918 and January 1919 Washington Gladden, Walter Rauschenbusch, and Theodore Roosevelt passed from the scene. Gladden was eighty-two at his death, but the others were two decades younger and hence disappeared prematurely from active srvice. Gladden, the "father of the social gospel," and Roosevelt achieved fame and recognition earlier than Rauschenbusch, although at his death the latter was properly

---

[25]*Annual of the Northern Baptist Convention* (1919), 168.

acclaimed by *The Nation* as "the one man who had done more than any other to change its [American Protestantism's] thought in the present generation."[26] As we have seen, other social-gospel writers and speakers attempted to shape the thought of the postwar era, yet none expressed the ideas of the troubled time with as much authority and dominance as Rauschenbusch, Gladden, and Roosevelt had done earlier.

More recently, Professor Henry F. May designated the years from 1912 to 1917 as "the end of American innocence." He maintained that the three central ideas of late-nineteenth-century America— moralism, progress, and culture—were disintegrating before the nation entered the war because intellectuals and radicals undermined their foundations. The war simply intensified the collapse that was already well under way.[27] Social Christianity was closely identified with each of the three concepts, as May indicated, but the movement's hopeful allegiance to them had not wavered, even by the close of the fighting. Instead, champions of the social gospel persisted in their optimism, broadening their ideology from a national to an international perspective. Had the momentum of the Progressive Era continued, perhaps their idealism might have endured. However, the mood of the nation did not remain constant, and a series of circumstances forced the churches to reexamine their social message and ministry. In the immediate aftermath of the war, the churches developed a program of social reconstruction built on optimistic beliefs and goals. Only the shaking of these foundations produced changes, and even such compulsion had difficulty assailing the inveterate optimism of social-gospel thought.

---

[26]*The Nation*, 20 July 1918; reprinted in *Rochester Theological Seminary Bulletin* (November 1918): 46.

[27]Henry F. May, *The End of American Innocence: A Study of the First Years of Our Own Time, 1912–1917* (New York: Alfred A. Knopf, 1959; pbk., Chicago: Quadrangle Books, 1964) 12-14, 121, 125, 361, 393-98, passim.

CHAPTER 19

A Chastened Mood

Those who have watched the current of religious thought since our country entered the great war realize that the Church is acquiring an enlarged conception of its mission in the world. . . .

But this puts upon the Church heavy obligations, much greater than in former times; and requires a new power of faith and an unparalleled heroism of large undertakings. We are in a chastened mood. We know these great evils cannot be removed nor these constructive tasks of social engineering accomplished without a mighty working of the spirit of God.

("Report of the Commission
on the Church and Social Service," 1920)

AFTER A PERIOD WHEN PROTESTANT SOCIAL ACTIVISTS had been able to lead their denominations to embark on more large-scale service than ever before, it was not surprising that the same leaders were able to transfer their enthusiasm, convictions, and organizing talents to move beyond social service into wartime service. Similarly, when the armistice ended the fighting on the battlefields, champions of social Christianity turned their talents to designing programs for social reconstruction to rebuild what had been destroyed in Europe and to solve the continuing inequities in the nation. In an age of social responsibility, both wartime service and social reconstruction seemed to be legitimate responses to the great needs of the United States and the world. With characteristic optimism, social-gospel leaders in Protestant churches and the Federal Council of Churches attempted to carry the duties imposed upon the world by both war and peace.

Their inherent optimism did not permit proponents of the social gospel to think that energetic efforts could result in failure rather than success. For more than a decade, their cooperative endeavors had produced slow but steady progress and even a few notable victories. Their movement had made a permanent place for itself within the bureaucratic structures of Protestantism. After such positive experiences, it was difficult for them to envision major failure and criticism. Nevertheless, a fickle national mood that suddenly shifted to conservatism in a country long dominated by active progressivism surprised religious as well as secular idealists in 1919 and 1920. As a consequence, some activities and ideas of social-gospel leaders in those years were attacked with such strong opposition that the cause of social Christianity in institutional Protestantism had to be modified.

Events on the national scene during 1919 indicated that the nation was in flux. In January President Woodrow Wilson and his associates arrived in Paris for the Peace Conference, while at home it was announced that the Prohibition Amendment to the Constitution had been ratified and would go into effect on 16 January 1920. By mid-February it was obvious that there was opposition to the League of Nations idea in Congress, and Wilson set sail for America. Throughout the year there was turbulence in industry, and four million persons were on strike or lockout. In September the Communist party held its first convention, which convened in Chicago. That month Governor Calvin Coolidge saw the Boston police go on strike and told Samuel Gompers of the American Federation of Labor, "There is no right to strike against the public safety by anybody, anywhere, anytime." On 22 September a massive strike against the United States Steel Corporation started in Gary, Indiana. Two months later the Senate rejected the Versailles Treaty for the first time. And in December, 249 Russians were deported as part of Attorney General A. Mitchell Palmer's "Red Hunt."

Problems were not limited to the social, economic, and political order; church leaders also complained about conditions. The editor of *The Christian Advocate* in New York had his own litany of complaints late in February.

> We have seen the Christian Church come upon times as troublesome as those of '76 and '61 [1776 and 1861]. . . . There is no use to blink the facts. The churches have been slackers at their task. The fires on the altars of faith have burned low. Prayer has become formal, and even ceased to be. . . . The membership of the churches, though waxing wealthy in this world's goods, make no adequate acknowledgement of their responsibility as stewards for all that they possess. The crowded cities, the immigrant populations, the swarming industrial towns, the neglected rural communities, call to the churches for immediate and lavish application of the individual and social gospel, and the Church has been standing with weak knees and hands down in the presence of these near-by fields, while abroad in India, China and Africa the harvest is only limited by the lack of reapers, and the wounds of France, Italy and Belgium are so many dumb mouths crying for pity and relief. Not

in the memory of living men did a situation call so insistently to organized Christianity to rise to a great duty and a great opportunity.[1]

Other Christians shared similar concerns after the war ended, but early in 1919 Christian optimism continued to dominate through the birth of the Interchurch World Movement. That program was a product of Protestantism's exuberant optimism, and its activities and propaganda during the year tended to obscure other troubling events that caused problems for the social gospel.

Inspired by a "vision of a united church uniting a divided world," a meeting of 135 representatives of Protestant mission boards and related benevolent agencies on 17 December 1918 put in motion the nascent ideas and organization that became the Interchurch World Movement. More comprehensive than any project yet sponsored by cooperative Protestantism in America, the movement attempted to unite all the work of 140 different boards representing 34 denominations at home and abroad into a single program covering the entire range of Christian activity. A vast plan of surveys, education, and publicity was to be carried on prior to a coordinated financial campaign to raise the then-awesome total of $360,000,000 in the spring of 1920.[2]

The general vision and plan was carried back to the boards and agencies, which one by one agreed to create their own machinery to participate in the project. The movement's General Committee drew on the successful Methodist Centenary campaign of 1918 by borrowing its organizational pattern, educational and office materials, and survey experience. They even hired its leader, S. Earl Taylor, as general secretary for the movement. Although it started as a voluntary enterprise, the new program grew expansively until it employed more than 2,000 persons and proposed to buy a large building to house its offices. Extensive surveys were initiated in foreign missions, home missions, and education. A vigorous publicity campaign in the daily and religious press kept the movement in the nation's attention. Enthusiasm reached a peak at Atlantic City 7-10 January 1920 as 1,700 delegates heard preliminary reports of the surveys and inspiring addresses that convinced them of the value of the enterprise.[3]

---

[1]*Christian Advocate* (New York), 20 February 1919, pp. 225-26.

[2]William Adams Brown, *The Church in America: A Study of the Present Condition and Future Prospects of American Protestantism* (New York: Macmillan Co., 1922) 115-19; Eldon G. Ernst, *Moment of Truth for Protestant America: Interchurch Campaigns Following World War One* (Missoula MT: American Academy of Religion and Scholars' Press, 1974) 51-52.

[3]Brown, *Church in America*, 117-18; Ernst, *Moment of Truth*, 53-58.

Maintaining this huge program became increasingly expensive, and by the fall of 1919 the movement had to secure financial support from the denominations. At that point the member churches required commitments for underwriting the finances that transformed the idealistic movement into a church federation. By design, the overall campaign was to produce its work first, which then would provide the scope of the needs as a challenge to donors. It was anticipated that all gifts for missionary needs in the nation and the world would go to those causes, with all operating expenses to be covered by donations of "friendly citizens" with wealth. In the meantime, denominational agencies borrowed the money for daily operations on their own credit. Consequently, the final financial appeal by the movement in April 1920 had to bear the weight of the entire campaign.[4]

As the denominations forced the Interchurch World Movement to become an ecclesiastical federation in order to maintain fiscal responsibility, it became apparent that the new organization conflicted with the already existing Federal Council of Churches. In April 1919 representatives of the two organizations agreed on a basis for cooperation that emphasized this distinction: the council was officially constituted by the denominations as a permanent ecumenical body while the movement was a temporary body with limited objectives that were nonecclesiastical in nature. With that understanding, the special meeting of the Federal Council at Cleveland in May endorsed the Interchurch World Movement, although it insisted that the movement clarify in its presentations "the distinction of function and field between it and the Federal Council."[5] By November it was obvious that such distinctions were vague and, in fact, the two bodies had become competitors in church federation, mission, and fund raising. When the council's Executive Committee met in December, Charles Macfarland's report devoted a major section to this problem. The report quoted documents concerning the agreement and expressed hope for continued cooperation. Advocating a need for "sympathetic and constructive" criticism, Macfarland evidenced the seriousness of the differences when he said that "it is an hour for statesmanship rather than for diplomacy."[6]

---

[4]Ernst, *Moment of Truth*, 78-79.

[5]Federal Council of the Churches of Christ in America, *Report of Special Meeting. Cleveland, Ohio. May 6, 7, 8, 1919* (New York: National Office, 1919) 27, 32; Ernst, *Moment of Truth*, 79-80.

[6]*Annual Reports of the Federal Council of the Churches of Christ in America* (1919), 21-25; Ernst, *Moment of Truth*, 80-82.

More was involved in the struggle than clarification of principles, although those were important to Macfarland after his years of careful negotiations with constituent churches of the Federal Council. Beyond the institutional issues were problems of functional overlapping and personal differences that tended to divide the once-harmonious social-gospel sympathizers who led the federated organization. In his report concerning the Commission on the Church and Social Service to the December 1919 annual meeting, Worth M. Tippy indicated that he had designed "a general plan for the organization of a Department of Industrial Relations for the Interchurch World Movement" and then assumed voluntary leadership roles in it in order to bind together the work of the department and the commission. During the summer these duties took him to Europe, where he conferred with church leaders concerning social and industrial conditions.[7] His quadrennial report in 1920 described his services to the movement as "a contribution by the Federal Council to the Interchurch, and it expressed not only its desire to help but its sense of the importance of cooperation."[8]

For Frank Mason North, the Interchurch World Movement proved to be a thorny problem that created mixed feelings, strained personal relationships, and added work. As one of the three executives of the Board of Foreign Missions of the Methodist Episcopal Church, he had to assume more administrative duties when his colleague, S. Earl Taylor, became general secretary of the Interchurch Movement. As president of the Federal Council of Churches, the movement caused him more anguish. When Tippy asked to be relieved from his job on a part-time basis in order to head the Industrial Relations Department of the movement, North felt deserted by another close associate. His concern to expand Methodist missions in Europe after the war put him in conflict with Macfarland, who helped negotiate an agreement concerning Protestants in France that excluded Methodist missions there. North's sharp criticism of that action cooled their relationship afterward, although the two remained outwardly courteous. The movement also put North at odds with his presidential predecessor Shailer Mathews, who favored the idea of the movement over the council. These problems were especially bothersome to North because they put his personal values and priorities into conflict; his commitment to missions and to ecumenism was frustrated by a movement that

---

[7] *Annual Reports of the Federal Council* (1919), 15, 100-102.

[8] "Report of the Commission on the Church and Social Service," *The Churches Allied for Common Tasks: Report of the Third Quadrennium of the Federal Council of the Churches of Christ in America, 1916–1920,* ed. Samuel McCrea Cavert (New York: Federal Council of Churches, 1921) 116-17.

threatened the Federal Council and his denominational mission loyalties while appealing to his desire to proclaim the gospel and serve humanity.[9] Despite the personal effects of these problems, the differences did not impede the momentum of the Interchurch World Movement.

During 1919 North was not the only Methodist leader who experienced difficulties because of the movement and a changing national mood. With the end of the war, unemployment rose as industries shifted to peacetime production. At the same time, unions resumed efforts to organize workers. Widespread labor discontent, and even riots, resulted. In the popular mind and the press, much of the unrest was attributed to the machinations of radicals. The American domestic scene felt the reverberations of the Communist revolution in Russia and shared the anxiety of world revolution. A fear of Communism combined with restless workers and economic recession to make the years 1919–1921 a troubled time in the nation. Not everyone shared these sentiments, but those who did not felt the displeasure of the growing sentiment, as Harry Ward discovered.

Harry F. Ward continued to serve as executive secretary of the Methodist Federation for Social Service, but by 1919 he had moved to New York City where he became Professor of Christian Ethics at Union Theological Seminary as well. On 25 January he mailed a statement on the "Russian question" to the editors of Methodist papers, alerting them to the fact that the January-February issue of *The Social Service Bulletin* would have a fuller treatment of the subject. In the 20 February issue of the New York *Christian Advocate* was a major article on Bolshevism that questioned Ward's press release and started a journalistic attack against him that continued through May. Not only was Ward criticized for his defense of the Communist form of government as "an experiment in direct democracy" and in accord with biblical aims, but also for the expression of his views in the name of the Methodist Federation for Social Service and on its letterhead. About the same time, the publishers of the Sunday School Graded Lessons announced that Ward's regular social interpretation of the lesson was being eliminated, and shortly afterward the *Adult Bible Class Monthly* indicated it was discontinuing lessons submitted by him.[10]

---

[9]Creighton Lacy, *Frank Mason North: His Social and Ecumenical Mission* (Nashville: Abingdon Press, 1967) 161-63, 191, 193, 206, 207-209, 223; Shailer Mathews, *New Faith for Old: An Autobiography* (New York: Macmillan Co., 1936) 165-66; Charles S. Macfarland, *Across the Years* (New York: Macmillan Co., 1936) 189-91.

[10]*Christian Advocate* (New York), 20 February 1919, p. 240; Milton J. Huber,

When the Executive Committee of the federation met 24 March, it reviewed what had occurred and discussed a plan for counterattack. A statement condemning the *Christian Advocate* editorial as "precipitate" and "unfair" was sent to editor James R. Joy, who had been among the first supporters of the federation in 1908. Efforts were also started to determine why the Sunday School Syndicate had acted to exclude Ward's contributions. At the request of ten prominent clergymen, among whom were Worth Tippy and George Albert Coe, Ward submitted to the *Christian Advocate* a letter explaining his views more elaborately. Although the tone of most of his long epistle was conciliatory and explanatory, it ended by affirming that the experiment in Russia was "in part the creation of Christian social ethics." While he did not agree "with the Russian definition of this ideal," he regarded it as a blundering attempt in the right direction that "flings a thundering challenge to our churches."[11] The next week a letter from Bishop Francis J. McConnell, as president of the federation, appeared in the same paper. While defending Ward, he disassociated himself from some of Ward's views and indicated that he personally was a capitalist and a stockholder. McConnell went on to suggest a possible connection between the actions to reject Ward's contributions to Sunday school literature and recent federation agitation to secure more democratic labor policies in the denomination's publishing houses.[12]

In an editorial titled "Defective Candor," which appeared in the 15 May issue, editor Joy responded to Ward's letter of explanation. Although expressing appreciation for his clarification of ideas, the editor reprinted part of an editorial that had appeared in *The Continent*, a Presbyterian paper. That journal not only questioned Ward's views about Russia but also stated that the *Social Service Bulletin* was not limited to Methodist readers and had Congregationalist Henry Atkinson and Presbyterian Paul Moore Strayer on its editorial board. Moreover, it was the responsibility of that editorial board to correct Ward's errors, a view with which Joy concurred. Furthermore, the editor asked why the federation's Executive Committee lacked the candor "to tell the public that at the same meeting in which this paper was condemned definite measures were taken to prevent any further presentation of Bolshevism in the Bulletin." Secret action was not enough. "The Church has a right to know that the

---

"A History of the Methodist Federation for Social Action" (Ph.D. diss., Boston University, 1949) 127-38; Robert H. Craig, "An Introduction to the Life and Thought of Harry F. Ward," *Union Seminary Quarterly Review* 14 (Summer 1969): 339-41.

[11]*Christian Advocate*, 3 April 1919, p. 434.

[12]Ibid., 10 April 1919, p. 450.

Federation disapproves of what was done in its name, for the Church, as well as the Federation, is involved."[13] For the editor, that issue was at the heart of the matter: the federation's responsibility to the Methodist Episcopal church for what it said and did. With the issue clarified, the *Christian Advocate* ceased its attack, but Ward continued his interest in Russia, for it was part of the subject matter of a new book he was writing.

Harry Ward's large book *The New Social Order* was completed in July. It was one of a flurry of books and pamphlets he wrote in 1918–1919, which included *The Gospel for a Working World* (1918), *The Christian Demand for Social Reconstruction* (1918), *The Opportunity for Religion* (1919), *The Religion of Democracy* (1919), and *Social Unrest in the United States* (1919). Ward's *New Social Order* built on arguments previously stated in these and other sources, but it was distinctive in carrying these ideas to more radical extremes. Although not repudiating evolutionary means, much of what he wrote in this book presumed revolutionary changes. Generally, the volume condemned capitalism for being outmoded economically and for preserving the old order in economics and politics. Additionally, the book was critical of the League of Nations because it sought to preserve the old order. In contrast, Ward praised Russia for carrying out a socialist program in practice and not just in theory as other European socialists did. His analysis and argument was developed on a world scale, seemingly answering many questions asked but not answered in *Christianizing Community Life*, which he had written earlier in collaboration with Richard Henry Edwards.[14]

Methodologically, Ward's argument was carefully developed. Starting with a basic conviction "that we have arrived at one of those conjunctions of economic pressure and idealistic impulse, which occasion fundamental changes in the organization of life," he maintained that recent events confirmed "the judgment that the beginnings of a new order are already with us." That new order was rooted in the past and was emerging through "a process of growth." Pointing to the emergence during and after the Great War of the idea of "reconstruction," he asserted the need to move beyond that. The term *reconstruction* suggested "a job of repairs" or "the replacing or rebuilding of something that has been destroyed," but more than that was needed. He cautioned those who would "maintain the present order" that the "working class the world over" had been awakened and was "determined to have a redistribution of power." "What is going on," he insisted, "is no mere tinkering with

---

[13]James R. Joy, "Defective Candor," ibid., 15 May 1919, p. 611.

[14]Harry F. Ward, *The New Social Order: Principles and Programs* (New York: Macmillan Co., 1919). See pp. 296-97 above.

the machinery of human society but one of those tremendous upheavals which mark a new period in human living." In a time when a world social order was forming, "the idealistic attempt to spread political democracy all over the earth" was the "last stage of our present political and social order." It was in Russia, where a social upheaval altered the capitalist order, that a truly new order was emerging as the working class seized power so it could "organize a social democracy around the principle of productive labor." Idealists of other classes and countries had joined them, but the outcome was unclear because forces of political nationalism, economic imperialism, and uncommitted intellectualism sustained the class conflict of the old order. The new order might come by revolution or evolution, but it would be achieved only when there was "a democratic form of economic organization" as well as "a democratic state."[15]

That analysis of "the nature of the new order" was followed by his description of the principles for the changed order, which included equality, universal service, efficiency, supremacy of personality, and solidarity.[16] Another extended section evaluated existing programs in light of his perception of the needs of the forthcoming social order. The British Labor party, he said, relied too much on gradual reform to be truly effective. The League of Nations was too concerned with preserving the existing old order in economics and politics. Socialist and labor movements in the United States failed to "fully understand their situation or themselves."[17] Only in Russia had socialists been able to attempt "an immediate economic revolution" by direct action; only there had something finally been done and not just discussed: "Whatever happens to the present Government in Russia from whatever cause, whether it fail because of the tactics of those who control it or because its principles are impossible, whether it be suppressed from without or overthrown from within, the record is written into human history that a government based on a socialist economic system once lived." For that reason, Ward concluded that "because the socialist theory has been taken off paper and made to live and move and have a being, all organized life will be quickened by what happens in Russia," whether it succeeded or failed.[18] In the more complete context of his book, Ward's socialist sympathies were more understandable than they had been in his premature press release and its resulting controversy in the pages of the *Christian Advocate,*

---

[15]Ward, *New Social Order*, v-vii, 3-32.

[16]Ibid., 35-183.

[17]Ibid., 185-224, 272-327.

[18]Ibid., 225-71. The quotations are on p. 227.

although the expanded ideas did not find widespread sympathy among Methodists or other mainline Protestants in 1919.

When Professor Ward discussed the role of the churches with regard to a new social order, his views did not seem as radical as his economic and political interpretation. He indicated the great change that had occurred in the past decade as Protestant churches moved beyond individual religion and adopted industrial and social standards in the Social Creed of the Churches. Quoting the 1912 recension of that platform in full, Ward said that most of the items were reform measures calling for immediate improvements. However, the points dealing with equality of rights and justice, division of the product of industry, development of the child, and acquisition and use of property were "general principles which if followed to their conclusion would result in a new social order." He interpreted the social-service movement as having a twofold task: to engage the churches in "practical tasks of community service" and to apply "the principles of religion in the organization of human society." Also, he envisaged the role of the church in social change as twofold: to be "a conserving institution in society" and yet to be "fundamentally revolutionary" in the sense that the Hebrew prophets were. If the churches were sufficiently prophetic, they would play a revolutionary role in creating a new social order. It was his conclusion that "an increasing section of the leadership of the church is accepting the responsibility which develops upon organized religion in a day when multitudes of men and women are longing for a new order of life."[19]

Due largely to his repeated assertions that capitalism was passing away and the working classes were growing in power, Ward's book did not find wide acceptance among American Protestants. Since his book identified the working class with the Russian Revolution and reached bookstores in November 1919, when a major steel strike was in progress, it was regarded as another evidence that his ideas were too radical for postwar America. Although its analysis was fresh and thorough, *The New Social Order* did not receive serious attention because its premises were not acceptable to the majority of Protestants and Americans at the time.

A third Methodist social-gospel leader to face difficulties that year was Bishop Francis J. McConnell, who became involved with what was called the Great Steel Strike. On 22 September 1919 a strike was called by Samuel Gompers's American Federation of Labor against the United States Steel Corporation, and approximately 300,000 workers walked off their jobs. As the weeks went by in the massive confrontation between labor and management, violence broke out and was ruthlessly suppressed in bloody

---

[19]Ibid., 328-51.

clashes. At issue were low wages, the twelve-hour work day, the seven-day work week, control of jobs, and the way all these were arbitrarily fixed.[20]

During October the Industrial Relations department of the Interchurch World Movement initiated a large-scale investigation of the steel strike. Bishop McConnell reluctantly agreed to head the nine-member Commission of Inquiry when other church leaders and prominent progressives avoided the controversial responsibility. A research staff was hired to assist with the investigation, but some of the interviewing was done by McConnell and other members. Despite a lack of cooperation on the part of the company, extensive interviews and surveys were conducted for the report. Elbert Henry Gary, chairman of the board of the United States Steel Corporation and an active Methodist layman, took an intransigent stand against the workers. With an immense cash surplus at hand, the company refused to negotiate on the issues. The steel corporation used strike breakers, police, spies, and "name-calling" to suppress labor during the strike. By the use of emotionally laden words such as *radicalism*, *Syndicalism*, and *Bolshevism*, the company played on popular fears and was able to turn initial public sympathy for the workers into irrational antagonism. McConnell and his commission were subjected to harassment and vilification. The bishop was publicly heckled, personally threatened, and had protests lodged against his appearances for public addresses. A former parishioner called him an "old Bolshevik." After 109 days the strike ended without a single concession by the company.[21]

Although the strike ended on 8 January 1920, the Commission of Inquiry did not publish its thorough *Report of the Steel Strike of 1919* until the following July. The investigation had ended in February, and the report was adopted unanimously by the nine members at the end of March. From the outset, its position was obvious: "The main issues were not settled. The causes still remain. Moreover, both causes and issues remain uncomprehended by the nation."[22] Since the report strongly favored the strikers, leaders of the Interchurch World Movement found

---

[20]The Commission of Inquiry, The Interchurch World Movement, *Report of the Steel Strike of 1919* (New York: Harcourt, Brace and Howe, 1920) 3-6, 11-16.

[21]Walter W. Benjamin, "Bishop Francis J. McConnell and the Great Steel Strike of 1919–1920," *A Miscellany of American Christianity: Essays in Honor of H. Shelton Smith*, ed. Stuart C. Henry (Durham NC: Duke University Press, 1963) 22-47; Francis J. McConnell, *By the Way: An Autobiography* (New York, Nashville: Abingdon-Cokesbury, 1952) 214-15.

[22]The Commission of Inquiry, *Report of the Steel Strike of 1919*, 3.

themselves in a dangerous situation at that time. Public opinion readily identified organized labor with social radicalism, and if the official report favored the workers it might alienate large numbers of people just when the movement's financial campaign was to begin. On the other hand, laborers might be offended if it appeared that the Interchurch campaign was identified too closely with big business. However, the movement could not afford to antagonize business leaders, upon whom it admittedly relied to make the fund-raising effort a success.

When Bishop McConnell presented the steel-strike report to the Interchurch Executive Committee on 10 May, a small committee was appointed to study it carefully and bring it back for unhurried consideration later. Rumors charged that the report was being suppressed, but it seems that the leaders were being cautious because of the seriousness of the findings and were limited in time because of dealing with difficulties in the fund-raising effort. When the investigation was reviewed, the subcommittee did not hesitate to recommend its publication. On 28 June that recommendation was unanimously approved by the Executive Committee, and the report was distributed late in July.[23]

"The report of this Commission of Inquiry is in effect a verdict against the Corporation and in favor of the strikers," declared *The Outlook*, which presented an accurate factual summary of it in its 11 August issue. An editorial in the same issue praised the courage of those who conducted the investigation but questioned whether the church should have undertaken such an inquiry. To the editor, it appeared that the church had attempted "to act as a judge in the controversy," since it heard witnesses, listened to arguments by both sides, and presented a verdict. That put the church in a vulnerable position, it was argued: "It becomes the church to take note of injustice, to be indignant against the unjust, and to use its moral power to rescue the oppressed; but it deprives itself of the moral power of its indignation and its influence when it sets itself up to determine for others what they shall count injustice and to set apart the just from the unjust." Although *The Outlook* agreed with the commission's overall evaluation, it concluded nevertheless that "it is the church's business to discriminate, it is not the church's business to judge." Admitting the difficulty "to see the distinction between discrimination and judging," the editorial believed that "the church is not relieved of a duty because it is not easy."[24]

Not all readers of the weekly journal were able to understand the editor's distinction. Two ministers wrote letters complaining that the

---

[23]Ernst, *Moment of Truth*, 124-32.

[24]*The Outlook* (New York), 11 August 1920, pp. 627, 633.

interpretation in *The Outlook* deprived the church of an active voice in Christianizing industry. One was John McDowell, who in 1919 had assumed the leadership for social service in the Presbyterian Board of Home Missions and had served as one of the nine members of the Commission of Inquiry. He insisted that it was impossible to determine "where and when injustice exists and who are the unjust" so the church could use its moral power to rescue the oppressed if the church was unable "to investigate industrial conditions." Another editorial, signed by the eighty-five-year- old Lyman Abbott, explained that "it is one thing to condemn injustice and another to determine who are the unjust." He argued that the church was well equipped to arouse the public conscience against injustice, but it was not as able "to investigate persons or corporations who are accused of wrong- doing." Using the occasion not to judge the Interchurch report but to restate the journal's "conception of the function of the Church of Christ," the patriarchal editor wanted the church and ministers to inspire workers rather than to do the work themselves. The church was losing its "moral power in the community because she is substituting the ambition to do the work of other organizations for the ambition to inspire all organizations to do their own work well."[25] Whether or not this argument convinced McDowell and other social activists was not as evident as the fact that champions of the social gospel were still not of one mind on how the church should proceed to Christianize the social order in the nation, or the world. According to Eldon Ernst's careful study of the movement, the majority of editorial opinion in the country accepted the commission report and reversed its earlier condemnation of the strikers and their cause.[26]

Shortly after the steel strike ended in failure on 8 January 1920, the intensity of the Interchurch World Movement increased. From January through April the churches attracted the attention of the nation through propaganda, conferences, and evangelistic meetings. Behind-the-scenes teams were trained for the financial campaign scheduled for the week of 25 April to 2 May. Despite the efforts of 5,000 canvassers, it was clear that the financial goals had not been met when the Interchurch Cabinet met on 4 May. General subscriptions reached nearly $124,000,000, and denominational subscriptions reached nearly $200,000,000, although both were below expectations. These unprecedented sums would have been acceptable, but a crisis was created by the poor response of the "friendly citizens." Of the $40,000,000 goal for that group only $3,000,000 was pledged. Since those gifts were projected to cover all the expenses incurred

---

[25]Ibid., 22 September 1920, pp. 157-58, 135-36.

[26]Ernst, *Moment of Truth*, 132.

in the surveys, publicity, programs, and fund raising, that shortfall was disastrous. The subscriptions did not nearly cover the $8,000,000 already expended, and the financial burden overwhelmed the denominations.[27]

On 17 and 18 May, exactly seventeen months after the movement was initiated, representatives of the denominations met with the General Committee to evaluate the situation. Their enthusiasm by this time had greatly diminished. A second campaign was attempted, but it occurred while several of the churches were in their national meetings and it failed also. Responses by denominations varied. Northern Methodists voted to continue to support the cause, but Northern Presbyterians and Northern Baptists authorized withdrawal from the campaign "as now organized and controlled."[28] The actions of the Baptists and Presbyterians made it virtually impossible to continue, but on 8 July members voted to reorganize the movement with the hope that denominational support would revive. It did not, and in effect the Interchurch World Movement was dead.[29]

As the religious counterpart of the idealism expressed by the League of Nations, the movement suffered a similar fate. Church leaders learned at the end of April that the political mood that led the United States Senate finally to reject the League of Nations in mid-March represented the dominant psychology of the country. The optimistic atmosphere in which both visions were conceived had disappeared and was replaced in the nation by a spirit of disillusionment, fear, and isolationism.

Any attempt to evaluate the role of social Christianity in the Interchurch World Movement is difficult because that project reflected the growing conservatism that characterized the churches as well as the nation in 1919 and 1920. An example of the complexity involved was the fact that both Worth Tippy and Harry Ward were members of the movement's Industrial Relations Department and its Executive Committee. Both were social-gospel advocates, but they differed in their basic approach and

---

[27]Ibid., 141-45. An account of the meeting of the Methodist Board of Foreign Missions, 19-22 November, reported that it "began in gloom, which deepened daily" as members were shocked to learn of the financial problems resulting from the movement. *Christian Advocate* (New York), 2 December 1920, p. 1603. This contrasted with the more favorable publicity announcement released earlier by the movement. Ibid., 3 June 1920, p. 763.

[28]*Journal of the General Conference of the Methodist Episcopal Church* (1920), 442, 684-88; *Minutes of the General Assembly of the Presbyterian Church in the United States of America*, n.s. (1920), 174-76; *Annual of the Northern Baptist Convention* (1920), 121-22.

[29]Ernst, *Moment of Truth*, 145-51.

understanding by this time. Tippy was sufficiently concerned that Ward's leftist ideas would lead "straight into the revolutionary movement" and embarrass the movement that he shared his fears with S. Earl Taylor and John R. Mott. Although Professor Ernst concluded that the role of the Industrial Relations department was "never more than an undercurrent within the Interchurch mainstream," these personal differences, along with those noted earlier in the chapter, evidence that the movement had a disruptive and divisive influence upon the champions of social Christianity who were affected by its dynamics.[30]

In retrospect, the collapse of the Interchurch World Movement, the rejection of the League of Nations, the vicious nature of the steel strike and resulting investigation, and the growing fear of Bolshevism quickly modified the optimistic mood of the country during 1919 and 1920. Looking back on these events in his quadrennial report in December 1920, Tippy declared, "We are in a chastened mood." An enlarged sense of mission following the First World War created a heavy sense of obligation for the churches, but new awareness that great evils could not be as easily removed as they thought led Protestant social activists to reexamine their tasks and reorganize their work.[31] The violence and antagonism throughout the nation, coupled with setbacks and criticism experienced in the churches, dampened the optimism and enthusiasm of the social gospel as it entered the decade of the twenties.

---

[30]Ibid., 133. William McGuire King, "The Emergence of Social Gospel Radicalism: The Methodist Case," *Church History* 50 (December 1981): 436-49 deals on a larger scale with this inner tension within the social gospel.

[31]"Report of the Commission on the Church and Social Service," *Churches Allied for Common Tasks*, 124.

CHAPTER 20

A Fundamental Reorganization

The Commission has nearly completed a fundamental
reorganization. . . . This makes of the Commission an official and
effective agency for denominational and interchurch purposes.

*("Report of the Commission
on the Church and Social Service," 1920)*

WITH THE DEMANDS OF THE WAR and its aftermath producing a changed
national mood and new conditions, social-service commissions were
required to adapt. They did so partly by expanding former teachings and
practices and partly by innovative responses. In this task they were
hindered not only by pressing needs but also by major adjustments in their
own institutional relationships. Between 1917 and 1920 every social-
service agency of the socially active Protestant denominations and the
Federal Council of Churches altered its functional organization.
Furthermore, these adaptations were accompanied by a greater change
in leadership than the social-gospel movement had previously
experienced.

The first reorganization occurred in the Congregational churches
during 1917. As noted earlier, that reorganization affected the Commission
on Social Service by making it a department of the Educational Society
when all Congregational general agencies were reorganized on 1 October
1917. Other than Henry Atkinson's becoming head of a department rather
than an independent commission, there was little effect upon the
denomination's social ministry beyond its more direct tie with education.[1]

Changes in the functioning of social service in other denominations
did not occur until 1919. Although it was not technically a structural

---

[1]*Minutes of the National Council of the Congregational Churches of the United States*
(1917), 221-38. See p. 273 above.

reorganization, the social ministry of the Presbyterian Church in the U.S.A. was revitalized that year by hiring John McDowell as full-time Secretary of Social Service within the Board of Home Missions. McDowell, like Stelzle, was the product of a working-class background. Despite a mining accident that crippled his arms, he had battled his way through school and had assumed national leadership for social and industrial relations after several successful pastorates in the East. In 1910 he had chaired the Special Committee on Social Problems that wrote and secured the adoption of the Presbyterian version of the Social Creed. Nine years later McDowell reminded the General Assembly of the duties now entrusted to its Social Service Commission. It was constituted to create better understanding of the social implications of the gospel and to help the church apply them "to the life of to-day, to the end that society may be reconstructed and the world reorganized so as to eliminate injustice and wrong and to make war forever impossible." Its goal was to create "a new state of mind in the Church" and to stimulate Presbyterians "to function in new and effective ways in the moral, economic and political life of the people." Since events the preceding two years had already created a sentiment for social service, it was necessary only to show how the church might definitely render service to the community. "It is not time to agitate, but to act," McDowell said. "What is needed is not an agency to educate, but one that can administer and direct the activities of a Church fully aware of its social responsibility."[2] With the hiring of McDowell, Northern Presbyterians returned to a more active role in the Social-Gospel movement.

During the months of the war the Social Service Commission of the Northern Baptist Convention had changed its work because new needs called it to serve in many capacities and to cooperate with numerous agencies. By May 1919, when the convention met in annual session, Samuel Z. Batten reported that the committee had negotiated a new working agreement with two other denominational agencies, the Publication Society and the Home Mission Society. Through this arrangement Social Service Education became a department of the Publication Society, while the Home Mission Society created a Department of Social Service and Rural Work to care for that neglected area of community service. Together the two departments planned to publish a Social Service Bulletin, conduct special investigations of "acute industrial situations," and work for better conditions. The convention's Social Service Committee served "in an advisory capacity to these two

---

[2]*Minutes of the General Assembly of the Presbyterian Church in the United States of America*, n.s. (1919), 176-78.

departments," with the two secretaries of the departments serving as chair and secretary of the committee. By this new plan it was anticipated that the field of social service could be greatly enlarged among Northern Baptists. Since the war had resulted in the "break-up in the ideas of men and the policies of states," the focus of this new organizational pattern was on social reconstruction. Batten and the committee also eulogized the departed Walter Rauschenbusch as "the most potent personality in America in the modern revival of the idea of the kingdom of God."[3]

In October 1919 the place of social service in the Protestant Episcopal Church was a subject of great interest at its General Convention. A bishop proposed that there be a canon providing for a General Board of Social Service, but this suggestion was withdrawn when the Committee on Canons felt that the subject was too "didactic and hortatory" for canon law. In the end, a general reorganization of the functional structure of the church placed the functions of Social Service, along with Missions and Church Extension, Religious Education, Finance, and Publicity under the control of the presiding bishop and council. The Joint Commission on Social Service continued independently until 31 December; at that time, it came under this new jurisdiction. By 1920 Frank M. Crouch was no longer listed as a member of the Secretarial Council of the Federal Council. Other than a general reaffirmation that social service was a "great field of Christian thought and effort," there was no indication of any new programs such as social reconstruction.[4] Perhaps anticipating a more restricted role for social concerns at the General Convention, several Episcopalian clergy and laity had formed the Church League for Industrial Democracy in May 1919.[5]

Meeting the same month, the National Council of the Congregational Churches heard its Social Service Commission commit itself to building the kingdom of God on earth by inspiration rather than by manipulation. Convinced that the Christian conscience demanded "a Christian world order which shall be the community of God on earth," the commission report affirmed that Christianity and a democratic social order were inseparable. Although Arthur E. Holt replaced Henry Atkinson, who had joined the staff of the Federal Council of Churches as Secretary for International Justice and Goodwill in 1919, the social thought of the denomination continued to reflect current emphases in social Christianity.

---

[3]*Annual of the Northern Baptist Convention* (1919), 166-68, 169-71.

[4]*Journal of the General Convention of the Protestant Episcopal Church in the U.S.A.* (1919), 70-71, 156, 158, 162, 216, 224-25, 515.

[5]Raymond W. Albright, *A History of the Protestant Episcopal Church* (New York: Macmillan Co., 1964) 316.

Reared in Colorado, Holt served pastorates in that state as well as in Kansas and Texas following doctoral studies at the University of Chicago. The influence of the West gradually became evident in his strong commitment to rural life, which was unique among social-gospel leaders during his years of national leadership. Under Holt's guidance the commission secured the adoption of a "Declaration of Principles" that called for "a new national order" characterized by justice. Recognizing that a new order could not be created instantly, the agency recommended a long list of beliefs about social service with the understanding that they had to be achieved "community by community, social situation by social situation." Such an approach was a large undertaking, and the General Council showed its support by authorizing increased appropriations for meetings and publications.[6]

This review of denominational general meetings during 1919 clearly shows that social-service reports were essentially positive and optimistic. The hiring of McDowell by the Northern Presbyterians and Holt by the Congregationalists indicated a continuing commitment to social ministry. Organizational changes affecting social service seemed to be parts of larger denominational adjustments rather than signs of a loss of dedication to the social gospel. A year later, however, when the national assemblies of the various churches convened, most reflected the more pessimistic mood of the time; and changes in social-service organizations were as responsive to altered conditions in the nation as to needs for structural efficiency by the parent bodies. The major exception to this general evaluation was John McDowell's report "Upon the Church and Industry" to the Northern Presbyterian General Assembly in May 1920. In contrast to his previous report, which was action-oriented, this report concentrated on affirming basic beliefs that undergirded social action. It reaffirmed and amplified the Presbyterian Social Creed adopted in 1910 to make it relevant to recent developments. These declarations ranged from "the supreme worth of personality" and the "brotherhood of man" to one day's rest in seven and the right of workers to organize. Essentially, the statement amounted to an updated version of the Social Creed of the Churches, although the items were not identical. Allowing for the significant impact of Charles Erdman's conservative attack against the social gospel, this renewed statement brought the General Assembly back to its standing ground before that assault. The pronouncement provided a platform on which McDowell could build social ministry again. While "the democratic control of industry" was mentioned, there were no references to social

---

[6]*Minutes of the National Council of the Congregational Churches of the United States* (1919), 33-38, 216-28.

reconstruction or a new world order.[7] Nevertheless, the General Assembly was well aware of current events, as its withdrawal from the Interchurch World Movement evidenced.[8]

Northern Baptists were reminded of world and national conditions several times during their annual convention late in June. Their knowledge of the Interchurch Movement failure was noted earlier, and the American Baptist Foreign Mission Society described the fiscal year that ended on 30 April as "a year of international disappointment and world-wide readjustment." That report's discussion of "almost unprecedented industrial turmoil, social unrest, financial collapse in many countries" was paralleled by the Social Service Commission's description of this "time of unrest and change." "We entered the war," said Samuel Batten, "to make the world safe for democracy," but "now the war is over and this exalted mood has passed." Reaction and greed were trying to restore the old order, which challenged Christians to find and correct "the defects of our present social order and political institutions." The need of the hour was "to frame a positive and constructive program of social salvation, and then to unite all the forces of good-will in behalf of a better and more Christian world."[9]

With reference to its work during the past year, the Committee on Social Service represented the convention in temperance and social work and served in an advisory capacity to the Department of Social Service and Rural Community Work of the Home Mission Society and the Department of Social Education of the Publication Society. Specifically, in the reorganized structure Batten worked primarily with industrial problems and social education. In the latter he indicated that studies in Britain and America showed that "the great mass of the people have no clear and definite idea with reference to the kingdom of God. Many have no conception of the Christian meaning of the great institutions of society." That admission must have hurt him, since he had labored for those ends for more than two decades. His report indicated that the denominational reorganization seemed to work, but social conditions had not improved.[10]

When the Methodist Episcopal Church assembled in quadrennial General Conference 1-27 May 1920 they were also frequently reminded of the changed and worsening national and world situations. At the outset

---

[7]*Minutes of the General Assembly of the Presbyterian Church in the United States of America* (1920), 181-86.

[8]Ibid., 174-76.

[9]*Annual of the Northern Baptist Convention* (1920), 242-43, 607-608.

[10]Ibid., 243-55.

Bishop W. F. McDowell's Episcopal Address described the social unrest of the time: "Economic, social and industrial conditions are volcanic. They go far beneath mere questions of wages, hours, and profits. They reach the roots of organized life, the basis of government itself, the province of law, and the stability of society as based on law. Everywhere free institutions are threatened. The church must not fail in the effort to preserve them." He felt that it was "part of our chief business at this Conference to declare anew our devotion to orderly government and our belief in legal processes in society; to declare against lawlessness, confusion, and anarchy." Thus, it was not surprising that he neither sympathized with nor approved of Bolshevism, "whether of the red-handed mob or the soft-handed sentimentalist." Both the "destructive radical" and the "unyielding reactionary" were condemned. In a world dominated by conflicting ideas and movements, Bishop McDowell asserted,

> The church must hold a steady course toward universal democracy based on right; a course that will save the world from the excesses of fanaticism, the unbridled sway of greed, the tyranny of the few or the tyranny of the many. To-day, as always, the church is for order, steadiness, fairness, and law; and to-day the church must speak that steady word to which the world will listen.[11]

In small ways the General Conference showed modest social concern. Early in the four-week meeting a layman in the manufacturing business introduced a resolution "For the Settlement of Industrial Unrest" that called for settling "social and economic misunderstanding and disorders . . . according to the teachings of our Lord" and it was adopted. The conference also approved a message of sympathy to Samuel Gompers regretting the death of his wife, but not until a clause expressing the sympathy of the Methodist Episcopal Church "with the legitimate demands of organized labor" was deleted.[12] A report on "The Spiritual Life of the Church" expressed the mood of the conference when it noted a turn to inner religious experience and away from social and industrial involvement.[13] Other than a celebration of "devout thanksgiving" for national prohibition, this General Conference seemed to avoid social, economic, and industrial problems, which contrasted with the three preceding quadrennial meetings of the denomination.[14]

---

[11]*Journal of the General Conference of the Methodist Episcopal Church* (1920), 166-67. The entire address is on pp. 145-98.

[12]*Daily Christian Advocate*, 8 May 1920, p. 144.

[13]*Journal of the General Conference of the Methodist Episcopal Church* (1920), 583-84.

[14]Ibid., 662.

Despite the absence of floor discussion of such issues, the standing Committee on the State of the Church had an active subcommittee on social service that functioned throughout the conference. Its members sometimes were divided in opinion, but three major reports were prepared for consideration and printed in the official daily paper of the General Conference: Report 19 recommended revisions in the Social Creed, Report 20 was an Economic Platform of the Church, and Report 21 dealt with the Methodist Federation for Social Service.[15] In the press of business at the close of conference, the sifting committee that was appointed to select the most important items for action before adjournment failed to recommend any of the three reports. A last-minute appeal was made on the floor to consider the report on the Social Creed, but it was voted down.[16] As a result, no action on social concerns was endorsed in 1920, which resulted in no mention of such matters in the *Journal of the General Conference* since it printed only actions taken by the body. An editorial in *The Christian Advocate* remarked that "the General Conference did not trust itself to discuss the social, economic or industrial problems in any of their phases. Nothing which it did is quite so surprising as that it left this work undone." Partly that was attributed to tardy committee work that delayed consideration until the last crowded week. "But there was also an evident willingness to 'let sleeping dogs lie,' " said the editor, "which kept off the floor of the Conference certain great matters on which opinion and feeling were known to be irrevocably divided."[17]

Report 21 concerning the work of the Methodist Federation for Social Service was particularly bothersome to delegates as they read it in the *Daily Christian Advocate*. That report, which was adopted by a vote of 22 for and 14 against, out of a committee membership of 269, reversed the action of a previous meeting. The losers submitted a minority report telling what was altered, twenty-eight others indicated they had not heard the meeting announced and did not concur with the majority action, and another thirteen asked to have the report recommitted because they also missed the notice. Such evidence suggested questionable parliamentary maneuvering concerning an organization whose leaders, Harry Ward and Bishop McConnell, had recently received critical attention and it probably led delegates to shun the report as controversial in its adoption as well as its content. Comparison of the majority and minority reports shows that the basic difference was in how much authority the Board of Bishops

---

[15]*Daily Christian Advocate*, 26 May 1920, pp. 535-36; 27 May 1920, pp. 570-71.

[16]Ibid., 28 May 1920, p. 596.

[17]*Christian Advocate* (New York), 10 June 1920, p. 781.

should have in the federation. The minority wanted all the members of its council appointed by the bishops; the majority wanted episcopal influence limited to three bishops as members who could see that actions were in accord with church authorization or withdraw the mandate recognizing the federation as "an executive agency of the church." In effect, no action by the 1920 General Conference left in place the provisions enacted in 1916 concerning the Federation and the Social Creed. According to Bishop McConnell, that result was better for the social-service program than if the organization had been subjected to the conservative mood of the General Conference.[18] Once again, the issue of the federation's unique autonomy among social-service agencies was in conflict with the feeling that it should have a more responsible official relationship to the denomination.

Since the Methodist Episcopal Church failed to tighten its control over the federation, the social-service organization itself was able to decide the nature of the relationship. Two weeks before the annual meeting of the Executive Committee and General Council of the federation on 22 November, Worth Tippy wrote to Harry Ward concerning their strained personal relations and what direction the group would take. In response Ward said, "I have come to the conclusion that the time has arrived for a reorganization of our Executive Committee. We have not the unity and the interest that is necessary for the effective prosecution of our work." He recognized "that some of the members of the Executive Committee are embarrassed by my policies," and others were "too much pre-occupied with other affairs to give us the interest and support that they formerly contributed." Two courses of action seemed possible to Ward: either those who differed or were too busy should resign, or the committee should be reconstituted and their names would be left off.[19]

When Bishop McConnell convened the meeting on 22 November, ten persons were in attendance, including Ward, Tippy, and George A. Coe. As Ward presented the need to reorganize the Executive Committee and council, he broadened the discussion to ask whether the federation "should continue its present relationship with the General Conference or should become a completely independent group." Even broader, he said, was the fact that such a change would involve the relationship of the organization to the Federal Council of Churches. Finally, it was decided

---

[18]*Daily Christian Advocate*, 27 May 1920, pp. 570-71; Milton J. Huber, "A History of the Methodist Federation for Social Action" (Ph.D. diss., Boston University, 1949) 139-40.

[19]Ward to Tippy, 15 November 1920, Worth M. Tippy Papers, Archives of DePauw University and Indiana Methodism, Greencastle IN.

"that the organization should continue in its present relationship to the General Conference and the Federal Council." With regard to the Executive Committee, there was a recommendation that it consist of the chairman and two others. Council membership should be increased to include those taking local initiative and responsibility and subdivided into geographic groups so more persons could participate actively. Members would be invited to submit names for both groups, and the chairman and secretary would select a list of nominees for election by the full membership.[20] Although appearing to broaden the base for decision making, real power was more centralized in the chairman, secretary, and two others who agreed with Ward.

Also at the meeting a pamphlet was approved that would contain the statements submitted by the federation to the 1920 General Conference, reports of the Committee on the State of the Church involving federation interests, plus an explanation of the relationship of the organization to the General Conference. Concerning the controversy over who was responsible for what was printed in the *Social Service Bulletin* or on federation letterhead in the Information Service, it was voted that the latter be discontinued "for lack of funds" and that the *Bulletin* and other printed pieces "carry a statement that the editors alone are responsible for the material which appears."[21] This decision was implemented immediately. Whereas the November issue of the *Bulletin* listed Grace Scribner as editor with an Editorial Board consisting of Ward, Arthur E. Holt, and John G. Shearer, the December issue listed the editors as Harry F. Ward and Grace Scribner, with no Editorial Board. Also in the December issue and each issue thereafter was the statement, "The editors alone are responsible for the material appearing in this Bulletin."[22] In light of the Russian Question controversy with the New York *Christian Advocate* and the problems the federation experienced at General Conference, the organization revised and clarified its organization, policies, and procedures.

There was no indication that the meeting did anything to heal the growing differences among Methodist social-gospel leaders. Earlier Frank Mason North's displeasure over Tippy's role with the Interchurch World Movement was noted. North was probably bothered too by the federation's 22 November meeting because the Board of Foreign Missions, on which he served as an executive officer, also met that day. Its agenda

----

[20]"Minutes of the Methodist Federation for Social Service, 1907–1930," typescript, Rose Memorial Library, Drew University, Madison NJ, 22 November 1920, 202.

[21]Ibid., 202-203.

[22]*Social Service Bulletin* (November 1920): 1; (December 1920): 1, 4.

was dominated by unpleasant financial news resulting from the Interchurch campaign that reflected unfavorably on North's administrative efficiency, although he had not created the problems.[23] Tippy's concern that Ward's Bolshevism might embarrass the Interchurch Movement also was indicated previously. A comparison of "The Church and Social Reconstruction" statement that Tippy wrote with Ward's *New Social Order* makes clear the basic ideological differences that had emerged between the two men since the war. While both sought social justice, Tippy's belief that social reconstruction should be achieved by constitutional and peaceable means rather than by class struggle and violence was a more conservative approach than Ward's. There is little evidence of the exact basis of their disagreement, but Tippy's name was removed from the Editorial Board of the *Social Service Bulletin* after September 1920. Although the three leaders continued to work with each other, it was clear that their social ideas had diverged and their relationships were strained.[24]

When uneasy relationships were added to the large turnover of social-gospel leaders since the war, there was less camaraderie among champions of social Christianity. The passing of Josiah Strong, Washington Gladden, and Walter Rauschenbusch removed renowned figures from the movement, and no replacements of comparable stature and influence took their places. By 1920, in the Council of Social Service Secretaries only Samuel Batten and Harry Ward remained from the first group in 1912. Alva Taylor of the Disciples of Christ in 1918 and Arthur Holt and John McDowell in 1919 joined them. In 1920 five additional representatives were selected by denominations, and the council was enlarged to ten members for the first time. These new persons carried social-service responsibilities in addition to other duties, representing broadening social concern although not laboring full-time for the cause. When the Council of Denominational Secretaries assembled, it was helpful that the members had experienced leadership in the Federal Council from Executive Secretary Worth Tippy and Research Secretary F. Ernest Johnson. By the end of 1920, Charles Stelzle and Henry Atkinson were no longer part of the Federal Council staff.[25]

---

[23]*Christian Advocate* (New York), 2 December 1920, p. 1603. See XX above.

[24]*Social Service Bulletin* (September 1920): 1; (October 1920): 1; Eugene P. Link, *Labor-Religion Prophet: The Times and Life of Harry F. Ward* (Boulder CO: Westview Press, 1984) 52, 54n. See pp. 298-300, 312-14 above.

[25]*The Churches Allied for Common Tasks: Report of the Third Quadrennium of the Federal Council of the Churches of Christ in America, 1916–1920,* ed. Samuel McCrea Cavert (New York: Federal Council of Churches, 1921) 411.

The fourth quadrennial session of the Federal Council of the Churches of Christ in America met in Boston, 1-6 December 1920. Tippy's report for the Commission on the Church and Social Service for the past four years recounted its wartime and peacetime work, the Statement on Social Reconstruction, the elaboration of the Social Creed, and the relation of the Commission to the Interchurch World Movement, all of which were discussed previously. In addition, the report listed publications, told of studies of industrial conflicts in Lawrence, Massachusetts, and Denver, Colorado, and indicated continuing cooperation with national social agencies, showing that the commission continued these basic components of its work. Continuity of its original interest in modern industry also was evidenced by Tippy's extended remarks concerning a new program: "The Church and Industrial Peace."[26]

This new effort was designed to move employers and employees from "the present industrial warfare" to cooperative relations based on "the teachings and spirit of Christ." A national Advisory Council comprised of business leaders, representatives of labor, ministers, and church officials was created. That group sponsored a trial conference in Atlanta that became the model for a series of local one- and two-day conferences on "Social and Industrial Relations" to be held during 1921. Emphasis would be centered on vital issues such as industrial disputes and conflicts, community relations, churches for industrial neighborhoods, and Christian principles in industry. On 17 October experienced leaders from important industries met in New York to give advice concerning the proposed program. According to Tippy, "The conference unanimously approved in principle the Commission's proposals." Moreover, its members affirmed that the project would be difficult, but it was possible if pursued with tact. "Most employers will oppose the effort," he was told, "but you must go ahead. We employers need pressure from our ministers."[27]

As this new program on "The Church and Industrial Peace" was projected into the next year, it was obvious that Tippy had shifted the emphasis from workers to employers. That in itself was a basic difference in approach from Ward. But it may well have been a new direction in light of the apparent failure of previous Protestant efforts geared to workers. At the 1917 National Council of the Congregational Churches, Henry Atkinson had been questioned as to whether or not laboring people had come into the church through its industrial programs, and he had responded that the

---

[26]"Report of the Commission on the Church and Social Service," ibid., 104-18.

[27]Ibid., 118-21.

purpose was not evangelism as much as social service. However, Atkinson said there was still "a distrust of the church in the minds of large masses of the people."[28] In 1918, in one of his last written pieces, Walter Rauschenbusch addressed the issue of the response of workers to social-gospel efforts in their behalf in a symposium entitled "The Path of Labor." "The church in recent years has not been lacking in earnest efforts to win back and serve the working people," he said. There had been devoted ministers and social workers, costly institutional church buildings, and evangelistic efforts. "Yet the situation itself has not changed," he concluded. Rauschenbusch was not certain whether laborers could be won back to the church unless there was "a democratic reconstruction of society" that substituted a single class in place of "the two antagonistic classes which now confront each other."[29] Since he wrote during the war and before the industrial strife that followed it, it is not certain whether he would have moved toward radicalism, as Ward did, or to moderation, as Tippy did. It seems clear, however, that Tippy decided to utilize the business contacts he had established when he chaired the Joint Committee on War Production Communities during the war.

It was noteworthy that Tippy reported to the Federal Council that the Church and Social Service Commission had "nearly completed a fundamental reorganization." Basically, the changes increased the number and importance of "official and delegated representatives from the denominational commissions and church boards responsible for social service" and reduced the number of at-large individuals who were personally but not representatively involved in the Social Gospel movement. Several at-large members were still provided for, but they were to be selected from interchurch agencies. A revised committee system also was created to divide the labor among standing rather than ad hoc committees. An Executive Committee of no more than twenty members was to replace the former Committee of Direction, and the majority were to be "denominational representatives responsible for social service." These changes, said Tippy, would make the commission "an official and effective agency for denominational and interchurch purposes."[30]

The new organizational structure, which was approved, was fundamentally different in that its membership and program would be "determined in general by the consensus of denominational

---

[28]*Minutes of the National Council of the Congregational Churches of the United States* (1917), 238.

[29]Walter Rauschenbusch, "Justice and Brotherhood," ch. 4 of *The Path of Labor: A Symposium* (New York: Council of Women for Home Missions, 1918) 185-87.

[30]"Report of the Commission on the Church and Social Service," 121-22.

representatives and the representatives of cooperating bodies as to the needs of their organizations." Rather than initiating its own ideas and activities, the work of the commission was "to be done mainly through denominational and cooperative organizations." Henceforth the future work of the commission would concentrate on research and educational work, providing assistance to local church councils, improving industrial relations through research and education, and maintaining contacts for the churches with national social agencies and movements, and with welfare departments of the federal government.[31] Whatever advantages the reorganization had representatively, it appeared to have the potential to stifle creativity and initiative, which formerly had been one of the commission's strengths.

While these changes of structure and function would produce basic changes for the Social Service Commission, more adjustments were in the offing as the Federal Council of Churches in 1920 proposed its own larger reorganization. Initiated at the December meeting, the alterations could not be worked out before adjournment and were entrusted to the Executive Committee for action. Part of the revised structure called for a reduction in the number of commissions and committees. In the original design, Social Service was to absorb works of benevolence and mercy in this country as well as Country Life responsibilities and was to be yoked with Temperance in what was designated The Commissions of Social Welfare. When the Executive Committee met on 21 January 1921, it could not complete all the changes and left it to the decision of the Administrative Committee whether to create a separate commission for benevolence and mercy or leave it with the Commission on the Church and Social Service.[32] Thus, at the end of our period of study, the fundamental reorganization affecting social-service responsibilities in the Federal Council was still in process, although the main pattern of the changes was already evident. As proposed, the changes seemed to limit the interdenominational commission and to increase the work and importance of the denominational commissions. Nevertheless, there was still a major place for social ministry built into the Federal Council structure.

News accounts of the quadrennial meeting at Boston indicated that social and industrial concerns dominated much of the attention of the delegates, beyond matters of changing organization. A reporter noted in the *Christian Advocate* that the middle sessions were devoted to "the industrial field and the enlarging social program for the Church." On 2 December, Methodist Bishop William F. McDowell spoke on "The Church

---

[31]Ibid., 122-23, 339.

[32]*The Churches Allied for Common Tasks*, 32-33, 356.

in Its Relation to the National Government," and Ohio State University president William O. Thompson presented an address entitled "The Enlarging Social Program of Christianity." Arguing that institutions were the substance of human history, Thompson likened Christianity at the time to that in the Middle Ages when it shaped institutional life and insisted that "today Christianity must determine the expansion of banks, schools, churches." Bishop McConnell reported on the steel strike, and delegates were intrigued with the street railway strike in Denver. On Sunday afternoon, 5 December, a special public meeting was held in Faneuil Hall on the subject "The Christian Challenge to Cooperation between Employers and Employees."[33]

Much of another day was devoted to a discussion of the future prospects of the church in the present world, which was led by Professor William Adams Brown and the Committee on the War and the Religious Outlook. They affirmed that questions regarding the economic and industrial situation were baffling, but they were so central to human life that they received much of the time of the study group and resulted in one report and two pamphlets. Trying to avoid the twin problems of uttering pious platitudes or taking sides in disputed issues, a subcommittee prepared a report entitled "The Church and Industrial Reconstruction." Instead of inquiring what social reforms were workable and then sanctioning them as Christian, the committee asked what Christian teachings required of persons and made this demand the norm for evaluating the existing social order. These questions led back to a more basic question of "the nature and function of the church in modern society." Facing this question proved so time-consuming that the project was not yet ended, although the result would determine the future of the church and of the Federal Council.[34] Two years later the results of that study were published as a book titled *The Church in America: A Study of the Present Condition and Future Prospects of American Protestantism*. In that volume, the section "The Church and the New Social Order" provided helpful perspective and definition for social action, but it lies beyond the periodization of this study.[35]

---

[33]Ibid., 303-309; *Christian Advocate* (New York), 16 December 1920, pp. 1679-80.

[34]"The Church Facing the Future," *The Churches Allied for Common Tasks*, 44-54.

[35]William Adams Brown, *The Church in America: A Study of the Present Condition and Future Prospects of American Protestantism* (New York: Macmillan Co., 1922) 153-72, passim.

At the end of 1920 the questions were real, but the responses were in process and not yet ready for action. The understanding of the social situation at that point was best expressed in the Federal Council's "Message to the Churches of America" adopted on the final day of the meeting.

> We are not blind to the difficulties which confront us. The mood of high resolve in which less than four short years ago we entered the war, the thrill of relief with which at the news of the armistice we welcomed the coming of peace have alike given place to a more sober and chastened spirit. Everywhere we find men conscious of aspirations still unfulfilled, longing for freedom, for comradeship, for the chance to be their own best selves without injuring or slighting their fellowmen, seeking for some solvent of the social evils of our time which science and statesmanship alike seem impotent to give. In church as in state we have seen great hopes, confidently entertained, fail of fruition because of the inadequacy of men. We realize as we have not realized before how stupendous are our tasks, how mighty the forces with which we must contend. But great as the difficulties which confront us, our grounds for confidence are greater still.[36]

With such confidence, the council resolutely proclaimed "a message of faith and hope and brotherhood which must be brought to a despondent and disheartened world." To produce deeds to match their words, they sought to minimize "competition and strife" between Christians so they could exemplify the unity that would break down barriers between classes, races, and nations.[37]

A newspaper correspondent looking at the quadrennial sessions of the Federal Council in December 1920 remarked that it had "more points of contact with a 'torn and bleeding world' than any religious convention of the past." It was marked by sensitivity, brotherliness, and spiritual vitality, but the council took "no initiative on questions that were divisive." It left delegates with their individual emphases, although it steadied their consciences and their judgment to meet the critical days ahead.[38] Robert E. Speer, a Northern Presbyterian who represented "a wise conservatism" that was "familiar with and responsive to the current movements of social and theological thought," was elected the new president.[39] For the first time in eight years, the Federal Council had a

---

[36]"A Message to the Churches of America," *The Churches Allied for Common Tasks*, 310-11.

[37]Ibid., 310-11

[38]*Christian Advocate* (New York), 16 December 1920, p. 1680.

[39]Ibid., 9 December 1920, p. 1635.

presiding officer who was not a social-gospel advocate, although he was an experienced Protestant bureaucrat. According to *The Outlook*, the spirit pervading the council was the most significant factor: "While not blind to present difficulties and dangers, the Council faces the future with a confident spirit promising well for 'the resolute and united advance' to which it calls the churches."[40]

Noting this bewildering series of changes in structure and personnel in institutional Protestantism, one wonders about the stability of the church following the war. But comparison with the social, economic, and political realm indicates that the denominations were not unique. In its year-end assessment of the nation, the *New York Times* said that "1920 put American institutions to a severe test." Defending against despairers who charged that the year was a time "of lost leadership, of lowered aims, of abandoned ideals," the editorial suggested that "perhaps our fall in 1920 was not so profound as alleged" because orators may have praised the "pitch of moral elevation in 1918 and 1919" too highly.[41] An editorial in *The Outlook* also saw the year in relation to preceding events, calling the time "the twilight of the war": "We are living in a time when the World War is ended and yet world peace is not come," similar to the period when the day is ended but night has not yet come.[42] When viewed amid a national atmosphere characterized in these ways, the course of social-gospel and general Protestant developments institutionally was neither as distinctive nor as depressing as it may seeem without such a larger comparison.

What happened at the Federal Council meeting appropriately climaxed the period of social-gospel development from 1917 through 1920. The interdenominational organization's perception of what had occurred in the world with America's entry into the war, the armistice, the expectant optimism of a hopeful new world, and the disillusioning series of postwar problems produced a chastened mood. Mindful of the rapidly changing circumstances in the world, it became obvious that the council and its member churches needed to change their ideas as well as their ways of functioning. But this was a monumental task, and the federation's unfinished agenda of reorganization and incomplete study of the nature of the church and its mission in the world reflected the instability of an age in transition.

---

[40]"Protestant Churches in Alliance," *The Outlook* (New York), 22 December 1920, p. 708.

[41]*New York Times*, 1 January 1921, p. 8.

[42]"The Twilight of the War," *The Outlook*, 22 December 1920, p. 708.

If the council generally mirrored the constantly changing scene since the United States declared war on Germany, Worth Tippy's report for the Church and Social Service Commission specifically identified the evolving role of social Christianity during the four years. There was the difficult but successful contribution of the social gospel to the war effort. Amid the promise of the months following the peace, there were ideas for social reconstruction that would create a comprehensive new social order that would approximate the kingdom of God more fully than anything projected a generation earlier. But then there was the disabling social unrest and disenchanted rejection of Christian hopes for world mission and world peace that purged the dreams of the social movement and led the churches to reorganize their structural machinery and reevaluate their basic purpose. Nevertheless, for Tippy, the social gospel's perennial optimism and concern with industrial problems were wrapped up in a new program for industrial peace that was still to be implemented. That unfinished project, like the incomplete reorganization of the commission, evidenced that the move from social service to social reconstruction was still in process as the period of study reached its end during "the twilight of the war."

CONCLUSION

We believe that the age of sheer individualism is past and the age of social responsibility has arrived.

("Declaration of Principles,"
Religious Education Association, 1914)

An evaluation of social Christianity at the close of December 1920 has to look beyond the structural reorganizations that claimed the energies of the movement at that time. When compared to its position in American Protestantism in 1900, the social gospel was more than an ideology proclaimed by a few individuals; it was a movement that had been incorporated into mainstream Protestantism. While that accomplishment hardly fulfilled all the expectations of social activists, official recognition of the movement by their denominations was a goal that had long eluded them. During these two decades the social gospel had erected a solid foundation institutionally and theologically. It had proved that it could inspire, organize, create, cooperate, and change. Moreover, it had demonstrated the ability to survive both internal and external attack by a combination of conviction and adaptability. Whereas advocates of social Christianity were like voices in the wilderness in 1900, they were represented by official staff from ten denominations on the Council of Social Service Secretaries of the Federal Council of Churches in 1920. While the core of the movement continued to center in five denominations, that growth evidenced a wider interest in the movement than has often been assumed as the social gospel entered the twenties.

When Walter Rauschenbusch urged future historians to study the influence of various denominations on the social awakening of the nation and the shaping of a new social order, he identified a fundamental component in social-gospel history. The recognition and stabilization of that movement within institutional Protestantism was one of the outstanding achievements of social Christianity during the Progressive Era. Of the many things that the socially active denominations did between 1900 and 1920 to establish a Christian social order, one of the most important feats was to include social ministry in the official structures of denominational and interdenominational Protestantism. The sanctioning of the social gospel by religious bodies not only provided the necessary recognition of the movement but also guaranteed its continuity. Absence of such approval in previous decades had limited the impact and growth of this distinctive ministry; working with this authorization during the period, and after, enabled social Christianity to survive despite apathy and attack.

Tracing the slow steps by which institutional recognition and status were attained has revealed that denominations followed diverse paths to the goal. Initially each Protestant denomination moved at its own pace, affected by its own dedicated leaders, polity, and tradition of social activism. With the emergence of new interdenominational organizations, leaders discovered that other persons held similar values, and a cross-fertilization of ideas facilitated the development of cooperative programs and action. The founding of the Federal Council of the Churches of Christ in America in 1908 created a new institutional framework that promoted the interaction of movements committed to ecumenism, mission, and social responsibility. Adoption of what came to be called the Social Creed of the Churches by the Federal Council provided a public symbol of the new cooperative commitment concerning both the church and the social order. Less obvious, but equally important, the new ecumenical organization created a Commission on the Church and Social Service and gradually developed a functional Council of Secretaries where employed leaders of denominational social-service agencies were able to plan and act cooperatively. By 1912 official denominational and interdenominational machinery existed to facilitate the development of social Christianity. Church approval and organization required denominational programs, but joint planning and effort produced results beyond expectations, proving that for the Protestant social movement the whole was greater than the sum of the parts. As a result, this minority movement was able to exert disproportionate influence on American Protestantism.

This influence was achieved as much by unheralded bureaucrats as by acclaimed leaders of social Christianity. The significance of Rauschenbusch, Gladden, Strong, and Mathews has long been recognized, but these popularly recognized champions of the cause were not the primary persons who slowly constructed the programs and organizations that solidified the social gospel in institutional Protestantism. Such leaders as Henry Atkinson, Samuel Zane Batten, Frank Crouch, Frank Mason North, and Worth Tippy were neither as renowned nor as radical as Charles Stelzle and Harry Ward, but together they willingly labored behind the scenes for the same cause. Largely through their efforts the organizational machinery of social Christianity was erected, adjusted, and oiled. In the long run, the ability of the social-action agencies to survive from this period to the present testifies to the solid foundation they laid for the social gospel in American denominational and ecumenical church life.

The recognition and development of social Christianity was enhanced by the coalescence of religious social reform with parallel moral remedies outside ecclesiastical circles. A broad progressive movement concerned with social, economic, and political amelioration had emerged before 1900 and continued in truncated form after 1920. Its interests were so akin to those of social Christianity that some historians interpret the social gospel as the religious phase of Progressivism, although the origin of the Protestant concern antedated that movement. The rambunctious writings of muckraking journalists captured the attention of the populace for half of the period of study and did much to convince the nation that a social crisis existed, whose causes had to be remedied. Muckrakers, Progressives, and social-gospel advocates interacted and together achieved more than any one of them could have achieved alone. In the first decade of the century, champions of social Christianity shared in one of those eras when things came together in "the fullness of time" and change resulted. What social activists had been unable to achieve in the Gilded Age was accomplished in the Progressive Era. And during the Wilson administration the spirit of cooperation enabled church activists to work with various social, labor, and government agencies to achieve similar purposes.

Particularly in the middle years of the study, the two movements cooperated so easily that they seemed to be two facets of one cause. The combined effect during these years was evident when the Religious Education Association declared, "The age of social responsibility has arrived." [1] Obviously, the basis for this affirmation was grounded in romantic idealism and only those wearing rose-colored glasses saw that reality. The close interaction of social Christianity and Progressive reform in 1913 and 1914 nurtured the hope to the point that believers made the assertion with conviction, but by 1920 the dream had faded. American involvement in the First World War and postwar pessimism undermined much of the common optimism. Although more an ideal than an accomplishment, the Age of Social Responsibility designation expressed the basic goal of the social gospel during the Progressive Era.

To a considerable degree it was true that the social gospel was a "response to the challenge of modern industrial society."[2] Protestant social

---

[1]"Declaration of Principles," March 1914, *Religious Education* 9 (April 1914): 98.
   [2]Charles Howard Hopkins, *The Rise of the Social Gospel in American Protestantism, 1865–1915* (New Haven: Yale University Press, 1940) 320.

prophets tried to arouse their denominations to action because of the social question and the social crisis, calling fellow believers to correct the evils so evident all around them. But, despite the dominance of industrial and economic issues, much of their argument was built also on the larger framework of building a Christian nation and implementing the church's role in the kingdom of God. These concepts were grounded not so much in the church's response to a troubled social order as in basic initiatives of Protestants to shape a Christian America that had existed since the time of the Puritans.[3] The message of the social gospel was both initiative and response, both social redemption and social reform. Christianizing the social order involved not just reconstructing old ways in purer form but erecting new patterns based on the social teachings of Jesus and the immanence of God in earthly affairs. This initiative and response methodology of the social gospel was as apparent after the overwhelming impact of World War I on the nation and the church as it was after social, economic, and political evils had reached crisis proportions nearly a decade earlier. Protestants responded to wartime needs, but they also held up visions of a new social order when the fighting ended. During the two decades of this analysis, the vision of social Christianity broadened from a Christian nation to a Christian world order, universalizing a nationalistic ideal.

Several times during the twenty-one-year period, circumstances changed and affected the development of the Social Gospel movement. The challenges of social service and social reconstruction differed greatly from those of the social question and evangelizing the world in this generation. This study identified and explained the crucial turning points in the evolution of social Christianity between 1900 and 1920. As the circumstances altered ideas were modified, perceptions were clarified, and leadership and organizations were changed. For example, Episcopalians, who pioneered the social movement in 1900, were the least active twenty years later. Northern Presbyterians, inactive in 1900, quickly developed the most effective and extensive social ministry by 1912, only to have the program disassembled by conservative critics. However, they were able to reestablish the work again by 1920. Although they did little before 1907, Northern Methodists quickly assumed leadership in 1908 and maintained it throughout the rest of the era. Only the Baptists and Congregationalists sustained a consistent, steadily developing social concern during the period. As years passed, the methods and ideas of Charles Stelzle and

---

[3]Robert T. Handy, *A Christian America: Protestant Hopes and Historical Realities,* 2d ed. (New York: Oxford University Press, 1984) ix-xi, 8-12, 23, 27, 56, 81, 99-100, 132-33, 143-47, *passim.*

CONCLUSION

Harry Ward became more intense and radical, causing problems both for themselves and for the groups with which they were affiliated. Despite these changes, the status of the social gospel solidified within institutional Protestantism. This was particularly evident in the perceptive understanding of Rauschenbusch: in 1912 he looked back to 1900 as a time of lonesomeness for social prophets and rejoiced in the social awakening of the time, and five years later he gladly proclaimed that "the social gospel is a permanent addition" to American Protestantism.[4] Social Christianity evolved rapidly during the Progressive Era, and consequently it was constantly in a state of flux.

Although circumstances, personnel, ideas, and moods changed, the underlying commitment of institutional Protestantism to the social gospel persisted once it was voted. Lines of authority, funding, and even names of organizations were modified, but once within the institutional structures of the denominations and the Federal Council of Churches, social-service agencies continued their identity and function. While the fortunes of the social Christianity movement ebbed and flowed like the tide, the agencies survived and, consequently, so did the movement. Recognition of the social gospel and its admission to church organizational life occurred during the Progressive Era, and it has continued to the present.

Intrinsic to the recognition of social-service agencies and to their place in denominational and ecumenical Protestantism was an undergirding sense of responsibility for the social order. Once the churches accepted the obligation they did not abandon it, despite changing moods and vacillating degrees of commitment. It was that sense of duty to which social-gospel advocates appealed repeatedly during these two decades. Thus, it was not surprising that Worth Tippy concluded his report to the Federal Council in December 1920 on that note. In light of the changing conditions after the Great War, he urged the church to acquire "an enlarged conception of its mission in the world" because God laid that obligation upon the institution. " 'The churches today recognize, as they did not a generation ago, that the Kingdom of God is as comprehensive

---

[4]Walter Rauschenbusch, *A Theology for the Social Gospel* (New York: Macmillan Co., 1917) 2.

as human life with all its interests and needs, and that they share in a common responsibility for a Christian world order.' "[5] To the end of the period, the goal of social responsibility continued to be the primary motive for social Christianity. Combining social reform and social redemption emphases, the social responsibility theme that ran through the era embodied the essence of this epoch in social-gospel history.

---

[5]"Report of the Commission on the Church and Social Service," *The Churches Allied for Common Tasks: Report of the Third Quadrennium of the Federal Council of the Churches of Christ in America, 1916–1920*, ed. Samuel McCrea Cavert (New York: Council of Churches, 1921) 124.

CONCLUSION

INDEX

party platform and the Social Creed, 184; responses to, 192-93; role of progressive and social-gospel advocates, 183-87. *See also* Church and politics

Ely, Richard T., 15, 46

Employers, 106-107, 174-76, 238, 331-32. *See also* Industry

Encyclopedia of Social Reform, 18

Episcopal Church. *See* Protestant Church in the U.S.A.

Erdman, Charles R., 229-31

Ernst, Eldon G., 317

Evangelical Alliance for the United States, 13, 27-28, 33, 90

Evangelism, 27-34, 155-63, 229-33. *See also* Social Evangelism

Evangelization of the World in This Generation, The, 28, 84

Everybody's, 52

Federal Council of the Churches of Christ in America: adopted four supplements to the Social Creed, 300; adopted the Social Creed of the Churches, 107-14; "Church and Modern Industry" report, 106-14; "The Church and Social Reconstruction" statement, 298-300; clarified its social principles, 222-25, 238-40; Commission on the Church and Social Service its only functioning agency, 150; convinced it was now stabilized, 264; cooperated with other social-service organizations, 251-54; created a Secretarial Council, 152; created a separate Temperance Commission, 202; discussed the nature and function of the church, 334; during World War I, 280-81, 282-86; efforts to placate differences, 225, 233-37; employed an associate secretary at Washington, 202-203, 225; employed Tippy as executive secretary of Church and Social Service Commission, 261-62; expressed confidence, despite unfinished agenda, 336; and the Interchurch World Movement, 308-10; its enlarged facilities, staff, and finances, 263; Macfarland became executive secretary of the Council, 178, 199-200; Macfarland elected secretary of the Church and Social Service Commission, 147, 150; organizing session, 105-106; poor health of executive secretary Sanford, 150; principles of social service adopted, 238-39; proposed a total reorganization of the Council, 333; quadrennial meeting, 1912, 174-79; quadrennial meeting, 1916, 238-40; quadrennial meeting, 1920, 331-36; revised the Social Creed of the Churches, 172-75; Secretarial Council affected by member turnover, 323, 330; social service the first area of council activity, 150-51; turnover of its social-gospel staff, 330

Commission on the Church and Social Service: added social-gospel advocates to its Committee of Direction, 151-52; Committee on Literature was productive, 147-48, 151-52; cooperated with other social-service organizations, 251-54; creation of, 109; during World War I, 282-86; Macfarland elected as its secretary, 147, 150; made denominational social-service secretaries its associate secretaries, 152, 200; North its chairman, 148; the only active department of the council, 149; planned to reorganize the commission, 332-33; policy, strategy, and methods of, 200-204; principles for social service recommended by, 238; proposed an industrial peace program, 331-32; recommended revision of the Social Creed, 174-75; sought closer relationship to denominational departments, 235; staff prepared the Social Reconstruction report, 298; staff provided stability during leadership changes, 330; Strong its chairman, 199; Tippy became executive secretary of, 261-62; Tippy replaced Strong as chairman, 236

Council of Social Service Secretaries (Secretarial Council): membership turnover, 323, 330; organized by Macfarland, 152; proposed a revision of the Social Creed, 172-73; purpose and work of, 199-200, 203, 204

meetings: (1908), 106-14; (1912), 174-79; (1916), 238-40, 262; (1917), 282; (1919), 298, 300; (1920), 331-36

See also Inter-Church Conference on Federation; Macfarland, Charles; Social Creed of the Churches; Tippy, Worth

Federation Chronicle, 48

Ferguson, Charles, 26

Folks, Homer, 90, 93

For the Right, 18

Fosdick, Harry E., 162

Fundamentals, The, 128-30, 229-31

General War-Time Commission of the Churches, 284, 287, 293

Gilbert, Levi, 97, 99, 101, 104, 148

Gladden, Washington: addressed the Religious Education Association, 82-83, 246-47; *The Church and Modern Life*, 71-72; "The Church and the Social Crisis," 67-70; condemned Rockefeller gift to mission board, 42; death of, 302; "father of the social gospel," 302; member, Columbus City Council, 38, 65; member, Committee on Industry, Congregational National Council, 141; member, Federal Council Committee of Direction, 151; and the Men and Religion Forward Movement, 159, 161, 163; on ministers and politics, 188-89; moderator, National Council of Congregational Churches, 41-42, 67-70, 79; and the muckrakers, 37n, 67; "The Nation and the Kingdom," 124-26; as pastor, 65-66, 69; and progressive reform, 38, 65; *Recollections*, 188; and Roosevelt and the Progressive party, 186-87, 189; *Social Salvation*, 30-31, 34; speaker, New York State Conference of Religion, 20-21; unable to preach at the inauguration of Atkinson, 141-42; worldwide perspective of, 302

Gompers, Samuel, 314

Mathews, Shailer: *The Church and the Changing Order*, 60-63; editor, *The World Today*, 47, 60; Federal Council representative to American Federation of Labor, 251; *The Individual and the Social Gospel*, 231; and the Interchurch World Movement, 309-10; leader, Religious Education Association, 46, 47, 243; member, Commission on Social Service, Northern Baptist Convention, 86, 137; member, Federal Council Commission on the Church and Social Service, 148; president, Federal Council of Churches, 177, 199, 239, 240; president, Northern Baptist Convention, 206; professor, University of Chicago, 46, 60-61; secretly visited the defeated Roosevelt, 193; *The Social Gospel*, 127-28; on the wartime activity of the Federal Council, 289

Maurice, Frederick, 15

May, Henry F., 3, 303

Men and Religion Forward Movement: evaluations of, 161-63; method and approach of, 156-57; origin and purpose of, 156; social-service component of, 158-61

Messages to Workingmen, 45

Methodist Episcopal Church, General Conference
  "The Church and Social Problems" report, 97-104
  "The Social Creed of Methodism," 99-104, 107-11
  meetings: (1892), 89; (1896), 89; (1900), 14; (1904), 43-44, 89; (1908), 97-102; (1912), 171-73, 177; (1916), 212-15; (1920), 325-28
  See also Methodist Federation for Social Service; National City Evangelization Union; National Conference of Methodist Social Workers; New York City Church Extension and Missionary Society; North, Frank Mason; Social Creed of the Churches; Tippy, Worth M.; Ward, Harry F.

Methodist Federation for Social Service: affected by differences between North, Tippy, and Ward, 328, 329-30; autonomy of, 104, 144, 213-15, 328-29; Bishop McConnell the new president of, 178; decided editorial responsibility of the *Social Service Bulletin*, 329; influenced the action of 1908 General Conference, 97-100; initial strategy and program, 95-97; involved in the Russian question controversy, 310-12; its leaders were at Brotherhood conventions, 209-10; lacked funds for a salaried secretary, 103; limited funds restricted the program of, 144-46; and the 1912 General Conference, 171-73; and the 1916 General Conference, 212-15; and the 1920 General Conference, 327-28; origin of, 91-93; outlook and motivation of, 94; publications were its early accomplishment, 145-46; recognized as "an unofficial Methodist organization," 101, 102, 104; recommended supplemental paragraphs to the Social Creed, 212-13; reorganized the executive and other committees, 103-104; shaped "The Church and Social Problems" report, 100-102; significant progress of, 210-14; sponsored National Conference of Methodist Social Workers, 102-103; Ward employed as executive secretary, 146, 178

Meyer, Donald B., 3

Millennialism, 129-30, 269

Miller, Robert Moats, 3

Moody, Dwight L., 27, 31

Moral revival. *See* Social awakening

Mott, John R., 28, 84, 319

Mowry, George E., 81

Muckrakers: exposed the nation's wrongs, 35-37; impact of, evident in 1905–1906, 52-53; influenced the Methodist Federation for Social Service, 94; influenced social-gospel leaders, 37, 37n, 57, 67-69; made a frontal attack on churches, 119-23; origin of the movement, 35-37; popular with Progressive

reformers, 37; social conscience of, was essentially Protestant morality, 37

My Religion in Everyday Life, 12, 128

"Nation and the Kingdom, The," 124-26

National Association for the Study and Prevention of Tuberculosis, 253

National Child Labor Committee, 201, 253, 257, 258, 284

National City Evangelization Union, 91, 92, 171, 231

National Civic Federation, 253

National Conference of Charities and Correction, 182-84, 201, 252, 253

National Conference of Methodist Social Workers, 102-103

National Education Association, 248, 249

National Federation of Churches and Christian Workers, 28, 31, 48-49, 90

National Housing Association, 120

National Municipal League, 253

National Organization for Public Health Nursing, 285

National Prison Committee, 253

National Purity Committee, 253

National Women's Trade Union, 251, 253

Neill, Charles Patrick, 84

New Era, The, 13

"New Nationalism, The," 124, 127, 185

New social order, 281-82, 292, 301, 302, 312-14. *See also* Kingdom of God

New Social Order, The, 312-14

Newton, R. Heber, 15

New York Association for Labor Legislation, 253

New York Charities Directory, 14

New York City Church Extension and Missionary Society, 91

New York State Conference of Religion: origin and purpose of, 19-22, 25, 90; recognized moral revival occurring, 88, 165-66, 181; urged moral revival, 21-22, 28-29, 33, 35, 40

New York State Federation of Churches, 20

New York State Woman Suffrage party, 284

Theological Seminary, 55; and the Religious Education Association, 46, 81-82, 248-49; on the role of ministers and church in politics, 190-91, 192; "The Social Revival," 175-77, 178-79, 194; *A Theology for the Social Gospel*, 265-70; "The True American Church," 198-99; "What Is a Christian Nation?", 81-82; worldwide perspective of, 302

Religion of Democracy, 26

Religion and public education, 248-50

Religious education, social theory of, 270-73. *See also* Democracy of God; Religion and Public Education; Religious Education Association

Religious Education Association: a barometer of social-gospel ideas, 119, 250; declared the age of social responsibility had arrived, 248; on democracy and religion, 291-96; emphasized social duty, 118-19; 1908 convention on national morality, 81-83; origin and purpose of, 46-48, 81; recognized the moral awakening, 165-66; said churches and schools shared the moral-education task, 249-50; saw moral awakening occurring, 117, 165-66; social interest of, 46, 47-48, 81; usefulness of, for social purposes, 272; and World War I, 281-82

meetings: (1903–1907), 46-48; (1908), 81-83; (1909–1910), 117-19; (1911–1912), 165-66; (1912), 244-45; (1913–1916), 245-50; (1916), 281; (1917), 281-82, 291-92; (1918), 292-94; (1919), 295-96

social themes of annual conventions: (1908) "Education and National Character," 81-83; (1909) "Religious Education and Social Duty," 117-19; (1910) "The Church and Education," 165-66; (1911) "Religious Education and the American Home," 166; (1913) "Religious Education and Civic Progress," 245-47; (1914) "Education and Social Life," 247-48; (1915) "The Rights of the Child," 248-49; (1916) "Religious Instruction and Public Education," 249-50; (1917) "Religious Education and the Coming World Order," 281-82, 291-92; (1918) "Community Organization," 292-94; (1919) "A Religious Interpretation of Democracy," 295-96

Religious Movements for Social Betterment, 11-12, 63

Report of the Steel Strike of 1919, 315-17

Riis, Jacob, 24, 147, 151

Roberts, William H., 106

Rochester Theological Seminary, 17, 19, 32, 55

Rockefeller, John D., 36, 42, 68

Rogers, Henry Wade, 50

Roosevelt, Theodore: articulate and activist president of the United States, 38; articulated progressive values, 38, 53; coined the term *muckraker*, 36; contributing editor, *The Outlook*, 124; death of, 302; differed with President Taft, 123; evaluation of, 302-303; envisioned a strong central government, 39; figuratively and literally a preacher, 38, 39-40, 133; governor of New York, 19, 24-25; helped by social-gospel leaders in 1912, 184-89, 193; hero of social-gospel advocates, 38, 123-24; his African hunting expedition, 123; his messages to Congress proposed reform legislation, 80-81; leader, New York State Conference of Religion, 19; "The New Nationalism" address, 124; preached at Labor Temple, 133; progressivism of, compared to President Wilson's, 257; vice-president of the United States, 23-24

Russell, Charles Edward, 52, 120

Russell Sage Foundation, 253

Russian question, the, 310-14

Sagamore Conference, 253

Sanford, Elias B., 150, 178

Scudder, Vida, 15

Shriver, William P., 132

Slum missions, 122

Smith, Fred B., 156, 157, 159, 162-63

Social Aspects of Religious Institutions, 90

Social awakening, 27-34, 165-79; Brotherhood of the Kingdom on, 83; election of 1912, a climax of, 193-94; Episcopal Church recognized, 142; Federal Council and, 175-76, 178-79; Gladden on, 30-31, 68, 71; Mathews on, 62; Men and Religion Forward Movement and, 155-56, 162-63; Methodist Federation for Social Service on, 96; *The Outlook* on, 83; Rauschenbusch on, 1-2, 167-68, 170-71; Religious Education Association recognized, 117, 165-66; the Social Creed as evidence of, 114; Strong on, 31-32, 34, 64-65; Welch on, 84-85; Whiton on, 40, 88, 165-66

Social Christianity. *See* Social gospel

Social conscience, 105-14; awakening of, in late nineteenth century, 30; developed by Federal Council efforts, 203-204; Gladden on, 42, 71-72; *The Kingdom* on, 88; Macfarland on, 244, 259; muckraker's sense of, 37; Religious Education Association on, 82, 119, 259; Social Creed of the churches as, 110; Strong on, 32, 64; Whiton on, 40

Social Creed of the Churches: in "The Church and Modern Industry" report, 107-11; contents of, restated without the title, 238-39; endorsed by denominations, 134-35, 136, 141, 143, 216; Federal Council avoided changes in, to preserve unity, 234; influence of, on 1912 political platforms, 182-84; 1912 revision of, 172-75; Presbyterians reaffirmed and amplified their version, 324; revised and enlarged the Social Creed of Methodism, 107-14; some preferred "social ideals" to "social creed," 234; supplemental paragraphs to, adopted by Methodists, 212-13; supplementary paragraphs added to, 300; symbol of social

and ecumenical movements,
111-14; title changed to Social
Ideals of the Churches, 300-
301; Ward's *The New Social Order* on, 314; written by North,
107, 112-13
Social Creed of the Churches, The,
113, 173-74
"Social Creed of Methodism,
The," 99-104, 107-11
Social crisis: after World War I,
298; Church Congress on, 87;
Federal Council on, 111, 114;
Gladden on, 67-71; ideas on,
compared, 72, 74-75; Mathews
on, 61-62; Methodists on, 101,
102, 104; Rauschenbusch on,
57-59; Strong on, 64-65
Social duty, 103, 118-19, 226-27,
307, 316
Social evangelism: Gladden on,
71-72, 74; Macfarland on, 232-
33; Men and Religion Forward
Movement, 160; Rauschen-
busch on, 32, 59; Ward on, 231-
32
Social Evangelism, 211, 212, 231-32
Social gospel: has multiple
meanings, 4; used inter-
changeably with the term *social Christianity*, 4. *See also*
Individual gospel and social
gospel; Social Gospel Movement; Social responsibility
Social Gospel, The, 127-28
Social Gospel and the New Era, The,
301
Social Gospel Movement: climaxed in the social revival, 194;
defined generally, 4; disproportionate influence of, 340;
enlarged its vision from nation
to world, 302; evolved rapidly
during Progressive Era, 343;
forced to reorganize, 321-37;
historiography of, 2-4; ideas of,
similar to those of the muckrakers, 37; inherent optimism
of, 303, 305, 307; institutionalized denominationally and
ecumenically, 153; leadership
of, greatly changed by 1920,
330; my periodization within,
2-4, 5; more latency than accomplishment, 19; optimism
of, modified by events and
mood, 305-19; overshadowed
by World War I, 274, 275, 279,

286; and politics, 182-93; a primary factor in the Men and
Religion Forward Movement,
157; Rauschenbusch's accurate description of, 269-70;
shaped by Federal Council efforts, 199-204; stability of, evidenced, 262, 263, 265, 266, 269-
70, 274-75; symbolized by the
Social Creed of the Churches,
112, 113-14
Social justice, 182-84, 248, 272,
300, 316-17
Social Ministry, 145-46
Social question, the, 22-23, 30, 75,
192, 300
Social reconstruction: in "The
Church and Modern Indus-
try" report, 109; "The Church
and" statement, 298-300;
churches to build a Christian
world order, 299; contention
over, by Tippy and Ward, 330;
emphasized by Presbyterians,
322; the focus of Baptist social
service, 322-23; inadequacy of,
for Ward, 312-14; method of,
gradual or violent?, 299-300,
312-14; by orderly, progressive means, 300; pastoral letter
on, issued by Methodist bishops, 301; urgent questions of,
noted by Baptist Convention,
302
Social responsibility: the age of,
has arrived, 248; broadened to
a Christian world order, 298-
300; brought churches and
schools into the same en-
deavor, 245; "the chief sacrament . . . in our age," 160;
conveys the essence of the period, 7-8, 344; Federal Council
expressed a cooperative view
of, 106, 111; Gladden on, 71;
Macfarland on, 244; Methodism assumes its, 103; Mott on,
84; Presbyterians on, 86, 226-
27, 322; produced by social
conscience, 82; symbolized by
the Social Creed, 114; was more
an ideal than an accomplishment, 341
Social revival. *See* Social awakening
Social salvation. *See* Social awakening
Social service: became a generally current phrase, 245; church

concerns broadened beyond
industry to, 134-53; conservative Presbyterians attack, 220-
22, 226-31, 240; Erdman critical of, 229-31; institutional implementation of, 197-218;
principles of, adopted by the
Federal Council, 238-39; Religious Education Association
exalted the ideal of, 248
Social Service Bulletin, The, 146,
211, 310, 311
Social settlements, 12, 122
Social Task of Christianity, The, 166-
69
*Social Theory of Religious Educa-
tion, A*, 270-73
Social unrest, 85, 86, 87; affected
Federal Council organization
and program, 331-36; after
World War I, 299, 302, 306, 310,
325; in the Great Steel Strike,
314-17
Socialized Church, The, 145
Society for Christian Socialists, 15
Southern Sociological Congress,
201, 252, 253
Speer, Robert E., 335
Spencer, C. B., 96, 97, 101, 104
*Spiritual Culture and Social Ser-
vice*, 151
Spiritual Unrest, The, 120-23
Steel Strike, the Great, 306, 314-
17, 319
Steffens, Lincoln, 36
Steiner, Edward, 141, 177
Stelzle, Charles: added an Im-
migration Department to
Church and Labor, 85-86;
added staff and a Church and
Country Life Department, 132;
*American Social and Religious
Conditions*, 158; *The Church and
Labor*, 132; criticized the Fed-
eral Council's social ministry,
235-36; early experience and
ministry, 44; elected to the new
Presbyterian Commission on
Social Service, 265; and the
Federal Council, 148, 149, 152;
a Federal Council representa-
tive to the American Federation of Labor, 251; founded
Labor Temple, New York City,
132-33; headed the Presbyterian mission to workers, 44; his
department changed to the
Bureau of Social Service, 135;

his efforts praised by other denominations, 80, 96; joined the Federal Council staff, 236-37; left the Federal Council staff, 330; and the Men and Religion Forward Movement, 157-58; Merrick lecturer, Ohio Wesleyan University, 84; *Messages to Workingmen*, 45; the mission was upgraded to the Department of Church and Labor, 45; praised "The Church and Modern Industry" report, 109; a Progressive party candidate, 185; recognized as the leading minister to workers, 45-46; resigned when his social ministry was attacked, 219-22; wartime activities of, 284, 286

Stewart, Lyman and Milton, 128-29

Strayer, Paul Moore, 285, 288, 311

Strong, Augustus, 19

Strong, Josiah: *The Challenge of the City*, 63-65; founder and president, League for Social Service, 11, 13; headed Research Committee of the Federal Council, 149; his death, 261; illness forced his resignation from the commission, 236; leader, New York State Conference of Religion, 19; member and chairman, Federal Council Commission on the Church and Social Service, 148, 199; *The New Era*, 13; *The Next Great Awakening*, 31-32, 34; *Our Country*, 13; praised Gladden's social-crisis address, 69; *Religious Movements for Social Betterment*, 11-12; secretary, Evangelical Alliance in the United States, 13; social-gospel pioneer, 11-13; *The Twentieth Century City*, 13

Student Volunteer Movement for Foreign Missions, 28, 84

Taft, William Howard, 80-81, 123, 186

Tarbell, Ida, 36

Taylor, Alva, 330

Taylor, Graham: director, Chicago Commons, 139; member, Federal Council Commission on the Church and Social Service, 148; member, Federal Council Committee on Litera-

ture, 147, 151; member, Industrial Committee of the Congregational National Council, 79-80; member, Religious Education Association, 46; and the Men and Religion Forward Movement, 158, 163; Merrick lecturer, Ohio Wesleyan University, 84; professor, University of Chicago, 139; reported for Industrial Committee at the Congregational National Council, 139-41

Taylor, S. Earl, 307, 309, 319

Temperance (Prohibition): Baptists and, 205-206, 325; a concern of social reconstruction, 299; Federal Council and, 202-203, 238, 264; Methodists and, 210, 213; Prohibition amendment to Constitution ratified, 306; Prohibition during World War I, 283, 288

Theology for the Social Gospel, A, 265-70

Tippy, Worth M.: on Christian cooperation with community agencies, 254-56; *The Church a Community Force*, 255; *The Church and the Great War*, 286-87; and "The Church and Social Reconstruction," 298-300; cofounder and secretary, Methodist Federation for Social Service, 91-93, 95, 97, 98; executive secretary, Federal Council Commission on the Church and Social Service, 261-62; helped to influence 1908 General Conference action, 95, 97, 98, 99, 100; his "The Church and Industrial Peace" program, 331-32; his 1920 report identified a changing social gospel, 337; his relationship to Ward, 311, 318-19, 328, 330, 331; increasingly involved in Federal Council activities, 261-62; and the Interchurch World Movement, 309-10, 319, 329-30; a pastor with social interests, 29-30, 90, 91, 256; replaced Strong as chair, Federal Council Commission on the Church and Social Service, 236; *The Socialized Church* (ed.), 145; wartime responsibilities of, 282-87; wrote the chapter on social

service, *Manual of Inter-Church Work*, 254

Trinity Church, tenements of, 119-21, 123

Twentieth Century City, The, 13, 63

Union Theological Seminary, 19, 247, 270, 293, 294, 310

"United Declaration on Christian Faith and Social Service," 226-28, 231

United States Department of Agriculture, 284

United States Public Health Service, 285

United States Steel Corporation, 314-16

Veiller, Lawrence, 120

Voluntary societies, 14-15, 208

Ward, Harry F.: Coe dedicated a book to, 270; cofounder and vice-president, Methodist Federation for Social Service, 92-93; concentrated on publications, 211-12; editor, *The Social Service Bulletin*, 146; executive secretary, Methodist Federation for Social Service, 146, 178; and the Federal Council, 147-48, 151-52; helped to influence 1908 General Conference action, 95, 98, 99; his relationship to Tippy, 311, 318-19, 328, 330, 331; *The Labor Movement*, 211-12; *The New Social Order*, 312-14; a pastor with social interests, 90, 92; *Poverty and Wealth*, 211; praised as "the greatest social prophet to-day," 215; primary emphasis on workers' conditions, 211-12; professor, Boston University School of Theology, 178, 211; recommended reorganization of the Methodist Federation, 328-29; recommended supplemental paragraphs to the Social Creed, 212-13; refused nomination as secretary of the Federal Council Commission, 236; and the Russian-question controversy, 310-14; *The Social Creed of the Churches* (ed.), 173-74; *Social Evangelism*, 211, 212, 231-32; *Social Ministry* (ed.), 145-46; wartime activity of, 284, 288; wrote "The Church and Social Problems" report, 99;

wrote "The Social Creed of Methodism," 100-101, 112-13; *A Year Book of the Church and Social Service in the United States* (ed.), 201, 203-204

War-Time Agencies of the Churches, 287

Welch, Herbert, 84, 113, 148; co-founder and president, Methodist Federation for Social Service, 91-93, 146; at the 1908 General Conference, 95, 97, 98, 99, 100

Wesleyan Methodist Union for Social Service (England), 91, 92

Western Christian Advocate, The, 96-97, 98, 99, 101, 110, 176

Weyl, Walter E., 187

White, Ronald C., Jr., 4

White, William Allen, 38, 39

Whiton, James M., 19, 21-22, 69; on the church's and nation's moral health, 21-22, 40, 46, 53-54; recognized a moral awakening, 88, 165-66, 181-82

Williams, Leighton, 17, 18, 19-20, 60

Wilson, Warren H., 132, 152, 225, 237-38

Wilson, Woodrow, 192-93, 233, 306; in the 1912 presidential election, 182, 192-93, 194; and Progressive legislation, 80-81,

257-58; and World War I, 280, 292, 296

Women workers: 84, 88, 251, 256, 299, 300; provision concerning, in the Social Creed, 100, 174, 175

Women's Trade Union League, 253

Workers: the church should inspire, 243-44; a concern of social reconstruction, 299; a continuous emphasis of social-gospel leaders, 251-52; Federal Council efforts for, 149, 201-202; and the Great Steel Strike, 314-17; not likely to turn to the church, 331-32; right of, to organize reaffirmed, 324; should receive adequate wages, 300; Social Creed and, 100-102, 109-10, 174-76, 238-39; Tippy shifted emphasis from, to employers, 331-32; in Ward's *New Social Order,* 312-14; Ward's primary interest in, 211-12

concern for

by Baptists, 16-18; by Congregationalists, 29, 41, 74, 79-80; by Episcopalians, 15-16, 29, 40-41, 80; by the Federal Council, 107-10, 113, 174-76; muckrakers, 36-

37; by Methodists, 92, 94, 96, 98, 99

ministry to

by Congregationalists, 139-42; by Methodists, 100-102; by Presbyterians, 44-46, 85-86, 132-33

World Today, The, 47, 60

World War I, 279-89; American involvement in, 279-80; denominations and, 283, 287-88; Federal Council and, 282-87; Macfarland and, 280-81, 282; overshadowed the Social Gospel Movement, 274, 275, 279, 286; Religious Education Association and, 281-82; social gospel little involved in, until the nation entered, 280-81; social-reconstruction concept emerged from, 298, 312-13

World's Student Christian Federation, 84

Yale University, 30, 50, 150, 209, 265

Year Book of the Church and Social Service in the United States, A, 201, 203-204

Young Men's Christian Association, 25, 84, 156, 201, 283, 300

Young People's Missionary Movement, 63

Young Women's Christian Association, 201, 283, 300

Zaring, Elbert Robb, 91-93

Donald K. Gorrell is professor of church history at United Theological Seminary at Dayton.